MEDIEVAL TRADE
AND FINANCE

MEDIEVAL TRADE AND FINANCE

M. M. POSTAN

CAMBRIDGE
AT THE UNIVERSITY PRESS
1973

Published by the Syndics of the Cambridge University Press
Bentley House, 200 Euston Road, London NW1 2DB
American Branch: 32 East 57th Street, New York, N.Y.10022

© Cambridge University Press 1973

Library of Congress Catalogue Card Number: 72–93136

ISBN: 0 521 08745 7

Printed in Great Britain by
Western Printing Services Ltd
Bristol

PREFACE

In the preface to a companion volume (*Essays on medieval agriculture and general problems of the medieval economy*) I have explained, and apologized for, my decision to fall in with the prevailing practice and to assemble for re-publication a number of my studies not available in book form. I should like now to cite the special reasons why the studies in this volume have been grouped together and apart from my other essays. A separate collection devoted to trade and finance can of course be justified by the conventional demarcations between different aspects of economic history. But my main justification is that the topics of commercial and financial history in this collection represent my earlier and, so to speak, preliminary approaches to medieval economic history. In embarking upon the study of medieval economic history I chose as my main subject the formation of capital and the role of capital in medieval economy. The use of money in the middle ages, the function and scope of credit, the machinery of investment, and the financial technique were all constituent parts of the main subject and were intended to lead up to its main theme – that of the sources of capital formation. I embarked on this last and most important stage by trying to compute the profits of the great estate owner who in my view controlled the bulk of productive capital. With this object in view I turned to the manorial accounts of the bishops of Winchester, the earls of Lancaster and the abbots of Glastonbury and Bury St Edmunds. But having enmeshed myself in manorial and agrarian topics I found it impossible to disengage myself from the study of agrarian history as key to medieval economy as a whole.

The essays in this volume, more particularly those dealing with finance, are thus mere components of an unfinished edifice. What the edifice would have looked like had I been able to complete it could perhaps be guessed from the components published here: from some of their arguments left over for further treatment, from some of their conclusions which I intended and promised to buttress up with evidence in later studies. I hope these gaps will be noted by students proposing to embark on the history of medieval capital, and may in this way help them to draw up their agenda of study. But I also hope that they will draw from this autobiographical diversion the consolation that unfinished enterprises need not be altogether fruitless, and that one can sometimes do as great a service to one's subject of study by deserting it as by remaining faithful to it to the end.

In the preparation of this volume, as well as that of the companion volume, the personnel of the Cambridge University Press were as helpful and efficient as only they could be.

January 1973 M.P.

Acknowledgments

The author and publisher are most grateful to publishers and learned societies for their co-operation while this volume was under preparation. They are further grateful to Thames & Hudson Ltd for permission to reproduce copyright material. Cambridge University Press has made every effort to trace copyright holders and it is regretted if any copyright has been unwittingly infringed.

CONTENTS

1
CREDIT IN MEDIEVAL TRADE[1]

The extent to which medieval trade was based on credit does not figure among the favourite problems of economic history. Not that it has been entirely neglected, since the economic theorists have been busy over it for more than seventy-five years: it is the historian who is guilty of neglect. In his absence the field has been entirely appropriated by the economic theorist; and the latter, unsupported and unrestrained by research, inevitably produced notions unrelated to historical facts. These notions spring from the source whence have originated so many current pre-conceptions about the economic nature of medieval civilisation – namely, speculations as to the 'stages' of economic development. In the nineteenth century sociologists and economists regarded their age as biologists regard the *homo sapiens*, as the culmination of an evolutionary process. To them epochs of history were successive stages in the uninterrupted ascent of mankind from the crude primitivity of prehistory to the complex per-fection of their own age. In accordance with this view, the economists have constructed a number of hypothetical models of the evolutionary ladder, in which every step differed from the one which followed in that it did not contain one or other element of the modern economic system, or else contained it in a less developed and a more imperfect form. As credit, especially in its alliance with trade, in fact constitutes an essen-tial principle of our present economic system it was inevitably drawn into the schemes of economic progress. The argument was simple. If mercan-tile credit was one of the basic principles of our economic civilisation, then every successive stage of economic revolution made some contribution towards it, and therefore the further back we went the less important the function of credit became, until we reached a time when there was very little credit or none at all. Hence the prevailing notions of the absence or the undeveloped state of credit in the Middle Ages.

This view was given its clearest and sharpest expression by Bruno

---

[1] This paper first appeared in *Economic History Review*, I, 1928. The following abbreviations have been used: E. Ch. Pr.=Public Record Office, Early Chancery Proceedings; M.R.=Public Record Office, K.R. Exchequer Memoranda Rolls; A.V.=Public Record Office, K.R. Exchequer, Accounts Various; L.B.=Calen-dars of Letter Books (ed. Sharpe); P.M. Rolls=Plea and Memoranda Rolls at the Guildhall; *V.S.W.G.=Vierteljahrschrift für Sozial- und Wirtschaftsge-schichte*.

Hildebrand, one of the fathers of the 'historical' school of political economy. He believed that the only differences between epoch and epoch which furnished principles of evolutionary classification were those relating to the methods of exchange. And from the point of view of the methods of exchange there were three main stages of economic development: the prehistorical and early medieval stage of natural economy when goods were exchanged against other goods; the later medieval stage of 'cash' (money) economy, when goods were bought for ready money; and the modern stage of credit economy when commercial exchange was based on credit.[2] The form in which Hildebrand expressed this view of the Middle Ages as the pre-credit era was too simple and straightforward to find general acceptance among historical economists. Karl Bücher, who on this question had a greater influence than any other of Hildebrand's successors, knew more about the Middle Ages and was careful not to make the presence or absence of credit the sole *differentia* between the various stages of economic development. But, in regarding the institutions of our civilisation as the product of a growth extending over the whole of European history, he was bound to assume that in the earlier stages credit could play only a minor part in economic life. There was some miscellaneous borrowing and lending in the Middle Ages, but it did not testify to the economic importance of credit. Medieval loans were always disguised into, or regarded as species of, other transactions with which the Middle Ages were more familiar, especially those of purchase and sale. Moreover, they were used not for production, but for consumption. 'It may even be doubted whether in medieval trade credit operations can be spoken of at all. Early exchange is based on ready payment. Nothing is given except where a tendered equivalent can be directly received.'[3]

Bücher's general theory of economic evolution now forms one of the axiomatic assumptions of historical research; and his views on credit were naturally adopted by historians with the rest of his theory. In England Dr Cunningham set out to describe the 'growth' of English industry and trade: the story of how England's economic power steadily waxed from the early Middle Ages. On the question of medieval credit he believed that only at the close of the Middle Ages did English foreign trade become important enough to afford an opportunity for the use of credit. Until then, notably in the thirteenth and the fourteenth centuries, the volume of English trade was modest and its methods primitive: the capital employed in it was very small, and there was hardly any room in it for credit. 'The demand for money for commercial and industrial purposes, at

---

[2] 'Natural-, Geld- und Creditwirtschaft' in *Jahrb. Nationalökonomie* (1864). For the theoretical criticism of Hildebrand's scheme, see Gustav Cohn, *System der Nationalökonomie* (1885), I, 454–5.

[3] *Economic Evolution* (English trans. by Wickett), 1901, pp. 128 seq. Restated in *Grundriss der Sozialökonomie*, I, part i (1924).

the only rates at which men were accustomed to lend, was practically nil';
'money-lending had nothing to do with commerce; wealthy men borrowed
in emergency, or to equip for a war'; 'it is very probable that even in
emergency merchants did not often have recourse to borrowing, as the
gild merchants made arrangements which enabled them, in some cases at
all events, to get temporary aid'. As to 'credit as a basis for transactions of
other kinds', 'there is a striking difference between those times and ours',
as 'transactions were carried on in bullion; men bought with coin and
sold for coin' – in other words, 'dealing for credit was little developed,
and dealing in credit was unknown'.[4] These views are still common.[5]

There cannot be many topics in the economic history of the Middle
Ages on which the evidence is as copious as on credit. The bulk of the
evidence consists of records of debts. Most numerous of all are the records
of 'recognisances' – i.e., debts acknowledged before judicial tribunals
and entered upon their rolls. After the passing of the Statute of Burnell,
1283, the entries began to be concentrated on special rolls kept by the
authorities empowered by the Act to receive recognisances. But before
1283, and to some extent after, recognisances were also entered on
various official registers: the Letter Books of London, the registers of other
municipalities, the Memoranda Rolls of the exchequer, and occasionally
on the Close Rolls and the other chancery enrolments, or the rolls of the
king's courts. The number which has survived amounts to several scores of
thousands. The second class of references to debts consists of entries and
documents relating to pleas of debt. Of these especially important are
the petitions on debts among the early chancery proceedings at the Public
Record Office; next come references to cases of debts brought before the
municipal authorities for trial, execution, or other purposes, and recorded
in various municipal registers, and above all on the Plea and Memoranda
Rolls at the Guildhall. Of considerable importance also are the numerous
Patent Roll entries of pardons for outlawry for not appearing before the
royal justices on plaints of debt and finally comes the uncharted sea of
the Plea Rolls and the various local court rolls.[6] The third class is composed of documents dealing with debts and credits, but not in connection
with their recording, enforcement, or adjudication. To this class, in the
first instance, belong the valuable inventories of debts and goods of
foreign merchants, or lists of their transactions, compiled on several
occasions in the thirteenth and the fourteenth centuries and now grouped
together in the 'accounts various' of the exchequer at the Public Record

---

[4] I, 362–4, 463.
[5] There are, of course, exceptions. See Thorold Rogers, *Industrial and Commercial History* (1892), 69; E. Lipson, *Economic History* (1915), I, 528 seq.
[6] Strictly speaking, to this class of judicial records belong also the statute staple
certificates at the Public Record Office – a multitude of documents judicial in
purpose, but identical with ordinary recognisances in content.

Office. To these one must add the various collections of non-official documents, illustrating the financial transactions of medieval merchants, such as the Cely accounts in the chancery files[7] and their letters in the volumes 53 and 59 of the 'ancient correspondence' at the Public Record Office; a ledger of a fourteenth-century merchant, a day book of a fifteenth-century scrivener[8] and a vast number of other miscellaneous documents at the Public Record Office showing the medieval merchants in their dealings with each other. Lastly, there are numerous references to debts and credit in the more general sources such as the parliamentary rolls, Statutes of the Realm, Rymer's *Fœdera*.

It would be possible to enumerate other documents where medieval borrowing or lending is recorded, mentioned, or described. Not all these references to debts relate to mercantile credit, but the proportion of the latter is very high. Many debts were never enrolled or officially recorded, especially in the earlier centuries when the tally was still the commonest financial instrument, and in the later Middle Ages when various forms of informal bonds came into use. It was in the second half of the thirteenth and the first half of the fourteenth century that official enrolments in the shape of recognisances were most commonly used for the recording of debts; and it is in the recognisances of the thirteenth and early fourteenth centuries that the prevalence of mercantile debts is most clearly marked. The preamble to the Statute Burnell, introducing that system of recognisances which prevailed all through the later centuries, expressly stated that the new order was instituted for the benefit of the merchants. That this remained the avowed object of the reformed recognisance was declared or implied in all the subsequent measures dealing with this financial instrument. Some non-mercantile debts found their way into the recognisance rolls, whereupon the Ordainers commanded in 1311 that the Statute Burnell should not hold 'except between merchant and merchant, and of merchandise sold between them'.[9] The ordinance remained in force only until 1326, but even a cursory review of the rolls will show that for a number of years after 1326 they continued to deal chiefly with debts between merchants, which presumably arose out of ordinary mercantile transactions. It is only in the second half of the fourteenth century that a change came over the character of the entries in the Recognisance Rolls – a change reflecting not the evolution of credit itself, but a certain new departure in the nature of financial instruments.[10]

The conclusions to be drawn from this evidence are obvious. The abundance of mercantile debts clearly demonstrates that credit commonly

---

[7] Public Record Office, Chancery Miscellania, bundle 37.

[8] A.V. 509/19 and 128/37.

[9] Edw. II, c. 33; L.B.E., pp. 53, 213; *Rot. Parl.*, I, 457.

[10] This and other questions relating to the employment of financial instruments in the Middle Ages lie outside the present article

entered into the commercial practice of the Middle Ages. At the same time it must not be taken to imply the rare use of cash payments, since debts were recorded while cash transactions were not. It affords, therefore, no indication as to the relative importance of credit in the total volume of medieval trade, or as to its part in the turnover of individual merchants. Nor does it solve any of the problems essential for the correct understanding of the nature and function of mercantile credit. Granted that credit transactions were frequent, does it necessarily follow that there was an organic connection between credit and trade? Did credit enter into the ordinary commercial routine, and was it equally common in every branch and at every stage of business? Was it adapted to the multifarious needs of commerce? Did it fulfil the various functions which mercantile credit is theoretically supposed to fulfil? And was there any connection between its functions, its forms, and its methods? The problems are many, and no attempt will be made here to exhaust them all; neither will it be possible to deal with any of them separately. All it is proposed to do here is to review the chief forms of medieval credit in the hope that this will in itself throw light on the problems enumerated.

SALE CREDITS

'Sale credits' – that is, credits in the shape of deferred payments for goods sold or advances for future delivery – enter into the actual exchange of goods more directly than loans of money; and it was sale credits, rather than loans, that Hildebrand and his followers had in mind when denying the existence of mercantile credit in the Middle Ages. Fortunately no other form of credit is better served by the surviving evidence, so that even a summary treatment of facts will demonstrate clearly enough the extent to which sale credits were common in the different branches of medieval trade.

We may begin with the trade in goods retailed, as some of the fullest and earliest collections of recognisances, notably those recorded in the early Letter Books and Recognisance Rolls of London, consist largely of debts for goods intended for consumption in this country. Some of these goods, whether imported from abroad or produced here, were sold directly to the consumer; but most of them to other merchants. German historians have debated whether the Middle Ages possessed a class of traders who could be labelled as wholesalers. One point, however, is not disputed. Whether a separate class of wholesalers existed or not, wholesale trade was common throughout the Middle Ages. Goods were often handled in bulk and sold, not to the final consumers, but to other merchants, and often changed hands several times before being retailed. Now, the evidence of debts makes it clear that credit was demanded and allowed at every stage through which the goods passed from importer or producer to consumer.

Of the foreign commodities retailed in this country, wine seems to have lent itself best to handling *en gros* and to successive sales on credit. The trade in wine, like that in wool and cloth, attracted a large amount of capital, and was apparently open to all – vintners, cordwainers, drapers, curriers, saddlers, mercers, even princes, nobles, and ecclesiastics. Some bought for retail, others for resale to merchants. And whenever wine changed hands an opportunity for credit arose. To begin with, wine was often, though not always, bought on credit from wine growers and wine merchants in Gascony and Poitou. Then the importers, whether English or foreign, sold it on credit to retailers or wholesale merchants in England. The transactions recorded in London recognisances show wealthy vintners of the thirteenth or the early fourteenth centuries, like William Barache, Simon of Farnham, Allan of Suffolk, and others, regularly buying wine on credit from importers and reselling it again to taverners and smaller vintners. Occasionally they formed partnerships with taverners, who retailed their wine for a share in the profits. But often the chain between the importer and the retailer consisted of several links; there was more than one middleman, and consequently more than one credit transaction.[11]

Similarly in other commodities. Goods in common demand, like corn, leather, woad, etc., whether imported from abroad or produced here, and whether sold at fairs or distributed from the larger towns, changed hands several times before reaching the consumer, and every time they changed hands credit could be demanded and conceded.[12]

The terms of payment in the principal export trades were similar to those in the internal trade. Exporters of cloth in the later fourteenth and fifteenth centuries made almost exactly the same use of sale credits, and offered the same scope for them, as the wine traders. In its passage from producer to foreign consumer cloth went through several stages, at each of which credit invariably appeared as the governing principle of the transaction. Clothiers would, as a rule, deliver cloth to drapers and other merchants for export or internal sale on several months' credit. Sometimes an additional middleman would intervene: a wandering chapman who had bought the cloth on his circuit, or a big wholesaler, or, what

[11] See L.B.A., p. 6 (Falco), *The Red Register of Lynn*, I, 33; Letter Books A, B, and C, and Guildhall Recognisance Rolls 1–4, *passim*; F. Sargeant in Unwin, *Finance and Trade under Edward III*.

[12] The early Letter Books and Recognisance Rolls at the Guildhall abound with references to chaloners, cordwainers, and leathersellers buying leather, yarn and other commodities from foreign importers. For credit in the fourteenth and fifteenth centuries between wholesalers and country retailers, see the very numerous references in the Patent Rolls (Pardons for Outlawry), also E. Ch. Pr. 6/20, 7/122, 9/382, 26/272, 46/144.

seems to have been quite usual, occasional speculators drawn from various trades and occupations. A Chancery petition of the beginning of the fifteenth century tells an interesting story of a quantity of blankets bought by 'certeyn chapmen', resold by them to two vintners, who in their turn resold it *in solido* to someone else. At each stage, except the first, of which we are told nothing, the cloth was sold on credit. And this was apparently quite an ordinary transaction.[13] Nothing can demonstrate better the dependence of the English cloth trade on the system of postponed payments than the failure of the Act of 1430 as to credit sales to foreigners. It was enacted then that no Englishman should sell his goods to aliens except for ready money and goods. A year later, however, the Commons petitioned and Parliament enacted that it should be lawful to sell cloth to aliens 'per apprest de paiement . . . de 6 mois a 6 mois', as otherwise the cloth 'could not be uttered or sold'.[14] But even in this form the statute could not be enforced. Goods other than cloth continued to be sold to foreigners on credit, while in the sales of cloth the terms often did not conform to the legal 'de 6 mois a 6 mois', and credit was allowed for a period of one, two, and even three years.[15]

It remains to show how this system of sale credits was applied to the wool trade, the oldest and the most important branch of English export trade. The financial methods of the English wool trade in the second half of the fifteenth century have recently been described by Dr Power,[16] whose account is largely based on the Cely accounts and correspondence. The Celys bought the greater part of their wool on credit from wool merchants in the Cotswolds, and in turn sold it on credit to foreigners abroad. This chain of credits, however, commenced before the Celys received the wool, for we know that at least one of their Cotswold woolmen, William Midwinter, himself bought his goods from local men on credit. Neither did the chain come to its end as the wool passed into the hands of wool merchants and clothiers in foreign towns. In other words, from the wool grower in the Cotswolds to the buyer of Dutch cloth in Poland or Spain there was one uninterrupted succession of credit sales. This practice was not confined to Celys, and it was certainly not a fifteenth-century invention. However different may have been the scope and technique of the wool trade in earlier centuries, the methods of payments remained very largely the same. As far back as we can trace the activities of the English exporters on the foreign wool markets, the transactions were commonly based on credit. That in the second half of the

[13] E. Ch. Pr. 20/2; the other references are too many to be enumerated.
[14] 8 Hen. VI, c. 24; 9 Hen. VI, c. 2; *Rot. Parl*, IV, 377, 509.
[15] Abundantly shown by the cases in the M.R. for 37 and 38 Henry VI, when the court of exchequer happened to obtain information about the credit transactions of a number of foreigners.
[16] *Cambridge Hist. Journal*, 1926.

thirteenth century English exporters were in the habit of selling their wool on credit is illustrated by a document in the archives of Ypres recording a debt owed by Boidin, son of Walter de Gaunt, to John Ludlow, an English wool exporter, for wool bought in July, 1291. Desmarez, who prints this bond, mentions also a number of other similar documents among the thirteenth-century obligations. One Nicolas Ludlow, of Salisbury, figures often in them: in 1277 he appears as creditor for £34 1s 6d; in 1279 he sells wool on credit to the value of £234.[17] In the fourteenth century the experiments with the Staple system several times threatened completely to disorganise the trade; yet so long as the English continued to export their wool, they regularly sold it on credit.

This close dependence of the wool trade at foreign marts on the smooth working of the machinery of sale credits was at times clear even to the blundering governments of the fifteenth century. But what the governments admitted only occasionally, the merchants demanded all the time. We find them in 1410 petitioning the Crown to put an end to the English piracy against the Flemings in the interests of the English merchants who 'have communication in the feat of merchandise with the inhabitants of the said country of Flanders, appresting them "selon la cours de la monde" their wool and merchandise, which cannot and never could be delivered at their true value to the common profit of the whole Realm without that they be apprested in instalments'.[18] And declarations of a similar nature occur over and over again in the fifteenth century in connection with the frequent interruptions of trade by war or the equally frequent anti-credit measures of the Crown. The failure of these measures, more than anything else, reveals the extent to which credit permeated the sale of wool abroad. The attempts to regulate credit in the wool trade of Calais had a greater chance of success than in other trades, since wool sales abroad were centralised and rigidly controlled through the machinery of the Staple. Yet here, as in the cloth trade, the official policy came to grief through the reluctance and inability of the merchants to carry it out. The so-called Ordinance of Partition of Wool of 1430, which introduced a rigid system of control over the transactions of individual merchants, provided that payments for wool should be in cash, and that the bullion be brought without delay to the mint at Calais to the amount of some 75 per cent of the value of wool sold.[19] The Ordinance could hardly have been obeyed to the letter; still it was effective enough to provide the merchants with a grievance.[20] In 1442 it was enacted upon a

---

[17] G. Desmarez, *Lettres des Foires*, no. 157.

[18] L. Gilliodts van Severen, *Le Cotton Manuscrit Galba B.*1 (Brussels, 1896), no. 101. See also ibid., nos. 127, 133, 135, 168.

[19] 8 Hen. VI, c. 17, 18. (Re-enacted for another three years in 1433, 11 Hen. VI, c. 13) *Rot. Parl.*, IV, 358–9.

[20] Ibid., IV, 490, 509.

petition of the Commons that the Staplers should bring to the mint only one-third of the bullion,[21] which virtually legalised the 'lending' of the remaining two-thirds of the cost of wool. But even this milder regulation was found to be unenforceable, and when in October of the same year the Crown approached the Company of the Staple for a loan, it was confronted by the demand that the 'merchants English mygt selle their wolles withoute that they shold to be arted to take the thirde part in bullion'. The question came up for discussion before the Council and the conditions of the Staplers were vigorously opposed by Cardinal Beaufort on the ground that their acceptance would be equivalent to a Flemish victory on this issue, as 'yif they could feele that the kyng for necessitee sholde thus dispense with the statute of bringing in of bullion . . . he sulde never hereafter by constreint make hem bringe in any bullion'. The Cardinal on this occasion was less of a business man than usual. He failed to recognise that the law could not be executed. When the Council met a few days later it had before it the statement of the Mayor of the Staple to the effect that it was impossible to bring in the third part in bullion, and that the Staple had 'of ther owne auctoritee . . . dispensed' with the Act of 1442.[22] Thus ended the endeavour of the Lancastrian government to restrict the credit in the wool sales,[23] in the interests of its bullionist policy. An attempt to revive the policy was made under Edward IV in 1463, when it was enacted that no merchant of the Staple should sell wool at Calais without that he 'take ready payment', of which one-half he must bring in bullion or English coin to England within three months following the sale. This Act sounded more formidable than it actually was, for in spite of its general prohibition of credit sales merchants could allow the buyer three months' credit on one-half of the price and unlimited credit on the rest.[24] But whatever the provisions of the law meant, they could not be of great importance, since the Staplers continued to sell as they thought best: the contemporary business of wool sales in Calais abounds with references to sales on credit; and in 1473 the legal restrictions of credit were swept away.[25]

So much for the foreign end of the trade. The issue becomes somewhat more complicated as we pass to the trade on this side of the Channel. What is striking about the sale credits in the English wool trade abroad is not only their frequency, but also their uniform 'direction'. As in other branches of trade, it was commonly the seller who gave credit: goods were sold for deferred payments, and the 'flow' of credit was from the seller to the buyer. The practice was not quite so regular and uniform in the wool

---

[21] Ibid., v, 64; 20 Hen. VI, c. 12.
[22] *Proceedings of the Privy Councils*, v, 216–19.
[23] For a fruitless attempt to revive the policy, see *Rot. Parl.*, vi, 256–76.
[24] 3 Edw. IV, c. 1.
[25] *Rot. Parl.*, vi, 60.

trade at home. The sales on credit were at least as common as in the foreign wool marts, but the direction of credit was not invariably the same. In the transactions between the exporters and the merchants who supplied them with wool deferred payments apparently formed the rule;[26] so much so that the very fact that the Italians paid *au comptant* more frequently than the English was regarded as an unfair advantage over the native merchant.[27] This rule, however, does not seem to have applied to every wool sale in England irrespective of who were the contracting parties. Mr Bond and Mr Whitwell have shown that in the thirteenth century the Italians, in their dealings with the monasteries, commonly paid for the wool before it was shorn or collected.[28] They advanced to the monasteries sums of money as payment, full or partial, for wool to be delivered in the course of one or several following 'seasons'. Transactions of this type were even older than the thirteenth century. The unique roll of debts to William Cade, a twelfth-century financier, records several advance payments for wool. 'Monaci de Parco de Luda debent 70 marcas quas receperunt de lana sua quam Willelmus debuit habere 6 annis post mortem Teobaldi archiepiscopi.'[29] The Curia Regis Rolls report what seems to be a similar transaction for the closing years of the twelfth century between William, son of Robert, and the Prior of Swine.[30] References of this kind become very common in the thirteenth century. The accounts of Flemish merchants whose goods and debts were arrested by Edward I teem with entries of sums owed to them on account of advances made to monasteries and others for wool of future growth. But it was the great Italian houses of the thirteenth and fourteenth centuries – the Riccardi, the Peruzzi, the Bardi, and others – which made a common practice of these transactions. The exact terms varied with each contract. Sometimes only the next year's wool was sold, sometimes the sale was made for four, six, and even twelve years ahead. Sometimes the advance payment formed only a part of the price, and the transaction was then commonly described as one of wool sale. Sometimes the payment represented the full value of the wool, or occasionally even exceeded it, and then the transaction could be described as a loan repayable wholly or partly in wool. But whatever were the forms in which these contracts were expressed, they all represented one and the same type of commercial

---

[26] Letter Books A and B, and Recognisance Rolls 1–3, *passim*; Cal. P. M. Rolls, p. 9, 262; Guildhall Plea and Mem. Rolls, A 23 m. 6 dorso, R 84 m. 5, etc.; E. Ch. Pr. 26/395, etc.

[27] *Rot. Parl.*, v, 334 (1455): a complaint against the Italians, who obtain their wool cheaper than the English because they pay for it in ready money, but wool sales to Italians on credit were frequent.

[28] *Archaeologica*, xxviii, 221–2; *V.S.W.G.* (1913).

[29] Jenkinson, 'William Cade', in *English Hist. Review* (1913), 209 seq.

[30] Cal. Curia Regis Rolls, I, 144; III, 27, 177.

transaction. They were credit deals in which not the seller but the buyer gave credit.[31] This variation in the direction of credit is a fact of considerable interest for the study of medieval economy, but it does not affect the conclusion that, whether the seller or buyer figured as debtor, sales credits entered into every stage of the wool trade.

LOANS AND INVESTMENTS

Sale credits by no means exhaust the forms of mercantile credit. Short-time loans and investments are at present likely to be regarded as equally common, if not the commoner, forms of alliance between trade and credit; and no description of a system of mercantile credit is complete which leaves them out of account.

The ordinary short-time loan had for its object to satisfy immediate want of cash. Sudden liabilities which could not be met from the regular resources of the business, payments impending before the corresponding receipts fell due, promptitude of creditors and procrastination of debtors – in short, all the maladjustments of the regular systems of sale credits – would create a demand for short loans. In a sense these maladjustments could be described as emergencies, but in so far as selling and buying was generally based on credit, they were both frequent and inevitable, and the 'emergencies' were therefore part of the ordinary commercial routine. The Celys borrowed and lent money for terms of two, three, and six months whenever they were either short of ready money or had a surplus, and they were regularly short of money on the eve of the payments to the woolmen, just as they always had a surplus of cash immediately after the payments at the great Brabant fairs. These loans were probably even more numerous and certainly less uniform than direct reference in our records to the *mutuum*, or loan, would lead us to think. Apart from the fact that a great many mercantile debts remained unrecorded, they often appeared in such forms as would leave no traces, or else very misleading ones, in the records of debts. A very obvious instance of this are the 'loans by sale'. Loans of money between merchant and merchant were sometimes disguised in the shape of ordinary sales. This was often done to conceal the charging of interest, as in those cases of 'false chevisance' which came before the city tribunals of the fifteenth century. On 26 June 1421, one John Sadiller, vintner, was attached to answer in several prosecutions for 'feigned sale'. It was alleged that he had sold on credit Spanish

---

[31] A.V., Foreign Merchants, 127/3, etc. G. Espinas, John Boine Broke in *V.S.W.G.* (1904), pp. 95, 221 seq. Espinas, *La vie urbaine de Douai*, III., no. 860. For the deals of Italian merchants see the Recognisances on the L.T.R. and K.R. Memoranda Rolls. Rose Graham, 'The Finance of Malton Priory, 1247–1257', (*Trans. Royal Hist. Soc.*, 1904), 148 seq.

iron for £25 4*s*, to one Richard Trogonold, and then repurchased it for £23 10*s* in ready money; and that to John Lawney, John Bernard, Robert Haxton, and even to Sigismund, the King of the Romans, he had lent money in a similar way.[32] If a fictitious sale of this kind could easily be distinguished from a legitimate commercial bargain, it had to be but slightly modified to become absolutely indistinguishable from a genuine sale. How could anybody detect the real nature of similar transactions when they were carried out by three parties instead of two, when goods were bought on credit from one man and sold for cash to another?[33] The raising of funds by means of a three-cornered sale was common both in this country and abroad. It was employed by Bruges, Leiden, and other continental towns, and by English kings, notably Edward III, in their transactions with wool.[34] There are on the whole surprisingly few references in English records to this method of raising loans; but the fact that these transactions were seldom recorded is less a sign of their rarity than of their identity with ordinary buying and selling. Every merchant who had bought goods on credit, and then, when in need of money, sold them possibly at a lower price than he had stipulated to pay for them, would be raising a loan 'by the means of a sale'.

Arguing from the very few instances that are to be found in the records, it would seem as if the concealment of interest was not always the only motive for the employment of this type of loan. Quite often goods were 'chevised' because they happened to be more readily available than money. This was certainly the reason why the English Crown and the foreign municipalities had recourse to this type of transaction, and this was the avowed motive of a number of private 'chevisances by sale'. Thus apart from their employment for the disguising of interest, they also had a legitimate and independent economic function, which distinguished them from ordinary money loans.

The 'loan by sale' has been described at length, not so much for the intrinsic importance of the transaction, but for its interest as a characteristic example. Other types of medieval loan, like 'chevisances by sale', often remained unrecorded or 'misrecorded' among the ordinary entries of debts. These different types of loan were therefore even commoner than the numerous references to them would suggest. What is still more important, every one of them, just as the 'loan by sale', or even more so, had a distinct economic function of its own to fulfil in medieval trade.

---

[32] Guildhall, P.M. Rolls, A 49 mm. 8–10; other cases, ibid. A 63 m. 7 seq. Thomas, *Cal. of the Plea and Mem. Rolls*, 270–80 (1364), etc.

[33] In 1390 a City ordinance made such sales punishable when they were carried out by two partners, one selling and the other buying: *Liber Albus*, III, 162.

[34] I am indebted to Dr Power for material throwing light upon Edward's transactions with wool merchants. For chevisances of wool by Henry VI's government see *Proceedings of the Privy Council*, IV, 291–3.

This will become clear from even a cursory review of the main types of loan.

A type of loan very common in foreign trade, especially in the fourteenth and fifteenth centuries, was the so-called 'loan on exchange'. The London members of the Cely family, when short of money, 'took up' from London merchants certain sums in pounds sterling and undertook to repay them in several months abroad in a foreign currency at an agreed rate of exchange. Similarly, the man who represented them abroad – George or William Cely – would periodically 'give out' to other English merchants sums he had received from his customers to be repaid in England in pounds sterling.[35] Transactions of this type seem to have been a part of the business routine of Staplers and English importers, notably the mercers of London, and references to them are very abundant.[36] These exchanges were essentially credit transactions, and would probably be classified by medieval legists as 'fictitious exchange'. We must not, however, take this description at its face value. It is true that the carrying out of an exchange was seldom the sole object of a transaction of this type. Nevertheless, it was not a 'fictitious exchange' in the sense of ordinary loans disguised as exchanges; it was more often a genuine exchange transaction employed for the purpose of credit. The difference is certainly only one of emphasis, but it is worth noting. The Celys and their other contemporaries did not adopt this method of borrowing money merely in order to disguise interest charges; and this was certainly not the only form of short loan which they employed. Over and over again we find them contracting ordinary loans repayable in this country, which they describe as 'lones', 'prestes', or 'chevisances'. It was only when the repayment of the loan really involved a transfer of money from one place to another, or manipulations with several currencies, that the loan was contracted in the form of exchanges. The only type of exchange loan which in all justice could be described as a 'feigned exchange' (*cambio fittizio*)[37] was the 'dry' exchange – a contract of loan which stipulated repayment in the same place and in the same currency in which it was contracted. The references to these 'dry' exchanges, however, are very few; they were apparently infrequent in medieval England, and the bulk of the exchange loans mentioned in the English records belong to the same type of transaction as those described in the Cely papers. The whole class of transaction as it figures in the medieval practice in this country was specially adapted to, and used in

---

[35] Cely Papers and Accounts, *passim*.

[36] E. Ch. Pr. 58/291, 64/614, 29/161, etc. Gilliodts van Severen, *Cartulaire*, II, 6, 12, 712. Guildhall P.M. Rolls, A 74, m. 2 and 4; A 43, m. 70; A 61, m. 3; A 57, m. 6; A 41, m. 76; A 54, m. 1, etc.

[37] For the medieval classification of 'cambio' and the meaning of 'cambio fittizio' see Tawney, *Discourse*, 72–8; Frendt, *Wechselrecht*, I, 1–5.

connection with, financial dealings between merchants in different countries.[38]

No financial transaction has attracted so much attention as the so-called sale of rent. Rents were sold commonly either for life or for a certain number of years in every country and all through the Middle Ages; in some of the continental towns they formed the basis of municipal finance. It is generally held that the buying and selling of rents was common, for the simple reason that it was a convenient method of disguising the interest on loans. Here, again, we have a case of misplaced emphasis. It is probably true that the selling and buying of rents was stimulated by anti-usury legislation. It would, however, be entirely wrong to ascribe the constancy with which the rents circulated in the Middle Ages entirely and chiefly to the evasion of the usury laws. The real significance of the rent sales and the explanation of their popularity in the Middle Ages lies in the fact that they had a place to fill in medieval economy which was very important and, in a sense, entirely their own. Their function was related not to the ordinary borrowing and lending, but to the mobilisation and demobilisation of capital, and was fulfilled by a group of transactions, all of which were connected with real property.

Recent investigators have been struck by the frequency with which medieval merchants bought and sold land. Whether mercantile capital in the Middle Ages originated in the profits of agriculture and the accumulated ground rent of urban landlords, which is Sombart's view, or whether it was drawn from various sources, including trade, which is the view of most historians, the fact remains that every merchant of substance was also a landlord. John of Northampton, the famous Mayor of London, possessed in 1384 – the year of his disgrace – over ninety tenements in the city to the annual value of over £150. William Eynsham, a wealthy wool exporter and cloth merchant of Edward III's reign, owned in London over seventy tenements to the annual value of c. £110. Stephen of Cornhill, one of the rulers of the City of London, a draper and an important exporter of wool, possessed at his death in 1295 some twenty-five rents in London to the annual value of £36 4s, and lands in various places outside

---

[38] Closely allied to the exchange loans were the so-called 'sea loans' (*foenus nauticum, Seedarlehn*). (E. Ch. Pr., 26/193, 11/38, Cely Accounts, chancery miscellanea, bundle 37, file 13, fo. 31; Year Book 21 Edw. IV, Pasch., pl. 23.) This was a loan to a merchant or a master of a ship proceeding to another port. The loan was commonly payable in the place of the boat's destination and in the coin current there; it was therefore very similar in function to the exchange loans (J. Goldschmidt, *Universalgeschichte des Handelsrechts*, 354, 413 seq.). But in so far as the risk was borne by the lender, it often served the purposes of maritime insurance. We shall also see that it was sometimes merely a modified type of an ordinary investment.

London; and he had sold, shortly before his death, a number of messuages and rents in the city to the annual value of £33 18s 8d.[39]

All these men were of course, magnates of the city; but their possessions differed from those of the other wealthy merchants in quantity rather than in kind. There was hardly a merchant of substance in the city who would not possess a certain amount of real property, including leases and rents, and there was certainly no merchant of substance who would not, from time to time, engage in transactions with real property, be it buying, selling, pledging, or letting it. There was a constant movement of mercantile capital out of and into real property; the pace of the movement may have changed from generation to generation, but it never ceased, and always claimed the attention of municipal administrators.

The motives which prompted the flow of investments into real property were many and various. Rural estates were often bought for no other purpose than social advancement. More than one city family of the fourteenth and fifteenth centuries ended in this way its connections with the city and entered the coveted circle of country gentry. The bulk of the investments, however, had a purely economic end in view, and served the same purposes to which investments into 'safe' and regular sources of income are now put: annuities for widows and orphans, dowries, endowments for charitable or religious purposes. And just as non-speculative securities are nowadays employed by merchants as one of the methods of holding reserves or temporary unemployed capital, so also in the Middle Ages the investment in landed property and rents was often merely a way of holding unemployed capital in readiness for needs to come.[40] Now, if the buying of lands or rents meant locking up for a time a certain amount of liquid capital, the selling or pledging of rents, like the selling and pledging of the land itself, was one of the ways in which capital, immobilized by investment into real property, could be released. It is therefore wrong to lump the 'rent sale' with all the different forms of loan and describe it as one of the many methods of disguising the interest. There were several varieties of rent sale, and only one of them could, with some stretching, be classified as a loan – namely, the sale of a newly constituted rent. A German or Flemish municipality could raise a loan repayable by annual instalments, and these instalments would often represent, not the rent levied upon property before the loan had been contracted, but entirely new charges upon it. The moment, however, the

---

[39] Northampton, Parliamentary and Council Proceedings, Roll 15; Eynsham, P.R.O. Rentals and Surveys, Portfolio 1/21; Cornhill, ibid. Roll. 797.

[40] R. Davidsohn has shown that the landed property of the great houses of Florence was in their hands merely one form of their mercantile capital: *Forschungen zur Geschichte von Florenz*, IV, 272–3. The same can be demonstrated for at least a dozen English merchants of the thirteenth, fourteenth, and fifteenth centuries.

'new' rent was sold and entered into the market of the town, its future sales were merely successive mobilisations and immobilisations of capital. In public borrowing today it is only the issuing of the stock, and not its subsequent sales by one holder to another, that constitutes a loan; similarly in the Middle Ages every sale of an 'old' rent, be it municipal or private, was not a loan, but a transfer of capital from a smaller to a greater liquidity.[41] In other words, the sale of rents had a function of its own in the economic life of the Middle Ages, and from the point of view of this function it resembled other transactions with real property and not loans. If it had any relation at all to the financing of trade, it represented the financing of a merchant's trade out of his own resources. It is the financing of trade out of the capital resources of other persons that constitutes a commercial loan.

Next to the rent sales the type of financial transaction in the Middle Ages most popular with the historian is the *societas*. Partnerships loom large in the records of medieval trade, and there is no wonder that they have attracted so much attention. Their abundance, however, called for explanation, and attempts have been made to find causes sufficiently medieval to account for the popularity of the partnership in the Middle Ages. Hence the view of the *societas* as one of the methods adopted by medieval merchants in order to circumvent the prohibition of interest. It has, however, been pointed out by both Ashley and Cunningham[42] that medieval partnerships were not merely devices for the concealment of interest on loans; they had a function of their own to play in medieval trade, for it was by means of partnerships that capital was commonly invested in commercial undertakings. With this conclusion every student of medieval finance will concur. The medieval partnerships, or, to be more exact, the institutions which were regarded as such in the Middle Ages, had a double function to perform. One was related to the financing of medieval trade, the other to its organisation. Like every association, the medieval partnership had its *raison d'être* in carrying out such tasks as were beyond the powers of a single person. A commercial undertaking would require greater capital than one person was able or willing to bestow upon it, or would require an amount or a type of personal service

---

[41] Even this distinction must not be carried too far. From the point of view of the economic process embodied in it, the constitution and the sale of a 'new' rent, representing a real profit of the land, and not a mere promise to make certain annual payments, was as much a 'liquefaction' of capital as the sale of an old rent. Then, as Desmarez and Généstal point out, even when sales of rents were employed for purposes of loan they differed from ordinary loans in that they did not entail the return of the principal, and were often contracted for a long or an indefinite term: R. Généstal, *Le rôle des monastères comme établissements de crédit*, p. x; G. Desmarez, *Etude sur la propriété foncière*, 339. But the difference was not so clearly marked as Desmarez thinks.

[42] Ashley, *English Economic History*, part II, 42; Cunningham, 364 seq.

which he himself could not give. Partnerships would therefore be employed to overcome either or both of these difficulties. A person possessing the capital, but unable to conduct the trade or do it alone, could associate with a partner who would contribute his services. A person able to do the work, but not to contribute the capital, or at least the whole of it, could associate with others ready to make the required investment. Thus theoretically it is possible to distinguish three types of partnership: (1) one in which the capitalist hired the services of a trader; (2) another in which the trader hired capital (the 'financial partnership' proper); (3) the 'complete' or 'real' partnership (*vera societas*), in which all the members contributed both capital and services, and which in its pure form was nothing else but a 'joint business', or a union of several undertakings.[43]

The distinctions are not easy to apply. The question as to who hires whom – whether the merchant hires his capital, or capital hires its merchant – cannot be decided by any general rule, and no single principle of classification would enable us to group finance partnerships separately from the rest.[44] The whole combination of circumstances must be taken into account whenever we try to discover the economic nature of a partnership. When a merchant received a 'stock' in goods or money 'to merchandise withal', and the stock was obviously too small to constitute in itself a complete business undertaking, or where we know that it merely formed a part of the capital employed, we may safely assume that we have before us, not the contract of service, but one of investment. We can assume the same in most partnerships in which the user of the capital is known to have been an important merchant, and the owner of the capital was a widow, an orphan, or a person otherwise prevented from engaging in trade – a prince, a lord, an ecclesiastic.

[43] In some cases the finance partnership bore a strong resemblance to the 'complete' one, since investors often could, and sometimes did, engage in management of the business.

[44] The classification to which most historians adhere is that which the Italian and the German writers have borrowed from the history of the Italian *societas*. Ashley, *Economic History*, part II, 411–16, and Mitchell, *An Essay on the Early History of the Law Merchant* (1904), 126, 138, contain the best accounts of this classification. Attempts have been made to treat the various classes of *societas* as 'labour' partnerships and 'capital' partnerships respectively (cf. Lastig in *Zeitschr. f. d. ges. Handelsr.*, vol. XXXIV, and his *Accomendatio* (1909), Introduction, and pp. 41 seq.; also A. Lattes, *Diritto Commerciale* (1884), 154). These attempts, however, were bound to end in failure. The principle by which partnerships are classified in the medieval sources is not that of 'economic function'; therefore partnerships fulfilling either the function of organisation or that of finance, or both, will be found in each of the traditional classes of *societas*: Silberschmidt, *Teilhaberschaft und Beteilung*, 12–13; also his *Kommenda*, 103 seq.). In England neither the law nor the terminology made any of the distinctions we see in Italy, so that the Italian classification into *commenda*, *collegantia*, and *compagna* not only fails to provide the key for the separation of the financial partnerships from the others, but is altogether inapplicable.

Financial partnerships so identified will probably be found in every class of *societas* recorded in the English sources. They were apparently quite numerous among the commonest and simplest type of English partnership – namely, in the occasional partnerships of 'joint purchase and sale', where two or more merchants associated to carry out an isolated transaction. John Croche, a petitioner in the chancery, was asked by one John Ellys, who had bargained with one Richard, a mercer of London, for £24 worth of merchandise, to be partners with him in the same, and 'to be bounde jointly with hym to the same Richard', and he became Ellys's partner in this bargain.[45] In this particular case it is clear that the arrangement was purely financial: Ellys wanted someone to shoulder a part of the financial responsibility involved in the transaction. But in the majority of the occasional partnerships our information is too scanty for the purely financial arrangements to be singled out, and it is difficult to say how far this practice of investment in the form of separate transactions was general.

The distinction becomes more marked when we pass to partnerships of a more continuous nature, founded on a more or less permanent 'joint stock', or where one partner delivered to the other a certain sum in money or goods to be employed in his business. Financial partnerships of this type were common in medieval Europe from the earliest days, and references to them abound in the earliest collections of commercial laws and records.[46] In this country William Cade, the first financier to figure in English official records, apparently was in the habit of investing different sums in the undertakings of merchants.[47] This practice, known to Cade in the twelfth century, was apparently common throughout the Middle Ages. There were *societas*-like investments of varying magnitudes and types; and investors could be drawn from every class and station. On occasions they were orphans, widows, princes, ecclesiastics, nobles; while foreigners figured both among investors and recipients of investments. But most of the financial partnerships on record represent transactions of English merchants with each other. A fifteenth-century case in the chancery describes a partnership between Nicholas Mylle and Richard West, both tailors of London, by which West invested in Mylle's business £400 and £900.[48] The counter-petitions, rejoinders, and replications in this case make it one of the completest records of financial partnership in existence, but similar transactions more scantily reported occur in the English records over and over again.

There is nothing surprising in the fact that investments were so

[45] E. Ch. Pr. 48/154.
[46] The 'continuous' partnership was sometimes, though not very often, merely a series of occasional ones – e.g., E. Ch. Pr. 46/238.
[47] *English Hist. Review*, 1913, p. 730.
[48] E. Ch. Pr. 59/160–5.

commonly made through the medium of partnerships. Investment, connecting as it does the interest of the lender with the fortunes of the business, is by its very nature not a loan, but a special form of association. It was always regarded as such, and it constantly found a congenial embodiment in the contract of partnership. As Ashley correctly observed,[49] modern investments in industry and trade also take, as a rule, the form, not of loans for fixed interest, but that of shares in joint-stock companies. Of course, the identification of investments with partnerships must not be carried too far: not every partnership represented an investment, and not every investment took the form of partnership. Yet there is little doubt that the bulk of investments were embodied in *societas*-like arrangements; and even investments which were treated as loans were often, probably, nothing else than partnerships miscalled or modified. The type of *societas*-like investment corresponding to the Italian *commenda* or *implicita*, where the investor 'entrusted' a stock to a merchant for a specified length of time, was often hard to distinguish from an ordinary loan. Whatever distinction existed was subtle enough to permit of conflicting interpretations of the same arrangements by the very people concerned in them.[50] Hence we find instances of investments, described as ordinary loans, which in reality were *commenda*-like contracts. To take an instance. A friar, John Woderowe, warden of the house of Deptford, sought to recover 'certain moneys lent to John Chynle, mercer, and his partner Ralph Knyghton, who had traded and profited by the money'.[51] Can we really be certain that this was an ordinary loan, and not a financial *societas*?

It was chiefly by the method of remuneration that the financial partnership was commonly distinguished from an ordinary loan. It was therefore sufficient for the contract of partnership to adopt a fixed rate of profit to become almost completely indistinguishable from ordinary loans, and it was not unusual for the medieval *commenda* to adopt these conventional rates of interest instead of fluctuating shares in profits. Weber has shown that the *fœnus nauticus* with fixed rates of interest was nothing else than a modification of the ordinary *commenda* resulting from the greater certainty of trade in the Western Mediterranean and the possibility of calculating the average rate of profits.[52] Sometimes this conventional rate of profits was the result of official action, as in the case of the rate fixed in the investments of wards' funds in London, which in all other respects preserved the traces of their *commenda*-like nature and origin.

---

[49] *Economic History*, part I, 435–7.
[50] Several such cases are recorded in the Early Chancery Proceedings – e.g., 46/306.
[51] Guildhall P.M. Rolls, A 13, m. 1, 1367. Cf. Year Books, 12 Hen. VI, Pasch. pl. 3.
[52] M. Weber, *Zur Geschichte der Handelsgesellschaften*, 109–10.

The investment of wards' funds was a practice frequent and important enough to deserve special consideration. If there was in the Middle Ages any fund that could claim to be the source from which the mercantile community drew its investment credits, it was the orphans' funds, and especially those administered by the municipalities. In most of the towns of Northern Europe the funds left to orphans were employed by the municipal authorities either as public loans or given out on long terms to private merchants. The London practice in the Middle Ages did not differ much from that of continental towns. The City of London claimed a number of rights with regard to the administration of the goods of orphans, especially when their parents died intestate. Guardians were appointed by the Mayor and Chamberlains of the city, and were accountable to them for the discharge of their duty to the orphans. A child could be committed to a guardian with or without its goods, but usually the former was the case, so that the acceptance of a ward became a financial transaction, the funds being handled like ordinary investments. The goods, and sometimes even the charge of the orphan's 'body', could change hands several times during the period of minority; on a number of occasions the goods were from the outset committed for a period obviously related, not to the duration of the child's minority, but to the financial exigencies of the borrower's business.[53]

Sir William Ashley has pointed out that these investments were a variety of *commenda*-like agreements.[54] It was very usual in Western Europe throughout the Middle Ages to 'commend' dowries and patrimonies to merchants for employment in trade,[55] and of this *commenda* the investments of wards' funds described above were merely a variant. In one respect, however, these transactions did differ from the ordinary *societas* – namely, in the fixed rate of profits. The distribution of profits was regulated by a reputedly old custom, according to which the average 'mesne' profits were estimated at a flat rate of four shillings per pound per year, of which the guardian had one-half and the ward the other half, minus the cost of his maintenance and education.[56] Thus, in spite of the fact

---

[53] The chief source of evidence is the Guildhall Letter Books. A few isolated entries of orphans' goods committed to merchants occur in the first two letter books among the miscellaneous recognisances (L.B.A., 177, 188; L.B.B.., 38); in letter books G and H, belonging to the second half of the fourteenth century, they become common; in letter books I, K, and L, belonging to the fifteenth century, they fill more than two-thirds of the contents.

[54] *Economic History*, part II, 417–18.

[55] For an early Italian instance see Lastig, *Accomendatio*, 72. For English instances see *Testamenta Eboracensia* (Surtees Society), IV, 207–10; Sharpe, *Calendar of Wills*, 393; E. Ch. Pr. 65/149.

[56] Riley, *Memorials of the City of London*, 378, 446; P.M. Rolls, A 19, m. 8 dorso; Letter Book G (MS.), 132, 169, 323, etc. Occasionally funds were entrusted *sine proficuo*. In the second half of the fifteenth century the references to profits in the entries become less frequent.

that the fixed rate of profits had converted it into ordinary annual interest of 10 per cent, the fiction of division of profits was still maintained to bear witness to the origin and economic essence of the transaction.[57]

To conclude: the use of partnership in medieval finance was determined by the same principles as governed all the other forms of loan discussed here. The choice of the appropriate form was in every case determined not by mere whim, fortuitous chance, or an incorrigible desire to cheat, but by the economic essence of the contemplated deal. Loans on exchange, rent sales, sea loans, partnerships, were not various devices indiscriminately employed by the medieval merchant in order to disguise his ordinary loans. Each of them embodied a type of financial transaction distinct from others both in purpose and method; each of them had an economic function of its own to perform.

CREDIT AND CASH

What has been said as to the ubiquity and variety of medieval credit does not yet solve the purely quantitative aspect of the problem – that is, the question as to the relative importance of credit transactions in the total volume of medieval trade, or in the turnover of individual merchants. For an inquiry of this kind we are singularly ill-equipped, as the surviving evidence consists chiefly of records of debts. Nevertheless, in several isolated instances the evidence of debts supplemented by other sources can be made to yield not merely a vague impression of abundance, but also something approaching a quantitative statement. For some individual merchants the records of debts are, or can be, so grouped as to throw a great deal of light on the relative importance of credit in their transactions. For some merchants we are given or are able to compile something like inventories of their debts, which can then be compared with what we know or can guess of the total volume of their trade. These instances, of course, are few, but their importance is heightened by the fact that they all tell the same tale. The Celys, who were apparently an average fifteenth-century Staplers' firm, sold wool on credit in eleven out of every twelve transactions recorded in their letters and accounts. Some of George Cely's notes about his financial transactions at the fairs of Antwerp and Bergen-op-Zoom show that he never had much ready money on his hands, and most of the firm's capital consisted of wool not

---

[57] There was much in common between the commitment of the wards' funds to guardians and the financial transactions accompanying the contract of apprenticeship. See G. Desmarez, 'L'apprentisage à Ypres' in *Revue de Nord* (1911), 41 seq.; also Epinas and Pirenne, *Documents*, etc., III, nos. 854, 855, 857, 864, 870; II, nos. 470, 482. Cf. also the employment of funds of gilds for the purposes of investment.

yet fully paid for, and of debts owing to them. The state of George's account in winter, 1482, was as follows: £50 in cash, £200 in goods, £663 in debts maturing in May, and £234 8s 3d in more recent debts.[58] In this state of account there was nothing extraordinary or exceptional. In 1424 the executors of William Lynn, a wealthy Stapler, submitted to the city authorities an account of his movables. The total amount left was £4842 7s 2d, of which about £965 was in coin, about £811 in merchandise, and about £39 in plate and utensils. The rest, about £3027, was in debts owing to him from various persons in England and abroad. In his turn, he owed various men £1637 1s 4d – that is, about as much as he had in cash and merchandise.[59] A day book of John Thorp, a London scrivener (1458–60), supplies somewhat similar information about the credit transactions of a number of English wholesale clothiers and pewterers.[60] Thomas Dounton, a cloth merchant of London, figures in the book twenty-six times between September 1458 and May 1460 as creditor of various German merchants for cloth bought from him. The total amount of debts is £1359 4s 5d, while the value of cloth was apparently in the vicinity of £1700.[61] It would, therefore, seem that these credit sales represented the bulk of Dounton's business, as he was not a city magnate and his annual turnover could not very much exceed £1000.

Instances of this kind are not confined to the fifteenth century, and certainly not to Englishmen alone. The transactions of foreign importers trading to England are well illustrated by the inventories of their debts made on several occasions during the later thirteenth century in connection with the arrests of their goods by the Crown. At the time of the royal confiscation, the firm of Burnettus, Johann Vanne and partners, merchants of Lombardy and dealers in mercery, had a sum of over £1100 owing to them for goods sold on credit to various English merchants. The other possessions of the firms in England ('bona et mercimonia') were estimated by the assessors at £1400.[62] A similar use of credit would probably be revealed by an analysis of the transactions of the better-known merchants of the thirteenth and early fourteenth centuries, English and foreign alike, such as Gregory de Rokesle, William Servat, Philip Tailor, William Trente, John of Burford, William of Done-

---

[58] Cely Papers and Accounts, *passim*, and Chancery Misc., bundle 37, file 12, fols. 38–9.
[59] Guildhall Letter Book K (MS.), fo. 16. The account shows the relation of credit to Lynn's turnover and not to his capital. As will be shown in another place, Lynn's real property, or most of it, would have to be included in his business capital.
[60] A.V. 128/37. I am indebted to Mr Hilary Jenkinson for the identification of Thorp.
[61] This statement is based on the assumption that an instalment, commonly one-quarter or one-third of the price, was as a rule paid at the time of the purchase.
[62] A.V. 126/6.

castre, Richard of Resham, William Hauteyn, John Boine Broke,[63] Wautier Pied d'Argent, the several Betoins, Basings, Blunds, etc., not to mention the de la Poles and other commercial magnates associated with Edward III's transactions. These individual instances, however, must not be misunderstood. Significant as they are, they do not prove the absence or the rarity of transactions for ready money, as merchants often paid for their goods 'on the spot', or even in advance, and there were also persons who seldom sold on credit. All they prove is that the medieval merchant displayed no preference for any particular financial method. His choice between purchase on credit or for ready money was not determined by any 'medieval' dislike or ignorance of credit, as Bücher suggests, nor by any special liking for it, as a hasty deduction from the evidence here presented might suggest, but by a very obvious economic factor which is as little medieval as it is modern. This factor was the amount of the available capital. It was the relative abundance or scarcity of capital at the disposal of an individual merchant that determined the employment of credit in selling and buying. An ordinary medieval merchant, a vintner like William Barache, or a Stapler like Richard Cely, obtained his goods on credit, and could therefore afford to wait for payment from his own customer. In its ideal form this type of trade needed very little capital. But the shorter and smaller the credit which the merchant received relative to the length and amount of credit he himself allowed, the greater had to be the capital engaged in trade, and the greater the capital at the disposal of the merchant, the more he was able – given the same turnover – to dispense with credit in buying, or even to pay for his goods in advance. Similarly, a wealthy seller was able to allow credit to his customers, while a needy one would require full payment or even pre-payment.

The sales of wool for future delivery described above[64] are a case in point. In seeking to explain why sale credit changed its usual direction in these particular transactions we may easily be led astray by the fact that they took place mainly in the late thirteenth and early fourteenth centuries; and that the debtors were chiefly monasteries and the creditors Italians. The temptation thus arises to explain everything by what we know of the financial domination of the Italians in the thirteenth century, their advanced commercial methods, and their pioneering work in the English wool trade; or else by the peculiarities of manorial economy which made it easier to collect monastic debts and papal dues in kind. Either explanation contains a grain of truth: neither contains the whole

---

[63] Accounts of Boine Broke's and Servat's activities are contained in the Articles of G. Espinas in *V.S.W.G.*, 1904; F. Arens, ibid., 1904, and Edmonde Albe, *Bull. de la Société des Etudes du Dep. du Cot*, 1908 (according to the latter there were two William Servats at the end of the thirteenth century).

[64] Above, pp. 10 seq.

of it. That the advance sales of wool were not peculiar to the thirteenth century is shown by the Statute of 1465 enacting that 'come per subtile bargains faitz en achater des laines devaunt que les berbizes, que ceo portent soient tondrez', none except spinners and cloth-makers shall be allowed for the next two years to buy 'unshorn' wools in the eighteen principal wool-growing countries.[65] Nor, again, can the transaction be described as exclusively Italian. While Italians often bought wool for advance payment or ready money, they were not the only merchants to do so. We find Flemings like Boine Broke and others buying wool from monasteries in the same fashion; and there is no doubt that some of the English merchants followed a similar practice.[66] Still less can this type of transaction be regarded as a peculiarity of monastic trade. First of all, there are numerous instances of similar advances made to laymen,[67] secondly, there was hardly a wool-growing monastery in England which would not at one time or another sell its wool for deferred payments. Frequently, monasteries combined both methods of payment, receiving a part of the price in advance and the rest some time after the delivery of the wool.[68] The real explanation lies in the buyer's abundance of capital or the seller's shortage of it. If the Italians made the widest use of the method of advance payment, this was merely because in the later thirteenth and early fourteenth century they were better provided with capital than most other wool exporters, while the monasteries at this period frequently found themselves in financial difficulties.[69] In other words, in a trade where demand was always keen, and supplies were more or less fixed, buyers who were powerful capitalists came into contact with sellers who were poor. Advance payments came as naturally, both before and after the thirteenth century, between lay sellers and non-Italian buyers, whenever the same conditions were re-enacted.

Thus far only are we justified in accepting the assertion that advance payments for goods constituted the rule in commercial dealings between agricultural producers and urban capitalists. As a statement of fact the assertion is more or less correct, for in the sales of agricultural produce advance payments were indeed very common, especially on the Continent. But as a scientific generalisation or an attempt at an explanation it

---

[65] 4 Edw. IV, c. 4.

[66] *Chron. de Melsa*, Rolls Series, III, 84–7, 144. Rec. Roll 1, m. 1 (Basing), etc.

[67] Rec. Roll, 1, m. 1 (Ricardi); A.V. 126/28, m. 2 dorso; Northumberland Pleas, p. 310 (1271); M.R. 52 (6 Edw. I), m. 11, 60 (15 Edw. I), m. 19 dorso and 20 (Holm and Tattershall), etc.

[68] The fifteenth-century views of hosts show a number of abbeys in the West of England selling their wool to Italians, obviously for ready money or deferred payments: A.V. 128/30 and 128/31; Whittaker, Craven, 449 seq.; *Chron. de Melsa*, III, 233, etc.

[69] R. Snape, *English Monastic Finances in the Later Middle Ages*, pp. 120 seq.; R. Graham, *St Gilbert*, pp. 136 seq.

is misleading. In the example already described, that of advance sales of wool, the wool growers frequently allowed credit to some of the buyers; nor were the recipients of advances always wool growers – there were numerous contracts for future delivery of wool between merchant and merchant.[70] But what is still more important is that even wool growers, lay and monastic, often sold not their own wool, but wool bought from others. We find monasteries selling for future delivery quantities of wool out of all proportion to the size of their flocks, and employing the advances received from merchants in buying wool on the local markets. The Cistercian and the Sempringham orders attempted to suppress this practice, as did also on one occasion the Crown, but for a long time their attempts apparently produced no immediate effects.[71] The monasteries continued to buy wool to fulfil their contracts with merchants; and the contracts frequently gave them the right or even made it their duty to supply wool not of their own growth.[72] It is therefore not as producers of wool that monasteries demanded or accepted advances. If agricultural producers and not merchant buyers accepted credit, this was because the latter were, as a rule, well supplied with capital, while the former were commonly short of funds. When these conditions were absent, when the trader was not an important capitalist, and the producer was not impoverished, the credit, if given, was likely to flow in the opposite direction –from the seller to the buyer. The occurrence of cash deals does not, then, constitute an exception to the practice of credit sales. The advances, the deferred payments, and the cash payments did not each represent a different financial principle in medieval trade: they were all various manifestations of one and the same elementary maxim that 'the rich lend, the poor borrow'.

There is yet another reason why 'cash sales', however frequent, cannot be contrasted with the employment of credit – namely, the connection between the different forms of sale credits on the one hand and investments on the other. We have said that the greater the capital at the disposal of the merchant the more credit could he allow in his sales and the less he would need it in his purchases. Now, if we remember that the trading capital of medieval firms often belonged to other people, we shall also understand the connection which sometimes existed between

---

[70] At Leicester and Northampton it was at one time usual for strangers to entrust money to local merchants, who bought wool on their behalf in the surrounding countries: *Records of Leicester*, 1, 88, 91, 93, 186–7, 201–2, etc.; *Records of Northampton*, 1, 230–1, cap. xlix. Most of these transactions represented *commenda*-like partnerships, but it was only a short step from them to ordinary advances from big wool merchants to smaller traders who collected wool from the growers: A.V. 126/128 (Bonaventura); M.R. 60; 15 Edw. I, m. 15 (Guidicione); and many other references in the M.R.

[71] Rose Graham in *Trans. Royal Hist. Soc.* (1904), 148; Whitwell, op. cit., 8–10.

[72] M.R. 60, 15 Edw. I, m. 16 d. (Rievaulx), m. 20 (Toteshale), etc.

investments and sale credits. The *Grosse Ravensburger Gesellschaft*, a great South German trading organisation, sold goods on credit, but as a rule bought them for ready money,[73] since it possessed greater capital than was usual in the fifteenth century, its capital being made up of deposits, investments, and special loans received from numerous persons. Thus its cash purchases, credit sales and investments were all parts of the same commercial policy: it preferred to owe money to its partners and depositors rather than to sellers of goods; but – given the same turnover – it would have needed a much smaller capital, and owed much less on account of investments, if it had bought goods on credit. Similarly, if it is true that the Medici, Spinelli, Strozzi, Contarini, and the other Italian merchants of the fifteenth century paid for their wool in cash more frequently than did English merchants, this was the result of, and a testimony to, their possessing larger capitals than the native wool merchants. And in so far as the trading capital of these firms was largely made up of other people's investments, their use of credit was not so very different from that of ordinary wool merchants. They merely borrowed from, and paid interest to, a different set of people. The same applies also to the Italian houses of the thirteenth century, which so commonly paid for the wool in advance.[74] Apart from what is known of the system of investment and deposits which these houses practised in Italy itself, there is also evidence of Italians accepting investments from people in this country. Mathew Paris, writing about the behaviour of the Italian usurers in England, alleges that even after their expulsion by Henry III a large number of them remained in England under the protection of the magnates who had invested their money with them 'after the example of the Roman Curia'.[75] That these investments – at any rate, in the late thirteenth and fourteenth centuries – were not unconnected with the wool transactions of the great Italian houses, and may have formed part of the capital which enabled them to pay for their wool in advance, is shown by an interesting thirteenth-century case relating to a sum delivered on deposit (*tradite fuissent*) by William Servat and another Anglo-French merchant of London to the Riccardi of Lucca, a firm most commonly mentioned as paying in advance for its wool.[76]

[73] A. Schulte, *Geschichte d. Grossen Ravensburger Handelgesellschaft* (1923), I, 123, 301, 458 seq., 472; III, *passim*.

[74] R. Davidsohn, *Geschichte von Florenz*, IV, 202–8; Giovanni Villani, *Cronica*, III (ed. 1844–5), libro xi, cap. lxxxviii, describing the loans of Italian banks to Edward III, says: 'E nota che i detti danari erono la maggior parte di gente che gli aveano dati loro in acomandigia e in deposito, e de più cittadini e forestieri.'

[75] 'Quia magnatum quorundam, quorum, ut dicebatur pecuniam ad multiplicandum seminabant, exemplo Romanae curiae, favore defendebantur' (*Cron. Maj.*, v, 245).

[76] *Rot. Parl.*, I, 43.

It is not always that the connection between investments and sale credits can be established. Theoretically, in most medieval trades, and especially in those in which the turnover of the individual businesses was more elastic than it seems to have been in the wool trade, the obvious connection was not between investments and sale credits, but between investments and the volume of trade, since the additional capital was more likely to be used for the extension of business than for the modification of the methods of payment. It is therefore impossible to speak of anything in the nature of a general and necessary connection between investments and sale credits. For our present purpose, however, no such general rule is required. It is sufficient to observe that very often a connection of this kind did exist; that the elimination, complete or partial, of credit in buying and selling was likely to be offset by borrowings in other directions; and that consequently 'cash deals', in some of those instances in which they were frequent, signified, not the merchant's dislike or disuse of credit, but merely a different choice between its various forms.

Several aspects of medieval trade have been neglected in this essay. To begin with, of Dr Cunningham's binomial formula – 'dealing for credit was little developed, and dealing in credit was unknown' – only the first element – i.e., the 'dealing for credit' – has been analysed here; the 'dealing in credit' – i.e., the selling and buying of credit and of financial instruments – still awaits examination. Secondly, there is the problem of chronology: the antiquity of medieval credit and its evolution from century to century. Thirdly, there is the question of interest, and of the public attitude towards credit and interest. Finally, no study of medieval credit is complete which does not describe the organisation of credit, the professional standing of the financial agents, and the social standing of the owners of capital. And this in its turn demands a preliminary study of the 'origin' of loanable capital. To these problems the present essay provides merely an introduction. Its purpose has been to show how the economists, and through them also the historians, have underestimated the volume of medieval credit and consequently misunderstood its nature. Sale credits, of which the existence has been generally denied, in reality formed the financial basis of medieval trade. As to the other forms of credit their existence was never doubted, but their function was wrongly interpreted. Because of its ubiquity, medieval credit displayed greater variety than is commonly supposed; and of this variety the multiplicity of forms was merely an outward expression.

2

PRIVATE FINANCIAL INSTRUMENTS IN MEDIEVAL ENGLAND[1]

Few problems of medieval credit have received more attention from continental historians than that of financial instruments. The medieval *tratta* (bill of exchange), its origin and diffusion, has been a special favourite with the student, and we now know more about its legal and diplomatic evolution in the Middle Ages than we do of its fortunes in modern times. But this added knowledge has had surprisingly little influence upon the relevant principles of economic history. In spite of the accumulating information the writers of economic history are still apt to represent the technique of medieval credit, especially in the transactions of the non-Italian merchants, not only as something far less elaborate and perfect than the modern technique (which would probably be true) but as its complete antipode: the embodiment of an entirely different economic principle, part of a different, 'medieval' order of things. To the present day the teaching of economic history in England conforms to the traditional notion which Cunningham has epitomised in his binomial formula: 'dealing for credit was little developed and dealing in credit was unknown'. By 'dealing in credit' Cunningham obviously meant the selling and the buying of credit: its transfer and circulation. 'Though bills were used for transmission of wealth, there is a striking difference between those times and ours in the absence of commercial credit (except what corresponds to book debts) as a basis of transactions of other kinds. We must remember that transactions were carried on in bullion; men bought for coins and sold for coins. Loans were made in coins and repaid in coins . . . There was no paper circulation of any kind.'[2]

---

[1] This paper first appeared in *Vierteljahrschrift fur Social- und Wirtschaftsgeschichte*, xxiii, 1930. Abbreviations: R.S.=Rolls Series; S.S.=Selden Society; E. Ch. Pr.=Public Record Office, Early Chancery Proceedings; P.M. Rolls= London City Records, Plea and Memoranda Rolls; L.B.=ibid. Letter Books; Cely Accounts=Public Record Office, Chancery Miscellanea, Bundle 37; Y.B.=Year Books; P. & M.=Pollock and Maitland, *History of English Law*; Holdsworth=W. Holdsworth, do.

[2] *The Growth of English Industry and Commerce during the early and the Middle Ages*, ed. 1910, p. 362.

This view rests on two major assumptions. Credit did not in itself constitute an object of commercial operations, first of all because its employment in trade was exceptional and irregular, and, secondly, because, whatever there was of it, was not yet embodied in efficient financial instruments. The first of these assumptions, the rarity and irregularity of credit in the Middle Ages, has been examined elsewhere;[3] the present essay makes the second assumption its theme – the technique of credit as represented by the English financial instruments of the later Middle Ages. The theme comprises a number of distinct problems relating to the functions of the different financial instruments, their relative efficiency, their development and evolution, and above all, the question whether and how far they served the purposes of circulation. But it is not proposed to treat these problems here in the systematic and analytical manner they deserve. All the present essay sets out to do is to give a description of the English financial instruments in use in the late fourteenth and fifteenth centuries, analogous and contributory to the existing descriptions of financial instruments elsewhere. It can only be hoped that the description will in itself supply a discerning reader with an answer to the problems enumerated here.

THE OBLIGATION (THE BOND, THE RECOGNISANCE, THE BILL OBLIGATORY)

Of the medieval English documents witnessing debts, the obligation (*littera obligatoria, escript obligatoire*, bond) was undoubtedly the commonest. The notched wooden tally, a handy evidence of debt, could not compete with it. Even if it were common in mercantile transactions in the earlier centuries, it certainly fell into disuse in the late fourteenth century, except in the financial business of the Crown. It had by then lost many of its old advantages, while preserving many of its old drawbacks. Though it had never been as full a record of the transaction as a written document could be, it probably commended itself by the ease and cheapness of its production. But in the fifteenth century the bond had shed most of its unnecessary verbiage and probably became a less expensive document to draw up. The bonds printed in Madox's *Formulare Anglicanum*[4] illustrate well the progress of this diplomatic economy, and the 1439 bond which he prints is fairly representative of the laconic form adopted for the recording of mercantile debts in the fifteenth century.

---

[3] M. Postan, 'Credit in Medieval Trade', (*Economic Hist. Rev.*, 1928) and Ch. 1 above. See also B. Kuske, 'Die Entstehung der Kreditwirtschaft und des Kapitalverkehrs' (*Kölner Vorträge*, Bd. 1, *Teil* 1, 1927).

[4] Nos. 631 seq.

Noverint universi me Robertum Tylney de Lenn Episcopi mercatorem teneri et firmiter obligari Henrico Foster de Newark draper in septem libris bone et legalis monete Anglie, solvendi eidem Henrico, heredibus vel executoribus suis, aut suo certo attornato in festo Translacionis Sancti Thome Martitis proximo futuro post datam presencium, sine dilacione ulteriori. Ad quam quidem solucionem ut predicitur bene et fideliter faciendam, obligo me, heredes et executores meos ac omnia bona mea per presentes. In cuius rei testimonium presentibus sigillum meum opposui. Datum tercio die Augusti anno regni Regis Henrici post conquestum sixti decimoseptimo.

At the same time, even in this laconic form the bond remained a full record of the transaction and a relatively full summary of the duties and stipulations involved in it – a thing the tally or some of the other medieval expedients could never hope to be. A typical document, like the one quoted here, contained the names of the parties, the date of its sealing, the amount of the debt, the date of payment. It might also contain clauses specifying the place of payment, the mode of payment (instalments, currency, rates of exchange) or stipulations which would make the payment contingent upon the fulfilment of certain specific conditions and thus convert the bond from an 'obligation simple' into an 'obligation conditional'. These conditions and stipulations would sometimes be set out on the back of the document ('bond endorsed') or in special documents, commonly indentures, but they could also be embodied in the text of the principal obligation.[5] Some bonds also contained clauses dealing with sanctions, i.e. penalties for non-payment. A common method of stipulating these was by means of a separate document, which contemporary sources sometimes describe as the 'penal bond'. By its very nature the 'penal' bond was not an obligation 'simple' but an obligation 'conditional'. It was as a rule made out for a sum larger than the payment stipulated, and the amount by which it exceeded the former constituted the damages for non-payment. Sometimes, however, the penalties and the damages would be enumerated in the original bond, and a careful survey of the diplomatic forms of the bond may reveal a close connection between the existence of a 'penal' bond and the absence of a sanction clause in the original obligation.

Needless to say, the 'fullness' of the bond was only relative. As a record of the transaction it was comprehensive, but not exhaustive. The most obvious omission, and the one of which the historians are most conscious, is the absence of any stipulations of interest. Another and a very important omission is that of collateral securities. The importance of these omissions, however, must not be exaggerated: they reflect certain peculiarities of medieval diplomatics and law, rather than the imper-

---

[5] Liber Albus (R.S.) p. 209, enumerates three types: 'simple ou endosse, ou par endentures'.

fections of medieval credit itself. That the absence of references in English bonds to interest charges is not evidence of the gratuitous nature of medieval loans requires no proof. In England, as abroad, it seems to have been a common practice to make out the bond for an amount representing the principal plus interest; and although this practice prevents us now from discovering the interest charges, it could not prevent the medieval merchant from making them.[6] The same argument applies to the omission of securities. That securities were commonly given cannot seriously be disputed. We know that the gage of land in the Middle Ages was very common; the records of mercantile transactions leave no doubt as to the frequency of pledges in the shape of goods; the same records testify also to the prevalence of personal sureties. We also know that the sureties, their quantity and quality, affected the terms of loans and must have figured prominently in the negotiations for them. The attempts of creditors to exact additional sureties from their debtors are invariably represented in the Chancery petitions as a contravention of the original terms of the bargain: which clearly indicates that the terms of a debt contracted on the debtor's own sureties were more onerous than they would have been had they been secured by additional pledges.[7]

The silence of the bond was not a sign of the rarity or novelty of securities. Nor was it a measure of the diplomatic efficiency of the document. The gage of land, especially in its late medieval form of 'conditional feoffment', was as a rule safeguarded by means of formalities and documents (covenants and charters) additional to those recording the debt itself; the pledge of goods was also recorded, if a record were wanted, on a conditional bill of sale; and in those cases, in which the hypothecation of land or goods was intended, a handy instrument was provided by the so-called Statute Staple.[8]

In short, the special nature of these pledges required a special record, and could safely be omitted from the principal obligation. The position

[6] The mercantile records abound with relevant instances, e.g. E. Ch. Pr. 43/262, 60/20, 64/119, 64/923, 28/452.
[7] E. Ch. Pr. 64/594–5; the petitioner was forced by his creditor 'to find other collateral sureties to keep his said days of payment, whereas in deed . . . petitioner would never have borrowed' if other sureties had been required of him. Cf. E. Ch. Pr. 48/25, 47/154. The custom of 'foreign attachement' in London and other boroughs (cf. W. Brandon, *A treatise upon the Customary Law of Foreign Attachment*, 1861, pp. 1–8, *Borough Customs* (S.S.) vol. 1, pp. 127–9; Liber Albus pp. 207–9) was often diverted from its original purpose and employed to force debtors to produce additional sureties.
[8] Separate conditional bonds; E. Ch. Pr. 59/113. Documents recording conditional feoffment for the purposes of gage (Verpfändung unter Resolutivbedingung): Madox op. cit. nos. 560–2; D. Hazeltine, 'Die Geschichte des englischen Pfandrechts' in Gierke's *Untersuchungen* etc., Hft. 92, appendices, pp. 333 seq. Conditional bills of sale: E. Ch. Pr. 26/272, 46/366, 62/251. For the employment of recognisances for the purposes of hypothecation of land see Hazeltine, op. cit., pp. 284–9.

was slightly, but only slightly, different with regard to personal sureties. These took the form of either an independent suretyship or a co-debtorship (*Samthand*). In the first of these two forms the sureties bound themselves to the creditor in separate obligations conditional on the non-payment of the debt by the principal debtor.[9] Much commoner was the co-debtorship: a transaction whereby the sureties bound themselves jointly with the actual debtor, and were in exactly the same position as he: they were bound jointly and severally, each was responsible for the whole sum 'as for his own proper debt' and the creditor could proceed against each of them separately for the whole amount. These bonds contained no security clauses, and for obvious reasons. From the creditor's point of view an obligation secured by co-debtorship was indistinguishable from a bond by virtual co-debtors. It was not his duty, nor his concern, to define the special position of sureties. This definition was a matter between themselves and the principal debtor, and the latter would sometimes undertake to render his sureties 'harmless' i.e. to compensate them for whatever damages his failure to pay might cause them.[10] This undertaking could be recorded in a separate document, but it would be omitted as irrelevant from the principal bond embodying the claims of the creditor. Thus the absence of security clauses from the medieval bond, as its silence in the matter of interest, meant much less at the time than it means to us now. The omissions certainly make the bond a less satisfactory source of historical information than a more explicit document would be. But its inconvenience to the modern student is not a true measure of its inconvenience to the medieval merchant; nor is it a true reflection of the imperfections of the medieval financial mechanism. Certain commercial practices present in a normal contract of debt failed to find expression in the bond, but the failure was not due to their rarity, nor even to the inadequacy of the diplomatic technique, but to considerations of legal and commercial expediency, which made their recording in the principal bond either redundant or irrelevant.

The advantages of the formal bond over other expedients, and above all over the tally, become more obvious still when we pass from its function as a record of the transaction to its value as evidence in courts.[11]

---

[9] E. Ch. Pr. 59/113.

[10] E. Ch. Pr. 51/236, 17/219. Normally if any of the sureties paid the debt he could proceed against each of the other pledgers, P.M. Rolls A 23, m. 6 d. In London this could be done by a special 'bill of contribution'. Lib. Albus, pp. 206–7, E. Ch. Pr. 48/9, 48/67.

[11] The position of the tally in Law Merchant was higher than in Common Law, cf. Y.B. 20–1 Edw. I. The custom of London regarded a sealed tally as binding as an obligation, Lib. Alb. p. 214, but even there the plaintiff was allowed to deny the day of payment. In Common Law even a sealed tally did not attain the full legal conclusiveness of a bond. P. & M. vol. II, p. 215 and footnotes 2 and 3.

From the legal point of view the bond was a 'specialty', a covenant under seal, the highest form of documentary evidence the English Common Law recognised. Although it may not have been by origin a '*dispositive Urkunde*', i.e. a document not merely witnessing a pre-existing obligation but in itself creating it, it came to resemble it in more than one respect.[12] The obligor could not deny or explain away any statement contained in it; the right witnessed by it did not expire until the document was destroyed or until the creditor released the debtor by a special declaration equally solemn and formal (acquittance). There was nothing to prevent a creditor who retained the bond after the payment of the debt from demanding payment for the second time, and a debtor who was unable to produce a formal acquittance had no remedy in Common Law. However unscrupulous might have been the conduct of the creditor in obtaining the bond, nothing save approved duress, could absolve the debtor from his liability. One course only was open to him, and that was to deny the authenticity of the document, but a bond proved to be his deed was conclusive against him to its last word.[13]

This exalted position of the commercial bond is not surprising considering that both in its origin and in its diplomatic structure it was merely a species of the 'carta', differing from the land charter only in its subject matter. Its universal address (*noverint universi*) and words of obligation (*me Johannem teneri firmiter obligari*), gave it the form and the meaning of a solemn, public and personal declaration of the obligor in recognition of his debt to the obligee; a declaration which, because it was solemn and public (i.e. 'open', patent) and because it was personal, had a greater legal force than a mere certificate, a *notitia*, modestly worded and telling the story of the transaction in the third person. But the feature

The final position as formulated in 1310 was that against the tally as against a deed there could be no wager of law, but an averment that nothing was due could be made: Y.B. Edw. II (S.S.), pp. 46–7, Holdsworth III, p. 417, n. 2. In the words of C. J. Beresford, *Eyre of Kent (1313–1314)*, vol. II (S.S.), p. 58, 'a tally is not a pure deed as is a writing, for what has been inscribed on a tally can be shaved off and something different from what was there before can then be put in its place at the will of the custodian of the tally, without anyone being able to detect it, which is not the case with a writing'. A similar argument is used by Belknap in a later case quoted by R. Bellew in his *Les ans du Roy Richard le Second*, ed. 1869, p. 158. For the evolution of the Common Law view prior to its definition in 1310 cf. the cases listed in the Y.B. 3 Edw. II, p. 47, n. 2, and the case in the *Eyre of Kent*, op. cit., p. 57.

12 The notion of the medieval *carta* as a 'dispositive Urkunde' (cf. A. Heusler *Institutionen*, vol. I, pp. 87–8, H. Brunner, *Carta und Notitia*, 1886, p. 574) has been subjected to a searching criticism by C. Freundt, *Wertpapiere im antiken u. frühmittelalterlichen Rechte*, vol. I, pp. 121–46. For the evolution of the English views in the Middle Ages see Holdsworth III, 418–19. The validity and the effect of the dictum that 'obligation est contract en luy mesme' (R. Bellew, op. cit., pp. 32, 111, 255; cf. W. T. Barbour, *The History of Contract in Early English Equity*, p. 21) still awaits examination.

13 Bracton, *De Legibus*, fo. 100b, P. & M., II, p. 220, Barbour, op. cit., p. 23.

primarily responsible for the exceptional validity of the bond in English law, and marking it off sharply from similar documents abroad, was the authentication by means of a seal. Abroad documents were usually authenticated by enrolment and registration by notaries and public authorities. In this country the same purpose was served by private seals. All persons of property possessed seals, and their employment became essential in the authentication of private documents.[14]

Whether as a result of this use of seals, or for other reasons, the official enrolment of debts fulfilled in England a purpose different from that for which it was employed abroad. It is not that official enrolment was not employed in this country for the recording or authenticating of private deeds. The clerks of the Chancery and the Exchequer, the town clerks of London and other towns, regularly recorded wills, donations and covenants of private persons on the official rolls of their departments. Nor can it be said that the notarial recording of deeds was entirely unknown in England. The institution of notaries probably remained throughout the Middle Ages an exotic custom, and derived whatever authority it possessed from Imperial and Papal grants.[15] But it would be wrong to suppose that there was nobody in England to fulfil at least some of the functions which the notaries fulfilled abroad. There was in England, from comparatively early times a class of professional 'scriveners' which reached, by the end of the Middle Ages, a position of great influence. They apparently monopolised the work of diplomatic composition, and private bonds were, as a rule, written by them. By the beginning of the fifteenth century, and possibly earlier, they seem to have kept a record of those private documents which passed through their hands, and the entries in the scriveners' books could play a part somewhat resembling that of notarial records on the continent.[16] Even if unrecognised by the courts of common law, they were apparently regarded as valid evidence in merchant custom, and possibly in the courts of the Chancery and the Exchequer. Nevertheless it remains broadly true that debts were rarely enrolled or recorded before official bodies or authoritative persons for the mere purpose of their authentication. Enrolment in

---

[14] T. F. Tout, *Chapters in the Administrative History*, I, pp. 121–3, P. & M. II, p. 224. On the legal consequences of the authentication by private seal see Holdsworth III, p. 417, n. 2, P. & M. II, p. 220.

[15] Tout, ibid.: J. Granstoun, *Brooke's Notary Public*, ed. 1925, pp. 8–16. For instances of notarial deeds see Madox, op. cit., nos. 25–7, P.M. Rolls A 14, m. 1 d., A. 73, m. 6.

[16] Granstoun, op. cit., 213; E. Ch. Pr. 63/119: an acquittance delivered in the presence of a scrivener 'as it appeareth in his book of records'. E. Ch. Pr. 10/217, 64/1046 & 64/1051 contain reference to bonds recorded in scriveners' books. In the Accounts Various of the K.R. Exchequer at the Public Record Office there is a register of a scrivener, John Thorp, (128/37) which looks like a 'book of records' referred to in the petitions.

this country had for its principal object the creation of a different and a more formal variant of the bond: it converted an obligation into a full legal recognisance.

The expression 'full legal recognisance' is used with a purpose, for a bond can also be called and regarded as a *recognitio*, though it lacked the power of a full legal recognisance. In medieval terminology 'recognitio' meant a formal acknowledgement by one party of the right of the other in an actual or potential law suit. This definition would partly apply to a bond in so far as it was a public recognition of the obligee's right. The production of a bond would consequently confine the judicial proceedings on a plaint of debt to the mere question of whether the writing were genuine. Once it was established and admitted as genuine, the judgement was given automatically, for the bond embodied a public recognition that the right was the creditor's. But even this preliminary investigation would be unnecessary if that public recognition could officially be placed before the court entitled to hear plaints of debt. One way of procuring a judicial recognition of a potential plaintiff's right was the so-called 'judgement'. The creditor could, with the debtor's consent, and even before the money was delivered, make a plaint of debt in court; the court would then give a judgement in the creditor's favour, who, being now a 'judgement creditor', could, if the debt were not paid, apply at once for a writ of execution.[17] But he could also obtain the same results by means of a 'recognisance' i.e. the formal acknowledgement of the obligation by the debtor before a judicial tribunal. The recognisance so acknowledged, and recorded upon the court rolls, was not merely an enrolled obligation, it was equivalent to a 'judgement'. By recognising the obligation before a court the debtor conceded to the creditor in advance the right to proceed with the execution as soon as he defaulted. At the conclusion of a typical recognisance the debtor would state that should he fail to pay ('*nisi* etc. . . .') execution could forthwith be had against his lands, goods and person. Armed with this executory power the recognisance became one of the favourite financial instruments of the Middle Ages, employed whenever even greater legal security was needed than that which an ordinary bond could provide.[18]

If a certain type of judicial enrolment produced a version of an obligation more formal and conclusive than the ordinary bond under a private seal, the absence of both a judicial record and a private seal converted the bond into one of those informal obligations which were so popular with merchants in spite of their uncertain position in law. Writing of the foreign commercial usages of the seventeenth century Malynes describes

[17] Hazeltine, op. cit., p. 88.
[18] Hazeltine, op. cit., pp. 284 seq. For identical instruments abroad see P. Huvelin, *Le droit des marches et des foires*, pp. 473–9.

at great length the use which the merchants abroad made of what he calls *bills obligatory*. 'The most usual buying and selling of commodities beyond the seas, in the course of traffik, is for bills of debt, or obligations, called bills obligatory, which one merchant giveth into another, for commodities bought and sold, which is altogether used by the Merchant Adventurers of Amsterdam, Middleburg, Hamburg and other places.'[19] These bills, he says, are quite informal documents 'which every man of credit and reputation giveth of his own handwriting . . . without any seal or witness thereunto'. Now, if we do not misinterpret the evidence of the English records, it seems that the English merchants also employed highly informal 'bills obligatory' of exactly the same type. The commonest way of describing them was simply 'bills' or 'bills of his own hand'.[20] Of course, medieval terminology was never exact, and the term 'bill' could sometimes be employed to designate, in a loose fashion, a short document, whatever its economic or diplomatic nature. It is nevertheless obvious that whenever a distinction between financial documents was drawn, and different terms were used to designate differences of diplomatic type, the words 'bill' or 'bill obligatory' were taken to mean what they meant to Malynes: an informal promissory note.[21] This is certainly what the Celys, a family of fifteenth-century staplers whose business correspondence now forms one of the principal sources of information upon the organisation and financing of trade in the fifteenth century, meant by the term, and their accounts contain what seems to have been a typical 'bill obligatory': 'Jorge Cely, Je vous prometz payer a votre volouir, ou au porteur de cests, six livres etc. gros mony de Flandres en moy rend(rent) cest sign de mon saign manuel. Le 25 May [14]79.' [Signature][22] The document is not sealed, while the handwriting, the spelling and the grammatical structure suggest that it was produced not by an experienced scribe but by the debtor himself. The diplomatic structure is not unlike that of a modern promissory note. It is not an open declaration (letter patent), but a statement addressed to the creditor (letter close); nor does it contain a definite clause of obligation, or in this particular instance, a definite day of repayment (au vouloir).[23]

These two deviations from the conventional bond – the formal recog-

[19] G. Malynes, *Lex Mercatoria*, ed. 1622, pp. 96–102; also quoted in Holdsworth vol. VIII, p. 149. These documents under the title of 'billets à ordre' are also described in J. Goris, *Les colonies marchandes meridionales à Anvers*, p. 340.

[20] It is not unlikely that the obligees own handwriting served as a formal proof of authenticity.

[21] Cf. esp. Cely Accounts 11/33–4. [22] Ibid. 11/35.

[23] Promissory notes of this kind were sometimes described as 'letters of payment' a title which was more commonly applied to the bills of exchange (see below). The confusion with the bill of exchange was quite natural: both were informal instruments not recognised in Common Law till quite recently, and for that reason lumped together by lawyers and legislators (Holdsworth, VIII, 170–1).

nisance and the informal bill – raise the difficult question as to the motives which determined the merchant's choice between them. It is not enough to say that the merchant made his choice in accordance with the economic nature of the transaction. This answer is obvious and true enough, but it raises a further question as to the grounds on which a certain type of obligation was considered suitable for one transaction and unsuitable for another. Legal security alone will not explain it. Had it been the only ground for the merchant's preferences we should have witnessed in some financial transactions a marked displacement of the informal obligation, and even of the conventional bond, by the recognisance. In reality nothing of the kind happened. The history of the recognisance suggests that, if in a certain group of transactions there was any displacement at all, it proceeded at the expense of the recognisance. That history may also indicate some alternative grounds for the merchant's choice of financial instruments.

The history of the recognisance is linked up with that of the Statute of Acton Burnell of 1283 (11 Edw. I), The meaning of this act and the history of the legislation that followed it has been repeatedly described by legal historians and offers hardly any new points of interest. We shall only note here that recognisances had been known in England prior to 1283. The last clause of the Statute stated that the Chancellor, the Barons of the Exchequer, the Justices of the King's Bench, and the Justices Itinerant were allowed to take recognisances of debts according to rules heretofore applied. In London, the City Courts which had a jurisdiction over plaints of debt arising within the City, had been in the habit of taking recognisances of debts prior to 1283.[24] What the Statute did was to establish an uniform order throughout the country for the taking and the execution of recognisances, and to adapt it to the requirements of commercial intercourse. The Statute *de Mercatoribus* enacted two years later reinforced the Statute of Acton Burnell by a number of new rules increasing further the creditor's powers of execution over the goods and the land of the debtor and providing for the effective control by the Chancellor over the due execution of the Act by reluctant sheriffs. It also extended the right to take recognisances under the Statute to fair courts. The provisions of this act were almost completely reproduced in the *Statute Staple* of 1353 (27 Edw. III), but the creditors' powers were extended still further and the right to take recognisances given to the mayors of the English Staple towns established by the same act.[25] It was confirmed by Richard II and in this form remained in force throughout the fifteenth century.

---

[24] L.B.A. fols. 1–35.
[25] The recognisances enrolled under the Statute Staple came themselves to be known as 'Statutes Staple'.

The order established by the Statute of 1283 and perfected by the subsequent legislation was meant to serve the conveniences of mercantile credit. But although this was clearly stated in the preambles to the acts, non-merchants also availed themselves of them. In 1311 the 'Ordainers' expressly laid down that the Statute of 1283 'shall not hold except between merchant and merchant and of merchandise between them'. The ordinance was revoked in 1326, but the recognisances in the municipal collections show that during the four or five decades following the enactment of the Statute of 1283 the new machinery of recognisances was employed principally for the recording of mercantile debts.[26] The Letter Books A and B in the London City records contain a very large number of recognisances enrolled in the last quarter of the thirteenth century. It is not easy to find which of them refer to mercantile debts, as many of the names appear only once and are not to be found elsewhere. Still, a necessarily imperfect analysis reveals that out of some 600 entries which yield themselves to such treatment over three-quarters seem to be related to debts 'between merchant and merchant and of merchandise between them'. The first three Recognisance Rolls seem to contain about the same proportion of mercantile debts for goods bought and sold, and the mercantile character of most entries is born out by the external features – if we may use the expression – of the debts. The amounts involved vary from a few shillings to scores and even hundreds of marks. Most of the debts, however, are relatively small and seldom expressed in round figures. There are odd pennies, half-pennies and farthings in most of them. In short, they have the unmistakable appearance of debts contracted in the ordinary course of buying and selling. This character of the entries changes according as we proceed from the earlier rolls to the later ones, until by the end of the fourteenth century they become almost unrecognisable. The proportion of debts contracted between merchants perceptibly decreases. For these later rolls no attempt has been made to form a numerical estimate of the number of entries in which merchants figure as debtors, but the general impression is that London merchants do not occur as often as before. A student familiar with the names of merchants of the last decades of the fourteenth century and the early part of the fifteenth may sometimes plod through long rows of entries without meeting more than a few stray names of people known as active traders. And when we at last strike a batch of recognisances with merchants as debtors or creditors we cannot fail to notice a striking change in their appearance. The odd pennies and halfpennies have gone, and debts are mostly expressed in respectable round figures. Debts for shillings, marks and pounds in scores and multiples of scores – that favourite round figure of the Middle Ages – are commonest of all. Most of the debts there-

[26] L.B.E. pp. 53 and 213; Statutes 5 Edw. IIc. 33, *Rot. Parl.* I, 457.

fore look as though they had not arisen in connection with the ordinary transactions of buying and selling. For we have no reason to assume that the merchant of the fifteenth century, as distinguished from his predecessors, had a special predilection for such deals only as would run into round figures.

What exactly this change meant we do not know. All that it is possible to do is to offer a guess based on the few scraps of information gleaned from elsewhere. To begin with, it seems as if one of the principal uses of the recognisance was no longer the recording of the actual debts, but the creation of that security of a 'penal' sum, of which more has been said above. In most of the Chancery cases between merchant and merchant in which recognisances are mentioned, they figure chiefly as sanctions for other obligations, or as securities for the performance of a contract. The consent to abide by the award of the arbitrators, a promise to deliver certain goods at a certain time, an obligation to restore the ward's fund in due time, an undertaking to carry out the formalities relating to the creation of an estate in land, and a variety of other obligations and undertakings seem to be at the back of many, possibly most, of the recognisances. Those recognisances which still seem to embody actual debts, appear to represent not liabilities arising out of the current commercial transactions, but something of a different economic nature. Recognisances, when not employed as sanctions and securities, seem to have been made out for substantial long-term loans, or, in other words, investments. For this no definite proof can be adduced, but that it was so is suggested by the large amounts and the long terms of the debts.

If this analysis of the fifteenth-century recognisance is correct, the reasons why it ceased to be employed for current mercantile debts are more or less obvious. It had lost most of its advantages while retaining most of its defects. Its power of execution tended to become less perfect through the growth of the Chancery as a court of appeal in equity. Complaints became common at the close of the fourteenth century and the beginning of the fifteenth that the writs of the Chancery deprived the recognisees of most of their rights. The writs complained against were the '*corpus cum causa*' by which the Chancery could virtually set the imprisoned debtor free pending its decision on his appeal, the writ of '*scire facias*' by which the Chancery could demand from the lower court an account of all the circumstances of the case and thus delay the execution of the recognisance, and the writ of *subpoena*, by which the parties could be brought before the Chancery and a formal hearing arranged. This jurisdiction of the Chancery had, to some extent, undone the work of the Statute of Burnell in that it deprived the creditor of automatic remedies against the defaulting debtor. On the other hand, the disadvantages of the recognisance remained as they were. The parties had to appear at the Guildhall, or before the clerks of the staple courts; fees were charged for the enrolment higher than the legal rates of $1d$ and $\frac{1}{2}d$. Furthermore, there was an inconvenience, probably the most important of all, connected with the difficulty of assigning a debt recorded on the recognisance rolls. The latter defect was common to all enrolled debts, for theoretically, the easiest way of assigning a debt is to transfer the actual instrument. An entry in a roll cannot be transferred except by a new and a similar entry. All these defects would probably be felt least when the debts were contracted for large sums and for long terms and were not meant to circulate. But they would be keenly felt in smaller everyday transactions, and especially in the fifteenth century. Willingly or unwillingly, the merchant had to use for his ordinary transactions the less informal, though probably less safe, instruments and confine his use of recognisances to his less liquid debts, to wit investments and securities: both of them financial contracts for which the ease of recording or of circulation, and the cheapness of production, were secondary considerations, while full legal safeguards were of paramount importance.[27]

THE TRANSFER OF OBLIGATIONS

The history of the recognisance in the version given here presupposes that the other financial instruments afforded an easier means for transference than did the recognisance, and that such transference of assignments was general and permissible. To the economic historian, to say nothing of the lawyer, these assumptions may seem unfounded. But in the light of the financial records of the fourteenth and the fifteenth centuries there cannot be any doubt that debts were regularly assigned by creditors to other persons, and that assignments were made to serve a number of different purposes. One of the purposes for which the debts were assigned was to facilitate their collection in the creditor's absence. In other words, the assignee would be entrusted with the cashing in of debts and would act merely as the assignor's receiver. It can, however, be doubted whether this was the real position of the assignee in all, or even in the majority, of those instances when receivers were appointed by merchants to collect their debts. On 15 November 1430 'came Bartholomew Contaryne, merchant of Venice and gave evidence that he had assigned to Stephen Foster, citizen and fishmonger, a debt of £152.10.6 which was owed to him by Saier Acre and Nicholas Wyford, citizens and grocers'. And again – 'assignment by Baptista de Nigris of Genoa, to William Estfeld, of a debt of £223.4.2 owed to himself and Laurence Markysano, merchants of Genoa, by Peter Jamys, burgess and

---

[27] Statutes 11 Hen. IV c. 10; *Rot. Parl.* IV, 20, 84, 121, 189, 501.

merchant of Southampton, and John Wayther of Winchester'.[28] It is possible that these entries embody nothing more than arrangements between the parties, by which the Englishmen undertook to cash in the debts for the Italian absentees, although what we know of the organisation of the Italian trade and finance in this country speaks against this interpretation of these particular assignments. Assignments for this purpose would be superfluous in places where merchants habitually traded and where they could be represented by their servants or agents. It is therefore not unsafe to suppose that in the dealings of the larger Italian houses with English merchants this use of assignments was very rare. The usual purpose for which debts were assigned was the settlement of other debts. A merchant contracting an obligation to somebody else would 'set over' to him his own debts, and thus effect a payment without the actual employment of coin. How general this practice was is demonstrated by nearly all the contemporary records relating to the activities of medieval merchants. In a letter from one Ralph Lemington to George Cely there occurs a characteristically matter-of-fact phrase. Lemington promises to pay George the debts he is about to contract. 'You shall not fault of your money in the Cold Mart . . . by such men as I shall have my money of.[29] The facts which we glean from the accounts and the correspondence of the time make it clear that the English exporters and importers, all merchants of substance, paid their debts 'by such men as they had their money of' almost as often as in coin.

A debt could be assigned in several ways. In transactions among people constantly associated with each other, or used to conducting their business in an informal way, debts may well have been transferred to other people by verbal agreements of the parties. A debt could also be assigned by a public attornment of the assignee for the purposes of receiving the debts owing to the assignor. In the fourteenth century this method of assignment was quite common, especially in liabilities created by public grants, or in other debts evidenced by entries on public records; it was the most natural method of assigning debts secured by recognisances.[30] But the commonest methods of assignment, especially in the fifteenth century, were: the transfer of the instrument, and the issuing of bills of exchange ('letters of payment', *tratta*).

'The transfer of the instrument' – the expression sounds almost heretical. Nevertheless it describes quite correctly a practice that was common

---

28 P.M. Rolls, A 57 m. 1 b, A 59 m. 6; also cf. ibid. A 23, m. 3, A 59, m. 2 b, E. Ch. Pr. 64/587, 46/256.

29 Cely Papers, Ancient Correspondence, vol. 59, fo. 22; Cely Accounts 10/8–10, 11/38–42, 16/50, etc.

30 L.B.A. a. L.B.B. *passim*, H. Ingleby, *Red Book of Lynn*, pp. 75, 136, 141, 147 etc., P.M. Rolls A 15, m. 4, A 23 m. 3. On the assignments of 'judgements' ('duty of condemnation') see E. Ch. Pr. 45/170 and 45/263, 264, 270.

enough throughout the fourteenth and the fifteenth centuries, if not earlier. Bonds were transferred in satisfaction of debts and accepted in payment for goods. Here are typical examples. A Chancery petition of the middle of the fifteenth century describes how one William Haydock of London had bought of one William Elliot of London merchandise to the value of £40, for the payment of which he, by the request of Elliot, was bound by an obligation to John Middleton and William Saunders, to the use of William Elliot, but afterwards the same obligation was delivered for payment to one Walter Walker. Then Walker made a deed of gift of all his goods and chattels to one Philip Malpas, and the obligation finally passed into his hands and was, as the petitioner alleges, duly paid by him.[31] Many more similar examples could be cited, for contemporary records are full of them; and in the light of this evidence there cannot be two opinions as to the extent to which the assignment by the transfer of obligations was practised.

The transferability of the obligations was far from perfect. The general attitude of medieval law to assignments of debts, and the special requirements which the transfers had to satisfy in order to be legally valid, made the emergence of fully negotiable paper impossible. But it is easy to overestimate the extent to which the transferability of medieval instruments was affected by the attitude of medieval law. The attitude of the law to assignments of debts was by no means a friendly one, but it was not so inimical as seriously to impede what must have been a common commercial practice. It is also quite true that the transfer of obligations was fraught with cumbersome formalities; but they were not so many and not so great as is commonly imagined.

The attitude of medieval law to the assignment of debts, and particularly to the transference of bonds, is very hard to define, for the relevant rules were few, and by no means general. The attitude of the Law Merchant differed from that of the Common Law, and the latter was not necessarily the same as that of Equity (the Chancery). The only definite and general thing that can be said about the legal attitude to assignments in the fourteenth and the fifteenth centuries is that, while it was far removed from the modern view of negotiable instruments the recognition it afforded to the transfers of obligations was sufficient to make them legally secure.

---

[31] E. Ch. Pr. 101/215; other characteristic examples, some of which illustrate manifold transfers are to be found in the Chancery Proceedings – 10/215, 11/356, 16/456, 39/289, 45/170, 48/3, 46/144, 49/66, 48/63, 48/93, 47/157, 63/161, 62/461–4, 67/99–102; cf. P.M. Rolls A 67 m. 7 b, A 56 m. 2. References to transfers of bonds for customs and subsidies are very common (E. Ch. Pr. 15/248, 26/341, 558, 583a) as the more substantial exporters, especially the staplers, often paid customs and subsidies by bonds of several months, which the customers often discounted with other merchants.

The freedom of transfers was most circumscribed in Common Law. The Common Law admitted the assignment of debts by the creation of attorneys who were to keep the money. But in connection with the fifteenth-century struggle against 'maintenance' the courts made use of the doctrine of the 'chose in action', i.e. the doctrine of the unassignable nature of mere legal claims, to confine valid assignments to those cases only in which the assignor and the assignee could prove a 'common interest'. The assignor's debt to the assignee was considered a 'common interest' so that a transfer of an obligation in settlement of a debt could be enforced in Common Law.[32] In actual practice assignments were largely made in settlement of debts, so that the licence accorded by Common Law did not fall short of the requirements of mercantile intercourse. But it would not have mattered much if it had. However wide the divergence between the principles of Common Law and the *desiderata* of merchants, it could hardly have constituted a serious impediment and a grievance, since there was no need for the merchants to bring their debts before the Common Law courts; more often than not they applied elsewhere.

To a modern student the first and the most obvious alternative to Common Law is Equity. It is the general view of the historians of English law that in the fifteenth century a remedy against the attitude of the Common Law to the assignments was provided by the equity jurisdiction of the Chancery, which for a long time remained the only court enforcing the *bona fide* assignments of debts. This view, though substantially true, suffers from a somewhat misplaced emphasis. In the post-medieval era the Chancery indeed became the one court for the enforcement of assignments, but this had not yet become its function in the fifteenth century. Whatever was the attitude of Common Law to the transfer of obligations and to other forms of assignment of debts, it was not yet in conflict with the attitude of the Chancery, for the Chancery had not yet adopted any attitude at all. Mr Barbour recently brought together a certain number of cases from the Chancery petitions intended to illustrate the enforcement of assignments through the Chancery, but a careful examination of these cases will reveal that the Chancery was asked not so much to enforce assignments as to uphold certain informal promises, most of which had been made by deceased persons during their lifetime.[33] If Mr Barbour had examined a few more petitions on matters connected with assignments he would probably have found that in a great number of cases the

---

[32] Holdsworth, vii, pp. 534–5, F. Pollock, *Principles of Contract*, 1921, pp. 753–4.
[33] Barbour, op. cit., pp. 107–10. Of Barbour's eight cases at least six relate to informal assignments of which the assignee had no documentary evidence; of these, three (6/141, 9/337, 10/17) relate to promises of assignments made by deceased debtors *inter vivos*, and one (11/47) is brought before the Chancery merely because the petitioner was a clerk of the Chancery.

Chancery was requested not to enforce assignments but to do the very opposite – namely to remedy the abuses resulting from the sale of bonds. The bulk of the relevant petitions is made up of appeals of debtors against the decisions of London courts enforcing the assignment of debts. Some of them are petitions of debtors whose bonds had been sold by their creditors and who were certain that the decisions of the London courts would go against them, and some, without complaining against the assignment, mention the decisions of the City courts upholding them.[34] It goes without saying that the evidence of these petitions would not be sufficient to prove that the Chancery functioned as a court of appeal against assignments; they only suggest what must be clear to every student of the fifteenth-century Chancery, that 'no regular judicial system at that time prevailed at the court; but the suitor when he thought himself aggrieved found a desultory and uncertain remedy according to the private opinion of the Chancellor'.[35] But what this evidence does establish is that the different forms in which debts were transferred and bonds sold in the fifteenth century were all sanctioned by the City courts. The Chancery had not yet become the natural alternative to the Common Law in the matter of assignments, for the simple reason that no such alternative was as yet needed. The courts, which commonly served the interests of merchants and to which the mercantile debts were commonly brought, apparently allowed as great a freedom of transfer as was needed. That that was so is also suggested by the direct evidence of the City courts. There is an early reference in the City records illustrating the attitude of the London courts to assignments. In a case before the Mayor's court in 1305 Raymond de St Clement was summoned to answer Reginald de Thanderle in a plea that he restore to him two bills of £70.15.11 which the plaintiff had bought from William Foundepe, merchant, and which the said William entrusted to the custody of the defendant for delivery to the plaintiff. The court found for the plaintiff.[36]

Our conclusions will be very much the same if from the general attitude of the medieval law we pass to the problems presented by the 'special limitations and formalities' imposed upon the transfer of bonds. An important limitation was the consent of the debtor. Bonds, so it is said, could not be transferred without the debtor's concurrence. The debt was a personal relation between the creditor and the debtor; the change of creditor altered the nature of that relation, and could not take place without the debtor's knowledge and consent. Obedient to this view and

---

[34] E. Ch. Pr. 32/19, 32/389–90, 47/101, 59/192, 9/236, 49/66, 64/1014, 64/624 etc.

[35] Blackstone, quoted by Holdsworth I, p. 154.

[36] A. H. Thomas, *Calendar of the Early Mayor's Court Rolls*, p. 172. There is also a fifteenth-century award in P.M. Rolls A. 56 m. 2, whereby a settlement between the parties was affected by a transfer of obligations.

anxious to safeguard the interests of the debtor, medieval law and practice made his consent an indispensable condition of a transfer, and thus raised a serious barrier to the circulation of bonds.[37] This seems to be the essence of the accepted view and there is a certain amount of contemporary evidence which can be cited in its support. Petitions in the Chancery would sometimes tell the whole story of how the debtor had been brought before the assignee and recognised him as his rightful creditor. Sometimes, even, a new bond would be made out so that the assignment would take the form of what is known as 'novation'. For example a Chancery petition recites that whereas the petitioner Thomas Kirkeby was bound to John Olney in £72, he paid £14.14.4 in cash, and for the rest gave obligations of the debt owing to him from Thomas and Nicholas Dey; and the Deys agreed to being 'set over' and offered to be bound to Olney by a new obligation.[38] The meaning of these examples, however, must not be misunderstood. They show that the consent of the debtor was commonly asked; they do not prove it to have been indispensable. There are many examples of bonds bought and sold without the debtor's concurrence, and even without his knowledge. In another Chancery petition John Beche complains that whereas one Richard Muswiche was imprisoned for his debt of 100 shillings to Walter Taylowe, the latter 'made a bargain of the said 100 shillings' with one Richard Playstowe who 'is a common buyer of such duties that pover men being in danger'.[39] Or let us take another instance. Richard Marshall writes that he was bound in £30 to one John Hill, and has paid his debt in full; Hill, however, gave him no acquittance, and did not return the obligation, but sold it to one Christopher Colyns who is now suing for the debt.[40]

The significance of these and other similar instances is only intensified by certain considerations of a purely logical order. There is not, and apparently never was, any theoretical ground for regarding the debtor's consent as the *conditio sine qua* of transfers. There would have been some, if the debtor's consent had indeed been intended to safeguard him against his new creditor: a condition serving his interests could not be discharged without his participation. But there is nothing in our evidence to support this construction. There are many instances of

---

37 J. Brissaud, *A History of French Private Law* (transl.), Boston 1912, pp. 531–2; cf. Holdsworth VIII, p. 115; V. Spence, *The Equitable Jurisdiction of the Chancery*, II, p. 848.

38 E. Ch. Pr. 16/229; also 64/567, 32/370, 17/43 u. 43 b, 19/74, 16/333, 63/148, 16/456.

39 Ibid. 17/44.

40 Ibid. 47/101; also 46/354 (bond 'delivered to a stranger' in the debtor's absence), 64/1014 (an obligation not returned on the payment of the debt, but sold to another man), 64/624, 32/19 (similar cases), 64/643 (Elisabeth Caniziani alleges that bills issued in her name by her factor are being bought up by a group of merchants).

transfers in which the debtor's consent was asked and obtained, but in which it was meant to serve not his, but the assignee's interests. If the evidence of the Chancery petitions does not deceive us, it was commonly the assignee who was protected by the debtor's acknowledgement or the 'novation'. The reason for which he would require the debtor to signify his consent would be quite obvious. Under the conditions of the fourteenth- and fifteenth-century law the debtor's consent would safeguard the assignee from a number of unpleasant surprises: the debtor might have paid the debt to the assignor or might have been released from the obligation. If the assignee were assured that his position was sufficiently safe, or were prepared to run the risk, he would accept the bond without troubling about the debtor's consent. But even if he were unwilling to shoulder the hazards of the transaction, the debtor's consent was not the only way in which the risks could be obviated, for the assignee could demand and obtain the requisite guarantees from the assignor himself. One John Fisher, accepting a bond in payment for goods sold to one Robert Ford, insisted upon Ford's giving him formal assurances that the drawer of the bond 'was sufficient for the said sum', that the amount of the obligation 'was then clear debt and duty to Robert Ford' (i.e. that nothing of it had been paid or was owing to somebody else), that he had made no release or acquittance of the same, that he would be ready 'to maintain all actions' against the debtor, and, generally speaking 'defend and save the same duty unto . . . the suppliant'.[41] Not every assignee demanded all these assurances, but if he had them, he was in an impregnable position and had no need for the debtor's consent. And there certainly were assignees who did not trouble either about the guarantees from the creditor, or about the consent of the debtor. Where the parties to the transaction were all substantial men, when the assignee knew, from his own experience or from other sources, that the debtor was solvent and the assignor honest, or when an allowance for the risks was made in the terms of the discount, no additional guarantees were likely to be demanded. The procedure was determined entirely by the commercial conditions of each particular transaction.

The same applies to the other limitations of the transfer, and above all, to the *attornatio* of the assignee. In the fifteenth century the transfer of bonds by endorsement had not yet been invented, and the assignee had to

---

[41] E. Ch. Pr. 67/99–102 and 59/192. Cf. also 49/57: Thomas Keston 'proposing to deceive fraudulently the said William Kylton, covenanted with him that where the same Thomas has an obligation wherein one Yowet Huetson of the town of Leyden was bounden in £50 to the same Thomas . . . the which obligation the said Thomas . . . warranted to your besecher to be good and the person therin bounden sufficient to content the said duty' and sold him the obligation, but the debtor turned out to be insolvent. For further details see Chancery Miscellanea 25/10(2): cf. E. Ch. Pr. 43/167.

be provided with a letter of attorney or another document witnessing the transfer. In a number of transactions we have direct evidence of documents of this type being employed to complete the sale of a bond, and in a number of other instances their existence can be inferred.[42] But common as these documents were, their function and importance must not be misinterpreted. The powers of attorney, it is said, were not a matter of private arrangement between the assignor and the assignee, but an act enforced by courts as a formal condition of the validity of the transfer. The indispensable nature of the attornment would alone have constituted a serious obstacle to the free circulation of the obligation, but the obstacle was raised higher still by the formalities attached to the creation of attorneys in the Middle Ages. The bias of medieval law was against representation in courts, and the right to appear in court by attorney was a licence to be asked and bought from the king. Moreover the formal letter of attorney was a cumbrous and costly piece of diplomatic composition hardly worth while except in large and important transactions.[43]

These views, cogent as they seem, are another instance of misplaced emphasis. Here, as in the case of indispensability of the debtor's 'consent', the effect of Common Law on mercantile practice is greatly exaggerated. But even if the connection between them were as close and direct as writers commonly assume, there is no reason why it should have produced all those effects with which it is credited. To begin with, the interest served by the attornment was the assignee's: in the fifteenth century his legal claim against the original debtor was insecure unless he could prove his *bona fide* possession of the bond, while in Common Law he could only sue for his debt as the assignor's attorney.[44] It was for the assignee, and for him only to demand a document witnessing the transfer or conferring upon him the powers of attorney, and there was no need for the assignor to produce the document when the assignee did not demand it, i.e. when he expected that the payment would be, as in most mercantile transactions it was, made payable without recourse to law, or when, as in the transaction between Fisher and Ford, the assignor himself undertook to 'defend and save the same duty unto him'. Further in those cases in which letters of attorney were demanded, the formalities involved were not so great and forbidding as they are alleged to have been. Whatever was the position in the early Middle Ages, and on this point more than one view is possible, in the fourteenth and the fifteenth centuries the right of appointing an attorney had ceased to be regarded as an exceptional

---

[42] E. Ch. Pr. 39/289, 46/298, 48/93, 64/452, 64/929.

[43] P. & M. I, p. 213, II, pp. 226–7; cf. E. Jenks, 'The Early History of Negotiable Instruments' (*Select Essays in Anglo-American Legal History*, III), p. 59; Heusler, *Institutionen*, vol. I, pp. 203 seq., H. Brunner, *Forschungen zur Geschichte des deutschen u. französischen Rechtes*, p. 423.

[44] Above, p. 43.

privilege to be bought of the king: nor was the appointment of a special attorney impossible out of court.[45] All that was necessary in order to create an attorney for the purposes of debt was to draw up a document of procuration. And there is no reason why the drawing up of the document should be regarded as a serious impediment to the transfer of bonds. In principle, the difficulty of using a separate piece of parchment to announce the transfer, was not much greater than that of using the back of the bond for the same purpose, especially as a comparatively short form of letter of attorney had been evolved by the fifteenth century.[46] Furthermore, in cases where a Common Law suit was not intended, and all the assignee wanted was a proof of a *bona fide* acquisition to serve in his direct dealings with the debtor, or in litigation before mercantile tribunals, the justificatory document need not necessarily have been a formal procuration: any writing under the assignee's signature announcing the transfer sufficed.[47] In Germany these writings were known as '*Willebriefe*', and usually took the form of letters addressed to the assignee. If we are right in the interpretation of certain expressions in contemporary English documents such *Willebriefe* were also in use in this country.[48]

[45] The prevalent opinion seems to be that for representation by attorney in courts the authority of a special writ ceased to be indispensable in a number of cases after the thirteenth century. 'The law upon the matter has never been directly changed, but . . . the statutory exceptions, extending from the reign of Henry III to the reign of Elizabeth, has practically eaten up the rule' (Holdsworth II, p. 316); cf. Sir J. Comyns, A digest, etc. 1827, pp. 743 and 746 n. b. Even if Britton's statement as to the right of the courts of record to admit attorneys without royal writ (Britton, ed. F. M. Nichols, II, pp. 356–61) be regarded merely as the lawyers *desideratum*, it was not far removed from what, if we are to trust the records of debt cases of the fourteenth and the fifteenth centuries, must have been the virtual practice of the law courts specialising in mercantile cases. Some local courts had by the beginning of the fourteenth century established an informal procedure for the receiving of attorneys: Liber Albus I 222, M. Bateson, *The Records of Leicester*, I, p. 161, and above all, The Domesday of Ipswich, the Black Book of the Admiralty (R.S.), v. II, p. 134 where *attornatio* could take place out of court; cf. Brunner, *Forschungen*, p. 435. The act of 1437 (14 Hen. VI) generalised and perpetuated the informal practices as to the judicial *attornatio*, whereby an attorney could be appointed without royal writ, out of court, and in *absentia adversarii*.

[46] Madox, op. cit., no. 619.

[47] It is apparently an informal letter of this kind that is meant in a petition in the Chancery (59/80) by one Richard Dawson, who received from Richard Sired, as security, an obligation of £20, by which one Collins was bound to Sired 'as bill written with the hands of the said Robert unto . . . said oratour more evidently it does appear'. Was anything more than a *Willebrief* meant in the 1285 entry in a roll recording an assignment by the executors of the Countess of Leicester to Baruncino of Lucca who was armed with 'litteras predictorum executorum dictam assignationem testificantes'? Bond, *Archaeologia*, xxviii, p. 282, also quoted in P. & M. II, p. 227 n. 3.

[48] The *attornatio* for extra-judicial purposes, the one Sir Edw. Coke describes as 'private' (Coke on Littleton 51 b) must be distinguished from *attornatio* for

The conclusions are clear. Not every bond could be bought with the same freedom and ease as a modern negotiable paper: indeed medieval law and practice piled up formalities and limitations which must have impeded the free circulation of the instruments. But it is equally clear that these limitations were not determined by a legal or diplomatic principle and did not develop into hard and fast rules. They were all practical considerations, determined by the commercial and financial circumstances of each particular case; and the conditions on which a bond would pass hands were very largely a matter between the assignor and the assignee.

The fact that the transferability of instruments was limited by considerations purely practical and informal, stands out still more clearly in connection with the informal documents described above as 'bills obligatory'. As they had little standing in common law, there was no need for them to conform to its rules and to be bound by its limitations. They were extra-legal instruments, devised solely for the purposes of mercantile convenience, and they served all those purposes which mercantile convenience demanded, including that of assignment. As in the days of Malynes, the bills obligatory were widely accepted in payment of debts by English merchants and their foreign clients, and changed hands without any of those formalities which often encumbered the transference of the formal bond. Here is a typical case. In the course of a transaction, in which a number of English merchants trading abroad in the years 1445–7 were involved, a foreign merchant made out a 'bill' to one John Felde for wool sold; the bill was originally delivered to Lowes Fyncham, Felde's attorney, who in his turn, passed it to one Laurence Parke, the latter delivered it to John Petite, and John Petite is alleged to have bought with this bill certain merchandise of one Jacob Flemming.[49]

A financial instrument which could pass hands so many times, and apparently without any formalities or additional documents, almost deserves the name of 'currency', which Prof. Holdsworth applies to its seventeenth-century descendant. With equal justice can the name be applied to certain credit instruments of a semi-public nature, which seem to have circulated in a way not very different from modern bank-notes. Of these, the semi-public documents of the Staple of Calais: the 'debentures', 'bills of the mint' and the 'warrants of partition' are

representation in courts. Heusler admits by implication the freedom of representation for extra-judicial purposes in German law (*Instit.* v. 1, p. 206). It was apparently fully admitted in the English law and practice in the later Middle Ages, cf. Comyns, op. cit., p. 770 and n. K., also Coke on Littleton 52a; the instances of private attornment mentioned by Coke, i.e. deeds of feoffment incorporating letters of attorney to deliver seisin, was familiar also in the Middle Ages; Madox, op. cit., nos. 351–4, 356, 390.

[49] E. Ch. Pr. 24/247–8 and 16/369.

probably the best known.[50] The 'debentures' of the Staple occur in most accounts of the financial dealings between individual merchants and the treasury of the Staple. The debts of the Staple to its members, incurred principally in connection with the loans to the king, were often recorded on certificates of debt handed over to each lender in lieu of an obligation or a receipt, and identical in economic use and diplomatic construction with the debentures employed by the clerks of the king's wardrobe to certify the debts from Wardrobe to various individuals.[51] The debenture states in an impersonal form that a sum of money 'is owing' (*debentur*) to the person named therein, and to use a somewhat foreign terminology, it was an evidence of debt not in the form of an obligation, but in that of a 'notitia'. Within the limits of its diplomatic conventions the 'debenture' of the Staple apparently admitted variations in the direction of greater and less formalism. Whether one of these variations was identical with the document described as the 'bill of the mint' of Calais we do not know; but even if the 'bill' had a diplomatic identity distinct from that of the debenture, its function was very much the same. Under the many bullionist acts of the government the staplers were compelled at certain periods in the fifteenth century to pay into the mint of Calais a certain proportion of the sums realised from the sales of wool. Against sums thus accepted the mint issued to the staplers certificates serving as evidence of its indebtedness to the owners of the bullion. Most merchants apparently had something in the nature of a current account with the mint; bullion was paid and withdrawn all the year round; and bills of this kind could be obtained almost automatically on the payment of the corresponding sum in metallic currency. The 'warrant of the Staple' – the third class of Staple instruments – was a document subsidiary to the obligations and certificates of debt. Whenever the Staple was in a position to make payments on account of its floating debt to individual staplers, in settlement of state loans or in connection with the compulsory pooling of profit it made a partition, or in other words, declared the size of the next payment, and issued to the holders of obligations and 'debentures' of the Staple the 'warrants of payment' setting out the fraction of the pound to be paid as the next instalment. The warrant was thus neither a bond nor a certificate, but an order for payment, and was akin to the bill of exchange – a document to be discussed in the next section.

Now, all these Staple documents, and above all the 'bills of the mint', were legal tender for payments to the Staple, and circulated among the merchants in Calais and the other fairs in a manner very similar to

[50] For references to these see Cely Accounts *passim*, also E. Ch. Pr. 43/4.
[51] Miss D. Leach, of the Institute of Historical Research (University of London), has kindly drawn my attention to a very good example of a Staple debenture, with notes of repayment entered upon it, in Chancery Miscellanea, 25/9/17.

modern negotiable paper. The manner of their employment by fifteenth-century merchants is well illustrated by a case which at the time formed a subject of a great deal of litigation and diplomatic correspondence. A certain Richard Whethecroft, a factor of several staplers at Calais, drew from the mint several bills for sums of £2 and £3, added the letter C (hundred) to each of the bills so as to convert them into documents of £200 and £300 and then cashed them in with certain Dutch merchants at Antwerp. When later the Dutch wool buyers presented them at Calais in payment for the wool, the forgery was discovered and proceedings were begun against Whethecroft and his accomplices.[52] In this incident the apparent ease with which the bills were obtained, passed to other merchants and then found their way back to Calais, affords an interesting indication of the part the financial instruments of the Staple played in the mechanism of commercial payments. Their employment in payments between stapler and stapler is illustrated by a number of characteristic entries in the Cely accounts. Thus the debt of William Dalton, a friend and an associate of the Celys, to the Staple on account of custom and subsidy was paid in the following manner: £15.16.8 'by a warrant from John Tate', £4 by a warrant of a 'partition of 4 shillings in the pound' of a 'debenture of William Dalton', £1.6.3 by a similar partition of a 'debenture of John Thorp' etc.[53] The documents of the Staple were thus freely transferable; but there was nothing extraordinary in this quality of theirs. To say that they were transferable merely because they were backed by the great resources of the Staple is to confirm their unexceptional nature. For this only emphasises what has already been pointed out: that the transferability of financial instruments depended on the financial and economic circumstances of the transaction, and above all on the financial reputation of the drawer. A bond, a bill, a debenture, call it what we may, would circulate freely among merchants if their drawer were generally known as a trustworthy and reliable debtor likely to honour his obligations. Diplomatic construction, or legal formulae, were, for the purposes of transfer, of secondary importance.

Nowhere has this importance of practical considerations been more neglected than in the discussion of the so-called 'bearer' and 'order' clauses. Most medieval financial instruments contained a clause promising payment to a third party appearing instead of the creditor himself: 'to pay to N. or his certain attorney', 'to pay to N. or the bearer of this letter'. These clauses naturally attracted the attention of historians, with the result that a theory of the 'clauses' has been elaborated, to which

---

[52] Letters and Papers of the reign of Henry VI (R.S.), v. I, pp. 464 seq., and 'Bronnen tot de Geschiedenis van den Handel met Engeland, Schotland an Ierland, uitgegeven door', Dr G. J. Smit (*Rijks Geschiedkundige Publicatien* 66, 1928) v. II, pp. 846–7.

[53] Cely Accounts, 15/37.

every textbook now finds it its duty to adhere. According to Brunner, the father of the theory, these clauses neutralised the effects of the usual limitations upon the assignments of debts. Brunner starts from the firmly established notion that the early Germanic law regarded debt as untransferable. But as the smooth functioning of exchange depended on facilities for the transfer of debts, a way out was found by inserting in the obligation a 'bearer' or an 'order' clause by which the obligor recognised in advance the obligee's right to appoint an attorney (order clause) or to grant the debt in full ownership to an assignee (bearer clause). The power to appoint an attorney for the purposes of debt was on the whole revocable and did not eliminate completely the connection of the debt with the original creditor. It was, therefore, not so serviceable as the bearer clause, which converted the medieval bond into a fully negotiable instrument. The bearer clause consequently became the common constituent of medieval instruments. It was not, however, allowed to fulfil this function for very long. Before the Middle Ages were over the lawyers, then already under the influence of romanist ideas, began narrowing down the meaning of the 'bearer' clause until they succeeded in reducing it to that of Roman 'procuration', or in other words, to that of the 'order' clause. The bearer became a mere agent of the obligee with powers that had to be proved and could be revoked; the bond again lost its negotiable characteristics and the commercial classes were forced to try other expedients.[54]

This account, in spite of its air of plausibility, cannot be accepted without a certain amount of rearrangement. Brunner's account, though substantially true, does not fully apply to English conditions in the later Middle Ages. If it did, we should expect to find in the late fourteenth and the fifteenth centuries at least one of the two uses of the 'clauses': Brunner's 'earlier' use, when the 'bearer' clause was distinct from the 'order' clause and converted the bond into a negotiable instrument; or his 'later' one, when it was employed in the same sense and for the same purposes as the 'order' clause. In reality neither are to be found. It can be doubted whether the 'bearer' clause ever possessed in England the features of the so-called earlier stage. Its purpose was to define the mode of authorisation: to make the possession of the document in itself a sufficient proof of the assignee's authority and *bona fide* acquisition. When we read that on Wednesday next after the Lord's Epiphany (1275) William Bukerell came to the Guildhall and entered a recognisance that he owed John de Schynen, merchant of Brabant twenty pounds to be repaid 'to the same or to the bearer of his letters in this city', the stipulation

[54] H. Brunner, 'Les titres au porteur' (*Nouvelle Rev. Historique de droit*, 1880), restated in a simpler and somewhat cruder form by A. Wahl, *Traité des titres au porteur*, vol. I, pp. 24 seq. In this country Brunner's theory has been incorporated with slight modifications by Pollock and Maitland, Prof. E. Jenks (op. cit.) and Prof. Holdsworth (vol. VIII).

must not be considered as in any way different from the informal instruction in a private letter to 'deliver the money to the bearer of my ring': it provided for a mode of authorisation different from the formal *attornatio*.[55] That this was the function of the bearer clause is suggested by its frequent occurrence in English records conjointly with the order clause: '*vel suo certo attornato litteram obligatoriam deferenti*'.[56] And a case before the fair court of St Ives in 1293 shows that this joint clause apparently dispensed the bearer from the necessity of showing a special letter of attorney.[57] This was as much as the bearer clause could do, but even this it could do only sometimes and in some places.[58] A stipulation between the obligor and the obligee was perfectly valid as long as the obligor was willing to respect it, but its validity ceased to be determined by the bare intentions of the parties as soon as the case was brought into the courts. There the substance of the bearer's rights and the correct mode of his authorisation were determined not by the presence or the absence of the clause, but by the actual powers conferred and conferable upon him by the obligee under the existing rules of law.[59] No bearer clause could convert a conventional bond into a fully negotiable instrument in Common Law; the absence of a bearer clause could not make an informal obligation untransferable in mercantile custom. In short, the presence or the absence of the bearer formula did nothing to alter the transferable potentialities of financial instruments. Brunner's 'first phase' was unknown in the English legal and commercial practice of the later Middle Ages.

It is equally doubtful whether the clauses conformed in their purpose and function to the pattern of Brunner's second phase. The very use of the 'bearer' formula as an external sign of authorisation differentiated it from the 'order' clause, and this distinction was further emphasised by the fact that in the late fourteenth and the fifteenth centuries each of the

---

55 L.B.A. p. 3; cf. C. Freundt, *Wechselrecht d. Postglossatoren*, v. II, pp. 18–19.
56 This is Brunner's 'mixed' clause; Brunner, ibid., pp. 162–8. It is to be found in the majority of the English financial documents of the thirteenth and the early fourteenth centuries, e.g. *Select Cases in Law Merchant* (S.S.) pp. 26, 59, 62, 65, 86, and all the early examples of obligation in Madox, op. cit. Indeed very few examples of the ordinary 'bearer' clause have survived for the period earlier than the end of the fourteenth century. The nature of the instrument to which Bracton refers as 'missibilia' (*De Legibus*, fo. 41b) is shrouded in mystery, but it is quite possible that he had in mind bearer instruments: 'item in incertam personam, sicut sunt missibilia'.
57 *Select Cases in Law Merchant*, pp. 65–6.
58 If we are to believe Freundt, this was also the original function of the clause on the continent: *Wertpapiere*, *passim* and esp. v. II, pp. 105 to 109 and 146–54; cf. his 'Das Wechselrecht d. Postglossatoren', ibid. 30 seq. u. G. Desmarez, *La lettre de foire à Ypres*, pp. 34 seq.
59 Not even in the continental mercantile courts, cf. G. Bigwood, *Le régime juridique et economique du commerce de l'argent dans la Belgique au moyen âge*, pp. 512 seq.

two formulas came to serve a separate group of documents. The 'order' clause in its conventional form (*vel suo certo attornato*) was employed principally in the formal bonds, while the bearer clause came to be confined almost exclusively to the informal obligations, such as the promissory note and the bill of exchange or the bond drawn abroad.[60] The reason for this specialisation in the employment of the clauses is easy enough to guess: it followed inevitably from the differences between their respective functions. The 'order' clause was employed in the formal bonds because these were, so to speak, Common Law documents, and in the Common Law of the fourteenth and the fifteenth centuries obligations could be transferred only to 'certain attorneys' armed with powers of procuration. On the other hand, the bearer clause was confined to informal obligations because these had no standing in Common Law and therefore could, if the parties so desired, include stipulations of a less formal and more elastic mode of *attornatio* than that required by the Courts of Common Law.

The conclusion is clear: neither the bearer clause nor the 'order' clause transformed, or was meant to transform, the legal nature of the obligation. Their employment did not determine the legal differences between the documents: it was itself determined by them. The obligations were transferable in practice in accordance with the financial and commercial circumstances of each particular case, and the transfers were enforceable in accordance with the varying attitudes of the different courts to the question of assignments. The legal and diplomatic formulae were of secondary importance.

THE LETTER OF PAYMENT ('TRATTA', BILL OF EXCHANGE)

The latest, and in a sense the most highly developed financial document of the later Middle Ages was the 'mandate': the 'leter of payment' of the English records, the '*tratta*' of the Italian records, the 'bill of exchange' of present-day nomenclature. As will be shown further, it originated in connection with long-distance trade, and in the first place served the purposes of international payment: it is no wonder that it became the most cosmopolitan of all the diplomatic inventions of the later Middle Ages. By the end of the fifteenth century it assumed a stereotyped form, and the form came to be observed all over Europe, not excluding England. The French example printed by Brésard typifies the

---

[60] Cely Accounts, *passim*: e.g. 12/13, 'item delivered to George 2 specialties of Henrykson etc. . . . one payable at pleasure of the bringer'. The only English 'bearer' bond in the Cely accounts and papers is the one drawn by Aldridge the purser of Cely's boat for a loan on bottomry; Cely Accounts 13/31: 'to pay to the foresayd Roger or to bringer of this bill'. But this may have had something to do with the fact that being a loan on bottomry, the transaction was outside the jurisdiction of Common Law.

fifteenth-century *tratta* of any other country. 'Payes pour ceste premiere lettres de change le 15 moys de may prochain venant a Nexy Capon etc. de Lyon la som de . . . pour semblable somme qui j'ai en de Albache Delbeue a Tours, le 10 d'Avril etc.'[61]

This fifteenth-century document already possesses all the features of the modern bill of exchange. Four persons are involved in the transaction evidenced by it: the man who drew it (drawer), the original creditor (Delbeue), the payer (the man to whom the letter is addressed), and the payee (Capon). The word *premiere* indicates the usual order of sending a second and a third bill if the first has not been paid. The bill contains the clause of 'value received' ('*pour semblable somme*') which came to be invested with important legal meaning. Further the whole of its diplomatic structure expresses and emphasises its economic purpose: its nature of an assignment by a written command to pay. Its principal use was in foreign exchanges, but it could also be employed in every kind of payment transacted by means of assignment. It could be used to settle sale debts, and still more, it could be handed over not only to pay debts, but to lend money. Its function was to effect a payment – the purpose was immaterial.

Its nature of a mere command to pay distinguishes it sharply from the obligation. We shall see further that the mercantile custom soon invested the *tratta* with the legal significance of a bond, but this was a derived function of the document, and was not universally recognised until the very end of our period. Hence the common use of the term 'letter of payment' to describe the *tratta,* and hence the clear distinction which contemporaries drew between the letter of payment and the letter of obligation. It would be safe to assume that in the majority of cases in the fourteenth and the early fifteenth centuries the actual testification and recording of the transaction was done by an ordinary bond, while the *tratta* was merely intended to transact the payment on the bond, if and when this had to be done by assignment. The records of 'protests' of Venetian bills in the English calendars of the Venetian state papers contain several entries showing that even in the sixteenth century the Venetian bill of exchange in England was often merely a subsidiary document effecting the payment on an ordinary obligation.[62] In the earlier centuries this must have been quite a general practice. One example will suffice. Clements Waldingfeld complained to the Chancellor that by her 'script obligatorie' she was bound to William Brynrag of London, mercer,

---

[61] P. Brésard, *La foire de Lyon,* p. 263.

[62] Cal. State Papers Venetian, vol. I, 317, 321, etc. This relation between the obligation and the *tratta* is in itself sufficient to destroy Dezmarez's contention that the latter was an Italian instrument, while the former was a 'North-European' one. G. Desmarez, *La lettre de foire à Ypres,* pp. 1–5; cf. D.'s article in *La Revue de droit international,* 1899, pp. 533–7. E. Ch. Pr. 64/106.

in £18 to be paid to him or to his certain attorney; the debt was paid at Bruges by her 'servant' Robert Holbeck, 'the which Robert Holbeck by a special commandment in writing from your said oratress by the said William to him brought truly paid and content him in Flemish money'.[63] This does not necessarily mean that every early *tratta* was based upon a bond. What was essential was that the debt, or the loan, should be in a sense pre-existing. In other words, the drawer would issue a letter of payment on the presumption – which might be purely theoretical – that the debt, or the loan, had been arranged before the letter was drawn. It was immaterial whether the parties had recorded their arrangement on a formal bond, or in an informal note or merely talked it over in the tavern. Some of the known instances of early foreign bills may well have been based on nothing more than a verbal agreement. Between parties used to informal dealings with each other this would not be an unusual procedure. And it was bound to become more common when the letter of payment came to be accepted in mercantile courts as evidence of the pre-existing obligation, and so worded as to bring the existence of the obligation into prominence. When this happened, and apparently it happened long before the fifteenth century was over, the *tratta* became an independent financial instrument.[64] Nevertheless the subsidiary use of the *tratta* was not given up until well after the period covered here. The wording of the letter also preserved for a long time its features of a mere 'letter of payment' and for a long time remained that of a private mercantile letter of command. Being a command it had to be 'directed' to the person who was to transact the payment; it was therefore not an 'open' declaration (letter patent), but a 'letter close' addressed to the payer. It is sometimes described in the English records merely as a 'bill directed to N.' or a 'letter missive',[65] and indeed from the point of view of diplomatic structure it was nothing more than a formalised version of a private mercantile letter embodying orders or instructions. The Cely papers have preserved a perfect specimen of a letter of payment in which this process of formalisation has not yet been completed.

Jhesu [1472]. Right worshipful and reverend master. I recommend me unto you and pleaseth it you to wit I have received by exchange of Thomas Kestevin attorney of Richard Cely, merchant of the Staple at Calais, fourty pounds

---

[63] Cf. Cely Accts, *passim*, P. Huvelin, 'Les travaux recents' etc. (*Les Annales du droit commerciel*, 1901), pp. 1–5, Freundt, *Wechselrecht*, vol. I, pp. 15 seq.

[64] Below, p. 57.

[65] E. Ch. Pr. 28/210, Wm Grene delivered £100 to Thomas Mollesley, as evidenced 'by a bill directed by Thomas to John Wade'. For other examples of bills or letters of payment 'directed, etc.' see Cely Accts *passim*; Cely Papers (*Camden Society*) nos. 150 and 18. For 'Letters missif' see Cely Accts 10/7: 'repaid by George Cely by a letter missif, directed, etc.'; also ibid. 10/2.

sterling to be paid to the said Richard Cely, or to the bringer of the letters, at London the 24th day of February next coming. The which 10 li sterlings, I pray you, may be well and truly content and paid at the day aforesaid by this my first and second letter of payment. In witness herof I, the said John Dycons, have written the bill with my own hand and have set hereto my master's seal, the 8th day of December in the year of our Lord God 1472 [Endorsed:] To my right worshipful master John Wode, merchant of the Staple of Calais at London [with Wode's trademark following].[66]

This document contains certain elements of a fully developed *tratta* (value received, bearer clause, first and second letter), it is handed over to the payee instead of being sent direct to the payer. But it is still far removed from the laconic bill of exchange reproduced above, and is worded as if it were an ordinary letter from a factor to his master. In language and structure it differs little from other semi-private, but un-mistakably formal, letters of instructions from a merchant to a merchant containing commands to deliver goods or perform an action. When Richard Cely wanted to furnish a debtor, who had delivered him a pledge, with a document releasing the pledge on the payment of the debt, he issued to him a letter strikingly similar to the informal *tratta* of John Dycons.

Jhesu 1479, I greet you well. I let you wit I have received of John Fomer and Harry de Morys for the full payment of Phillip Seller's letter of payment wherof I will that you deliver to the said John or Harry, or to the bringer of this bill the pledge of Harry's the which Phillip Seller left with you at Calais. Writ at London the lath day of December, by your father Richard Cely [trade mark follows].[67]

The *tratta* was thus a letter of payment: an assignment by a written command to pay. This elementary truth we must remember, and remem-ber well, if we are to find our way through the labyrinthine ramifications of the problem of 'origins'.[68] The question of the rise of the international

[66] Cely Papers, Ancient Correspondence, vol. 53, no. 1.

[67] Ibid. no. 34; cf. P.M. Rolls, A 66, m. 3.

[68] The theories of 'origins' are exceedingly numerous. Attempts have been made to show that the *tratta* was borrowed by Europeans from the oriental peoples, Arabs and Jews; others would trace it back to the Hellenistic era. Of those who have explored the European sources of the 'invention', A. Schaube 'Einige Beobachtungen zur Entstehungsgeschichte der Tratte' in *Zeitsch. d. Savignystiftung*, Germ. Abt. vol. 14, and 'Anfänge der Tratte' in *Zeitsch. f. d. ges Handelsr.*, 1894) tries to prove by deduction from the correspondence of the Cerchi and the Tolomei, that the *tratta* originated from the *avisa* (letter of advice) which was originally a part of the general business letters of merchants in Italy to their agents abroad. G. Lastig (*Zeitsch. f. d. ges. Handelsr.* XXIII and XXV; incorporated into K. Lehmann's *Wechselrecht*, pp. 32 seq.) connected the rise of the *tratta* with the recording of debts in the books of early banks; as a rule, notices were issued on the strength of the entries resembling in many respects the late medieval *tratta*. Max Neumann (*Geschichte des Wechsels im*

tratta, of how and why this particular document made its appearance in Western Europe does not directly concern us here. It is irrelevant to the English evidence and unrelated to the English reality, for the *tratta* had been evolved in the commercial practice of other European nations long before the English began using it in their own commercial transactions. Embryonic bills of exhange have been found in the Italian correspondence of the late thirteenth century,[69] and the document was certainly employed by Italians and by the merchants of Southern France throughout the fourteenth century. On the other hand the English letter of payment, with an English drawer or an English payer does not appear before the fifteenth century, or at the very earliest the close of the fourteenth. To a student of English commercial and financial usages the problem is not one of origins. His question is not how and why did mankind invent the bill of exchange, but how and why did the bill, hitherto employed by others, come into general use in transactions between Englishmen. It is only by answering this question, that we can also hope to shed light, albeit an indirect and reflected one, upon the more general problem of origins.

How then did the English come to adopt the *tratta*? Let us begin with those answers to the question which to our mind do not answer it. Of these the most popular and the least satisfactory is the one which ascribes the adoption of the tratta in England to the imitation of the Italian precedents: the tratta was 'borrowed' from Italy. This theory, like most theories of 'borrowing', evades the problem it sets out to solve. It is time that historians realised, as certain sociologists did some time ago, that the transmission of an institution does not in itself explain its emergence at a given place and time. Things are never borrowed unless the borrower wants them: institutions are not transmitted unless they have a definite purpose to serve in their new home. When a new need produces a new tool or custom, that tool or custom is either 'invented' or 'borrowed', but the significant explanation elucidates the need which called it into being, rather than the manner in which it was adopted. The question whether it was invented or taken over from somebody else is in itself insignificant,

Hansagebiete) prepared the way for a theory which now holds the field. According to him, the *tratta* was originally an instrument of assignment subsidiary to the ordinary obligation employed for the purposes of exchange (Eigenwechsel). This theory has been elaborated and modified by Goldschmidt (*Universalgeschichte des Handelsrechts*, pp. 405–12) who links up the development of the *tratta* with what he calls the 'passive order clause' in the ordinary exchange obligation (domizilierter Eigenwechsel). The clause stipulated that the payment could be carried out by the debtor or his assigns, and when the latter was expected to make the payment, the obligor addressed to him a 'mandate to pay' which was handed over to the payee with the obligation. Lately, G. Freundt, has tried to derive the *tratta* from the *liberate* writs of the Norman and English Exchequer (*Wechselrecht* I, pp. 1–82).

[69] Schaube, op. cit.; Goldschmidt, op. cit., p. 439; Holdsworth, VIII, p. 131.

the more so in that the difference between social 'invention' and social 'borrowing' is merely one of terminology: the adoption of an imported social contrivance to meet a new need contains in itself all the essential elements of an 'invention'. With regard to the *tratta*, and its emergence in the English mercantile practice of the fifteenth century, the question to be answered is not whether it was invented at home or taken over from abroad, but whether anything occurred in English life at that time which necessitated and facilitated its appearance. For even if the bill of exchange were first evolved by Italian merchants, and the English *tratta* reproduced all the forms and formulas of its Italian predecessor, this would not yet explain why, of all the different things invented and evolved by Italian merchants, it was the *tratta* that was borrowed, and why it had to be borrowed in the fifteenth century and not in the fourteenth or the sixteenth. Schaube has shown that the Italians used something like bills of exchange in their dealings with their agents in England as early as 1260.[70] The Mayor's Court Files and the early Plea and Memoranda Rolls in the City records and the Exchange Rolls (Close Rolls Supplementary) at the Public Record Office show that Englishmen constantly made use of the Italian letters of exchange, especially in their transfers of money to Italy. But they did not begin drawing bills themselves until much later. The borrowing from Italy, far from explaining anything, itself demands an explanation.

The bill of exchange became a favourite financial instrument because it answered a serious need, and the real problem is to find what that need was. That this was the real problem was well understood by a number of older writers, above all by Brunner. Unfortunately Brunner, right as he was in posing the problem, was undoubtedly wrong in answering it. According to Brunner the bill of exchange became indispensable in the later Middle Ages all over Europe for the simple reason that it provided merchants with a negotiable instrument at a time when the older instruments had lost their negotiable characteristics. When the jurists, working under the influence of the renascent Roman ideas, succeeded in narrowing down the rights of the bearer to those of a *procurator*, the old 'bearer bond' ceased to be negotiable and the merchants were forced to try other expedients. The most important of these new expedients was the *tratta*.[71] This theory of Brunner's has no foundation in the English evidence. That the evolution of the *tratta* was intimately connected with the assignment of debts is obvious and has repeatedly been stressed here, but that the *tratta* itself possessed a fuller negotiability than some of the other and older financial instruments, and that it could be used as a substitute for a negotiable bond, is very largely a legend. The position of the bill of exchange in English law was little

[70] A. Schaube, *Anfänge*, etc.   [71] Holdsworth, VIII, pp. 125–6.

different from that of any other informal instrument: it was recognised by the mercantile courts, neglected by the Common Law and protected by the Chancery on those occasions when it embodied what appeared to be an equitable arrangement. That this was so even a cursory review of the legal position will show.

The attitude of English Merchant Law is rather difficult to ascertain. In so far as it is possible to judge from the few surviving cases, the mercantile courts in the fifteenth century recognised the letter of exchange and enforced the two principal obligations implicit in it. A case before the Mayor's Court of London in 1437 suggests that in common with some continental tribunals the City courts acted on the assumption that the 'payer' having 'accepted' the *tratta* entered thereby into an obligation to the payee. On that occasion the court upheld an action against one Elias Davy concerning a debt of £30 on a bill of exchange between one John Burton and John Audeley, Davy's factor, executed in Bruges and not yet paid by Davy.[72] The position is somewhat more certain with regard to the drawee's claim on the drawer in cases when the payer did not accept the bill or was insolvent. If we remember that in the fifteenth century and later, the bill of exchange was often merely a *documentum referens* to a pre-existing bond, it will be clear that the failure of the payer to honour the bill, would merely restore the same relation between the drawee and the drawer which had existed before the issuing of the bill, and the debtor would still be bound under the original obligation. The drawer's position was not quite so simple under 'independent' bills, i.e. those based not on a pre-existing bond but on a verbal arrangement. In Bruges, as indeed throughout North-western Europe, bills were accepted as evidence of the drawer's debt to the drawee; and the lawyers have, so to speak, localised the legal power of the bill in the clause of 'value received' which, as they argued, fulfilled the functions of an independent bond.[73] In England we can hardly find any traces of a similar legal theory: the English evidence on Law Merchant is too scanty. Nevertheless the judicial practice, whether based on the theory or not, seemed to conform to the continental deductions from it. As early as 1414 the Mayor's Court was called upon to adjudicate on a claim of one Richard Ikelington against Tidman Hansard arising from the defendant's bills of exchange (*litterae solucionis*) upon one John Maltby. The bills having changed hands a number of times were acquired by Ikelington, the plaintiff, who apparently failed to obtain payment from Maltby, and

[72] L.B.K., p. 208, cf. MS for terminology. The attitude of the mercantile courts abroad was largely the same. The Bruges tribunal apparently admitted in the first half of the fifteenth century that the payer having 'accepted' the *tratta* entered thereby into an obligation to the payee: Gilliodts II, pp. 6 and 12 (drawers Englishmen) as to Bergen-up-Zoom see E. Ch. Pr. 29/161.

[73] C. Freundt, *Wechselrecht* I, pp. 74 seq., Goldschmidt, op. cit., p. 447.

was now suing the drawer. In the course of the proceedings it turned out that the letters were issued on conditions which now made the claim invalid, and the case consequently went against the plaintiff, but its other particulars make it more or less clear that had the drawer been unable to prove the special conditions attached to the letters he would have been held responsible for the payment.[74] In other words the bills of exchange seem to have won for themselves a recognition in the City courts of London. The significance of this recognition, however, must not be misinterpreted or overestimated. The Law Merchant was merely another word for the 'custom of the merchants'; everything which entered into the everyday practice of merchandise and was indispensable for the efficient conduct of trade was, *eo ipso*, part and parcel of merchant custom and thereby sanctioned by Law Merchant. And in so far as bills of exchange were in common use at the time, their recognition by the Law Merchant was natural and obvious.

The attitude of the Common Law also presents no difficulties. The courts of Common Law ignored the letter of payment, as they did other writings which were not formal bonds or covenants under a seal. They probably had very little opportunity for evolving any separate doctrine as to 'letters of payment'. Apart from the fact that mercantile cases came comparatively rarely before the Common Law courts, the letters of payment, in so far as they were used for exchange purposes, were, in common with other contracts concluded abroad or stipulating a payment outside the Kingdom, supposed to be outside the jurisdiction of Common Law.

Thus the position of the letter of payment was little different from that of the informal bond; and the similarity was only emphasised by the ease with which letters of exchange seem to have circulated among merchants. For in this respect the *tratta* was similar to, and not different from, the informal obligations, and even sealed bonds. The Ikelington case quoted above shows that mercantile courts recognised the sale of bills of exchange, but we have seen that it also recognised the sale of bonds. In Common Law their transferability would be even smaller than that of ordinary bonds, for they were not even recognised as financial instruments. Nor was the 'bearer' of a letter of exchange in a stronger position than the 'bearer' of a bill obligatory. Most of the bills of exchange referred to in this section were drawn to bearer: but this apparently affected very little the degree to which they were transferable. In the same Ikelington case the plaintiff mentioned the fact that he had 'acquired' the letters to show that they had come into his hands in a legal and honourable way, but said practically nothing about their being drawn

[74] P.M. Rolls A 43, m. 70; cf. ibid. A 61 m. 3, A 74, m. 2.

to bearer. This he would certainly have mentioned if the bearer clause had been an important consideration.

It is, therefore, hardly right to suggest that the appearance of the bill of exchange and its wide use by merchants had anything to do with the alleged 'search for a substitute for the once negotiable bond'. The bond never was a negotiable paper; but it was freely transferable and remained so till long after the bill of exchange had become popular. On the other hand, the bill of exchange enjoyed no legal privileges over the older documents, and though freely transferable, did not become fully negotiable till late in the modern era.

The causes responsible for the popularity of the *tratta* in the later Middle Ages were not legal but economic: a conclusion obvious to the point of truism, indeed obvious even to historians. More than one historian has thought of economic reasons instead of, or in addition to, the legal argument of 'greater negotiability', and some of them, including Professor Holdsworth in this country, came very near to what seems to be the correct answer. According to Professor Holdsworth the *tratta* was born and popularised in the exchange transactions of medieval bankers, and above all, the Italian *campsores*. It 'originated in the method employed by the Italian merchants who had entered into a contract to transport money . . . The method employed to carry it out was by writing a "letter of payment" to a correspondent living in the place where the payment was to be effected.'[75] This view approaches the crux of the problem, since there undoubtedly was a close connection between the adoption of the document and the exchange transactions of bankers. It falls short of the desired solution only in so far as it misplaces the logical emphasis. The Italian banking societies indeed used the *tratta* for exchange purposes not only because it was specially suited to employment in exchanges but because it was an ideal instrument to employ when a person other than the drawer was expected to make the final payment; and especially when the sums assigned were not strictly speaking debts owing to the assignor from his creditor, but funds actually belonging to the former and kept in his name, or on his behalf, in another town. These conditions were almost invariably present whenever a commercial firm undertook regular exchange business by means of *tratta*. It was easy and natural for a society with partners trading on its behalf in different parts of the world to accept money on exchange in one place repayable by its agents in another; and to carry out the transaction by means of a written assignment. But it was easy and natural to do so not because the transaction was one of exchange, but because the firm had constant business dealings with foreign centres and had funds there to its credit. The identity between the business of exchanges, and the function of the *tratta* has been exaggerated.

[75] Holdsworth, vɪɪɪ, pp. 130, 132, 136.

Just as exchange was not the only transaction in which the *tratta* could be employed, so too the *tratta* was not the only instrument employed in exchanges. If exchange was taken up by a merchant without an organisation abroad or without funds to his credit in foreign towns, he would draw not a bill of exchange, but what the Germans call an 'Eigenwechsel', an ordinary bond payable by the drawer himself, who expected to be present in the place stipulated in the bond on the date of payment. It was not the business of exchange that was responsible for the rise of the letter of payment, but the fact that it was a payment to be made not by the drawer himself but by his partners, agents or debtors abroad, and it could be employed in all such payments, whether connected with exchange or not. In other words, the rise of the letter of exchange was due to the rise and development of that type of commercial organisation of which the Italian banking houses were a specimen: we mean the appearance of firms with permanent connections abroad.

This is the chief reason why bills of exchange came to be regularly employed by English merchants in the fifteenth century. It was in the second half of the fourteenth and the fifteenth centuries that much of English foreign trade came to be actively borne by English merchants. The wool and cloth exporters on the one hand, and the miscellaneous importers on the other, became the principal dealers in exchanges. The nature of the Staplers' business necessitated the constant presence abroad of a factor or a partner. They always had sums abroad in the hands of their agents or foreign debtors, and it would be as natural for them to 'take up' money in London and direct a bill of exchange to their agents abroad instructing them to repay the debt, as it was for the Bruges or Antwerp agents of the big importers to 'take up' money from the Staplers and draw bills on their masters or partners in England.[70] We find indeed very few instances of bills of exchange drawn on anybody who was not a factor or a *socius*.

The causes of the adoption and the spread of the *tratta* in England were thus economic, and the key to these causes is provided by the nature of the *tratta* itself. The *tratta* spread in England acording as the conditions of trade, and above all in its organisation, necessitated and favoured assignments by means of commands to pay. If this conclusion be accepted, it may also provide a glimpse into the causes of the rise of *tratta* elsewhere, i.e. of its 'origin'. By the same reasoning it is possible to show that the *tratta* in the other countries of Western Europe, or indeed in the world in general, arose in connection with the form of business organisation which

---

[70] Cf. A. Sayous, *Le Commerce des Européens à Tunis* pp. 45, 58–9, for connection between the *tratta* and the separation between exports and imports. Cf. also E. Power, 'The English Wool Trade in the reign of Edward IV', *Camb. Hist. Journal*, 1926.

made that particular form of assignment necessary and easy. Of that new type of business organisation, the firm with permanent connections in different places, the *tratta* was a product and a symptom. To try to trace, as many historians do, the origin of the document to its diplomatic predecessors, and to demonstrate the descent of its diplomatic forms from the corresponding formulae of older documents, is a task as unhelpful as it is unreal. The document was a formalised command to pay; informal commands were probably as old and as common as the art of writing itself, certainly as the art of letter writing. It required no special gifts, nor a long evolution, legal, economic or diplomatic, for men to ask or command somebody to transact a payment for them. What distinguished the *tratta* from these informal commands was the greater rigidity and conventionality of its form; that formalisation was impossible and out of place as long as the transaction it served was exceptional and irregular; it became possible with the growing frequency and regularity of the transaction, in response to the needs and the facilities of the new business organisation. Thus the same cause which explains the spread of the *tratta* in England allows us also to shed a light – and we have promised only an indirect and a reflected one – upon the origin of the *tratta* itself.

3
PARTNERSHIP IN ENGLISH
MEDIEVAL COMMERCE*

1

Societas in its various forms has always been a favourite topic with historians of medieval trade. Considering how important partnerships were in the organisation and finance of commerce, and how abundant is the historical literature dealing with them, it is surprising to find the subject almost wholly by-passed by English economic historians. Even Sir William Ashley, who was well-acquainted with the medieval *Societas* and fully aware of its importance, described it with hardly a reference to English doctrine and practice. As we shall see further, the obscurities of English medieval law and terminology are largely to blame for the silence of modern historians. But whatever its explanation, the silence does not mean that in this respect the practice of English merchants in the Middle Ages was fundamentally at variance with that of Italian or German or Flemish traders. For, looked at more closely, English records reveal the partnership and *societas*-like associations operating and covering a range of transactions as wide as that which the *societas* embraced abroad; fulfilling roughly the same functions and appearing in roughly the same forms.

To some extent, however, this gap in English historical literature is the fault not of English historians, but of the continental students of *societas*. The parallels between English and continental developments might not have escaped attention had continental practice and doctrine been presented in the shape recognisable by English lawyers and economists. Therefore, at the cost of appearing to labour the obvious, I propose to preface my description of English partnerships by a brief recapitulation of existing knowledge of partnership in Italy and Germany. The object of the recapitulation is to bring out those variations of form and function which English historians should hope to find in English records.

According to one view, partnerships were numerous in the Middle Ages because they supplied the most popular and least objectionable method of financing trade. This is not the same as to say that partnerships were common merely because they were used to disguise loans on

* This paper has appeared in *Studi in Onore di A. Sapori* and in *Rivista della Societa*, 11, 3, 1957 (in Italian).

interest.[1] Partnerships, according to this view, did not disguise the charging of interest, but legitimised it by converting it into dividend. Partnership was not a fictitious arrangement to cloak the ordinary loans on interest; it was merely a legitimate form of commercial loan.[2] According to another view, the partnership was a symbol and a consequence of the primitive organisation of medieval trade. The medieval merchant was primarily, and very often exclusively, an artisan, and had little more than his labour to employ. The necessary capital had to be supplied not by the merchant himself but by nobles, ecclesiastics and rich townsmen who were not merchants, and whose association with professional traders took, as a rule, the form of partnership.[3]

To some extent both views belong to the *ancien régime* in the study of medieval economy, when historians were mainly interested in the medievality of things medieval and tried to bring out the contrast between medieval institutions and our own. This bias apart, the two theories are compatible and both true in part. If we go behind the distinctions of law and form to the economic functions of medieval partnership we shall discover that they had two main purposes in medieval economic life. One was related to the financing of medieval trade, the other was related to its organisation.

To understand this twofold nature of the medieval partnership one has to start from obvious considerations: obvious almost to the point of triviality. Mercantile partnership was an association, and like every association it had its *raison d'être* only when there was a task which a single person could not carry out. A single person might find himself unable to engage in a commercial undertaking for two reasons – first, because the nature of the undertaking required the services of more than one person; secondly because it required greater resources than one person was able or willing to bestow upon it. By associating into partnerships men sought to overcome one or both of these two impediments. If so, it should be possible to distinguish three types of partnership – (1) in which 'capital' hired the services of a merchant, and which we shall call a 'service partnership', (2) a partnership in which the merchant hired capital, and we shall call a 'finance partnership', and (3) the 'complete' or 'real' partnership into which all the partners contributed both capital and service. The partnership of the first type came very near to the

[1] Cf. M. M. Postan, 'Credit in Medieval Trade', *Economic History Review*, 1927 and Ch. I above.

[2] W. Endemann, *Studien in d. Romanisch Kanonistischen Wirtschafts – u. Rechtslehre etc.*, Berlin, 1874–83, pp. 343–87 and esp. 370–1; Cf. P. De Peismaeker, 'Les formes d'association à Ypres', *Revue de Droit International*, etc. (1904), p. 640.

[3] W. Sombart, *Der Moderne Kapitalismus*, 5th edition, München-Leipzig, 1916–1924, I, pp. 300–2.

ordinary contract of service and was often indistinguishable from it. The partnership of the second type came equally near to ordinary loans. The third type was theoretically nothing more than a combination of the first and the second. The whole problem of partnership thus lies on the border between that of commercial organisation and that of commercial investment.

These two functions were not, of course, always identical with the actual motives which prompted the establishment of this or that partnership. Now and again, medieval partnership could be made to serve objects which had very little in common with the economic nature of the *societas*. In places where strangers were not allowed to trade freely or were highly taxed, partnerships could be employed to 'colour' strangers' goods. Sometimes they concealed a transference of a mercantile privilege or licence, as when a merchant shipped goods or obtained an exemption from duties under a royal licence on the pretext of his being a partner of the person who was the nominal beneficiary under the licence.[4]

But apart from these purely fictitious and fraudulent uses, medieval *societas* was in substance as well as in form a true partnership of service or finance. It may have been used to facilitate loans on interest, but it did so by changing the nature of the loan and assimilating it to partnership not only in form but also in essence. It may have been employed for purposes of maritime insurance, and certain types of Italian *commenda*, in which one partner bore 'the adventure' of the whole capital, lent themselves easily to such use. But here again the insurance transaction was a contract of partnership in essence as well as in form.

Needless to say, the distinctions of function do not necessarily correspond to the differences of form, according to which medieval partnerships have been grouped by lawyers and historians. Some of the founders of the modern school of the history of mercantile law attempted to identify the chief forms of medieval partnership as labour partnerships and capital partnerships respectively.[5] These attempts have not been very successful,

---

[4] In London the avowing of stranger's goods apparently involved in the majority of cases a relation between the owners of the goods and the 'avowers' not unlike those of German *Sendeve*. From fourteenth-century Lynn we have a direct statement that the merchant strangers were in the habit of sending their merchandise 'ovesque leours lettres a diverses burgeitz de lenne de vendre lour ditz merchandizes' so as to avoid the exceptionally high taxation of alien goods. This was probably one of the reasons why partnerships with aliens were prohibited in the majority of English and foreign towns.

[5] G. Lastig, *Die Accomendatio*, Halle, 1907, *passim*, Lastig's classification was in its essential features reproduced by A. Lattes, *Il diritto commerciale*, p. 154. R. Schmidt-Rimpler, in his *Geschichte d. Kommissionshandels* (Halle, 1915), also adheres to this distinction. He separates the *Anlagegeschäft*, that is, an investing partnership, from *Sendeve*, which was identical with commission (pp. 199–218). For criticism of this classification see W. Silberschmidt, *Die Commenda* etc., Würsburg, 1884, pp. 103 ss.

and no wonder. The way the partnerships are classified in medieval sources and modern books is more historical than logical, but in so far as it follows any logical principle at all, it is not that of economic function but that of 'relations between partners' as expressed in the legal construction of partnership. In each of the legal classes so defined partnerships will be found fulfilling either the function of organisation or that of finance or both.

The usual legal and formal classification to which most historians adhere is that which Italian and German writers have borrowed from the history of Italian *societas*. The Italian sources distinguish, roughly speaking three chief types of partnership: the *commenda*, the *collegantia* (*societas maris*), and the *compagna*.[6]

The *commenda* was a contract of 'sleeping' partnership, by which the *commendator*, or the sleeping partner, delivered goods or money to the *tractator*, or the active partner. The chief characteristics of the *commenda* were that the *commendator* contributed capital and no labour, while the *tractator* contributed labour and no capital; that the goods as a rule remained the property of the *commendator*; and that it was on his behalf and to his use that the *tractator* was supposed to be trading. The *commenda* was consequently employed most frequently as a labour partnership, and the 'labour' was frequently that of a 'factor' or 'commissioner'. A merchant, who had goods to sell at a distant place and could not go there himself, entrusted them to another person to be sold on his behalf. Indeed sometimes the *commenda* was merely a *societas*-like form of ordinary hire of service. A merchant engaging a servant in a managerial capacity would very often conclude with him a contract of *commenda*, in which the goods or the funds of the business constituted the stock managed by the *tractator*.[7]

---

[6] In English historical literature these three types have been admirably described by Ashley, Holdsworth and Mitchell. W. Ashley, *An Introduction to English Economic History and Theory*, London, 1894, I, pp. 411–42; W. Holdsworth, *A History of English Law*, London, 1925, VIII, 196; W. Mitchell, *An Essay on the Early History of the Law Merchant*, Cambridge, 1904, pp. 126–9.

[7] W. Silberschmidt, op. cit., pp. 71–4. Silberschmidt seems to think that, on the whole, the *Commenda* was in the majority of cases fulfilling the labour function. See also idem, 'Das Sendegeschäft in Hansagebiet', *Zeitsch. f. d. ges Handelsrecht*, vol. 68, p. 403. The contract of *commenda* was sometimes employed even in those cases in which the *tractator* was to receive a fixed remuneration for his service: see G. Lastig, op. cit., pp. 78–9 and L. Goldschmidt, *Universalgeschichte d. Handelsrechts*, Stuttgart, 1891, p. 245. Sometimes what prompted the employment of *commenda* for contracts of service was the managerial independence conferred by it on the *tractator*. It is possible that with the development of the law of agency, the *commenda* might have been used merely in order to relieve the principal from the full responsibility for his agent's action on his behalf. The importance of this motive, however, ought not to be exaggerated, for the responsibility of the *commendator* for the actions of the *tractator* who was his factor, was not always and not everywhere different from the responsibility of a principal for the actions of his servant.

Sometimes, however, *commenda* could also be used to serve the function of 'finance partnership' and also that of 'complete partnership'. A merchant could accept from other persons sums of money, sometimes goods, which remained the property of the investor, and ensured for him a share in the merchant's profits. Financial *commenda* of this kind (*participatio*) was relatively more common in Italy in the later Middle Ages when the function of 'service' *commenda* had come to be discharged by certain more advanced types of commercial organisation.

In principle this difference of function is very clear, but in practice formal distinctions were not drawn between the *commenda* which was essentially a contract of investment and that which was essentially a contract of service, and historians are as a result left without any formal indications of the economic purpose of any given *societas*. In each case the real clues to the nature of the partnership must be sought in the economic relations. When the *commendator* was a widow, an orphan, or an administrator of a dowry, or when the *tractator* is known to have been an important merchant carrying on a large business, the *commenda* obviously represented nothing else than a contract of investment. Similarly it is safe to assume that in a vast majority of cases in which the *tractator* was not a *chef d'entreprise*, whereas the *commendator* was a business man of substance, the partnership embodied a contract of service. In short, what commonly determined the nature of the *commenda* was the economic status of the partners. If the *tractator* was the head of the enterprise the *commenda* was a finance partnership, but if the actual *commendator* was the entrepreneur, the presumption is that the *tractator* was merely his agent and that the *commenda* was one of service.[8]

This discussion will help us to understand the economic nature of the second type of Italian partnership, which is commonly described as *societas maris* and *collegantia*.[9] By this term modern historians understand that kind of partnership in which both – or all, if there were several – parties contributed capital, and only one, or some, contributed labour. This was very frequently, but not always, a financial device. Just as the ordinary *commenda* was best suited to being employed as a contract of commission or service, so was the *collegantia* best suited to be employed as a finance partnership.[10] At the same time, however, it would be just as wrong to regard the *collegantia* as exclusively a finance partnership as it is to regard the *commenda* as exclusively a service partnership. The economic nature of the arrangement depended entirely on the personal standing and substance of the partners. The fact that in the *collegantia*

8 W. Silberschmidt, *Teilhaberschaft u. Beteilung*, Halle, 1915, pp. 12–13.
9 *Collegantia* is a Venetian term, but it is employed here instead of the rather misleading *societas maris*.
10 W. Ashley, op. cit., pp. 414–15; this is a restatement of Weber's arguments.

the *tractator* had to contribute a certain amount of money himself indicates that he was in most cases a man of some substance, and would therefore be likely to be the 'entrepreneur'. But the *collegantia* could also embody a contract of service. For could not a servant, still more a factor-*tractator*, contribute a certain amount of money to a business which, whatever its form, was in fact the undertaking of the *commendator*?[11]

Very little need be said of the third main type of Italian partnership, the *compagna*. According to the accepted view this term applied to partnerships in which all the participants contributed capital and labour and were jointly and severally liable for debts. According to the accepted theory, these societies grew out of family unions and were more common in industry than in trade.[12]

These Italian forms of partnership were matched by parallel arrangements in Germany. If, for the time being, we leave aside the German *compagna* – the *Offene Gesellschaft* – mercantile practice of the North German towns would appear to distinguish two types of partnership or quasi-partnership: the *Sendeve* (*Sendegeschäft*) and the *Wederlegginge* (*Wiedelegung*).

The nature of the *Sendeve* has long been a bone of contention among German legal historians. The word *Sendeve* apparently means 'goods sent out' ('Sende-vie'), and the *Sendeve* was in fact most frequently used in commission trade. A German merchant entering into his books that he had goods on Sendeve with X, meant that he had sent goods to be sold on his behalf. But it is obvious that this type of entry, especially when the *Sendeve* consisted of money, could also refer to *commenda*-like partnerships employed for the purposes of investment.[13]

Wederlegginge, on the other hand, stood for that type of partnership in which all the parties shared in the capital, and was therefore parallel to the Italian *collegantia*. Like the latter it was most frequently used for investment purposes. But there can be no doubt that in spite of its mutual character it was sometimes nothing else than a special form of 'service' partnership. Many of the Lübeck *Wederlegginge* (and practically all the

[11] The twofold economic nature of the *societas maris* was nowhere clearer than in Pisa. The *Constituum Usus* of Pisa gives to it a legal expression, in that it deals separately with the *societas maris* in which the *socius stans* is the entrepreneur, and that in which he is a mere investor. The latter type was described by a special name of *capitania*: Max Weber, 'Zur Geschichte d. Handelsgesellschaften', in *Collective Papers*, Tübingen, 1924, pp. 389–90; see G. Lastig, op. cit., pp. 109–10.

[12] However, there are some grounds for doubting the validity of all the accepted views as to the nature and origin of the Italian *compagna*. The accepted theory was brilliantly stated by Weber and was more recently supplemented by W. Silberschmidt in *Zeitsch. f. d. ges. Handelsrecht*, vols. 68–9. The English evidence suggests some correctives to the family theory of the *compagna*.

[13] W. Silberschmidt, *Teilhaberschaft u. Beteilung*, cit., pp. 50–61.

instances of *Wederlegginge*, described as such, come from Lübeck), were concluded between master and servants.[14] True servants sometimes contributed their share of the capital, but more often they borrowed from their masters the amount representing their share, so that the mutual nature of the *Wederlegginge* was largely fictitious. 'Mutual' contributions in these cases merely afforded a convenient basis for the servant's participation in profits and safeguarded the master's capital.

Some of these objects could also be achieved by means of a South German variant of *collegantia*, the so-called *Fürleggung*. Under this arrangement, the master earmarked for his servant the profits on a certain share of the capital. This share, however, never became the servant's property, but continued to be owned by the master. The *Vergeld* of the servant consisted solely in the right to the profits, but not to the principle sum itself.[15] This contract, therefore, fulfilled exactly the same function as the North German *Wederlegginge*, although it differed from it in legal form and constitution. Both were contracts of service in the form of partnership.

Certain types of the *Wederlegginge*, however, could approach very closely that type of complete partnership which we meet in the Mediterranean regions under the title of *compagna*. Rehme was one of the first to draw attention to a number of societies in which both the partners (or all, where there were several) contributed both labour and capital.[16] According to him, these partnerships were the prototype of the modern German *Offene Gesellschaft*. But whether we agree with Rehme or not as to the modern descendants of the *Wederlegginge*, there is not the slightest doubt that it could serve the same purposes as the Italian *compagna* and the modern English partnership as long as it fulfilled at one and the same time the functions of finance and those of service.

---

14 R. Keutgen, 'Hansische Handelsgesellschaften' in *Viertej. f. Soz. u. Wirtschaftsgesch.*, IV, pp. 492–502.

15 It was, it seems, J. Strieder who first drew attention to the prevalence of the *Fürleggung* in South German partnerships: 'Die sogennante Fürleggung' in *Viertj. f. Soz. u. Wirtschaftsgesch.*, vol. X. But he regarded it as the southern counterpart of the Hanseatic *Wederlegginge*. Cf. W. Silberschmidt, *Teilhaberschaft u. Beteilung*, cit., pp. 63–5. On the employment of *Voraus* by the great Ravensburg Society, see A. Schulte, *Geschichte der Grossen Ravensburger Handelsgesellschaft, 1380–1530*, Stuttgart–Berlin, 1923, I, p. 63.

16 German legal historians, and especially Weber, differentiate the *Offene Gesellschaft* from other types of partnership, by the full liability of every partner for the debts of the society. P. Rehme, however, argues – and in our view quite rightly – that the various types of partnership were distinguished in the Middle Ages not according to the nature of their contributions and their mutual relations to each other: 'Geschichte des Handelsrechts,' in *Handbuch d. ges. Handelsrechts . . .*, hrsg. von V. Ehrenberg, vol. I, Leipzig, 1913.

2

The various types of partnership in use abroad had their parallels in medieval England. A different terminology and possibly a different attitude of law may have distinguished the English partnership from its continental counterpart, but its economic nature, its functions, and, above all, its part in the commercial life of the country were essentially the same in England as in the rest of medieval Europe. There were in England combinations of the 'one-sided' type, much akin to the *commenda* and the *Sendegeschäft*, and there were also 'mutual' associations, both of the *compagna* type and of the *collegantia* type. There were also the same functional differences of 'finance' and 'labour' as abroad, cutting across the differences of terminology and legal construction. Indeed, considering the national peculiarities in the development of English trade, it is remarkable how fully the international practice was reflected in the English use of partnerships.

If this is not the impression which the standard histories of English law may convey to the uninitiated, the explanation will probably be found in the peculiarities of English legal attitudes towards the *commenda*. Common Law, and to some extent even the customary law of English towns, did not recognise the sleeping partnership as such. Where and when the sleeping partnership was one of service, the remedy in Common Law lay in the various actions which applied to the relation of master and servant: mainly that of 'action of account' by which the master could sue his servant or bailiff to render account for the goods or property entrusted to him. In this way Common Law and most of the urban laws assimilated the legal position of the *commendator* to that of a master or a landlord and that of the *tractator* to that of a servant or bailiff.[17] When the *societas* fulfilled the purposes of investment, the legal remedy lay in the action of 'debt' as well as in that of 'account', and thus the parties were disguised as ordinary debtors or creditors. And then, in the late fourteenth and the fifteenth centuries, the emergence of the equitable jurisdiction of the Chancellor and of the doctrine of trust enabled merchants to find additional legal protection for *commenda*-like contracts of every kind. But here, too, protection was not in the form of a legal doctrine comparable to the law of *societas* abroad.

It is only by going behind legal forms that historians can hope to discover the real essence of partnerships. Unfortunately the records of Common Law courts – and it was from these that English legal historians derive most of their facts and ideas – do not provide us with much opportunity for seeing through the legal formalities of 'actions'. But in

[17] T. F. Plucknett, *The Medieval Bailiff*, London, 1954, esp. pp. 22 seq.

the more informal pleadings before urban courts, and, above all, in appeals to the equitable jurisdiction of the Chancellor in the fifteenth century, the real relations sometimes break through the fiction of 'debt' and 'account', and an insight into the variety and ubiquity of English *societas* can be gained. From these sources a highly developed and differentiated system of partnerships can be reconstructed.

Most difficult to observe are the functions and attributes of the English *commenda*, but once observed they fall into roughly the same categories as abroad. In our general discussion of partnership abroad we have shown that the *commenda* could be made to serve two different functions, the function of finance and that of service. In the English mercantile practice of the fourteenth and fifteenth century, *commenda*-like arrangements fulfilling either or both these functions were also very common.

In the absence of clear legal and terminological distinctions the demarcation between ordinary contracts of service or loan, and those of partnership does not come through very clearly. In fact there are bound to be a great number of embryonic cases which neither contemporaries nor modern historians could classify with any precision. Thus, many of the *commenda*-like agreements for the purposes of service were often temporary and occasional. One merchant would deliver to another a quantity of merchandise with instructions to sell them on his behalf. We read about one Robert Rowchester of London, who delivered divers merchandise to Hugh Cokke to sell on his behalf;[18] about John Henlowe of Bristol who went to London to sell his cloth and took also fine cloths of William Richardes for sale on the same terms as his own.[19] A merchant by the name of Imond Champayne complained to the Chancellor that one William Vyncent sold a 'certain parcel of woad of [the] . . . said besecher in the shire of Wiltshire to the use of the said besecher'.[20] These occasional arrangements served the purpose of modern sales on commission, and were of course most common in foreign trade. In a Chancery petition one Thomas Neweland of Colchester, 'using the feit of merchandise as well beyond the seas as on this side' alleged to have received from Symond Smyth of London, Grocer, cloth to the value of £40 to be carried beyond the sea and there to be sold by Newelands to the use and 'behove' of Smyth.[21] John Lokkys, petitioner to the Chancery, alleged to have received of one Robert Briklisworth ten woollen cloths of different colours within the city of London to convey and carry over the sea into Brabant and there 'to selle and to utter to thuse and behove of the seid Robert as the seid John would selle and utter his owne goods'.[22] Sometimes the man entrusted with the goods was a foreign merchant.[23] Peter

[18] Public Record Office, Early Chancery Proceedings (E. Ch. Pr.), 64/482.
[19] E. Ch. Pr., 60/251.   [20] Ibid. 17/356.   [21] Ibid. 46/287.
[22] Ibid. 64/613 and 625.   [23] Ibid. 64/766.

Gracian, a Venetian, received ten cloths from John Andrew 'to merchandise and sell them in Venyse and other places to the most availe
that he coulde to the seid John and to pay unto hym all such money as
he should receyve . . . deducting hys costis and reward'. Sometimes the
agreements of commission were mutual and the merchants undertook to
sell each other goods. One Bernard Beust (alien), petitioner to the
Chancery, delivered in London to John Pynne merchandise (herring)
worth £59 to sell 'to the best avail and profit of [the] . . . oratour', while
John on his part delivered to Beust other goods to sell in Flanders 'to the
best avail of John'.[24]

However, the records also reveal numerous arrangements between
parties which were much more regular and continuous. In most of these
regular 'commitments' of goods, the 'commissionaries' were described as
'servants' or 'factors' but we must be very careful not to take the medieval
appellation of 'servant' at its face value. Sometimes the *tractator* was
indeed an ordinary servant, but in the great majority of cases the words
'factor' or 'servant' were employed to describe the relation of agents and
principals. The so-called 'servant' or 'factor' might be an independent
merchant, sometimes of greater substance than the so-called master; very
often, as we shall see further, he was his partner. Thus, when we
read that John Coldwell of Ipswich 'made one William Boldry of Ipswich,
merchant, his factour and attorney and to him delyvered 4 pakkes of
woollen cloth unto the valuor of £200 to carie them to Spruce and from
thens them to retouure with marchaundise of the seide country to the
moust profite and availe of the seid John Coldewelle'[25] there is no
reason for doubting that Boldry, described as a merchant, was a man of
considerable substance. In an early fourteenth-century letter to the Mayor
of London, one William de Branghiay, is described as a factor of Osbern
de Bray, merchant of Berwick. What was Osbern de Bray's economic
standing we do not know, but we know that Branghiay was a man of
importance and a well-to-do merchant. At one time he was exercising on
behalf of the City the jurisdiction of the City at the fair of Boston.[26]

We must, therefore, be very careful not to take the medieval appellation
of servant in its modern sense. When a person in a managerial capacity
was described as a 'servant' he was often a merchant in the position of a
tractator in a *commenda*. This relation is more obvious in cases when a
man was described as 'servant and merchant' of X. In the London records,
the Recognisance Roll, the Letter Books, and the Plea and Memoranda
Rolls, we find this description applied very frequently to persons acting on

---

[24] Ibid. 15/185. [25] E. Ch. Pr., 16/427.
[26] London City Records (MSS.), Plea and Memoranda Rolls, A. 1 (b). m. 376:
see also E. Ch. Pr., 78/114; *Myses Contarin and Ric. Palmer, merchant of
Bristol,* his factor.

behalf of foreign merchants; and we find it also applied to Englishmen. John Goldsmyth of Melton Mowbray alleged to have sold to William Soakes, 'servant and chapman' of John Trewe of Colchester merchant 3½ quarts of woad 'al seys et profyt de mesme le John Trewe'.[27] One John Cadon described himself as 'factour and marchant of one Gylbert Debenham into Pruce'.[28] What did this description mean? A servant in a position of an independent merchant, or an independent merchant representing another person and, therefore technically his servant? This question is difficult to answer,[29] but whatever the answer, the relations probably were identical to those of ordinary *commenda*.

In the earlier centuries – thirteenth or early fourteenth – various persons, vintners and non-vintners alike, often engaged in retail trade in wine through the medium of 'merchants' or 'servants' to whom they 'commited' their wine to be retailed. William Barache and Richard Hedreste, rich London merchants of late thirteenth century, had at one time several merchants retailing their wine, and to some of them they even supplied all the requisite equipment of a tavern, a house, cups, etc., thus establishing a precocious prototype of a 'tied' house.[30] Arrangements of this kind were by no means infrequent in other branches of trade, but apparently throughout the Middle Ages they continued to find special favour with the taverners. In a late fifteenth-century Chancery Petition, William Lanplay, servant to John Walshe, vintner, describes an arrangement by which one William Payn 'commyted certeyn wynes to [the] . . . oratour to sell and utter and yeld unto hym accompte of the money thereof comming'.[31] In another petition, Cornel Gesebright, brewer of London, stated that he had agreed to serve William Clement, 'draper, who kepeth a berehous' as his drayman for 'certain wages'. The petitioner served for a year and was willing to render a true account, but Clement would not pay the wages and sued the petitioner on action of account. It is obvious that Gesebright was more than a mere 'drayman'. He apparently had the charge of the tavern, and the fact that he was an

---

[27] E. Ch. Pr., 7/112. [28] Ibid. 16/469.

[29] Earlier evidence is also ambiguous. We read in the 'London City Recognisance', Roll II, 19 Ed. I, of 'Arnold Monedour burgess of Bordeaux' and 'Peter Moreve his merchant'. One Johan Pelden is described as a 'negociator' of a Cologne burgess Gerwin Pot, B. Kuske, *Quellen zur Geschichte Kölner Handels und Verkehrs im Mittelalter*, Bonn, 1917–34, vol. VIII, no. 96.

[30] *Calendars of Letter Books* (ed. R. R. Sharpe, London, 1901), Letter Book A, pp. 65 and 92 (John Skip), pp. 41–3, 102–3 (Barache). Also pp. 83–4: on Monday, 28 May 1284 came Richard de St Botulph, taverner, to the Guildhall and acknowledged himself bound to Richard de Hedreste 'doorkeper in the Exchequer' in the sum of 100 *s.* for the rent of Hedreste's house in Chepe. On the same day, we read further, the same Richard de St Botulph received from Richard de Hedreste 4 casks of wine to sell on his behalf; and St Botulph 'acknowledged himself to be servant to Hedreste for one year'.

[31] E. Ch. Pr., 48/167.

ordinary servant working for 'certain wages' seems to have been denied by Clement. The transaction resembles closely those of the wine importers of the thirteenth century, who could not, or would not, run taverns themselves and so 'committed' their wine to retailers.

In this transaction the sharing of profits and losses was made the test of the relationship: and a test it certainly was. We have seen that in Italy goods could sometimes be 'committed' to an agent who was paid by a fixed wage. However, it is certain that in the overwhelming majority of cases it was the partitory principle that turned the *commenda* into a *societas*. It may well be that in some of the English *commenda*-like arrangements fixed wages were paid. It is also possible that sometimes (as in the Hanseatic *Sendegeschäft*) the services of 'commisioner', or even those of a permanent 'factor', were discharged without any apparent remuneration.[32] But in a number of cases the 'factors' or 'servants' fulfilling the function of 'managers' or *tractators* were undoubtedly participating in profits. In a few early fourteenth-century records the factors resident abroad were sometimes described in terms leaving no doubt as to the existence of 'partitory' agreements between them and their principals. In December 1300, one John Heyron was attached to answer Peter Adrian in a plea that he rendered account for the time when he was the plaintiff's receiver and traded for their common profit from Michaelmas 1296 to Michaelmas 1300.[33] But an even more conclusive example will be found in the records of the fifteenth century. In a Chancery Petition belonging to the last decades of the fifteenth century the executors of William Haddon, a rich merchant of London, complained against William Botyller 'factor for . . . William Haddon in Bilbao', who had sold

---

[32] W. Silberschmidt, *Das Sendegeschäft*, cit., p. 140: I am stressing the word 'apparent' for there were different ways of obtaining an indirect remuneration for these services. The recipient could at some other time avail himself of similar services on the part of the sender. A merchant could also enter into a agreement with another merchant by virtue of which the latter became his partner with respect to a certain stock on conditions very favourable to one of them, and that favourable position was sometimes construed as an advance payment for the services of general commissionary in goods not pertaining to the stock. Thomas Keston, the factor of the Cely's, apparently had a sum of money advanced to him by Richard Cely senior, which may have taken the place of ordinary remuneration for his services. This was certainly so in so far as the relations between Richard and his two sons are concerned. They acted as his factors seemingly for nothing: at the same time they appear to have received from him a capital sum to be employed by them jointly in trade for their own profit.

[33] *Calendar of Early Mayor's Court Rolls* (ed. A. H. Thomas), Cambridge, 1924, 1, p. 104. City of London Records (MSS.), P. & M. Rolls, A, 1 (a) m. 36 contains an entry dated 23 Aug. 1326, relating to the arrest of Henry le Bere of London on the supposition that he was a certain Reginald le Ropere, or else 'factor and partner' of Ropere and one John Pik. However, 'factor and partner' was rather an unusual appellation, and, if it meant anything at all, it may well have referred to a real, i.e. a mutual, partnership between the principal and the servant.

Haddon's goods worth £260 but refused to pay over to the executors the sum realised. The plaintiffs, however, admitted that Botyller may have had a right to a *halvendell*.[34] However, even when such direct indications of a partitory remuneration are missing, it is not at all certain that the 'factor' or the 'servant' was not entitled to share in the profits. The expressions which may be interpreted as precluding any such arrangement, such as to 'the sole use of his seid master', 'to his best avail', 'to his use and behove' had hardly any bearing on the question of relations between the principal and the factor, and need not necessarily have implied something opposite to the expression 'common profit' or 'to the best avail of them bothe'.[35]

So much for *commenda* contracts of service. As we have already indicated they were also employed for investment. 'On Monday the morrow of mid-lent (1292) . . . Walter le Mouner . . . acknowledged that he had received from Geoffrey le Norton the sum of 10 marks to put out to merchandise to the use of the said Geoffrey, for which he will answer within the quinzane of Easter unless prevented by tempest of the sea . . . which peril will rest with the said Geoffrey, and at his risk.'[36] This is a typical English *commenda* embodying an investment, and at the first sight it differs from the service partnerships described above only in so far as Monner received not merchandise to sell or a whole mercantile undertaking to manage, but a sum of money to employ in trade.

This difference strictly speaking does not constitute the exact line of demarcation between a *commenda*-like agreement for the purposes of investment and a similar agreement embodying a contract of service. Galyone, the servant of Agnes Saye,[37] administered a stock expressed in terms of money; yet, if the relationship between him and Agnes was, as it well may have been, one of *commenda*, it served the purposes of service and not those of capital. Conversely there are numerous instances of financial *commendas* in which the stock entrusted was expressed in terms of goods. In 1365 William de Whetele cordwainer was summoned before a London court to render an account to the executors of Henry Sket, another cordwainer, of certain skins of leather entrusted to him 'to trade withal'.[38] If the plaintiff's version of the facts was correct, the transaction undoubtedly represented what we should now call an investment. The

34 E. Ch. Pr., 66/98. There is also an indication of a partitory arrangement in E. Ch. Pr., 16/427.

35 With reference to Germany cf. R. Schmidt-Rimpler, op. cit., pp. 131–3.

36 *Calendar of Letter Books of the City of London* (ed. R. Sharpe), vol. A, London, 1899, p. 139.

37 City of London Records, P. & M. Rolls, A, 1, m. 19. There is a similar instance of a 'stock' of £300 delivered by one merchant to another in the shape of cloth in E. Ch. Pr. 37/41. See also P. & M. Rolls A. 24. m. 13.

38 *Calendar of Plea and Memoranda Rolls of the City of London, 1364–1381,* (ed. A. H. Thomas), Cambridge, 1929, p. 46.

skins were not merely handed over to Skit by Whetele to be sold; neither did Skit engage Whetele to trade on his behalf and to his use. The transaction represented a long-term investment, although it was made in the shape of goods.

What constituted the external characteristic of an investment arrangement of this sort was the delivery of a 'stock'; and if a stock took the shape of goods, the goods were merely a substitute for money. They were not delivered, as in the case of commissions, merely to be sold on behalf of their owner, but to be turned over, to be employed continuously over a certain period of time. When a merchant received a stock 'to traffick withal', he thereby assumed the right of full discretion over its employment, and was, therefore, either a 'servant' in a managerial capacity, or else an independent entrepreneur accepting an investment. The difference between the two was of course one of degree, but in cases about which we are certain that the stock was too small to constitute a complete business by itself, or where we know that it merely formed a part of the recipient's business, we may safely assume that we have before us not a contract of service but one of investment.

Investments of this type were known in this country from the earliest days of its foreign trade. William Cade, the first financier to figure in English records, apparently was in the habit of investing different sums in undertakings of English and foreign merchants. Robert de Courçon, writing in 1302, quotes Cade's financial transactions as an example of the type of *foenus* which he is engaged in analysing.[39]

This practice, known to Cade in the twelfth century was apparently common throughout the Middle Ages. The Mayor of London wrote on 15 February 1328 to the Mayor of Rouen to assist John de Wrotham and Adam Hurel to recover money entrusted to Massiot le Mariet of 'Ducleer-sur-Seine' to trade therewith.[40] A few years later the Mayor wrote to the wardens of Berwick desiring them to arrest the property of John Turgis, chandler, inasmuch as the latter had received certain moneys from Thomas Otewy, draper and merchant of London 'to trade therewith' and rendered no account of the same.[41]

The clearest and fullest records of this type of investment, like the fullest records of other types of partnership, will be found in the Chancery proceedings of the fifteenth century.[42] Nicolas Mylle, tailor of London, submitted a long petition to the Chancellor with an eloquent tale of his grievances against one Richard West, also a tailor of London. Mylle alleged that

[39] G. Haskins, 'William Cade', *English Historical Review*, vol. 28, 1913, p. 713; full reference to William Cade and the documentary evidence relating to him is in M. M. Postan, op. cit.

[40] City of London Records, P. & M. Rolls, A, 1 (b) m. 19.

[41] Ibid. m. 34.　　　　　　　　[42] E. Ch. Pr., 59/165.

where he through grete request and special labour made to hym by . . . Richard West . . . the 14 day of December [1470] . . . covenaunted with the seid Richard West by deed identified that is to wete that the same Richard shulde deliver to the seid Nicolas a stocke of woollen cloth to the value of £400 to bye and selle and merchandise therwith from the fests next following to the ende of the terme of 12 yeres . . . ferthermore it was covenauntyd that the seid Nicolas Mylle shulde in eche yere duryng the seid terme make a full and true accompte unto the seid Richard West as well of the . . . stokke of £400 as of the encrece that shulde come of the seid stocke, and that the seid Nicolas Mylle yerely wulde have the thridde parte of the encrece of the seid stocke to his proper use, and the surplus of the encrece certyn costes deducted the seid Richard West shulde have to his parte. And over that at the ende of the said 12 yeres the said stokke of £400 to be relyveid to the seid Richard West or to his executores the seid Richard West standing to no jobardy nor adventure of the seid stokke nor of any parcel thereof.

After an interval of 5 years, continues the petitioner, West, plotting to defraud him, offered to deliver a stock of £900 on condition that the petitioner took one John Maydwell as his 'parternyng fellowe in bying and selling' and 'to take the forseid stooke of £900 ioyntly with the seid John Maydewell and it to occupie in such forme as is bifore specified'. The petitioner agreed to the new proposal, and an agreement to that effect was concluded between him and Maydwell on the one part and West on the other. Then West

through ruse and covyn hadde betwene hym and the seid John Maydwell . . . affermed a playnte of dette against the seid Nicolas Mylle and John Maydwell yointly bifore the sheriffs of London . . . £1000 and by vertue of the seid playnte the seid Richard West hath causid to attache and arreste all the seid stokke whiche he hadd delyvered to the said Nicolas Mylle and John Maydwell, and . . . the seid Richard caused to arrest all other goodis that the sid Nicolas Myelle your besecher hadde or was possessid . . . to the value of £400 and was in these actions supported by Maydwell.

West's answer and Mylle's replication appended to this petition help to elucidate some of the causes of the quarrel, but they add nothing to the nature of the arrangement as stated by Mylle. He was obviously a merchant with an independent business of his own[43] and it was into his business that West invested money.

A transaction of this sort, in the description of which all the terminology of the *societas* was employed (the 'entrusting of stock', of a 'stock . . . to merchandise therewith', of which the owner was to have 'a parte of the encrece'), could be and was clearly distinguished from an ordinary loan, and would be classed as *commenda* even by those historians

[43] E. Ch. Pr., 159/160. In his replication Nicolas, among other things, emphasises that he was West's servant: he mentions a 'place of his own' in Chigwell, Essex, to which he was in the habit of going to 'oversee his workmen'.

who do not trouble to go very far beyond the appearances of the contemporary terminology. The use of the *commenda* for the purposes of investment, however, was wider than the verbal form of our records seems to suggest.

The distinction between an ordinary loan and a *commenda*-like investment was, indeed, too subtle to be clearly discernible in each case. It is subtle enough to have enabled conflicting interpretations of the same arrangement by the very people concerned in them. Doubtful cases of this kind regularly came before the Chancery. Thus, William Gogyn of Norwich, vintner, had a dispute with Richard Whynborrogh, a clerk of the court of the Sheriffs of Norwich over the latter's investment into his business. According to Gogyn, Whynborrogh, 'by his own motion seyeng to your seid oratour that ha had money lyeng by hym which did hym noon ease offred . . . as moch as he occupied byeng and sellyng, to lende [to the petitioner] . . . such mone as he had'. The petitioner borrowed the money, occupied them in 'byeng and sellyng', and after some time returned them to Wynborrogh, but now the latter 'hath attained an action of dette before the shireves of Norwich for the somme of £30 and therupon hath hym arrest surmythyng by the same accion that ha had taken to [the petitioner] a certayn somme of money to employe in merchandise to his use, so that gayne and encrease of the same money in the meane tyme should amounte to his parte to the seid somme of £30' whereas the petitioner never 'toke the seid lone of money to no such use'.[44]

The transaction as represented by Whynborrogh, was one of *commenda*; Gogyn made it out to have been an ordinary loan. The distinction – apart from the question of remuneration – was not merely one of a legal verbiage. Even if we disregard the method of payment for the money, the financial *commenda* was not an ordinary loan. We are told of a stock entrusted and not of money 'loaned', and the subtle emphasis laid on the question as to whose use the investment was to serve, was not purely academic. The assumption apparently was that an ordinary loan became the borrower's property and was employed to his own use, while in a financial *commenda* the borrower merely held another man's stock to his trust. This distinction would have been meaningless if it had not been reflected in some of the material conditions on which the *commenda*-like investments were made. As we shall see presently the notion of 'trust' placed the investor in a position different from a mere lender; for one thing, it entailed the right to demand periodic accounts, and it probably had its effects on his rights of legal action. And then there was also the characteristic method of payment. The investor had a claim to a share of profits, he participated in the fortunes of the undertaking and thus

[44] E. Ch. Pr., 31/456.

found himself in a position of a partner not by a mere legal fiction, but by virtue of his economic connection with the business.

We must not therefore expect a *commenda*-like terminology in all *commenda*-like transactions. If the *commenda* terminology is a safe indicator of a like substance, the absence of this terminology is not evidence to the contrary. The legal form of the transaction, which was that of a loan, could sometimes overshadow the distinctions of ownership and remuneration. We find in the records of the fourteenth and fifteenth centuries numerous references to transactions described as loans but in reality identical with ordinary financial *commenda*. There is one such case in the Year Books.[45] A man brought an action of account against another in £100. There had been an agreement between the plaintiff and the defendant by which the defendant had undertaken to make to the plaintiff an obligation for £100 'afore received' and the 'profit' on the said £100. The fact that an action of account was granted and that profits were so freely spoken of before a fifteenth-century court makes it possible to conclude that the loan was one of partnership, in spite of the fact that not a single word is recorded in any way reminiscent of the ordinary *commenda*.

We must therefore be very careful to remember that many of the transactions recorded as mere loans may well have embodied a *commenda*-like agreement. We read, for instance, that Friar John Woderowe, warden of the house of Deptford, sought the aid of the Mayor's Court of London to recover 'certain moneys lent to John Chynle, mercer, and his partner, Ralph Knyghton, who had traded and profited with the money'.[46] Can we be really certain that this was a loan and not a financial *societas*?

Least certain were the border-line transactions. For it was not wholly impossible for medieval *commenda* sometimes to evolve into a fixed-interest loan. Weber has shown how the *fœnus nauticus* with fixed rates of interest was nothing else than a modification of the ordinary *commenda*, resulting from the greater certainty of trade in the western Mediterranean and the possibility of calculating the average rate of profits. Sometimes this conventional rate of profits was the result of official action. Such, at any rate, was the origin of the rate fixed for the investments of the London wards' funds, which in all other respects were allowed to preserve traces of their *commenda*-like nature and origin. But, apart from these and other rather unusual arrangements, the test of investment partnership, like that of service partnership, was one of 'participation'. A share in profits was a mark – one of the marks – of *commenda*.

[45] *Year Books*, 12 H. VI. (Black Letters edition), Pasch. Pl. 32.
[46] City of London Records, P. & M. Rolls, A. 13 m.1, 1367.

If it was not the sole mark it was because in medieval terminology and law even more important than the test of remuneration was that of the title to the money and the goods. In all the examples quoted above the expressions 'to his best avail', 'to do his best', 'to sell as he would have sold his own goods' are invariably employed. The form of words is very similar to the formulae habitually employed by Hanseatic merchants in their instructions to persons entrusted with *Sendeve*. Almost invariably the sender requested the recipient of the goods that he would 'de beste doen'; and this expression seems to have assumed an almost technical meaning of a formula constituting a *Sendeve* arrangement. It may well be that this technical sense did not attach to some of the formulae current in England. One of them, however, undoubtedly acquired a definite quasi-legal meaning. In so far as the recurring expression of 'to the use of', 'to the best avail', 'to the use and behove', had any definite purpose at all, it was to describe the title by which the factor had the possession of the goods, or by which the recipient of the investment held the 'loan'. As Maitland rightly pointed out, the phrase 'to the use of' was the untechnical designation of a trust: to possess goods 'to the use of' somebody else meant to hold them on trust. And this probably explains why the *societas*-like nature of these arrangements was not insisted upon in England. The early development of the English 'trust' made it possible to 'commit' goods to other persons without the risk of losing the rights of ownership over them. Thus one of the legal causes for which abroad the contract of *societas* had to be invoked when goods were commended was absent in this country. Here goods could be safely given over in a *commenda*, without a formal contract of partnership. Maitland has shown how the trust often dispensed with the necessity of forming a legal corporation.[47] It may often have dispensed also with the necessity of forming a legal *societas*.

It is, therefore, hardly right to conclude from the silence of English records that, unlike the rest of Europe, England made very little use of the *commenda*. The somewhat narrower application of the term 'partnership' by English courts, and the absence of an English technical term for the *commenda*, have led the historians to overlook many an arrangement that fulfilled the same economic function and was put to the same use as an ordinary *commenda*. *Commenda*-like arrangements, employed for the function of 'service' were assimilated to ordinary relationships of master and servant; *commenda*-like arrangements for the power to loan were assimilated to ordinary loans or trusts, but *commenda* partnerships they nevertheless were.

---

[47] F. W. Maitland, 'Trust and Corporation', in *Collected Papers*, Cambridge, 1911, vol. III, p. 333 and *passim*.

3

Fortunately the difficulties and opacities of legal form and the jurisdictional fictions do not obscure the history of 'mutual' partnership as they do that of the English *commenda*. This type of partnership is frequently described as such in contemporary records, and is treated as such by English medieval law. There is therefore no difficulty in finding its various forms clearly reflected in our records. We find among them the partnerships familiar on the continent as *collegantia, societas maris,* and *Wederlegginge,* as well as the partnership in which both parties contributed labour as well as capital, and which is known to continental historians under the names of *compagna, Offene Gesellschaft,* or *société en nom collective.* There is, however, little doubt that the form of mutual partnership which the English merchant of the late Middle Ages employed most frequently was one of rudimentary *collegantia*, i.e. that of 'joint sale and purchase'; and in this form partnership was probably as old as English trade itself.

The joint purchase and sale was what we should call an occasional partnership. It was confined to one transaction, and one only. The partnership began with the purchase of a 'certain merchandise' and ended with its division or joint sale. Each time a transaction was carried out jointly by two or several partners, the partnership had to be formed anew even if the partners and the terms of sharing remained the same. When the same partners 'went shares' in two simultaneous transactions, they formed two simultaneous partnerships. They regarded themselves as partners in a specified deal, or as they preferred to describe themselves 'partners in *certain* merchandise'.

There is little doubt that the primary and the essential function of this type of partnership was financial. It had for its purpose to enable a large purchase to be made by persons who were unwilling to do it themselves or on their sole responsibility. This was certainly the object of the earliest known instances of such joint partnership transactions, recorded, so to speak, *en masse* in English records. These partnerships were those entered in the earliest Recognisance Rolls in the city of London Records, and notably those in Roll 1, of the late thirteenth century. These recognisances record numerous transactions of London merchants, and especially their purchases of commodities recently imported, mainly from Spain and France. Over and over again we see groups of Londoners, often chaloners, acknowledging jointly a debt to an importer. At the very beginning of the Roll we read of Hugh the Kent, and two others, all chaloners of London, owing a sum of money to a merchant of Spain; and entries of this kind occur over and over again in the Rolls.

Their meaning is of course quite clear. To begin with, it is obvious that the recognisances represent commercial transactions, and more especially, the purchases of imports by merchants and artisans. This is shown by the fact that debtors in many of the early entries were chaloners and that the creditors were mostly Spaniards. In some instances we are told that transactions related to imported wool or yarn from Spain. Secondly, these joint acknowledgements probably represent real debts and not 'sureties'. The amounts of such debts were not usually large and there is no reason why they should have been guaranteed by three, four or even five co-sureties, while other and often larger debts recorded in the Recognisance Rolls seldom mention more than two persons. Finally, it is obvious that the chaloners did not act as members of permanent combinations. One and the same name may occur in several entries, while some appear only once and do not reappear again for the rest of the Roll. In short these entries represent occasional partnerships for a joint purchase of goods.

These occasional partnerships in purchase and sale were still very common in the fifteenth century. Thus according to a Chancery Petition, Robert Pulton of York, vintner, and John Howland were jointly bound in a sum to John Burnley of York, mercer, for merchandise bought. Petitioner had half of the merchandise and paid half of the cost. Howland had the other half.[48] In another petition one Richard Wistard stated that he and one John Rise 'deled in comyn upon certeyn merchandyse'.[49] In still another petition Henry Galyot alleged that he was 'partyng . . . in biyng and selling in certeyn merchandyses with one John Taynggy', and Taynggy obtained from a purchaser of their joint merchandise £10, half of which had to be, but was not, paid over to the petitioner.[50]

We find these partnerships in large numbers in the fifteenth-century customs accounts where shippers often occur in couples and sometimes in larger groupings. Most of the names appear coupled once and once only, and in these cases obviously represent occasional partnerships of purchase or sale.[51] These couplings mostly occur in entries of wool exports, though in this respect the difference between wool exports and

---

[48] E. Ch. Pr., 32/367.   [49] Ibid. 64/627.

[50] Ibid. 29/516.

[51] The partnerships in custom accounts are too numerous to be enumerated, but here are some examples. Boston: John Challey and Thomas Smyth, Henry Wiske and Richard Curson, and many others, K.R. Exchequer Customs Accounts (Particular) Boston, of the second half of the century (*passim*); Hull: William Thorp and Robert Morlan, John Furnace and Robert Mason, etc. Ibid. Kingston-Hull, 2 Edw. IV; Lynn: John Jenyer, Mather Forster and William Herde, John Malster and William Houghton, Thomas Norton and Edward Pepyn, John Finkel and John Motte, John Broun and Robert Motte, Robert Ferre and Hammond Claxston, etc. ibid., King's Lynn, *passim*. All these and many other 'couples' occur together as importers or exporters only once. As a rule, each of these merchants ships separately.

other branches of foreign trade may have been somewhat fictitious. The obvious reason why in wool accounts partnerships occur more frequently than in other custom accounts is the fact that the custom and subsidy for wool seem to have been generally paid in instalments, and the shipper was obliged to deliver to the customers obligations for the amount still due from him. It was therefore natural that if partners shared in the financial responsibility for the business, as they did in mutual partnerships, the names of both partners were declared to the customer and a joint bond entered into. With regard to other wares, for which duties were very much lighter, postponement of payment was less general, and there was often no need for the names of all the partners to be declared.

Some of the coupled names may appear to represent permanent partnerships: George and Richard Cely, Brothers Dalton, whom we know to have been partners from the Cely papers, Sir William Stonor and Thomas Betson, whom we know to have been partners from the Stonor papers; William and John Stoker, whose names occur together over and over again, similarly Robert and John Tate, John and Richard Oneley, Thomas Granger and Richard Drake, John Parker and Philip Hadeben – all these and a number of other more or less continuous couplings occur repeatedly in the custom accounts.

It is probable that some of the recurrent associations were nothing more than a series of occasional partnerships between the same merchants. Two or more persons, relatives or friends, could form a habit of buying and selling in common, and could trade jointly for a number of years. Theoretically, their association could be resolved into a number of separate transactions, and would be regarded as such by the partners themselves. John Lawrence of Winchester, in stating his case before the Chancery wrote that he and one John Hethe had 'long tyme ben in feloship both upon the see and on thys syde for divers merchandyses', and that recently they again bought a certain merchandise in common.[52] In other words, Lawrence and Hethe seem to have been partners 'in merchandise', but as they had been that 'for a long tyme', they were partners not in 'certain merchandise', but in 'divers merchandises'.

There were, however, partnerships which were permanent or continuous by their very nature. These were the partnerships of 'joint stock'. They differed from partnerships in 'joint merchandise' not only in terminology but also in principle. We read of John Chester, stapler, and Robert Stone, mercer, who are alleged to have 'covenaunted and agreed to merchandyse together and to be partners together either with oder of such wynnyng and losyng as should happe to be growe of such stokke as they bothe shuld togeder putte forthe and occupie'.[53] The nature of this

---

[52] E. Ch. Pr., 46/243.   [53] Ibid. 64/1038.

arrangement is obvious. The transactions to be carried out by the partners were not separate and not specified. A joint stock was formed for general trade for a term of years, or for an indefinite period. It was no longer a joint adventure, but a joint business.

The best known and the best documented of these partnerships was that between the brothers Richard and George Cely, which existed both during their father's lifetime and after his death.[54] We learn from a petition in a chancery dispute over the Cely inheritance that the two brothers had a common stock employed in wool trade, and that their partnership was consequently one of joint stock.

So far the examples quoted have been those of 'complete partnership', i.e. of the one in which the partners contributed both capital and labour. There was nothing in the English usage or law to distinguish this type of 'mutual' partnership from the one that corresponded to the Italian *collegantia*, where all the partners contributed the capital, but one of them contributed his skill and labour. This distinction was apparently not regarded in this country as determining the relations between the partners or their position in law. Chancery Petitions – and they are our chief source of evidence – made a special mention of the common stock or the common merchandise, as the case might be, but they hardly ever state who of the partners did the actual work. But in so far as we can judge from circumstantial evidence, when such is available, the *collegantia* type of mutual partnership was by no means uncommon in this country. It could be found both among the occasional partnerships (joint merchandise), and the permanent ones (joint stock).[55] Here is a typical example. Thomas Kirke of Coventry, hosier, before going to Ireland for a long sojourn, left in the hands of William Lancastre, his apprentice, merchandise to the value of £10 to 'chafer witherto', on the condition that each partner had half of the profits. William Lancastre contributed to the stock £6 of his own money.[56]

Somewhat different from the typical 'mutual' partnership were those forms of association in which all the partners contributed capital though none engaged in actual trading. The best instances of this will be found among the records of co-ownership of boats. The habit of investing into boat shares seems to have been especially common both in Italian and in Hanseatic towns where the values of boats were often divided into portions as small as one sixty-fourth, and sold to all sorts and conditions of men –

[54] *Cely Papers, passim.*
[55] E. Ch. Pr., 28/378, 19/26.
[56] Ibid. 9/131; also 9/382, 6/290: C. Gross, *Select Cases in Law Merchant*, (Selden Soc. Pub.), vol. 23, p. 77: an early case of an alleged partnership between two *socii ad lucrandun et perdendum in mercandisis faciendis in partibus Scotiae*, both of whom contributed capital, but only one of whom had to go to Scotland.

merchants and non-merchants alike.[57] In this country the habit of investing in boat shares was never so widely diffused as abroad. It was
nevertheless common and well-established throughout the centuries for
which mercantile records are available.

This co-ownership of boats, like all other forms of mutual partnership
so far described, could serve the function of finance and that of labour.
Its financial function is obvious. Investment in ships was both too heavy
and too risky for one person to shoulder the whole cost of a boat. If a
person wanted to invest a large sum of money into shipping he would
often prefer to own shares in several boats rather than acquire one boat
all to himself. It would, however, be wrong to describe this method of
ship-owning as insurance, for the sharing of the cost of a boat insured
nobody against anything. All it did was to spread the burden and the
risk of the enterprise and thus to facilitate an undertaking which was
costly and hazardous and therefore unsuitable to single-handed investment.

In these purely financial co-ownerships all the co-owners stood to each
other in the same position. It is obvious from the Cely Accounts that
George and Richard Cely and William Maryon possessed their *Margaret*
on these terms. To Aldridge, the purser, all of them were equally masters.
Now a boat was not an undertaking to be run by joint management. If
all the partners were equal, management devolved upon the hired
master or the purser. Very often the co-owners let their boat out to the
master, or to another merchant, or even to one of themselves. We read
of Thomas Bell and Nicholas Borell, merchants, who possessed a ship
called *James of Yarmouth* and let it 'to ferme' for the sum of eight marks
6s 8d[58] to Robert Heygham and Ricard Gardner, described as ship-
man and mariner respectively. But it was apparently much more common
for one man to farm the boat from its collective owners or to receive it
from them on a *commenda* basis.[59]

The establishment of boat-partnerships for labour purposes was less
common, though quite familiar to English merchants. The masters
(skippers) were often shareholders in their boats. In most cases it is impossible to tell whether their share was merely allocated to them by the
owners of the boats in *lieu* of an addition to their wages, or whether they
were the principal owners of the boats, somewhat in the position of the

---

[57] C. Sattler, 'Handelsrechnungen d. deutschen Order', *Verein für die Geschichte
von Ost- und Westpreussen*, 1887, *passim*; W. Vogel, *Geschichte d. deutschen
Seeschiffahrt*, Berlin, 1915; R. Hagedorn, 'Betriebsformen u. Einrichtungen d.
Emdener Seehafenverkehrs', in *Hansische Geschichtsbl.*, XVI.

[58] E. Ch. Pr., 36/430.

[59] Ibid. 7/291, 31/36. There is an early instance of a similar transaction in the
letter book A, but in that case the owner was a single person, and the farmers
formed a partnership. *Cal. Letter Book A*, p. 61, 2 Feb. 1281.

tractator of the *collegantia*. But on the whole *collegantia* seems to have been very common. Several persons put together the money necessary for the building or the purchase of the boat, while only one of them was given 'the full guidance, rule and employment'.[60]

Boat societies supply a very typical instance of a joint stock partnership, but they also demonstrate how difficult it is to distinguish between the *collegantia* and the 'complete' partnership and how very little has this distinction to do with the economic purpose of any given partnership. It was the joint stock, or a joint merchandise, whatever the motive for which it was formed and whatever the method by which it was governed and employed, that in the opinion of medieval people constituted a 'mutual' partnership. Very often in describing the economic status of partners records may confine themselves to appending to their names the appellation *socii* or *socius suus*, and give no other clue as to the character of the *societas*. The distinctions which historians have built up or even the distinctions with which contemporary lawyers and writers occasionally made play, were neglected by men who formed the partnership or those who recorded their transactions and suits. The only fact we are entitled to infer from the appellation *socius* is that a person so described belonged to a 'mutual' society of one of the types described here: to an occasional or a permanent one, to a *collegantia* or a complete partnership, to one of labour or one of finance.[61]

It was apparently in this wide and vague sense that the term 'partner' was applied by mercantile courts. It seems clear that the London courts accorded a very wide recognition to the contract of mutual partnership and regarded 'partners' as liable for debts incurred in connection with the common transactions of a partnership. In a fourteenth-century suit before a London court, John Wroth merchant of London, sued William Tong, merchant of the Staple, for £617.10.0 due for one hundred sacks of wool to Thomas de Nothingham, his partner, and secured on a bond. In his declaration he pleaded that according to Law Merchant, when one of the partners bought goods for their common profit, the other was equally responsible for the debt. The defendant did not deny this rule of law but merely alleged that he had no knowledge of the bond.[62] That Wroth's declaration was not altogether unfounded can be seen from a

---

[60] E.g. Richard Blackburn and Richard Newland, tailor of York, had in common a boat which was 'en la possession et en la governaunce' of Newland alone 'al use et comon profit de lui et du dit suppliant', E. Ch. Pr. 7/186. See also ibid. 7/291, 27/184, 29/521.

[61] For reference to *socii* who might have belonged to any of these types of *societas*, see *Cal. Letter Book* B, p. 208 (William Finchingfield, and compare with pp. 52–3); C. Gross, op. cit., p. 26, 59; City of London Records, P. & M. Roll, A, 24, m. 2b mem. 22b.

[62] *Cal. P. & M. Rolls*, 1323–64, pp. 262–3.

number of other cases before the same courts. In 1365 Thomas Atte Nashe, mercer, a partner with Thomas Umphray was committed to prison at the suit of Thomas Kynebelle for debt obviously contracted on behalf of the partnership. In 1367 Friar John Woderowe sought the aid of the Court to recover certain money pledged to him by John Chynle, mercer, and his partner Ralph Knyghton who had traded and profited with the money and refused to repay it. Ralph was the only defendant to appear and denied that he was Chynle's partner. In 1362 Thorold de Gascogne claimed from Fride, an executor, of Robert Peryn, a partner of the late Matthew Forteterwerre, the sum of £475 for goods delivered and money lent to the partners.

Evidently there was a presumption that each of the partners was liable for the whole amount of the debt contracted on behalf of the partnership. Therefore, if we are right in thinking that the appellation *socius* referred to all these types of mutual partnerships described above, it will follow that the unlimited liability for debt which modern historians have construed as the hall mark of the Italian *compagna* and of other forms of 'full partnership' was applied by the Law Merchant of England to the whole of that indefinite group of multifarious partnerships which were recognised as such by medieval merchants and lawyers in this country. Unlimited liability need not therefore go together with complete partnership of labour and capital which is supposed to have sprung from the family union. Men in the Middle Ages did not notice any difference between this kind of society and a partnership of a less complete nature. Joint stock or joint merchandise was apparently the essential, if not the only, substance of a partnership, and was sufficient ground for regarding its members as jointly and severally bound for its debts.

Now if the joint stock and common merchandise was often the constituting element of mutual partnership, or at least of some mutual partnerships, another distinction recently fabricated will also fall to the ground, at any rate in so far as English partnerships are concerned. Modern lawyers have sometimes tried to underline the 'modernity' of the modern joint stock company by drawing a distinction between medieval partnerships which were essentially relationships between persons, and modern companies in which the rights and obligations of partners are enshrined in the stock. This distinction is somewhat fictitious. In most of the English instances of mutual partnerships, their members were described as 'partners' in 'merchandise' or 'in a stock'. Their relationship as partners did not extend beyond their common ownership of a certain amount of goods or money. A merchant could simultaneously form independent, even though permanent, partnerships with several different persons. The shares of a stock could be alienated and bequeathed, so that an acquisition of a share conferred on its new possessor the position of a partner. This was especially so in the case of boat shares, which were regarded by the courts as corporeal things.[63]

For this and other reasons it is impossible to regard the joint stock company in a way different from other types of mutual partnership. This is hardly the right place to describe the rise and the nature of the early joint stock companies since this institution belongs mainly to the post-medieval era. It is nevertheless worth noting that, among the different varieties of mutual partnership known to the Middle Ages, there were some which differed very little from the joint stock company as we find it in the Elizabethan era. The most typical example of these is offered by the Iceland ventures of the merchants of Hull and Lynn.

The English traffic to Iceland in the fifteenth century possessed many features of the early colonial enterprises. The sea journey was long and the risks were great: partly because navigation to Iceland was hazardous and partly because the expeditions were often undertaken in defiance of the authority of the Danish kings. It is therefore not surprising that the expeditions, like the colonial voyages of the sixteenth and seventeenth centuries, should have been organised on a joint stock basis. On 1 June 1565 a boat of Hull left the port laden with eighty lasts of barley flour, seventy lasts of beer, four lasts of butter, 260 quarters of malt, 100 horse shoes, 200 ells of linencloth, 200 lb of wax, forty lb of thread, some wainscots, four lasts of osmond, three lasts of pitch and tar, and other miscellaneous commodities. The cargo belonged in common to William Eland, Nicholas Elys, Edward Compyndale and Thomas Eton, burgesses of Hull.[64] Two years later (6 June 1567) the same four men exported another shipload of the same commodities.[65] On the same day another partnership of burgesses of Kingston exported a similar 'assortment' of commodities in another boat. In Lynn in April a group of merchants paid custom on four boats laden with similar goods obviously belonging to all the shippers in common.[66]

In Kingston-on-Hull these shipments seem to have been often connected with, and formed part of, what to all intents and purposes was a

---

[63] E. Ch. Pr. 69/122; see also 28/84, 60/118, 69/112, 15/147; City of London Records, P. & M. Rolls, A. 91. m. 5; *Cal. of Early Mayor's Court Rolls*, p. 235; *Testamenta Eboracensis* (Surtees Soc. Publications), vol. II, p. 98.

[64] E. Carus Wilson, 'The Iceland Trade', in E. Power and M. Postan, *English Trade in The Fifteenth Century*, London, 1933, pp. 155ff. *K.R. Custom Accounts* (Particular), 6–7 Edw. 4.

[65] Ibid. 9–10 Edw. 4.

[66] Ibid. 9–10 Edw. 4. (Lynn). It is clear that the cargoes were intended for Iceland. A considerable part of the cargoes consisted of commodities usually imported into England from abroad, and chiefly from the Hanseatic Towns and Flanders. There was therefore no sense in shipping these cargoes to any port in the North Sea or the Baltic. In most of the customs accounts quoted we find a couple of months after the date of exportation, the same boats, and often the same merchants, importing cargoes consisting almost entirely of stockfish.

municipal trading expedition. By a Royal grant, the mayor and burgesses of Kingston-on-Hull were allowed to ship annually free of custom a certain amount of goods, and under the cover of this grant the city fathers organised expeditions to Iceland. They took out commodities of English and continental origin and imported Icelandic goods, mostly stockfish. Sometimes the exports were communal, while imports were brought in by individuals banded into small partnerships. But occasionally it was the other way round: separate groups of merchants exported to Iceland, but imports to Kingston were communal.[67]

There was apparently little difference between ordinary joint stock shipments and the partnerships of four or five merchants, such as were formed for export and import trade to Iceland; there was equally little difference between these partnerships of four or five and the still larger combinations in which the whole of the community seems to have participated. These latter in their turn differed very little from the joint stock companies of the sixteenth century. Were not the Elizabethan companies formed for the separate expeditions in the same way as the Kingston partnerships? The difference between the partnerships of Hull merchants for the trade in Iceland differed from the expeditions of the East India company chiefly in the size of the capital invested and the numbers of participants. The much larger size of the post-medieval companies was due partly to the nature of colonial ventures which required large investments and carried great risks, and partly to Royal grants incorporation which banded all the traders into comprehensive companies. The Hull example shows that when similar conditions appeared in the Middle Ages, either because of the quasi-colonial nature of the trade or because a Royal grant conferred a monopoly, the partnership assumed a striking resemblance to the full-fledged company of a later age.

[67] Thus in the second year of Ed. IV's reign a boat of Hull arrives at the port with stockfish belonging to 50 burgesses of the town, practically all the merchants engaged in maritime trade. Ibid.

4

THE TRADE OF MEDIEVAL
EUROPE: THE NORTH*

I. THE TRADE IN GENERAL

(1) *Commodities*

1

The international and inter-regional trade of Northern Europe and
its principal industries bear little resemblance to the conventional image
of medieval economy. The traffic across the continent of Western Europe,
or between the European mainland and the lands immediately to the
north and to the north-east, evokes in a modern reader none of that
romance which clings to the trade of Southern Europe. The latter
brought to Western Europe exotic goods of every kind: pepper, ginger
and other spices of the East Indies, silks, brocades and tapestries, sweet
wines, oranges, raisins, figs and almonds. It enticed the merchant into the
mysterious lands of the Near and Middle East, to Byzantium and Syria,
often to Africa, and sometimes even to China. It was also the trade of the
caravans, the galleys, the junks; and of the Venetian, Genoese and Florentine adventurers and merchant princes. This was the medieval trade as
popular writers know it, and this is the trade which some serious writers
have in mind when they insist on the luxury character of medieval
commerce.

The trade of Northern Europe was quite different. It was not greatly
concerned with oriental and Mediterranean commodities. At various
times between the sixth century and the tenth, traders and warriors
brought goods from the extreme north of Europe to Byzantium and re-
imported Byzantine goods into Northern Europe. In later centuries
Italian merchants frequently sailed into the harbours of England
and Flanders, bringing with them all the infinite variety of Levantine
and oriental products. Still more regularly – in fact throughout
the Middle Ages – Italian merchants and the men of the North,
Germans, Flemings, English and French, mingled in the great inter-

* This essay first appeared in M. Postan and E. E. Rich, eds., *The Cambridge
Economic History of Europe*, vol. II, Cambridge, 1952.

national marts of Central and Northern Europe: in Champagne during the twelfth and thirteenth centuries, in Bruges in the fourteenth and the early fifteenth centuries, in Geneva, Antwerp and Bergen-op-Zoom in the fifteenth, and there exchanged the Italian and the Italian-borne products for other goods.

Yet generally speaking, in the economic life of Northern Europe these contacts were of secondary importance. The main currents of trade across Northern Europe and between Northern Europe and other countries flowed with products of the northern hemisphere, cruder, bulkier and altogether more indispensable than the luxuries and the fineries of the text-book convention. This convention is not altogether true even of the South, for foodstuffs or raw materials also entered into the trade of the Mediterranean region. Nevertheless, what gave the southern trade its peculiar character was not the trade in the bulky essentials, but those luxury trades which we associate with it. By contrast, the trade of Northern Europe was almost exclusively devoted to the necessities of life.

Of the luxuries originating in the North and circulating in Northern Europe furs were probably the only one worth noting. Modest furs of local origin – the 'conies' of England, the Low Countries and France, the goatskins and the sheepskins of peasant wear – could perhaps be counted among the modest pre-requisites of humble existences. Not so the rare and rich furs of Scandinavian and Russian origins – fox, bear, beaver, sable, ermine. They were ceremonial wares, an insignia of wealth and standing; they rivalled the senatorial purple in the early Middle Ages, the Italian brocades and oriental silks in the later centuries, as marks of rank and worth. And so important did they become in European trade that by the end of the thirteenth century they formed one of the mainstays of Hanseatic commerce and wealth.

Furs, nevertheless, were something of an exception, for the main articles of northern trade were bulkier and cheaper necessities of life. Its main, and certainly the most permanent, branch was traffic in food. The very conditions of Germanic settlement in North-western Europe made it inevitable that some areas should early in their history have come to depend on food imports. Throughout the Middle Ages large portions of Scandinavia could not grow on the spot all the food they needed. Ever since the early days of the great migrations a relatively large population settled in the water-logged and sandy lands of the estuary of the Rhine – the Frisian country of the seventh-century nomenclature – which could not raise crops large enough to feed their population in normal years. Later in the Middle Ages, i.e. from the middle of the twelfth century onwards, the regions of the North-western littoral, Flanders, Brabant and Holland, maintained an industrial population which they could not feed out of their own agricultural production. If we are to believe a fifteenth-century description, the Dutch of that time still largely subsisted on dairy produce, birds and fishes. Farther south and west, on the Atlantic coast of France, lay the rich lands of Gascony which specialised in wine and had to bring in some of their food from outside.[1]

What made it possible for these needs to be covered was that side by side with the regions deficient in foodstuffs there were to be found regions with exportable surpluses of food. It is doubtful whether the estuary of the Rhine before the ninth century and the flourishing areas of Flanders and the Netherlands in later centuries could ever have fed themselves had not rich grain-growing areas existed at their very back-doors. In the early Middle Ages grain came down the Rhine from the rich agricultural areas served by the upper reaches of the river. In the later centuries some grain came from the agricultural areas bordering on German Rhineland (Gelder, Gulik and Cleves), but the bulk came from Northern France. The valleys of the Somme and the Seine were the granaries of Northern Europe. The agricultural surpluses of the lower Seine went mainly to the south, to feed Paris. But the wheat of the rich loam lands of Santerre, Vermandois and Cambresis, went not only by the Oise to Paris, but along the Scheldt to Flanders and along the Somme to Rouen and overseas. Amiens, Abbeville and St Valéry became the *foci* of grain trade between France and the Low Countries, and the trade continued till the very end of the fifteenth century. Throughout the earlier Middle Ages, but more especially in the thirteenth century, England was an exporter of foodstuffs, including grain. Later still, another and much more important source of grain appeared. As a result of German colonisation of the Slavonic lands beyond the Elbe vast new agricultural resources were opened up, and from the end of the thirteenth century onwards East German and Polish rye flowed to the West. By the beginning of the fourteenth century Baltic grain began to contribute to the Flemish food supplies, and by that time also it ousted English grain from the Scandinavian markets.[2]

Grain, however, was only one of the essential foodstuffs carried across the continent and the seas of Northern Europe. The history of European dairy farming and milk trade is a somewhat neglected topic of economic history, but the importance of butter and cheese as articles of international commerce is now beyond doubt. There were apparently several regions of specialised butter production whence butter was exported to other countries: Holland, Scandinavia, Southern Poland, and

[1] Quoted in J. E. Niermeyer, *De wording van onze volkshuishouding* (The Hague, 1946), 34.

[2] W. S. Unger, 'De Hollandsche graanhandel en graanhandelspolitiek in de middeleeuwen', *De Economist* (1916). Also Z. W. Sneller in *Bijdragen tot de Vaterlands. Gesch.* VI, 2 (1925).

to a smaller extent England. In historical records of the late thirteenth and fourteenth centuries butter appeared so suddenly as to suggest to some historians that there was a sudden change of diet among the inhabitants of Northern Europe as a result of which oil was displaced by butter. In England, however, the high-water mark of the dairying industry is in the earlier centuries – a time when the Earls of Lancaster pastured vast herds of cows on their *vacaries* in Lancashire and Yorkshire and when Ipswich, Boston and Lynn exported butter and cheese by the ton.

Even more important was fish, for the consumption of fish in the Middle Ages was high, and sea fisheries were many. Some fish was caught in and off all the estuaries of Europe and along its sea coasts. In the early Middle Ages the fishermen of Brittany and Normandy may even have brought in the flesh of whales and seals. But great international fishing grounds were relatively few. One such fishing ground was largely exploited by English fishermen: it was the herring fisheries off the coasts of Norfolk and South Lincolnshire. Its centres, and especially Yarmouth and its fishing suburb of Gorleston, became famous as the home of England's herring, though it is doubtful whether the red herring of Yarmouth, so important in the food supplies of England, ever figured prominently in international commerce. More international was the Scandinavian fishing industry, that of the white herring and the stock-fish. From Norway the art of 'white' curing or salting spread to other countries, and it was very largely from Iceland that the bulk of medieval supplies of stockfish came. Farther south, the estuary of the Rhine formed throughout the Middle Ages another centre of the fishing industry. In the sixth and seventh centuries much herring must have been fished by the Frisians in their estuary waters and exported from there all over North-western Europe. But throughout the greater part of the Middle Ages, and certainly from the thirteenth century onwards, by far the most important of the fishing grounds of Europe and also the busiest centre of the curing industry and of the herring trade were the Baltic fisheries of Skania off the south coast of what is now Sweden. They rose to prominence at the turn of the thirteenth and fourteenth centuries, and as late as 1537 more than 90,000 tons were still salted there. By that time, however, the herring fisheries off the coasts of the Northern Netherlands, modern Holland, had risen to rival those of Skania as the main source of fish supplies.

It would not be difficult to catalogue a whole list of other staple foodstuffs which entered the international trade of North European countries. In the twelfth and thirteenth centuries England exported bacon from her eastern counties, largely from Ipswich. Throughout the later Middle Ages vegetables, especially very large quantities of cabbages, garlic, onions and onion seed, regularly came from France and the Low

Countries, and apples – the pippins of Normandy – from Norman ports. Towards the close of the Middle Ages hops and beer began to come in from Holland and West Germany. Indeed so important had become the beer traffic that historians have sometimes ranked it among the primary causes of Holland's rise in the fifteenth century.

Nevertheless, with the exception of grain and fish, no other comestible product was more indispensable to medieval diet, or was carried in larger quantities than wine. Large quantities of wine were apparently drunk in Europe as well as in the wine-growing areas of France and Germany. In the eleventh-century *Colloquium of Alfric*, Alfric did not drink wine because he was not rich enough to buy it. Four centuries later, on the morrow of the battle of Agincourt, Henry V would not allow his soldiers to celebrate on the heavy wines of Champagne, for they had been brought up on ale and beer and were not used to strong wines. But men of all stations above the lowest drank it in large and, as far as England goes, increasing quantities.

The significance of wine in international trade was not only in the quantities in which it was drunk, but also in the conditions under which it came to be produced. In the course of centuries the commercial production of wine, once widespread over the face of Europe, gradually concentrated in regions of highly specialised viticulture. There had once been vineyards in what would now be regarded as most unpropitious parts of England and the Low Countries. In France itself wine of some repute was grown everywhere. But by degrees the wines of three or four areas – Poitou, Gascony, Burgundy (Auxerrois) and the Moselle – all of them seats of flourishing viticulture since the days of Rome, rose to dominate the international demand. In a thirteenth-century *fabliau* narrating the combat of wines an English priest is made to pass in review some thirty or forty regional vintages. Having excommunicated a dozen or so of unworthy wines he leaves the field of battle to the northern vintages of Argenteuil, Meulent, Auxerre, Soissons, Épernay, the various wines of Guyenne and Limousin, and above all, the wines of Angoulême, Saintes, Bordeaux and Poitou. The prize goes to what were undeniably the most highly valued of medieval wines, the sweet wines of Cyprus, and the troubadour himself shows a true gift of prophecy in preferring the white wines of Chablis and Beaune. But the wine most generally drunk 'all over England, among Bretons, Flemings, Normans, Scots, Irish, Norwegians and Danes' and bringing in return good sterling is the wine of La Rochelle.

Had the *fabliau* been written a century or so later, it would not only have excluded from the list a number of local vintages, but would also have placed La Rochelle as a source of sterling-earning wine in a second place after Gascony. By the beginning of the fourteenth century these two regions had come to supply the bulk of wine entering into international trade. But whereas the products of Poitou and La Rochelle went mostly to other parts of France and to the Low Countries, the clarets of Gascony went mostly to England, forming a close and continuous link between the two countries.

As a result of the wine trade the two countries developed economic systems which were mutually supplementary. Wine was Gascony's chief product, and she was not self-supporting in either food or textiles, while England was one of Europe's chief importers of wine (she imported over four million gallons in 1415), and was also from time to time able to supply Gascony with grain – with her own in years of good harvests and with re-exported Baltic grain in other years.

Yet although the 'French' wines flowed between countries in quantities far greater than any other, the wine of other nations also contributed their quota. There was a regular flow of sweet wines from Spain and the Eastern Mediterranean to the countries of Northern Europe: the 'Malmsey', the 'vin muscadet', and a few others. Above all, there were the wines of the Rhine valley. They were one of the staple commodities of Frisian trade in the sixth and seventh centuries; they were also one of the principal commodities imported into this country by the merchants of Cologne when they began to come here in large numbers at the end of the eleventh and twelfth centuries. And it was Rhenish wine that German merchants sold in Scandinavia before they had large surpluses of Eastern grain to dispose of.

2

So much for trade in food. It was large and, being food, was indispensable, but both in value and in bulk it was rivalled by the trade in basic raw materials. Of these, one of the most important and certainly the bulkiest was timber. Timber resources were unevenly distributed over the face of Europe, and were all but lacking in the areas where the population was at its thickest: in Flanders, in the Netherlands, and eventually in Southern England. As a rule, timber was becoming scarcer as the countries of Western Europe were getting settled and as forest was giving place to fields and pastures. But even in those regions of Northern Europe which were still well wooded, as in parts of this country, hardwoods predominated, and 'tall timber' suitable for shipbuilding and for standard domestic structures had to be brought in by water. In this trade water transport was even more important than the ecology of native forests. Timber growing away from navigable rivers and seaports, such as the timber in the forests of the West and North Midlands of England, was often more difficult to transport to other places within the country and much costlier than timber imported from abroad by sea.

Timber was therefore an important article of water-borne trade. In the earlier centuries, from the eleventh to the thirteenth, the chief exporters of timber were Scandinavia and the wooded regions of South Germany; but in the fourteenth century, with the opening of the Baltic, this trade, like the grain trade, changed in direction and volume. The vast coniferous forests of Eastern Europe including Russia, Poland and Livonia now became available, and from the middle of the fourteenth century onwards eastern timber shipped from the Baltic, and more especially from Danzig, all but ousted from the western markets the other types of 'white' timber. Pine, yew and fir of Baltic origin and occasionally some birch, both in logs and in sawn boards – 'wainscot' and *Klapholz* – became one of the main articles of Hanseatic imports into this country and also one of the chief magnets which drew English merchants to the Baltic regions. At one time in the fifteenth century hulls of boats and whole ships came to be imported from Prussia in lieu of shipbuilding material. Some wood shipped from Baltic ports may have come from countries even farther afield. The bowstaves which won the battles of Crécy and Agincourt probably came from the Carpathian mountains and were shipped to England through Hungary and Prussia.[3]

The forest resources of Eastern Europe and Scandinavia were not exploited for timber alone. Russia was by far the most important source of medieval pitch and tar, and pitch used in this country in the later Middle Ages was nearly all of Baltic origin, though a little came also from Bordeaux and Bayonne. From Russian and Polish woodlands also came potash, obtained by the burning of wood.

The industrial raw material *par excellence* was wool. The cloth industry was the first, and for a long time the only, medieval handicraft to grow into a *grande industrie*. It was also the first industrial occupation to transform whole parts of Europe into specialised manufacturing regions. In Southern Europe specialised industrial centres of this kind sprang up in Florence, and centres of cloth industry were also to be found in Champagne and the south of France. But it was mainly in Northern Europe, at its north-western corner, that an industrial society wholly based on the cloth industry came into existence.

Industrial societies, in the plural, would perhaps be a better term. Several contiguous regions of Northern Europe became successively industrialised as the Middle Ages drew to their close, and all this

---

[3] Th. Hirsch, *Danzigs Handels- und Gewerbgeschichte unter der Herrschaft des deutschen Ordens* (Leipzig, 1858). For a comprehensive, though possibly exaggerated, survey of Norwegian timber exports, see A. Bugge, *Den Norske Traelasthandels Historie,* I (Skien, 1925).

industrial activity – ever shifting but never broken – grew up on imported wool. Some of the wool came from Central France, and the original prosperity of the Artois cloth industry was largely based on the wool of Auvergne and the Cevennes. But by far the most important centre of wool, a source which at the turn of the thirteenth and fourteenth centuries overshadowed all others, was Britain. By the second half of the thirteenth century the average annual exports of wool from England averaged more than 30,000 sacks, or about seven million pounds. Some of it went to Italy, but most was worked into cloth in the North – in the Low Countries and later, to an ever-increasing extent, in England herself.

Cloth, thus made, was in itself a very valuable and by far the most important example of a 'wholly manufactured' export. In the seventh century we hear of English cloth exported to Carolingian Francia, and throughout that and subsequent centuries we find in the records stray references to traffic in Frisian cloth, which may have been cloth made in the Frisian lands and in their immediate vicinity or English cloth distributed on the continent by the Frisians. Various other regional varieties of cloth entered into the international trade of the ninth, tenth and eleventh centuries. But from the end of the eleventh century onwards, Flemish cloth began to overshadow all other cloths of Europe, and by the end of the thirteenth century we find it exported to the remotest corners of the then known world. In the later centuries it became the chief commercial *quid pro quo* for the grain, furs and timber products which the Baltic countries yielded up to the West, and therefore one of the pillars of German strength in Novgorod, Riga and Reval. When in the late fourteenth century English and Dutch cloth began to appear in large quantities on the continent it naturally flowed in the wake of the Flemish exports, gradually replacing them in all their ancient channels. Like the Flemish cloths they were soon to be found all over the civilised world – in Hungary, Russia and the Asiatic East as well as in countries nearer home.

Compared to cloth, the other textiles, though worn by men of all ranks, were not of very great importance in the inter-regional trade of Northern Europe. Silks and other luxury fabrics of Byzantine, Italian and oriental origin came in from the South throughout the Middle Ages. More important were linen and flax of northern growth. The damp and cool flax-growing areas of Europe were as clearly defined as its sheep-farming regions. They were as a rule to be found on land ill-suited to the growing of good quality wool, just as the chalk uplands and the salt marshes of Europe, which carried the largest and the best flocks of sheep, were ill-suited to the cultivation of flax. Hence the broad geographic demarcation between the flax areas of the Low Countries, North-west France, Poland and Russia and the wool-growing areas of England, Central France and

Spain. Yet in some areas the two textiles were mutually competitive, if not mutually exclusive, and in no other country were they more so than in Flanders. Parts of the Low Countries were well suited to the growing of flax and in fact grew and worked it throughout the Middle Ages. From the end of the eleventh century, however, the making as well as the wearing of woollen cloth spread so rapidly that to an observer the change might well appear as a combat between flax and wool. In a rhymed pamphlet of the eleventh century an anonymous pamphleteer defined the problem as *conflictus ovis et linis*. In the end, linen became one of Flanders' secondary exports. Some linen goods were still imported from there into England in the fourteenth and fifteenth centuries, but by that time the bulk of linen imports came from other sources; mostly from Northern France and from regions of Central and Eastern Europe controlled by the German Hanse. From Brittany and Baltic regions came also most of the canvas for sails and much of the hemp for ropes and cordage.

Wool and flax, however, were not the sole raw materials needed for the manufacture of northern textiles. Other subsidiary clothmakers' materials entered into northern commerce, and chief among them were woad and madder, the two commonest dyes of the Middle Ages. Both were to some extent grown in Northern Europe. Some woad came from Italy and was in the late fourteenth and the fifteenth centuries carried in Venetian galleys. A great deal of woad for English use came also from the region of Toulouse via Bordeaux. But before the fourteenth century Picardy was the chief northern home of the woad industry, and it was on woad that the economic prosperity of Amiens and Corby and the fame of their merchants were based. More exotic dyes especially the much valued and highly priced *granum*, came from Portugal, the still more precious ultramarine came from the East. Of the other materials used in the making of cloth, alum, black soap, mostly Spanish, and potash, mostly Eastern European, were the most important.

3

Potash, though a product of the Baltic timber industry and a raw material of the clothmakers, should perhaps be classified with the next important group of commodities in northern trade – the minerals. The basic mineral of modern times, coal, was worked in Northumberland throughout the Middle Ages – certainly in the thirteenth century – and was carried from there by sea to London and to the Low Countries. From the thirteenth century onwards coal was also mined in Hainault and, perhaps, Westphalia and elsewhere.

By far the most important of the mineral products was salt – one of the essential ingredients of medieval food, the indispensable preserver of meat and the mainstay of the great fish-curing trades. Salt was both mined and obtained by evaporation from salt pans, and local centres of both kinds of salt industry were to be found all over Europe. The economic rise of Venice in the ninth century may well have begun with the development of local salt supplies. Farther north the salt deposits of the Eastern Alps, already exploited in prehistoric times, revived in the closing stages of the Middle Ages. In this country the salt deposits of Worcestershire were also worked throughout the Middle Ages. But for the purposes of North European trade the most important salt-producing areas were the Lower Saxon region of Lüneburg and, still more, the Bay of Bourgneuf on the Atlantic coast of France. The Lüneburg salt deposits were conveniently situated for export to the Baltic as well as to the Netherlands. But in the course of the late fourteenth and the fifteenth centuries Lüneburg deposits, like most other important salt industries of Europe, shrank in importance by comparison with those of Western France. The shallow waters and flooded areas between the mouth of the Gironde and the Isle of Oleron – mainly in the Bay of Bourgneuf – formed natural salt pans of great extent and remarkable productivity. They were worked from early times, but it was not until the later centuries of the Middle Ages that they began to attract buyers from all over the world. In the first half of the fifteenth century, when our documentary evidence about Bourgneuf becomes most abundant, we find it frequented by great salt fleets of all the northern nations. Hanseatic 'Bay fleets' sailed there several times a year, and Dutch and English ships and merchants also resorted there in large numbers. By that time Bay salt also entered northern politics as well as northern trade. The lawless and riotous life of this salt 'Klondyke' generated international conflicts and quarrels, and the safety of the 'Bay route' preoccupied the Hanseatics throughout the fifteenth century and gave rise to at least one war – that between England and the Hanse in the middle of the fifteenth century.[4]

Relatively less prominent in the annals of northern trade and in the records of its shipping were the exports and imports of metal. The mining of precious metals, especially of silver, was a great industry, and its products played a part in economic development of Europe so crucial that they should not perhaps be treated as mere items in a list of commodities. But bullion was not the only metal worked. Some ironstone was mined in most places, and some iron was smelted in almost every great country in the Middle Ages. But of important centres there were only three or four; one was Westphalia, others were in Saxony, in the Basque country in the Pyrenees, and above all in Sweden. It is doubtful whether there ever was a period since the twelfth century when the high-quality

4 A. Agats, *Der Hansische Baienhandel* (Heidelberg, 1904). About the importance of salt from Zeeland, see H. J. Smit in *Bijdragen etc.*, VI (1930).

iron of Swedish origin, the 'osmund' of medieval records, was not exported from that country to other parts of Northern Europe. We find it in the documents referring to Swedish trade in the twelfth century, in the records of Westphalian trade to Sweden in the thirteenth and fourteenth, in the English customs accounts of the fourteenth and fifteenth centuries. It was the most highly priced and internationally the best known of medieval irons.

Of other metals and metal wares, copper, mostly of Swedish and Hungarian origin, and lead and tin, mostly of English and German origin, were distributed all over Northern and Western Europe by Hanseatic merchants. So were also other miscellaneous metal goods, mostly produced in the area of Liège, Dinant and Cologne, and pewter goods of English make – altogether a current of trade not very abundant in comparison with grain, wool or timber, yet sufficiently important to attract the attention of the makers of commercial treaties and of legislators.

This catalogue of goods entering the commerce of Northern Europe could be continued almost indefinitely. Miscellaneous commodities of European origin crossed and recrossed the frontiers of northern countries and passed its tolls. Bricks from the Low Countries, swords and helmets from Cologne, tapestries and painted images from Flanders, books from France and the Low Countries, amber 'paternosters' from Prussia, wax and honey from Russia, thread and lace from Cologne and Brabant, hawks from Bruges and Calais, feathers for pillows from all over Germany. But it is not from these commodities, whether luxuries or playthings, that the commerce of Northern Europe took its colour. Its essential feature was trade in bulk, its characteristic commodities were the necessities of life and industry, its economic function was to bind the peoples of Northern Europe by real economic ties – ties without which life in many places would have been difficult if not altogether impossible.

(2) *Quantities*

1

The catalogue of commodities cannot be complete, and as long as it is confined to the main branches of trade it cannot be even wholly representative. Above all, it cannot do full justice to the complexity of medieval commerce. The regions of Europe depended on each other's products or, to use the jargon of the economists, benefited from the geographical division of labour, to a far greater extent than a mere list of commodities would suggest. In spite of all the difficulties of long-distance trade the network of commercial exchanges had in the course of the Middle Ages come to be woven into a tight and complicated mesh. That whole industrial societies, like those of Flanders and Italy and later also that of Holland, should have come into existence even though the essential raw materials, as well as food, had to be imported, is an instance familiar enough. Less familiar, but equally characteristic, is the example of the export of beer from North-western Germany and later from Holland where it was brewed from grain imported from abroad. But nothing illustrates better the complexity of multi-lateral exchanges than the various secondary currents of trade which crossed and recrossed the main lines of commercial traffic. In the same years in the fifteenth century we find England exporting grain through Chester and Bristol to Ireland; importing grain through the eastern ports from the Baltic; exporting red herring from Yarmouth (to Holland of all countries!) and importing white herring through every port; exporting malt and ale and importing beer; exporting faggots and stakes and importing every other kind of timber; exporting figures made of alabaster and importing saints carved in wood; importing wax and exporting tallow; exporting pewter and importing Dutch pottery. And although these subsidiary currents were all small, they went far to give the economic geography of Europe the shape it has borne ever since.

Eloquent as these facts are, they cannot provide a full substitute for the missing statistics. They might, however, be sufficient to demonstrate how wide was the range of needs which inhabitants of Northern Europe covered by purchases from outside, and they might even support the surmise that the volume of the trade must have been high. For bulky goods would not be worth exporting or importing except in bulk, and a regular trade in essentials over long distances presupposed exporters relying on regular and substantial deficiencies in the importing countries as well as importers relying on a regular and substantial flow of supplies from abroad.

Here and there this general argument can be illustrated by numbers drawn from an occasional *cache* of figures. Thus the English trade returns, which are more abundant than those of any other country – they will be discussed later – make it clear that in the first half of the fourteenth century the value of British exports was at times not less than £250,000, or the equivalent of about $1\frac{1}{2}$ million quarters of wheat or $2\frac{1}{2}$ million quarters of oats at prices prevailing in the last decade of the fourteenth century. The evidence of the Hanseatic *Pfundzoll* – a war tax on sea-borne imports – suggests that in the seventies of the fourteenth century the annual value of the taxable sea-borne trade of the principal Hanseatic ports for which evidence is available was in excess of three million Lübeck marks or about 600,000 of contemporary pounds sterling.[5]

[5] The value of seaborne exports of the four Hanseatic ports listed by Stieda

Even more concrete, though not necessarily more precise or relevant, may be the few surviving figures of individual commodities imported and exported. We are told that the total amount of herring salted on the fishing grounds of Skania in a good year could be as high as 120,000 tuns and that some 24,000 tuns of salt were imported in a curing season. In some years at the beginning of the fifteenth century Dutch grain imports by the Somme route may have been as high as 230,000 quarters. At the beginning of the fourteenth century wine exports from Bordeaux reached 100,000 tuns (some 25 million gallons)[6] per annum. In 1334 a few English merchants received royal licences to export to Bordeaux more than 50,000 quarters of grain. The English records show that in the late thirteenth and early fourteenth centuries this country at times exported as much as 35,000–40,000 sacks, the equivalent of about 15 million lb of wool. In the good years of the fourteenth and fifteenth centuries this country exported more than 50,000 pieces of cloth of 28 yards per piece, and it is possible that at the height of their prosperity the Flemish cloth towns turned out a number of cloths at least three times as great.[6]

2

Similar estimates could be cited for a number of other places and other commodities, but however varied, they cannot and perhaps need not be turned into true measurements. The show of precision which they may impart to the history of trade is largely deceptive. Some of the figures are, to say the least, ambiguous; but even those which are not, have survived more or less in isolation and cannot be fitted into reliable estimates of total trade and still less into measurements of social income. It may be significant that in a fourteenth-century parliament it was confidently asserted that the wool of England represented half the total produce of the land; but what was the total produce of the land? It might also be important to know that the value of English exports in the thirteenth century was probably equivalent to the annual earnings of approximately 100,000 agricultural labourers. But even this figure, large as it is and close as it comes to a real measurement, does not mean very much unless related to the total size of English population or to the distribution of income between the various classes of the English people: a subject still shrouded in darkness.

The most that these figures can do is to build up in a cumulative and circumstantial fashion the general impression that the volume of medieval

approached 1.5 million marks in 1370. W. Stieda, *Revaler Zollbücher*, lvii ff. The other German figures in this and preceding paragraphs come from G. Lechner, *Die Hansische Pfundzollisten des Jahres 1368*, 57–8.

[6] Below Table 4.3; also M. Gouron, *L'Amirauté de Guienne*, 47.

trade was considerable; the least they can do is to make it unnecessary to disparage the part trade played in medieval life. No doubt, in comparison with the nineteenth and twentieth centuries, medieval trade at its highest would appear very small. But why compare with the nineteenth century, and indeed why compare at all? For all we know, the record of international trade in the nineteenth century may well turn out to have been a mere aberration in the economic development of the world. It has been argued that in the course of that century factors of production – land, labour, capital – were distributed more unequally over the face of the globe than in any other period of world history. As a result, interregional trade may have been greater in relation to total income than it would have been had the movable resources and especially capital been more evenly spread. By the same argument the international flow of resources has been slowly reducing the relative importance of trade, even though it may have raised its total volume and value. But even if the argument with all its implications were not accepted, it would still remain true that in the nineteenth century foreign trade was so great that, by comparison, the trade of all other centuries, the seventeenth and eighteenth as well as the thirteenth, would appear insignificant. And if historians and economists insist on matching century against century, they would be less open to accusation of irrelevance if they compared the Middle Ages with the earlier centuries of the modern era, the sixteenth, the seventeenth, the eighteenth. Thus compared, medieval trade of European countries would appear (and the argument is one of appearances and not of measurements) both smaller and greater than that of, say, the seventeenth century: smaller in the fifteenth century, greater in the thirteenth.

All such comparisons, however, are highly questionable. Not only must the magnitudes of commercial exchanges always be matters of vague surmise, but they must remain mutually incomparable even if they were capable of exact estimate. From this point of view more relevant than any attempt at a measurement of foreign trade are the simple historical facts indicating the place of trade in medieval life – the existence of specialised economies, the number and relative wealth of towns, the attention paid by kings and parliaments to trade and navigation, the readiness to engage in political and military conflicts on behalf of trade. The geographical and political implications of medieval trade will be discussed separately, but they must also be borne in mind in considering the problem of quantity. Did not the wool trade supply a link between Flanders and this country stronger than political, dynastic or cultural ties with France? Did not Gascon wine trade to England forge a link of political loyalty stronger than affinities of race, language and distance? In the twelfth century interruption in English imports could produce famine in Western

Norway. In the early fourteenth century disturbances in Northern France could produce famine in the Low Countries. In the fourteenth century conflicts with England resulted in mass unemployment all over the Low Countries. And in the fifteenth century the seizure of the salt fleet homeward bound from the Bay of Bourgneuf could produce a major political crisis all over Northern Europe.

The economic interdependence of distant regions and the essential character of certain branches of trade may appear out of scale with the small quantities of goods in fact exchanged. In the middle of the sixteenth century, Thomas Barnaby, an enthusiastic sponsor of the coal trade, could argue that 'the thing that France can live no more without than the fish without water; that is to say the Newcastle coals, without which they can neither make steel work nor metal work nor wire work nor goldsmith work nor guns nor no manner of things that passes the fire'. In the Middle Ages coal exports were probably smaller than in the sixteenth century. The French were as yet rare visitors to the coal wharves of Newcastle: their calls there did not become at all frequent until about 1500. And before the advent of the French, the Flemings and the Zealanders did not apparently take out of this country more than about 10,000 tons in a good year. Yet, even then, coal was, as in the nineteenth century, a bulky return cargo without which the voyages might not have paid and would not have been undertaken.

It is therefore not surprising that in time of war some countries appeared to be even more vulnerable to blockade than in more recent times. The readiness with which embargoes and economic boycotts were used as political weapons is in itself evidence of the store men laid by foreign trade: indeed, of foreign trade in its most specialised manifestations.

(3) *Impediments and facilities*

1

The scope of medieval trade is all the more remarkable for the various obstacles which beset the merchant. It is perhaps true that medieval commerce could not have functioned as it did, had the obstacles in its way been quite as formidable as their history might suggest. Yet formidable they doubtless were, and none more so than the innumerable payments on the frontiers, along the rivers and roads, on town markets and in sea ports: payments which must have burdened commerce nearly as much as similar payments were to burden the trade of France on the eve of Colbert's and Calonne's reforms, or the trade of Germany on the eve of Napoleon's conquest.

England was perhaps the largest area of Northern Europe in which trade was free from any but small tolls. If tolls were paid at all, they were usually in the nature of a *pontage* or a *viage*. Like the turnpike tolls of a later age they were levied to defray the cost of constructing or of maintaining a road or a bridge. As a rule, the king's government seldom granted the right to impose a toll except in exchange for a true equivalent in road service; and grants were frequently preceded or followed by inquisitions into the revenue of tolls and their employments.

By comparison with these service tolls, or 'tolls-thorough' as they were known to a later age, the 'tolls-traverse' – payments based on ancient right and functioning as a customary source of revenue irrespective of the road service rendered – were not many. They were remarkably few in comparison with similar tolls in medieval and post-medieval France and Germany. There, at the best of times, no major trade route was entirely duty free. Even the much frequented international land routes from Flanders to France in the thirteenth century had to pass numerous toll stations, of which several, those of Bapaume on the French border and those of Péronne, Nelse, Compiègne, and Crépy-en-Valois on the roads of Northern France, were more or less inescapable. There were also provincial tolls all over the internal roads beyond Paris, and there were payments at the frontier stations on the south and the east leading to the upper Rhine and the main Alpine passes. Above all, there were innumerable tolls on the Loire, the Somme, the Oise, the Rhône and the Garonne. The allegation that towards the end of the fourteenth century there were 130 toll stations along the Loire is probably far-fetched. But it is known that the tolls on the Loire, such as there were, grew as much in the following 25 or 30 years as they had grown in the preceding fifty. The Garonne and the Rhône were no freer than the Loire, and even on the Seine the toll charges on grain shipped in the late fifteenth century over a distance of 200 miles equalled more than half of its selling price.

The German picture was less uniform, for the country contained the relatively free arteries, like the great Hanseatic routes to the East, as well as the much taxed and restricted roads which connected the route with the interior. The surviving lists of tolls along the main German rivers may exaggerate the actual weight of impositions, but however much discounted, they make formidable reading. At the turn of the thirteenth and fourteenth centuries there were said to have been more than 30 toll stations along the Weser and at least 35 along the Elbe. In the middle of the thirteenth century there were more than fourscore tolls along the Austrian stretch of the upper Danube and a score of tolls on the river Main. But the most advertised, the most bitterly resented and, from the point of view of trade, the most damaging, were the tolls on the Rhine.

According to a recent account there were about 19 toll stations along the Rhine at the end of the twelfth century, about 35 or more at the end of the thirteenth century, nearly 50 at the end of the fourteenth, and more than 60 at the end of the fifteenth century; mostly belonging to the great ecclesiastical princes of Western Germany. Writing in the middle of the thirteenth century, an English chronicler, Thomas Wykes, could find no other way of describing the system on the Rhine than 'the raving madness of the Teutons' (*furiosa Teutonicorum insania*).[7]

The total weight of the internal tolls was thus heavy and growing and may in part account for the gradual clogging of internal trade in the closing centuries of the Middle Ages. At the same time it is important not to misunderstand their incidence and their effect on commerce. The system as a whole may have been sufficiently exorbitant and sufficiently anarchical to impose here and there a weight of charges greater than the traffic could bear. Yet the yield of the main toll stations on the Rhine, the Main, and the Elbe remained to the end sufficiently valuable to justify their owners, and especially the great ecclesiastical princes, in fighting for their retention to the bitter end. The presumption, therefore, is that, generally speaking, they did not choke trade altogether. Extortionate as were the lords of the Rhine tolls, the trade of certain towns, and Cologne in the first instance, remained relatively free over long stretches of the river. And although in the later Middle Ages grain from upper Germany was eventually forced out of the river and took to the land route, timber could still be floated downstream to Holland. The same is broadly true of the Elbe, for the merchants of the Wendish towns never ceased to use the river for the bulkier goods originating beyond Magdeburg and for shipments of fish and salt up the river.

The general impression is that the main weight of the toll taxes fell upon local traffic, thereby reinforcing the particularism and self-sufficiency of local economies. Their chief effect on long-distance trade was to raise local prices for imports and to reduce local prices of exportable surpluses. This in turn may have reduced production for exports and narrowed down the markets for imports. But how great the reduction in fact was in different fields of trade will not be known until local prices have been studied in greater detail than has so far proved possible. The general impression is that among the factors, which at times held back the output of industry and agriculture, high tolls *en route* to distant markets were of relatively little importance. The ability of medieval agriculture to yield surpluses for export, or its failure to do so, depended much less on differences in costs of distribution (including tolls) than on variations of climate, of soil, of seasons, and above all, of social structure. The same argument may not apply to products of industry and mining.

[7] *Annales Monastici* (Rolls Series), IV, 222.

The supply of most industrial products was greatly affected by costs, and the demand for textiles, metal articles and luxuries was apparently quite elastic. Everything that helped to raise their final costs was therefore bound to restrict the volume of production and sales. But for reasons to be expounded later, long-distance trade was not as a rule greatly affected by local taxes, from some of which it was exempted and most of which it could avoid.

From the point of view of inter-regional and international trade, more effective because more unavoidable, were the national or princely taxes at the frontiers or the great international toll-stations, like those of Bapaume. But in the nature of things these taxes were not as a rule so high as to be crippling. Among the highest was the English export duty on wool in the late fourteenth and fifteenth centuries. The taxes, i.e. customs and subsidy, rose to, and at times exceeded £2 to £2 13s 4d per sack, to which about 1s should perhaps be added for various local dues in English ports and 6s 8d for customs charged in Calais and sometimes levied as a special excise on wool shipped to Italy. The total customs payments thus computed exceeded 20 per cent of the value of good quality wool in Calais. The tax in the end penalised British wool exports and greatly stimulated production of cloth at home, but it never stopped the wool exports altogether; and had it threatened to do so it would almost certainly have been moderated. Tax on cloth exports at a rate which varied from 1s to 2s 9d or from about 1.5 to 4 per cent *ad valorem* was not much higher than stamp duties and registration fees were to be in the free-trade decades of the nineteenth century. Miscellaneous imports paid a tax of 3d in the pound, to which frequently the poundage of 1s in the pound was added. The additional duties levied on imports and exports were on the whole very small. Local dues such as 'anchorage' on boats or tolls on merchandise brought into ports varied from place to place and, on the whole, fell less heavily on distant trade than it might appear from the toll lists. In the Cinque Ports in the thirteenth century the tolls on wine, their main imports, varied from 2d to 4d per cask. The charges in Southampton averaged about 2d per pound worth of merchandise; in Winchester they were at the rate of 1d per cwt of wool. But in all these ports most merchants and merchandise coming from other English towns were exempt from local tolls by royal charter or else paid reduced tolls by inter-urban agreements. In a port like Yarmouth where remission was not so general, local dues might vary from about 2d per cloth to 4d per pipe of wine or a last of herring: by no means an exorbitant charge. No doubt in a number of foreign ports, where local taxation was employed as a means of enforcing the monopoly of the residents, the taxes could at times be much higher than they were in English ports. The various dues which were levied on strangers along the roads leading from the vineyards to the port of Bordeaux were sufficiently high to deter them from buying wine directly from the growers. But customs in Bordeaux itself were not such as to impede the flow of wine exports.

2

There was indeed every reason why most taxes and tolls actually borne by long-distance trade should not have been as heavy as those which weighed on local trade. Where princely authorities were so many and so ill-coordinated, as on the Rhine, the total weight of dues might in fact pass the limit of what the international traffic would bear. Yet even at times and in places where this limit was passed, trade was merely forced into alternative routes.

For alternative routes there always were. In considering the much misunderstood history of medieval trade routes, it is important to remember that what made a route was not the physical attributes of a road – a stretch of tarmac or an immovable railway track – but a combination of conveniences, mostly of political and social character: residential and trading facilities *en route*, guarantees of safety and security, and above all, comparative freedom from imposts and taxes. Geographical and physical conditions were of course essential; mountains could only be crossed by passes, rivers by fords and bridgeable places. In general the medieval carrier stuck as long as he could to navigable rivers and to the greater ancient highways, some of which were Roman in origin and construction, and most of which contained sections made and maintained by the work of men. But within limits set by geography, the man-made conveniences – even such conveniences as bridges – could be duplicated and multiplied, and their sites could be shifted. In a famous capitulary Charlemagne had to lay down that if the twelve bridges over the Seine were to be reconstructed they should be placed *ubi antiquitus fuerant* and not moved to new sites. The same motif recurs more than once in the history of European bridges, as in the clause of the Magna Carta providing that no man should be distrained to work on bridges on sites where they had not been *ab antiquo*. When in the later judicial proceedings we find the parties pleading that the bridges in question still were in *locis quibus esse consueverant tempore Ioannis regis* the main object was to prove that the bridges still had to be maintained, but the presumption was that the permanence of a bridge site could not be taken for granted.

What is true of bridges is even truer of the social and institutional components of a trade route. These could be combined and re-combined into linked chains stretching across the face of Europe in double, treble, and multiple strands. Thus between England and Flanders on the one hand and the Mediterranean on the other there were during the Middle Ages at least a dozen of geographically feasible lines of communication from which merchants could take their choice. There was, in the first place, the major alternative of land routes and sea routes. The latter did not become important until the closing of the Champagne routes by the action of the French kings in the late thirteenth and the fourteenth centuries; but eventually they rose to great prominence. In the last hundred years of the Middle Ages the bulk of English wool exports to Italy went that way, and whereas in the early fourteenth century the Genoese wool importers paid toll on wool in Milan, in the fifteenth century the merchants of Milan paid toll on their wool in Genoa. Among land routes, the Italians and the other merchants trading to the south rang the changes over a wide scale of trade routes across Flanders and France. There were in the first place the main lines of the Flemish rivers, and there were routes which were wholly or largely land-bound. In the thirteenth century, in addition to a number of secondary routes, there were two main arteries – that of Arras and that of Douai – which crossed Flanders to the south; and there were also at least several routes from Brabant to France which grew in importance in the later Middle Ages; a network of routes across Northern France, most of them converging on Compiègne and Troyes, and spreading out from there to Paris or to Saulieu, Dijon and the other places *en route* for the south-east. Marc Bloch has drawn attention to the several routes between Paris and Orléans, but a cursory study of French internal trade would reveal the several variants forming the routes between Paris and Brest, Paris and Lille, Paris and Rouen, Paris and La Rochelle, some following the main rivers of France, others mainly land routes.[8]

The same variety of routes traversed the continent from the west to the east. The time when the *Hellweg*, which bisected Northern Germany from Dortmund in Westphalia to Magdeburg or Bardowiek on the Elbe, was the sole line of communication to the Slavonic East passed away (if such time ever was) with the twelfth century. In the thirteenth and later centuries there were at least four transcontinental routes between Bruges and the Baltic: the sea route by the Sound, the two older land routes via Lübeck and via Münster and Stettin, and eventually the new southern route via Frankfurt-am-Oder. Historians have uncovered at least six main routes between the German ports on the Baltic and South-east Europe; two in a northerly direction: one by Gnesen and Posen and the other by Kalisz and Breslau; four in the south: by Sando-

---

[8] H. Laurent, *La Draperie des Pays-Bas en France*, 48 ff., 246–53; Armand Deroisy in *Revue du Nord* (1939), 40 ff.; F. Imbertin in *Les Annales* (1939); and M. Bloch's postscript, ibid. 416.

mir, by Cracow, by Lwow, and by Oposzno; and a network of other routes to and beyond Bohemia, round and into Hungary.[9]

The feasible lines of transcontinental traffic, whether complementary or competitive, were so many as to defeat the attempts of many a hopeful beginner at an exhaustive list or a comprehensive map. In this maze trade could be relied upon to pick its way and to shift when necessary. The history of the embargoes and staple laws imposed during the Middle Ages is one continuous record of old routes abandoned and new routes opened up. If some arteries of trade were closed by excessive imposts and restrictions (as the Champagne route across France was closed by the vexatious policy of the French Crown), others could be opened up by free-trade treaties negotiated between the interested parties. The early development of Brabant in the thirteenth century is generally ascribed to the liberal commercial policy of the far-seeing Counts of Brabant; the use of the eastern artery from Brabant via Lorraine in the late Middle Ages was made possible by 'free-trade' treaties which extended in an unbroken series from the fifties of the fourteenth century to the sixties of the fifteenth, and above all to the agreements between the merchants of Milan and Rudolf of Hapsburg for the remission of tolls and duties along the route which led from Bâle to Brabant. The Venetian merchants for a time developed the Bavarian route to the Alps, through Nuremberg, as an alternative to the French route, and there too the way was 'made' by agreements with princes for remission of dues and for greater safety of traffic.

3

The freedom of long-distance traffic was thus in essence a freedom of choice between routes. It was therefore imperfect and unstable and, from every point of view, inferior to the great liberty which European trade was to enjoy in periods as truly free as the honeymoon decades of the Victorian *laissez-passer*. For not only were routes newly chosen sometimes more expensive than the routes which had to be abandoned, but the whole system of communications suffered from lack of permanence and stability. In addition it was often insecure. Political conditions on which it depended changed frequently; princely whims and aims were often unaccountable; and above all wars were apt to break out at all times. And the crippling effect of war on trade must not be underestimated. Here and there war demands might inject a stimulating dose of inflationary expenditure into certain branches of trade; but on the whole

---

[9] Th. Hirsch, *Danzig's Handels- und Gewerbgeschichte*, 178–80 and *passim*. G. Köster in *Forschungen zu Brandenburgischen u. Preussischen Gesch.* XLVIII (1936), 120 ff.

war meant taxation, forced loans, monetary disturbance and physical hazards. Contrary to all the current notions, medieval conflicts could approach very closely the recent models of total war, for medieval princes did not as a rule hesitate to sacrifice their long-term economic prospects to the strategic or fiscal necessities of war. It was not so much the mere fact of annexation by France as the exposure to the demands of Philip le Bel's war strategy and war finance that ruined the cloth industry of Artois, the transit trade of France and the prosperity of the fairs of Champagne. It was Edward III's war finance that brought havoc into the English wool-growing and wool trade and into the Italian investment in this country. It was the Hanseatic war policy and its accidents that all but ruined in the fifteenth century the German position in Eastern Flanders.

Above all, in time of war and within the range of its operations, pillage and piracy reigned. Piracy and robbery along roads and rivers could at times develop into a major disaster, and it is therefore no wonder that it has now become one of the major themes of medieval history. The records are full of the complaints, petitions and counter-petitions arising from the seizure of ships and goods on the high seas, and it is doubtful whether there was any major act of piracy which remained unrecorded in the surviving medieval evidence. It is therefore not surprising that in modern accounts of medieval trade piracy figures very conspicuously.

It may even be that piracy has received more attention than it deserves. For if on some continental land routes ambushes and attacks on convoys were endemic, piracy on the high seas was not. Generally speaking it was much less a permanent feature of the medieval scene than an accident of war. In some parts of Europe, on the south-west coast of England, on the west coast of Brittany, and along the creeks of Normandy, and no doubt elsewhere, there was to be found a sea-faring population who at all times engaged in occasional piracy. But most of the piratical acts in medieval records were committed not by professional pirates practising their occupation in all seasons, but by merchants who turned pirate and sometimes acted as privateers under official letters of mark. They either were pressed into service by their princes or turned to privateering while trade was at a standstill, or were trying to recoup themselves for acts of piracy they or their compatriots had suffered at the enemy's hands. Pirates and privateers preyed on the French and English shipping in the Channel every time war between France and England broke out; with the result that during the Hundred Years War, i.e. for nearly 150 years, the sea-borne trade between Brittany and Normandy on the one hand and the English south coast on the other was reduced to a small and fitful trickle. The North Sea was thrown into a chaos of universal and promiscuous privateering of this kind in the fifties and sixties of the fifteenth century, and there were occasional outbursts of wholesale piracy in the disturbed periods in Anglo-Flemish relations in the early fourteenth century. But in the times when wars were not raging and in areas outside the range of privateering bases, the main channels of sea-borne trade were maintained more or less open.

On land the only true remedy was the enforcement of the king's peace. When and where the princes were strong enough to keep the roads safe – as in Flanders and Champagne in the eleventh, twelfth, and thirteenth centuries, in Burgundy in the fifteenth century, in Prussia and Livonia in the fourteenth and early fifteenth centuries – merchant traffic flowed unmolested both in peace and in war, and the wealth of their countries grew at the expense of lands and routes not so blessed. In Germany the safety of the routes was sometimes enforced by the action of the towns. In the later Middle Ages the great Hanseatic routes to the East were almost wholly free from the dangers of piracy and robbery. Somewhat more restricted and on the whole less successful were the activities of the inter-urban police unions (*Landfriedensverbände*) of the thirteenth and fourteenth centuries, which, with the occasional assistance of local princes, waged battle against the robber barons and their nests along the West German rivers.

On the high seas, however, the security of traffic was almost entirely the concern of the merchants and shippers themselves. Where shipments were valuable and regular and followed established sea lanes, they were as a rule made in convoy. The English wool was shipped in two great bi-annual convoys elaborately organised and controlled. The German and Dutch ships carrying salt from the Bay also as a rule sailed together, and so did often the English cloth boats sailing to the Baltic and the Prussian and Dutch boats plying between Danzig and the West. The system must have been effective, for very few of the great convoys were ever seized or disturbed. There was hardly any instance of the Venetian galleys being seized or plundered in northern waters on their annual visits to England and the Low Countries; not one of the great wool fleets which sailed from the main wool ports of England was ever seized; and of all the great Bay fleets, which regularly passed through the Narrow Seas on their way from the Atlantic coast to the Baltic, the first ever to be attacked was the great Bay fleet which was seized by Warwick in 1449. In short, piracy even more than the other disturbances of trade was a characteristic feature of the Middle Ages only in so far as the Middle Ages were specially prone to war. When and where peace prevailed trade flowed unhindered.

(4) Transport

1

In times of war and on routes which happened to be no more than ordinarily insecure the dangers of the routes must have added to the cost of trade. But in most years and especially in the years of peace they were by no means the main constituent of costs and could not be blamed for the high expenses of distribution. Commercial distribution was bound to be a costly service, but – tolls apart – the main element of cost was undoubtedly transport. It is not that transport was as primitive as it is sometimes represented, but like all transport of the pre-railway age it was wasteful of time, equipment and manpower.

On land routes goods were carried by horse and ox, but not necessarily by pack. Carrying services on medieval estates in this country and abroad consisted of both summage, i.e. carriage by horseback (indeed sometimes on human backs), and cartage; but English manorial accounts make it quite clear that, for bulky goods or for carriage over distances, carts and, where suitable, boats were used. On some stretches, e.g. across mountain passes, pack animals might be the only feasible means of transport, and the *vectuarii* of Genoa and Asti who ran the traffic across the Alps to Champagne at the end of the thirteenth century apparently employed horses for the purpose. But carts of varying sizes as a rule made up the bulk of medieval trade caravans. A thirteenth-century tariff of Péronne suggests that the purposes of local traffic were served by the *colliers* – the medieval coolies – who drew barrows and other small vehicles *ad collum*; and that some local traffic also went by pack-horses. But the bulk of the traffic was apparently borne by the *bronnette*, a cart on two wheels, which according to a text of 1327 was capable of carrying a fardel of thirteen cloths; and more still by *car* or the *carrette* on four wheels capable of carrying a cargo two or three times that of the *bronnette*.

The Péronne cart was not substantially different from the vehicle commonly used by peasants in the daily routine of their agriculture, and peasant carts therefore provided the main reserve of medieval transport. Wherever the accounts of local bulky traffic have survived, more especially of stone, brick, wood, or charcoal, we find it carried by horse and cart or ox and cart hired or requisitioned from nearby villages. Peasant carting was, however, in the nature of things seasonal and could not supply the needs of trade all the year round. It is therefore not surprising that regular traffic along the main lines of communication was in the hands of men who specialised in the business of transport and acted as common carriers. English records have preserved evidence of common carriers traversing the country in the thirteenth, fourteenth and fifteenth centuries from Southampton to Winchester and Oxford, from the Cotswolds by road and river to London, from the midland counties to the Stourbridge Fair near Cambridge, from Westminster and Oxford to York and Newcastle-on-Tyne. In towns like London there was a recognised profession of 'brokers of carts' who acted as intermediaries between carters and owners of cargo. Sometimes whole rural areas specialised in carting services. In the middle of the fourteenth century the carriers who transported wool from Flanders to Bâle were mostly Alsatians and Saarois; the Brabant route to the South was used mainly by carters from Lorraine, and the overland routes from Toulouse to the Atlantic seaports mainly by the wagoners of Béarn.

2

Wheeled traffic could not have been so general had roads been as impassable as some of the roads which Arthur Young depicted in the eighteenth century. Judged by modern standards they were certainly bad beyond all comparison, and most local roads were no more than mud tracks barely usable in bad weather. To conclude, however, that every King's road 'made and maintained itself', or to argue, as so well-informed a historian as Marc Bloch did, that medieval roads in general were no more than *l'endroit où on passe*, barely differentiated from fields and field tracks, is perhaps too disparaging a generalisation.[10] It may be true of the very early local example Bloch quotes: the village road which, in Flodoard's story, St Theodulph prevented from being ploughed up. On the other hand it could not possibly have applied to at least one local road in thirteenth-century Cheshire. For when the Cistercian abbey of Vale Royal in Cheshire was erecting its buildings, peasant carts transported stone from the quarry at Eddisbury about eight miles away, and made thousands of journeys, most carters managing to make two complete journeys – a distance of about 30 miles – per day for months at a time: and winter months at that.

The generalisation applies even less to main roads. Main roads artificially levelled and drained were not universal; roads with artificial metal or paved surfaces must have been very uncommon. Yet road approaches to a number of towns were frequently paved, and artificial road beds were also to be found in the open country. In origin they were mostly Roman, for in spite of all the shifts and changes in medieval routes,

---

[10] C. T. Flower, *Public Works in Medieval Law*, II, xvi, Selden Soc. Publications, vol. XL for 1923.

Roman roads were used whenever possible. In England ancient Roman ways shared the medieval road system, and some main roads on a surviving fourteenth-century map were little different from what they had been ten centuries earlier. Nor were they in this respect much different from what they were to be four centuries later, and it is also doubtful whether their surfaces were much worse. Their foundations were that many centuries 'newer' than in the eighteenth century, and in addition the average medieval cart was probably lighter than the later wagon. It was seldom furnished with metal tyres, which the Elizabethan legislators found so destructive of road surfaces.[11]

It is also probable that in England, parts of France and the Low Countries, surfaces and drainage were kept up to a standard well above that of a mere track. In most European countries the law of the road and the surveyance of roads were lax and rudimentary. Yet to assume, as Marc Bloch did, that roads were not subject to special legislation and control is not altogether true, even of France. For the legal notion of *strata publica* was part of the legal doctrine of thirteenth-century France, even if it may not have been greatly respected in practice. In this country, where documents have survived in greater abundance, they contain numerous indictments of people guilty of obstructing public roads, encroaching on them, or neglecting their duties of maintenance. And the indictments are evidence not only of the disrepair and neglect of roads but also of the legal and administrative provisions for their upkeep. In Common Law, as defined by Bracton and enforced by royal courts, the definition of the King's highway included not only military roads but all roads leading to ports and markets, and their destruction or obstruction was an offence against the King. In addition, law and custom charged landlords and vills with the maintenance of the *via communis* in good passable order.

That the law was not always enforced may be taken for granted; and at certain periods the gap between law and practice was bound to be wide. In England the work of maintenance was as a rule confined to the upkeep of drains and ditches, and a road was not deemed impassable except when flooded or barricaded. Moreover, in the late fourteenth and fifteenth centuries the system, linked as it was with feudal obligations and manorial dues, may have suffered from the commutation of services and from the general tendency on the part of the landlords to cut their capital investments. The Royal commissions of walls and dykes to some extent succeeded in checking the deterioration of bridges

11 Lamprecht in his well-documented appendix on roads in Rhineland (*Deutsches Wirtschaftsleben im Mittelalter*, II, 236 ff.) emphasised the continued use of Roman roads in the early Middle Ages; but his evidence does not support his argument that as time went on waterways replaced the Roman roads.

as well as of the main sea walls and dykes, but could not and were not expected to establish an effective national control over roads.

Yet, if in some respects daily practice fell short of legal ideal, in one
or two respects the ideal was sometimes outstripped by practical achievement. Thus substantial towns paved their roads and levied a special
pavage tax for the purpose. Roads across moors and fens often included
causeways and reinforced beds which cost much to build and to maintain.
The causeway by the Holland bridge near Boston was made up of thirty
bridges; a road across Sedgemoor near Glastonbury was built of stone on a
foundation of brushwood and alder sleepers held together by oak balks.

Some of the road works were carried out by princes. The French kings
may have neglected to enforce the law of roads, but English thirteenth-
century records have preserved evidence of work on roads and bridges
undertaken by the Crown on its own initiative. In England the Crown
in preparation for its military expeditions often undertook works on a
very great scale, as in 1277 when Roger Mortimer was appointed to en-
large and widen roads and passes into Wales, or in 1283 when Royal
Commissioners were appointed to widen the passes into Wales to a bow-
shot in width. But not all road works were fruits of state initiative.
Religious houses, municipalities, landlords and private benefactors, all
made their contributions. The Holland causeway was built by a religious
house; the Glastonbury causeway was in fact maintained by another
religious house. The Stecknitz canal which in 1398 cut across the base of
Jutland peninsula was a part of Lübeck's endeavour to support the land
road in competition against the sea route by the Sound. Similarly, when
in 1332 the town of Ghent busied itself with the repair of a distant stretch
of road near Senlis in the neighbourhood of Paris, this was taken for what
it was – an act of enlightened self-interest of a community dependent
upon traffic across France. History has not preserved the names of the
anonymous masons (some writers thought they might have been smiths) or
donors who by 1237 opened up the pass of St Gotthard by constructing a
road and a bridge across the gorges at Schöllenen, thus establishing a great
new line of communication between Italy and Europe. But records of all
European countries have preserved scores and hundreds of references of
charitable gifts, by will and otherwise, for the building and improvement of communications: gifts which contributed as much as acts of
municipal and princely governments to the main system of European
communications.

In the main, private enterprise and private benefactions were primarily
concerned with bridges and causeways: so much so as to suggest to one
historian of public works the generalisation that, whereas the Romans
were road-conscious but were quite prepared to cross rivers by fords,
the men of the Middle Ages were essentially bridge-conscious. The

writer has cited the part bridges played in the ancient feudal obligation of *trinoda necessitas*, as well as the frequent references to pontage, a local tax levied for the upkeep of bridges.[12] But he could also have cited, if he wished, the English evidence of the building and repairs of bridges and the more stringent enforcement of legal obligations for the upkeep and maintenance of bridges. And if there is anything in this generalisation, it may well be connected with what is now known about Roman inefficiency in the use of draught animals. Where the Romans moved themselves and their goods on horseback, medieval men used carts.

3

The main alternative to wheeled traffic, however, was not the packhorse but the barge and the boat. Here and there records have preserved curious instances of short sea routes for a time becoming unaccountably dear, but generally, in the Middle Ages as in modern times, carriage by water was much cheaper than by land; and this was one of the reasons why river traffic was able to bear the heavy tolls which weighed on it in so many countries. Traffic in heavy goods, such as timber and coal, over long distances was only possible where cheap waterways were available. Mineral coal was known as 'sea coal', not because it was necessarily mined by the sea but because it came to the south by river and by sea. Water transport explains also why in the south and east of England it was cheaper to import timber from the Baltic and Norway than from the North-west Midlands and why it paid to import building stone from Normandy for the erection of cathedrals and castles in southern England.

Sea transport was cheap in spite of the small size of the medieval boat and in spite of the costly methods of navigation. Medieval shipping was as a rule coastal. Whether because navigation was mainly by sounding, or whether because the high seas were thought dangerous, masters preferred to hug the coasts. Whenever possible they left the sea and sailed by internal waterways, and Holland owes much of its importance as a centre of entrepôt trade to the medieval seaman's liking for the shallow and sheltered waters of Dutch rivers and canals stretched along the east to west route. Farther east and west along the same route ships plied when possible in the narrow waters between the islands and within sight of dry land. As long as these methods prevailed, sea transport was bound to be relatively expensive, for it involved constant reloading at points where the coastwise route was interrupted by land masses. Lübeck and Hamburg were two such reloading places half-way from Bruges to Danzig. Amsterdam and Rotterdam, the two terminal points of the Dutch waterways, were two other ports serving the same function. There was also a great

[12] C. T. Flower, op. cit., xix.

deal of reloading into lighters in sea ports which, like Bruges, happened to be situated in silted-up river estuaries. Cranes – and they were to be found in a number of large ports – lightened the labour, but they could not do away with it altogether.

Both the size of the boats and the methods of navigation may have improved as the Middle Ages drew to their close. The history of the shipbuilding industry in the Middle Ages has not yet been written, and the technical history of medieval ships, though better known, is still incomplete. But in so far as it is possible to generalise from the present state of knowledge, it appears that in the later Middle Ages more merchant ships were carvel-built than in earlier centuries and that clinker-built boats were being ousted from the main trade routes across the north seas. The Genoese and Spanish carrack, a swifter though not necessarily a larger vessel, did not as a rule go much farther east and north than the ports of Flanders and Southern England, but towards the end of the Middle Ages it dominated England's western approaches and the sea-borne trade to the Mediterranean. In addition, in the later Middle Ages once a year there came into Southampton and Bruges the great Venetian galleys. But the mainstay of the new merchant shipping in the northern seas were the slower and roomier boats of local origin. The typical ships of the English wool and wine fleets and of the Dutch and Hanseatic shipping in the North Sea and the Baltic were the cogs and hulks frequently displacing as much as 100 or 200 tons and sometimes approaching the 400 and 500 ton limit.

Whether as a result of these improvements or through the spreading use of the compass or through the growing knowledge of their element, the seamen of the later Middle Ages ventured more frequently than before into the open sea. Such voyages had, since times immemorial, been occasionally made by Irish, Scandinavian and English merchantmen trading to Iceland, but from the economic point of view the most important instance of navigation not wholly coastal was the *Umlandfahrt* – the route to the Baltic round the Sound which was probably opened by seamen of Zealand some time in the middle of the fourteenth century. The direct routes as well as the larger ships must have helped to reduce the freights, and it was on lower freights that the Dutch established their sea power in the course of the fifteenth century.

In addition there were the internal waterways. The classical country of river navigation was east of the Elbe and more especially east of the Oder, in Lithuania, Poland, Galicia. Among the Western Slavs there were whole societies – villages and regions – which lived on and by their broad and sluggish rivers. In the course of centuries the Lithuanian and Slavonic peasants and fishermen had developed a system of river navigation ideally adapted to the transportation of timber and other bulky cargoes. The

usual transport was by a local variant of a raft – the Slavonic *dubassy*
– large timber platforms capable of carrying temporary huts and a great
deal of miscellaneous cargo as well as large quantities of timber. Hence
the importance of eastern river ports like Thorn, Kovno and Brest-Litovsk.
Hence also the prominence which rivers and weirs occupied in the
records of Eastern European trade and in the trade treaties between the
Germans and the Slavonic princes.

It is doubtful whether rivers were equally important in the West, but
here and there they formed essential links in transcontinental routes. The
Seine was a great trade artery of Northern France and one of its main
grain conduits, served and largely dominated by the rival companies of
riparian traders of Paris and Rouen. The part which the Somme and the
Oise played in the grain traffic has already been mentioned; the
Scheldt and the Meuse never ceased to serve the needs of Flemish traffic.
At times most of the great rivers of Europe, the Rhine, the Main, the
Weser, the Elbe in Germany; the Loire, the Rhône, the Garonne in
France, carried much of the heavy long-distance traffic. If they did not
always do so and if, in spite of the greater economy of water carriage,
traffic was at times apt to desert the great waterways, the fault lay with
the owners of tolls who preyed upon them. It has already been
shown how the general tendency was for the river tolls to multiply and
how at times some rivers, mainly German, came near to being deserted
by the merchant and the barge-man. Yet even in the later Middle Ages
they were not deserted altogether. Traffic was reduced but never stopped.

In England rivers were freer than in most other parts of Europe and
formed an organic part of the English route system. The Thames, the
Lea, the Stour, the Wye, the Severn, the Avon, the Humber, the Trent,
the Yorkshire Ouse, the Witham and other rivers were busy trade
arteries reaching far into the interior. The Thames was navigated well
into Oxfordshire, although in the fifteenth-century wool from the Cotswolds was as a rule loaded on barges no farther west than Henley. Not-
tingham was connected with the sea through the Trent and the Humber.
In conjunction with the Ouse and the Fossdyke the Trent formed a
chain of waterways from York to Boston. The Humber was also a great
waterway serving places as far inland as York and Beverley. Other and
smaller rivers with their estuaries were linked to the main rivers and
marked the points at which England's inland ports sprang up in the
course of the Middle Ages.

In England, in Flanders, in the northernmost reaches of the North
German rivers the waterways were kept up more or less continually
and more or less efficiently. We read of course of mills and fishing weirs
obstructing the passage, of mudbanks allowed to form, but we also read of
dredging operations, of repairs to banks and embankments, of prosecutions

for neglecting and obstructing the care of the waterways. Indeed in this country the very frequency of complaints shows what medieval men expected from their waterways and bears indirect witness to the use men made of the transport facilities they found.

4

Viewed in retrospect, medieval trade seems abundantly provided with means of communications – roads, sea lanes, rivers. Drawn on the map the network may indeed appear more imposing than it in fact was, for the final test of a transport system is not its density on the map but its effects on costs; and the costs were doubtless higher than the plethora of routes and quasi-routes might suggest to the uninstructed. What the average costs in fact were, no historian could now so much as guess, and it is doubtful whether the guess would be worth making even if it could be made. The most salient feature of trading costs in the Middle Ages was their infinite variety – a variety which would distort and falsify any attempt to strike an average for the system as a whole. Even a cursory survey of freights and charges would reveal striking contrasts in costs at one and the same time along routes of equal length and of similar physical character. In times unfavourable to commerce and on routes least favoured by governments, the charges could be very high and indeed prohibitive. But it would of course be a truism to insist that being prohibitive they must not be taken to represent the average costs of trade along the main lines of communication. For on routes which were so heavily taxed, or were so badly served by transport, or were so profoundly disturbed by war and piracy as to be unsuited to active trade, traders were not in fact active. They frequented instead those routes on which transport was relatively free and cheap. In theory this may have raised the costs of trade higher than they might have been had the merchants' choice of routes been unrestricted and had all the potential trade routes been in service; but in practice merchants engaged in the main branches of medieval trade could in most times find routes which were reasonably cheap or at least not so costly as to justify excessive 'traders' margins' or greatly to restrict the demand for commodities and their supply.

Thus the few surviving figures of costs of cartage in and around the Hanseatic towns suggest that in the second half of the fourteenth century it was sufficiently low to make it possible to divert the grain trade to land routes at a time when the river traffic was being choked up by tolls and taxes. The same conclusion also emerges from the English evidence which is sufficiently abundant to justify an impression more nearly statistical. The manorial rolls and other surviving accounts suggest that the existence of the peasant reserve of carts kept the level of cartage costs low. In

1278 a long and expensive transport operation on the King's behalf from Rhuddlan via Chester to Macclesfield, a distance of about 70 miles, was carried out an average cost of 6*d* per day per cart with two horses. The average charge elsewhere appeared to be from 3*d* to 4*d* per carthorse per day. Thorold Rogers computed that where the service was carried out over long distances by common carriers, who bore the legal responsibility of bailees of the goods and had to undertake loading and unloading, the charge worked out at about 3½*d* per ton per mile for the double journey. But the services of peasant carts were much cheaper. According to Thorold Rogers a peasant cart could be hired at any time of the Middle Ages at an average charge of 1*d* per ton per mile when the journey there and back was made in a day, and the charge did not appreciably rise even after the price revolution of the sixteenth century. For Norfolk a local historian has assembled the local carting charges in the fifteenth century, and these often worked out if anything lower than Thorold Rogers's penny. At these rates the cost of transporting goods over 50 miles would in the middle of the fourteenth century be rather less than 1.5 per cent of the value of the cargo if it were wool, and about 15 per cent if it were grain.

Sea transport was even cheaper, so long as it followed the well-established and regular sea lanes. The cost of shipping a tun of Gascon wine to Hull or Ireland at the end of the thirteenth century worked out at about 8*s* per tun or rather less than 10 per cent of its f.o.b. price in Bordeaux. It appears that in the late fourteenth and fifteenth centuries the transport charges in relation to the f.o.b. prices were if anything lower than a century earlier. In the fifteenth century the transport costs of wool from London to Calais, including the costs of convoy, worked out at about 4*s* per sack or rather less than 2 per cent of its f.o.b. price in London or Dover. A weigh (400 lb) of coal cost about 2*s* to transport from Newcastle to the South, presumably to the Low Countries, whereas transport charges of a certain shipload of about 200 tons of miscellaneous, mostly valuable, cargo from Bergen-op-Zoom to London in the middle of the fifteenth century worked out at £20, or 2*s* per dead-weight ton.

These charges were not very high, and may largely explain why it was that, in such active and well-established branches of trade as English wool exports to the Low Countries or the Gascon wine exports to this country, the distributors' margins were not exceptionally high even if judged by modern standards. The surviving evidence of the wool contracts and the figures given in a fifteenth-century treatise, the *Noumbre of Weyghtes*, make it possible to estimate the average cost of handling wool on its way from the grower to the foreign buyer. The total cost of packing, transport from a midland county to London, custom and subsidy (the latter at the lower English rate), amounted to

about £2 13s 4d per sack. To this there has to be added the freight from
London or another wool port to Calais, including the expenses of the
convoy, which in the second half of the fifteenth century worked out at
about 4s per sack (6s 8d per sarpler of rather less than two sacks). The
average price which an English exporter was expected to pay for a sack
of high quality wool in the Cotswolds in the second half of the century
averaged about £8, so that the total expenses would amount to about
40 per cent of the inland price and would bring the total cost of a sack
to a stapler in Calais to rather more than £11. The selling price of the
fine Cotswold wool in Calais and Bruges fluctuated between £12 and
£13, thus leaving a nominal profit of £1 to £2 per sack of fine wool. A
certain amount of disguised profit was also made on various allowances
and premiums for differences of weight, wastage, etc.[13]

It is also possible to estimate with some accuracy the cost of distribution of Gascon wine. We are told that the f.o.b. prices at Bordeaux
in the second half of the fourteenth century established themselves somewhere in the neighbourhood of nine Bordeaux livres and were made up of
5 li. paid for grapes, for the making of wine and for brokerage, 1 li. 10 sous
paid for transport to Bordeaux, and 2 li. 10 sous for Great Custom from
which the merchants of Bordeaux and the privileged merchants were exempt. Sea transport to English ports of the south and east coast varied
between 2 li. 10 sous and 5 li. per tun and about 1s 6d had to be paid for
various dues in English ports. The costs in England therefore worked
out somewhere in the neighbourhood of 14 livres or about £5, and the
wholesale price for Gascon wine in London appeared to be not greatly in
excess of that figure. Considering the length of the route and the many
hands through which the wine had to pass on the way from the Gascon
grower to the English vintner, the added charges were by no means out
of proportion to the costs of transport and handling which were to prevail in the wine trade of later ages.[14]

A somewhat similar conclusion would probably emerge from the study
of other 'regular' branches of northern commerce – Baltic timber, Skanian
herring, Bay salt. In the first half of the fifteenth century the price of salt
in Danzig immediately on arrival of the Bay fleet was barely twice that
which, following Warwick's attack on the Bay fleet in 1449, the merchants claimed to be the cost of the salt at Bourgneuf. What is more, it
competed in price with salt originating from Saxon and other nearby
sources. Transport and expenses of handling were obviously not the main
constituent of costs.

[13] 'The Noumbre of Weyghtes', Brit. Mus. Cotton, Vespasian E. ix; E. Power and
M. Postan, *Studies in English Trade in the Fifteenth Century*, 70–2.
[14] R. Boutruche, *La Crise d'une société*, 151, n. 1; Francisque Michel, *Histoire du
Commerce et de Navigation à Bordeaux*, 1, 123, 127.

On the other hand, the trades which did not happen to enjoy the advantages of relatively free and cheap lines of communication could at times be weighed down with vast expenses *en route*. What is more, even in favoured trades, like the English wool exports or the Gascon wine trade, war and commercial conflict sometimes obstructed the normal channels and added greatly to costs. Whereas in normal years, e.g. in the first two decades of the fifteenth century, the wholesale prices of Baltic timber in English ports were barely twice those in its Polish places of origin, in the years of 1437 and 1438, when trade between England and Danzig was opened after an interval of embargoes, prices were exceptionally low in Poland, very high in England, and the distributive costs and profits were inordinately high. Wainscoting then cost little more than 2 marks per hundred in Poland and 5 marks in Danzig and fetched 24 marks in Yarmouth; bowstaves which cost 14 marks per great hundred in Danzig were 51 marks in England; planks (*Klapholz*) about 10 marks in Danzig and 35 marks in England.[15] Similarly, in the middle and second half of the fifteenth century, when direct relations between England and Gascony were broken by war and French occupation, and Gascon wine had to find its way through neutral countries and neutral hands, the cost of transport and of handling was so high as greatly to increase both the price in Bordeaux and the price in England and indeed to reduce the English wine trade to a mere shadow. Even in the English wool trade the costs were not elsewhere as low as they appeared to be along the route which led from the wool grower to the stapler in Calais. Thus, the Italian merchants and the Englishmen who sent wool to Italy in the fifteenth century must have found transport and other charges very high. To begin with, the Italian merchants in England had to pay what amounted to disguised bribes for licences to avoid the staple of Calais and they also had to pay higher export duty. The transport was also costlier. According to the record of expenses incurred in the shipment of the King's wool to Italy in the late seventies and early eighties of the fifteenth century, the freight of a sack carried by a galley to Venice amounted to £3 3s 4d – which was much less than the costs by the land routes – and the total cost of a sack of wool to the exporter came to well over £14. The wool then sold in Venice at about £20 per sack, and the profit of £5 to £6 per sack was much higher than that earned by staplers on their shorter and safer route.

In short, medieval communications, like other trading activities suffered much more from instability and uncertainty, political in origin, than from high costs of an inefficient transport service. Inefficient the service certainly was, wasteful of manpower and other resources; but so was also medieval industry and agriculture. Judged by modern stan-

[15] Th. Hirsch, *Danzig's Handels- und Gewerbgeschichte*, VIII.

dards the making and growing of goods for sale may well have been costlier than the carrying of the goods to the consumer. To put it more abstractly, the proportion of trading costs to total costs was probably less in the Middle Ages than it is now, which is merely another way of saying that far greater economies have resulted from industrial revolutions of the eighteenth and nineteenth centuries than from the corresponding improvements in transport and distribution. If so, this may be one of the reasons why men in the Middle Ages found it not only necessary but also possible to trade and why commerce played the part it did in the economic life of the Middle Ages. And if it can be shown – as it appears probable – that local taxation, war and piracy became more disturbing and more difficult to circumvent as the Middle Ages drew to their close, this may also help to account for some of the 'long-term' trends of medieval trade. These trends will form the subject of the remaining sections of this chapter.

II. THE AGE OF EXPANSION

(1) *The origins*

1

The goods entering northern trade were as a rule products of local agriculture and industry and were often sold and bought in small quantities out of current production. From this point of view the great inter-regional currents differed in little but magnitude from the operations on the local markets. The staple commodities of international trade were handled in bulk and travelled over longer distances, but there was no hard and fast line between local and international trade. Both depended upon the surpluses of local production, rural and urban, and both grew with the general expansion of population and production.

It should therefore be possible to account for the 'origin' of northern trade without invoking any special cause not inherent in the general economic development of north-western countries themselves. Inter-regional trade, like the local trade from which it developed, was more or less endemic in the history of European society. Its use was familiar to prehistoric man, and there is therefore no reason why at the beginning of the Middle Ages men should have had to learn anew the lesson of its necessity and convenience. It has already been suggested that in the very choice of their *habitat* the tribal groups of Northern Europe appeared to assume the existence of inter-regional exchanges. For otherwise it would be very difficult to account for their deliberate migration into the water-logged plains of the Rhine littoral, the fiords and uplands of Norway and the fenlands of Britain; or for the emergence at the very dawn of the Middle Ages in most European countries of specialised communities of sheepfarmers, fishermen, charcoal burners, saltmakers, and miners. It could of course be argued that in the early stages of medieval settlement men were able to wring a balanced supply of necessities from lands which eventually supported specialised economies. But some regions – fishing areas like the estuary of the Rhine, wool-growing areas of Northern England were fully specialised very early in the Middle Ages; and regional specialisation implies inter-regional exchange.

This does not, however, mean that specialised societies were the only ones to engage in trade. Some trade must have been essential even to agricultural areas capable of highly variegated cultivation and of a highly self-sufficient economy. For, however self-sufficient the large estates or the villages in the continental interior of North-western Europe in the Dark Ages, they were never entirely independent of commercial supplies from outside or unaffected by division of labour within. Few agricultural villages themselves produced their salt, their iron or all their textiles. And however self-sufficient a village, not all households in it were equally self-sufficient. From the earliest centuries of the Middle Ages there were to be found in the medieval villages and estates crafts-men – smiths, potters, and sometimes even carpenters and weavers. Among the peasant cultivators themselves there always existed small-holders, who had to work for wages, and substantial peasants, who had surpluses to dispose of. Rents, reckoned and often paid in money, were older than the oldest manorial documents; while wages were seldom paid wholly or entirely in kind. In order to pay rents the peasants had to sell their produce; and whenever wages were paid in money the wage-earners presumably spent them at the market. Indeed an unbiased student of medieval agriculture cannot avoid the conclusion that social existence in medieval villages would have been impossible without some market and some trade.

This conclusion is in the nature of things hypothetical, but it is sufficiently obvious to shift the onus of proof from those who assume some trade at all historical times to those who wish to deny its existence at any period of the historical, as distinct from the prehistorical, past.

2

In this sense medieval trade never 'arose'; but it undoubtedly expanded and contracted. During the six or seven centuries of its documented history the quantities of goods entering European markets grew and declined; and so did the area in which they circulated. But whereas the territorial scope of medieval trade is on the whole easy to trace on the

medieval map, the changes in the volume of northern trade are very
largely a matter of guess. So scanty is the quantitative evidence of medieval trade that it is not surprising to find historians still differing about
the scale as well as the chronology of economic growth. As late as the
eve of the first Great War they were still able to assume a trend which
closely corresponded to the distribution of the evidence. The paucity of
records of trade in the early Middle Ages was taken to signify the scarcity
of the trade itself, while the wealth of evidence in the fourteenth and
fifteenth centuries was taken to mean that trade had grown in the intervening centuries. In dealing with individual regions historians may sometimes have been unable to fit them into the general curve, but when it
came to the trade of Western Europe as a whole they invariably represented the course of commercial development as a line steadily rising
from the Dark Ages, when trade virtually disappeared, to the sixteenth
century when it flourished abundantly.

Most obvious of all appeared to be the starting point of the story. Historians could take it more or less for granted that the irruption of the
barbarians meant a complete break with the economic civilisation of the
Roman Empire. The trade of Rome died a violent death, and with its
demise, European economy sank into a 'natural' condition innocent of all
industry and exchanges. Under the late Merovingian kings the Germanic
societies were supposed to have moved forward far enough to acquire
some trade and the rudiments of a settled urban life, but the advance did
not become really rapid until the so-called Carolingian Renaissance.
Soon after, the trade may for a time have been held back by the Norman
and Saracen invasions and by the feudal anarchy of the ninth and tenth
centuries. By the eleventh century, however, the pressure at the frontiers
eased, and economic development and commercial expansion could be
resumed and continued without break till the age of the 'great discoveries'.

The line, thus drawn, is straight and continuous – too straight and continuous for the present generation of historians. It is no longer possible
to believe in the continued expansion of trade throughout Europe in the
closing centuries of the Middle Ages, and more will be said about this
later. There are also reasons for being doubtful about the beginning of the
story. The starting point of the old version has been assailed and, probably, destroyed by converging attacks from two co-belligerent, though
not necessarily allied, historical schools: Dopsch's and Pirenne's. Alfons
Dopsch and his followers, basing themselves on their own interpretation
of the literary evidence (principally Tacitus) as well as on recent archaeological evidence (principally the excavations in the Roman *Limes*), have
attacked both the notion of the primitive barbarism of the German invaders and that of the complete break with the material civilisation of
Rome. Dopsch found no difficulty in showing that in the 150 years be-

tween Caesar and Tacitus the Germanic societies had acquired most of the attributes of a fully articulated economic civilisation, including the use of coinage and the dependence on trade. He also discounted the accounts of the total destruction wrought by the barbarians upon the material fabric of the Roman countries in which they settled. Urban life in the older Roman towns had declined but had not wholly disappeared. The Merovingian age, having thus inherited some of the commercial life of Rome, carried it on until it merged into the ascending movement of the Carolingian age.

But for this assumed continuity between the Carolingian and the Merovingian ages, Pirenne's view of Merovingian trade is not much different from Dopsch's. He also found it easy to show that the economic life of the Roman provinces in Western Europe continued uninterrupted, even if impoverished, throughout the Merovingian age. Commercial relations with the East persisted; Syrian merchants and their goods circulated throughout Europe; and Marseilles still remained Europe's doorway into the Mediterranean and the Levantine world. A break did occur in the end, but according to Pirenne it took place not at the outset of the Dark Ages, but in the Carolingian epoch. In the eighth and ninth centuries Saracen invasions and Muslim domination in the Mediterranean broke Europe's commercial links with the South, while in the North, economic life – including urban life in general – dwindled and declined under the stress of Viking raids and conquests.

The difference between the two points of view is thus largely focused on the exact role of the Carolingian age, and to that extent has not yet been fully resolved. The weight of the argument, however, appears to be against the theory of a violent break in the eighth and ninth centuries. The commercial links with the East and the traffic of costly luxuries may have suffered from the Muslim conquests and from the general insecurity of the times. But economic activity – settlement, colonisation, agricultural production – continued to expand; and in the history of European trade, economic activity within Europe mattered more than ease of communication with the outside world. For it has already been shown that northern trade was more dependent on the production of Northern Europe itself than it was on the conditions in the Eastern Mediterranean. The recurrent periods of disorder and anarchy during the Norman raids may have interfered with economic activities of every kind, but recent evidence from the north of France suggests that the ruin and devastation which the Norman invasions brought with them did not break the continuity of urban life in places like Arras. On the British side, the accumulating evidence points not only to the early development of trade across the Channel but to its continued functioning throughout the Dark Ages.

Yet, whatever is the final verdict on the Carolingian 'break', there can be little doubt about the continuity of development between the fourth and the seventh centuries. In Europe no violent break had intervened between the centuries officially Roman and those officially Barbaric, and there is equally little doubt that from the end of the tenth century onwards trade, like economic life in general, entered upon a period of rapid and general expansion.

(2) *The growth*

1

The course of medieval trade from the tenth century onwards can be traced both in its changing volume and in its expanding geography. From both points of view the trade grew until some time in the fourteenth century. The volumes of medieval production and of trade were on the increase, but quantitatively considered expansion was not its only significant feature. During this period northern economy was, so to speak, formed, for it was then that its separate regions, its trade routes and its commercial connections, composed themselves into a single trading area. In addition, throughout this period the trading area gradually spread eastwards and ended by absorbing the whole of Central and Eastern Europe.

The expanding volume of trade was a part of an economic process so general and so all-embracing that its story is easier to tell as an episode in the history of population and agriculture than as part of a narrower history of trade. For it was in agriculture and settlement that the signs of expansion were most obvious. In countries like England, where from the beginning of the thirteenth century onwards manorial documents can be made to yield something in the nature of statistical evidence, the growth of output can be traced for at least a century. But here and there, as on the estates of the bishopric of Winchester in 1209, production at the beginning of the thirteenth century already stood so high that the historian cannot fail to discern behind the later figures the dim outlines of an earlier increase stretching far back into the eleventh century and beyond.

The impression is greatly reinforced by what can be learned about settlement and population all over North-western Europe in the eleventh, twelfth and the thirteenth centuries. England and the continent west of the Elbe were rapidly filling up. In England the comparison of the population data in the Domesday Book with that of the manorial surveys of the twelfth century and the early thirteenth century, and of the latter with the Hundred Rolls of 1279 and the later manorial documents (rough and ready as such comparisons are bound to be), will show agricultural holdings multiplying manifold, and areas under cultivation growing apace. French evidence, mostly monastic, from Burgundy, Normandy and elsewhere in the tenth and eleventh centuries, German evidence from the Rhineland, Westphalia, Lower Saxony and Holstein; and, above all, the evidence from Flanders, tell the same story of growing population and expanding cultivation.

By the turn of the twelfth and thirteenth centuries the process had gone far enough for the surplus population to break out of the confines of what was now an old and relatively over-populated land and to spill over into new 'colonial' lands east of the Elbe. Here and there – as in Artois in the late eleventh and twelfth centuries, Flanders in the late twelfth and thirteenth, and possibly in parts of Champagne at the turn of the twelfth and thirteenth, and parts of westernmost Germany in the thirteenth – population was so abundant as to seek a solution to its economic problem in general industrialisation. It will be shown later that this period saw the rise of most of the great regional industries – that of cloth in Artois and Flanders, and probably Champagne; that of metal goods in Cologne, Liège and Dinant; that of iron and coal, lead and tin, in England, Hainault, Eastern France and South Germany. But even in those parts of Europe, which did not industrialise during this period, the towns were receiving great and ever-growing reinforcements from the surplus population of the countryside.

This was indeed the time when the whole of Western Europe became urbanised. Towns large and small sprang up all over the continent; most of them, whether old or new, grew fast throughout the period. In Flanders and in North Germany surviving topographical evidence, chiefly early maps, has enabled students to lay bare the main stages of urban expansion in the Middle Ages and to show how growing settlement added suburb to borough and repeatedly burst through successive girdles of urban fortifications. Elsewhere, and more especially in England and Central France, the evidence of urban growth is less direct, but is none the less convincing. In the rural records of the time, as well as in its literary sources, the town figures as the place of opportunity to which the villein might flee in search of freedom and wealth. That in most of the greater towns of the eleventh, twelfth and thirteenth centuries opportunities were more or less unlimited is indirectly borne out by the prevailing freedom of immigration – a freedom which was not to be regulated and restricted until much later in the Middle Ages.

2

Growing production, both agricultural and industrial, and increasing population were bound to lead to greater trade and are sufficient to account for its expanding volume. Other favourable developments, more purely commercial and more directly involved with the processes of trade, may also have made their contribution; and one of them – the influx of bullion – may have played an important and certainly a conspicuous part. Increasing supplies of precious metals and their expanding circulation, may at times have influenced the prices of commodities (and more about this will be said presently). Now and again they may also have influenced agricultural and industrial investment, and may thereby have given a further stimulus to both prices and production.

Recently, historians have laid special emphasis on the part which gold played as a means for the settlement of international accounts. It was Marc Bloch who first drew attention to the part which gold played in commercial exchanges between East and West, and it was he who first connected the main phases in the early history of international trade with the redistribution of gold in the world. Other students have supplemented Bloch's thesis and tried to show how dependent was the trade of the Roman Empire on Rome's ability to pay for eastern supplies in gold. In the last two centuries of the Empire supplies of gold dwindled away and Rome's purchasing power in the East declined; yet in the early centuries of the Merovingian era enough Roman gold was still available in the West to make it possible for the Frankish society to make some use of the as yet open channels of travel and commerce with Byzantium and the Levant. With the Muslim conquests, however, the world supplies of gold were radically redistributed. The Muslim conquerors acquired both the accumulated stocks of precious metals and the monopoly of supplies of newly mined gold. Starved of gold, European commerce with the East languished, and its *malaise* continued until the tenth century. It was not until the turn of the millennium that Muslim countries began to import slaves, metal goods, timber, and other commodities of European origin in quantities large enough to change the direction of gold movements. Eastern gold entered again into circulation, trade between West and East was resumed, and through it the whole economic life of Europe revived.[16]

This thesis, however questionable in detail, has been supported by a certain amount of evidence and frequently accepted as a working hypothesis. Yet, even if it were fully borne out by further researchers, it would still be insufficient to account for the evolution of northern trade. The commercial currents directly dependent upon supplies of gold were those which flowed to and from the Eastern Mediterranean. They doubtless

---

[16] M. Bloch, in *Annales d'Hist. Econ. et Sociale* (1933), 4 ff. M. Lombard, ibid. (1947), 143 ff. In England the issue of 1343 is generally regarded as the first effective gold coinage in the Middle Ages, even though gold coins had been minted some hundred years earlier by Henry III.

touched economic life in the North at many points. Northern and Western Europe as a whole may now have enjoyed (if 'enjoyed' is the right term) an active balance of trade, with the result that gold was now coming into many a country producing raw materials. Italian florins and ducats and perhaps Byzantine and Arabian gold coins now augmented the local resources of currency – mostly silver – and gold coinage began to be minted. But more important than the Italian supplies of Levantine and Byzantine gold was the real wealth which growing commerce generated. Much of it found its way into the hands of merchants all over Europe and could now be invested in industry and trade. Its chief beneficiary was doubtless Italy and, more especially, its great commercial cities, but from there radiating circles of investment and prosperity reached the outlying countries of medieval Europe, and it is doubtful whether any part of the continent escaped their effects altogether.

Yet, the effects on the trade of Northern Europe could only be indirect. The opening of the Levant added relatively little to the demand for raw materials and manufactured commodities of European origin (metal goods being the chief exception). Slaves were the commodity which was most in demand in Islamic lands in the early Middle Ages and which, if we are to trust some recent studies, was mostly responsible for starting and maintaining the flow of gold from the East. But the traffic in slaves touched the economy of Northern Europe at very few points, if at all. In the Dark Ages, i.e. between the seventh and eleventh centuries, the trade was largely in the hands of Jews and Syrians who took their 'cargoes' across Russia, Poland and Western Germany to Spain and countries farther east. Here and there they may have formed commercial *nuclei* within Europe: we are told that Verdun was an entrepôt centre of the slave trade, and it is possible that merchants resident there took part in the traffic. But from the point of view of Western Europe generally, this was merely a transit trade skirting the outer fringes of its territory and leaving behind very little oriental gold. Later, from the eleventh century onwards, other commodities of European origin, such as cloth (and furs!), found their way east, and raw materials imported from the North went into the making of the Italian goods exported to the Levant. Yet the total quantities of continental goods thus exported were as yet barely sufficient to redress the entire balance of Europe's trade with the Muslim world and to support the commercial prosperity of the North.

Did the crusades make much difference? The idea that the crusades were a turning point in the history of European economy is one of the most cherished notions of economic history; and so also is the belief that having conquered the Holy Land the northern world proceeded to help itself to the wealth of the Levant. How true it is and whether true at all is a problem which more properly belongs to the history of Mediterranean trade. The repercussions of the crusades must however be mentioned here, even if the mention can only be of the briefest and vaguest.

An economic history of the crusades has not yet been written, but until it has been written and the economic balance of the crusades has been struck, it will be difficult to say whether their consequence was to augment the flow of gold from Italy and the Levant to the continent of Europe, or on the contrary to drain the continent of its precious metals. Most probably the trickle of gold frequently changed direction, and at times contrary movements cancelled each other out. The occupation of the Holy Land may, to begin with, have brought in booty and ransom, and so must also have done the sack of Constantinople in 1204. On the other hand, ransom sometimes had to be paid and booty yielded. Similarly, crusading expeditions more often than not set up a drain on the western means of payment. The countries which sent them out financed them with levies and taxes; crusading nobles raised funds at home in many and various ways, but mostly by loans on which they could draw abroad. These methods of financing must have helped to mobilise the hoarded reserves of gold and silver, and thus indirectly to quicken the circulation and to influence prices and economic activity in general. Yet they must also have depleted the total supplies of gold in Northern Europe, since they sent precious metals moving away from continental Europe towards Italy and the Levant. Ecclesiastical taxation in support of the Latin kingdoms, the voyages to the Holy Lands, the military and religious activities of the Templars and the Hospitallers, must all have acted in the same fashion and added to the continental debit balance with Italy and the East.

This does not of course mean that the crusades did not stimulate the economic development of Europe, but the stimulus, such as it was, must have come from factors more general than the mere importation of bullion. If Northern Europe felt it at all, it must have received it in the course of ordinary trading activities of the Italian merchants and through their expanding commercial and financial operations. In this revival bullion played its part, but it did so not by virtue of its function in international accounts, but as a result of its internal circulation and investment. And here again the Levantine current was a mere tributary, and probably a small one, of a far more abundant flow. Although Italians brought into Champagne, Flanders and England a certain amount of gold, mainly of their own coining, the bullion most in circulation was not Levantine or Byzantine and not even predominantly Italian. What is more, it was not gold.

Throughout the Middle Ages, and more especially in their earlier centuries, the precious metal most commonly used in coinage and in everyday payments was silver. The coins of Northern Europe until the second half of the thirteenth century were all silver, and continued to be predominantly silver until the end of the Middle Ages. The evidence of mints, such as the accounts of the royal mints of England and the surviving registers of urban mints and exchanges, makes it quite clear that silver formed the bulk both of existing stocks of money and of the new accretion of metal. Gold and gold coins were relatively more common in international dealings presumably because gold was more convenient to transport and also somewhat more stable in value. In addition gold coins had the advantage of being as yet few – mostly Italian – and therefore free from the curse of variety and heterogeneity which afflicted the silver currencies of Europe. For these and other reasons, in clearing accounts of Italian merchants at the Champagne fairs of the thirteenth century as well as in commercial dealings of Italian merchants in other parts of Northern Europe, payments were apt to be reckoned in gold coins. Similarly, royal debts to Italian bankers in England and France were frequently reckoned in ducats and florins. Yet there is no evidence that the Italian bankers in fact delivered equivalent sums in gold cash, and there is unmistakable evidence that loans reckoned in gold coins, such as the Frescobaldi loans to Edward I and the Bardi loans to Edward III, were often made and repaid in silver and in goods. And in international payments between merchants of other nationalities active in Northern Europe silver pounds and marks, English and Flemish, were most commonly used both as units of account and of payment. So even if it remains true that gold figured prominently in international payments it did not displace silver even there.

The bullion in circulation was thus predominantly silver, and it is very probable that the amount of silver circulating in the twelfth and thirteenth centuries increased. How large the increases were cannot be said with certainty, but it is obvious that the increases came from several sources. Some new silver doubtless originated from mines recently opened up. Although silver must have been mined in Europe throughout the Dark Ages, the main sources of European silver, in Hungary, in Saxony, in the Harz mountains and elsewhere, were not fully developed until the tenth, eleventh and twelfth centuries. Mines, however, were not the only and may not even have been the chief source of additional silver, for even in the earlier centuries of the Middle Ages the volume of currency depended not only on the additions of newly mined metal but also on the uses of accumulated stocks of bullion. For it appears highly probable that the economic changes of the twelfth century set into motion a great deal of wealth previously immobilised in hoards, plate or ornaments. And that the bulk of the bullion thus 'de-hoarded' must have consisted of silver is clearly brought out by the evidence of wills and mint accounts.

· So whether any came in through the early medieval contacts with the

Levant, or during the crusades, imported bullion could not be held responsible for the revival and growth of medieval trade. Some of the other monetary factors were more important, but even they were not and could not be decisive. Their influence on trade would normally be transmitted through changes in price levels; yet even changing prices had a limited effect.

3

The problem of prices is, in Italy at least, closely involved with that of monetary circulation. We know now that during the earlier centuries of the Middle Ages, i.e. before the thirteenth, some prices changed a great deal. From the very moment at which documentary references to them become at all frequent, i.e. from the late twelfth century in England, and from the middle of the thirteenth century abroad, until the first quarter of the fourteenth century, food prices appeared to move steadily upwards. The English prices alone have so far been assembled for the earlier period. The work of collection and tabulation is as yet far from complete, but Thorold Rogers and later Lord Beveridge's team of archivists and historians have been able to analyse their data in a manner which enables a statistical trend to be traced.

Expressed in percentages the prices of 1150 were about 30 per cent of those in the first quarter of the fourteenth century; in other words the price rise in the intervening period was about three-fold. The price rise did not, moreover, begin in 1150, and, as far as the scanty evidence suggests, it went beyond that date. In so far as the meagre data of South-western Germany collected by Lamprecht can be trusted, it suggests a progressive rise in prices from the eighth and ninth centuries to the tenth and eleventh, continued, though not so violently as in England, to the early thirteenth. Yet even Lamprecht's figures show a rise of at least 50 per cent between the second half of the twelfth century and the first half of the thirteenth.[17] (Table 4.1.)

This was a veritable price revolution. Yet, in considering its economic effects, it is important not to argue by analogy with price revolutions of later centuries. For reasons which will have to be mentioned again more than once, the effect of price changes could not have been very general or widespread.

Agricultural output was bound to react to a secular rise in grain prices so steep and continuous, but its reactions may have differed from region to region. In the wine- and wool-growing areas of Europe, where the rural economy was one of cash crops, and even in certain areas pre-

---

[17] K. Lamprecht, *Deutsches Wirtschaftsleben im Mittelalter*, II, 512 ff.; esp. tables, etc., on pp. 612–13.

dominantly arable, such as parts of Western and Northern France and above all Southern England, estates continued to be run as large units producing mainly for the market, and even peasants marketed a considerable proportion of their output. And where the proportions to be sold were high, rising prices must have favoured and stimulated both output and sales. Indeed, the social historian of English agriculture cannot escape the conclusion that the high prices of the late twelfth and thirteenth centuries and the commercial boom in agricultural produce were to some extent responsible for the continued survival of the large-scale units of agriculture.

TABLE 4.1   *English wheat prices, 1160–1939*[18] (twenty years' means)

Period	Wheat price in shillings (per qr)	Wheat price in grains of silver (per qr)
1160–79	1.89	534
1180–99	2.60	744
1200–19	4.33	1082
1220–39	4.19	1047
1240–59	4.58	1144
1260–79	5.62	1404
1280–99	5.97	1491
1300–19	7.01	1734
1320–39	6.27	1547

To this extent the agricultural boom left its impression on European trade. As cultivation of cash crops expanded, larger quantities of agricultural products came on the markets; as rural wealth grew, opportunities for miscellaneous trade widened. Thus far the effect of prices is clear enough. What is not so clear is whether regions where the bulk of agricultural production was in the hands of peasants were equally affected. And it is not known how far industrial commodities, industrial raw materials and industrial regions were directly involved in the price changes. Historians do not even know how the prices of non-agricultural commodities moved, if they moved at all. Evidence is very scanty and difficult to interpret. Such as there is, suggests that prices for commodities like cloth and iron goods rose less steeply and less continuously than food prices. Prices for some commodities like coal and timber may even have fallen.

It is thus probable that price movements of the twelfth and thirteenth centuries were not 'general' in the sense in which the term is sometimes employed to indicate more or less simultaneous and synchronous shifts

18 Cited by the courtesy of Lord Beveridge.

in the price levels in all the main groups of commodities. If so, the probability is that such changes as there were were not due to monetary causes. Not only the influx of foreign gold but even the far more important supplies of silver and the still more important changes in its employment and circulation, could not have been the prime movers in the great economic transformation of the period – a transformation of which the expansion of trade was merely a part.

There is no need, however, to end the discussion of prices on this agnostic note. For even if the price movements fail to establish bullion's responsibility for the commercial efflorescence of the age, they can still reveal the action of other and perhaps more effective causes. More especially, steep and continuous changes in food prices unaccompanied by similar changes in other prices make it more or less certain that the relative costs of agricultural production were rising, and this again indicates a growing pressure of population against land.

This is not the place to discuss general problems of medieval land and population; in so far as they are relevant to the history of trade they will be discussed again in a later section. Here it will suffice to note that all available evidence, especially for France and England, shows land rents, land prices, and entry fines rising on a scale fully consistent with the hypothesis of 'pressure of population'. In this way the discussion of prices merely brings the argument of this chapter to the point at which it digressed to gold and monetary causes. Trade grew because Europe expanded. The lands of continental Europe carried an ever-growing population; growing population, in its turn, meant that agricultural production increased, that industries developed and that whole regions became industrialised. And growing wealth of rural Europe and economic specialisation of its regions meant bigger and better trade.

(3) *The professional merchant*

1

Growth quantitatively considered was by no means the only important change in the history of medieval trade in its age of expansion. It was accompanied by other phenomena, less material, and more obviously related to the condition and behaviour of men.

One of them was the extension of professional trade. In general, the part which full-time merchants played in economic life, very insignificant to begin with, was becoming more important as time went on. Doubtless, some professional trade there must always have been. We are told of the Syrian and Jewish merchants visiting Gaul at the dawn of the Merovingian age, and probably forming in the predominantly rural societies of

Western Europe alien *nuclei* of resident merchants, not unlike the Jewish towns and townlets in the eastern states of nineteenth-century Europe. A travelling Jewish merchant of the eighth, ninth and tenth centuries arriving in Western Europe from the East counted on finding there his coreligionists with whom he could trade, live and pray. When we are told by Gregory of Tours that, on his entering into Orléans, King Guntram was welcomed in Syrian, Latin and Hebrew, the presumption is that in the sixth century these were the native tongues of the merchants of Orléans.

Yet be it noted that merchants whose tongue was Latin were not altogether absent from the rudimentary communities of merchants. Evidence of indigenous merchants is scanty but is not altogether absent. We may know little about Philo, the merchant, whom Ausonius knew, or about Euphron of Bordeaux or about Eusebius of Paris, both mentioned by Gregory of Tours – their names like their age still appear to belong to Rome. But from the seventh century onwards evidence of merchants wholly indigenous becomes more frequent and more certain. In the seventh century King Dagobert founded the Fair of St Denis which Franks, Frisians and Saxons (Anglo-Saxons?) frequented; in the same century we hear of Frankish merchants travelling into the lands of the Slavs and Avars.

Some of the indigenous merchants were doubtless men of substance, like Christopher of Tours, who, we are told, speculated in the wine of Orléans, but in the main they must have been small fry, travelling hucksters of foreign wares. Their stock-in-trade must have consisted almost entirely of the small luxuries required on the medieval estates and villages: spices, silks, and other exotic fineries. For when it came to the buying and selling of agricultural commodities or of industrial articles locally produced, the services of the merchant were not always necessary. In medieval Europe, as in agricultural areas of our own day, the average producer was able to dispose of the petty surpluses of his household (eggs, cheese, hens, vegetables, milk, cattle and even grain) without the assistance of a professional trader. Similarly, wherever an industry happened to be organised in small handicraft units and goods were made in small quantities or to order, producers and consumers could deal with each other without the intervention of a trader. Not only the village smith and potter, but the urban butcher, baker and candlestick-maker themselves disposed of their produce. Even in the later centuries of the Middle Ages the distinction between craftsman and trader remained a very nebulous one, and men commonly traded with goods they themselves produced.

Merchantless trade, moreover, was not confined to transactions which were purely local. Manorial produce often travelled over long distances, and manorial trade in the early Middle Ages was sometimes in the hands of manorial officers themselves. Some of the larger estates were sufficiently large, and the quantities of marketable commodities which they produced were sufficiently great, to enable them to do their own selling, though perhaps it would be rash to assume that they always did so. Historians have made great play of the monastic *negotiatores* of the early Middle Ages, who were trade representatives of monastic houses selling their output in distant markets and sometimes making there the necessary purchases for their communities. The term *negotiatores* must not however be taken too literally. Some of the *negotiatores* were monks and manorial officials, but some may well have been professional merchants acting in the name of monastic houses and under their protection, just as the 'king's merchants' of the English kings of the thirteenth century traded under the protection of king's letters, but in a manner and on a scale wholly professional.

Much more important were certain other forms of non-professional or not wholly professional commerce, and most important of all was the commercial activity of certain semi-rural communities. There was nothing to prevent the members of the fishing and seafaring communities of Zealand and the Rhine estuary from venturing far away from their homeland in pursuit of markets and goods. The sea could not by itself provide for all their needs, but it enabled them to go anywhere they pleased in search of customers and supplies. Similarly, the fiords of Norway could neither feed nor occupy all the population throughout the year, and there was nothing to prevent the free Norse peasants from roaming the seas and visiting foreign lands. In this way a great deal of trade could be conducted all over Europe by men who were, so to speak, part-time merchants.

There was thus a great deal of non-professionalised commerce: rather more in the early Middle Ages than later. Indeed, what historians sometimes describe as the period where medieval trade 'arose' may merely refer to the time when conditions favouring part-time trade disappeared and a professional merchant class spread.

Some such unprofessional commerce could of course be found even in the later Middle Ages. Monastic communities acted as traders whenever and wherever they happened to derive their income from large and regular production of marketable commodities. The English wool-growing monasteries of the twelfth, thirteenth and fourteenth centuries not only sold their wool clip regularly to foreign exporters but often undertook to supply them with *collecta*, i.e. wool they themselves bought up from the surrounding countryside. We can also find English landlords dabbling in wool trade in every century of the Middle Ages; squire and squireen of Gascony taking a hand in wine trade, landlords on both sides of the English channel – in Devon as well as in Brittany – maintaining ships for piracy and trade. Similarly, seafaring communities of Zealand, Holland, Normandy and Brittany continued to combine a little trade and occasional piracy with their main occupations of fishing and shipping.

Broadly speaking, however, conditions in the later centuries were less favourable to part-time commerce than they had been at the dawn of the Middle Ages. In a number of medieval towns production of some commodities soon outstripped the potentialities of the local market. Cloth of the principal cloth-making towns of Northern France and Flanders, metal goods of the towns of Western Germany – to name only two most obvious instances – came to be made in large quantities for the distant and unknown demand; and whenever this happened the petty producer could not market his output, and the services of a merchant intermediary became unavoidable.

Still more significant and less obvious were the similar developments in the countryside. Feudal society and feudal law soon made it impossible for the average members of a rural community to combine agriculture with trade, while the passing of the large-scale demesne economy removed the *raison d'être* for the manorial *negotiatores*. In England it is possible to lay bare in the records of the wool trade the process whereby the social changes in wool-growing areas called forth a new merchant class. As the number of small sheep-farmers grew, so professional wool merchants interposed themselves between wool growers and wool exporters. The history of the grain merchant and fishmonger has not been investigated as fully as that of the wool merchant; but it seems more than probable that a similar connection was also to be found there.

2

The development of trade as a whole-time occupation played its part in the rise of towns. The story of the towns, their appearance and growth, does not belong to this chapter. Growth of towns has so far been mentioned as evidence of the general expansion of medieval economy, and need not be mentioned again except in so far as it was linked with the social transformation of trading activities. For so linked it doubtless was. Most historians are now agreed that the towns multiplied and grew in the two centuries following the tenth, for the simple reason that trade grew. Yet the logical and historical connection between growing trade and emerging towns is by no means an inevitable one. The Norsemen proved capable of engaging in active trade without towns; it is not at all certain that Dorstad and some of the other places mentioned as centres of Frisian trade in the seventh and eighth centuries were towns in the medieval and modern sense of the term and not merely clusters of fishing and seafaring settlements. At the very close of the Middle Ages most of the English wool trade was in the hands of merchants living in the country, and the bulk of cloth industry was in the hands of men who combined spinning and weaving with some agricultural pursuits and lived in what still were essentially rural habitations.

Indeed as long as industry and trade could remain part-time occupations and be in the hands of men who were also peasants, fishermen, landlords or monks, there was no need and little opportunity for commercial and industrial towns. The reason why at the height of the Middle Ages towns became necessary and indeed inevitable was not merely that trade expanded, but also that conditions of feudal society made it difficult for the expanding trade to remain in the hands of the rural classes and to be combined with other rural pursuits. At a time when life and all its vocations had become wholly professional, when war and government had become the exclusive occupation of the landlord and the freeholder, and when agriculture had become the whole-time occupation of the semi-servile peasant, trade had to become equally professionalised. Gone were the times when farmers from Norwegian fiords, fishermen of Frisia, and monk procurators of monastic estates or privileged officials of the Carolingian estates were able to run all the trade there was. Trade was becoming to an ever-increasing degree the affair of whole-time merchants and artisans trading in a professional way.

The effect on towns was obvious. In order to be professional and to conduct trade all the year round merchants and artisans had to be exempt from the ties and liabilities which restricted the liberty of movement and freedom of contract of the lower orders of feudal society. Their houses and tenements with their shops had to be free from the obligations which burdened the rural tenures; their transactions had to be judged by a law better suited to dealings between merchant and merchant than were the feudal custumals and common law. Hence the essential function of the medieval towns, as non-feudal islands in feudal seas; and hence their appearance in large numbers in the eleventh century – the time when trade grew and feudal order matured. Hence also the crucial part which the charters of privilege (which were nothing else than guaranteed exemptions from feudal order) played in the origin and development of towns. Charters of this kind created boroughs out of villages, and cities out of castle suburbs; and charters of this kind punctuated the subsequent progress of urban communities on their way to full urban status. The rising town was thus essentially a political and legal phenomenon, even though it served an obvious economic function.[19]

---

[19] This argument is not affected by the well-known fact that agriculture continued to play a part, often an important part, in the economic activities of smaller towns. However agricultural the small town was, what differentiated it from the regions purely rural was its nucleus of traders and artisans.

3

The argument is obvious enough, yet it may at first sight appear to clash with what historians have recently discovered about the social history of the early medieval towns. The growing volume of historical studies of the so-called patrician families suggests that the upper layers of urban society in the Middle Ages sprang from the families which happened to own land in the towns in the early stages of their history, and got rich as the rents and land values of town property rose. In detail the process may have differed from region to region, but in general, towns as different as Arras in the eleventh century, Barcelona in the twelfth century, and Lübeck in the early thirteenth seem to conform to the common pattern. In all of them political and economic power in the early phases of their history belonged wholly or in part to the urban landowners or their descendants. Indeed, so general and so obvious was the landed interest in medieval towns that a generalising sociologist like Sombart was able to base on it his entire theory of medieval capitalism and to find in rising land rents the chief source of the 'initial' capital of medieval industry and trade.

Stated in terms so general and so simple the theory may indeed be difficult to reconcile with the impression of the town as the seat of a professional merchant class. But was the history of the 'patriciate' in fact so uniform and so simple? In the first place not everywhere in Northern Europe was the citizen landowner a lineal descendant of the original owner of town sites. Some towns in the early Middle Ages had grown up on land belonging to their feudal overlords, whether kings or great feudatories. In some towns feudal landlords proceeded to alienate the income from urban property by sub-infeudation, by sub-letting and by outright sale of full property rights (burgage tenures in England, allodial tenements in France). But in some places, especially in the *Villes Neuves* of Western Europe – artificial foundations of a somewhat later age – the feudal founders sometimes retained the superior title to property as well as its income. In the English boroughs and in some towns abroad, e.g. Bordeaux, the freehold and burgess tenures of urban sites were as a rule shared among a whole number of manorial landlords of the surrounding countryside: a fact which stimulated several German and English lawyers, and Maitland among them, to propound the famous garrison theory of borough origins.

Wherever the land was in feudal hands, and as long as it stayed there, the rising profits of urban landownerships largely by-passed the burgess inhabitants. Yet even in towns, where in the twelfth century the burgesses owned or otherwise held most of the land, they did so not so much by succession from the original landowners as through later investment. The famous history of the market of Lübeck, as expounded by Rörig, may indeed prove that the great Lübeck families had all sprung from a narrow circle of men who had taken part in the founding of Lübeck and owned the sites of the market place. But the same history also makes it clear that the urban landowners of Lübeck had come from merchant families of Westphalia and that their venture into landownership was merely an investment and part and parcel of their great commercial speculations beyond the Elbe.

Altogether the distinction between investment in trade and investment in land in the early medieval town can be drawn too rigdly. Not only did investments in land and urban rents come naturally to medieval merchants, but the reverse process – the investment into trade of wealth mainly derived from urban rents – was equally common and equally easy. Commercial partnership serving the purposes of investment had been known to European law since times pre-medieval. The sleeping partnerships of the *commenda* type were the general practice in Italian towns in the eleventh century; and the life of St Godric, which will be mentioned again presently, shows that the commercial partnerships were an established practice in eleventh-century England. And commercial partnerships, especially of the 'sleeping' kind, made it possible for urban wealth to be employed on a large scale in foreign trade, even if it happened to be derived from land.

Indeed this employment of wealth in speculative ventures to distant lands was more characteristic of the leading figures in medieval towns than their connection with land. If we are to trust Pirenne, the typical representatives of North European trade in the eleventh and twelfth centuries were the men he calls 'early capitalists', but who should be described more exactly as merchants trading abroad on a large scale. The trace they left in records is very faint, but here and there Pirenne was able to discern behind the fog and silence of early sources the fleeting shadows of the early capitalists. In one instance he was even able to draw a full-scale portrait of a merchant engaged in far-flung speculative trade. Godric, a trader of East Anglia at the turn of the eleventh and twelfth centuries, began as a beachcomber, became in the fullness of life a substantial merchant and a member of a partnership, and ended his life by becoming a saint and inspiring a *Vita*.

In this the merchants of this age differed both from the class of small pedlars from which some of them must have originated and from the more sedate and less adventurous burgesses who were to dominate the trade in a later age. They were not primarily interested in the daily trade of the local market, and their indifference imprinted itself on the very economic character of towns. As long as they formed the governing group, the economic and social policy of the town itself was one of expansion, free immigration and relatively free trade. Our direct evidence of free immigration and free trade is of course very scanty: perhaps because it is in the nature of free trade to leave behind scanty traces in documents. But had settlement and local trade been as restricted as they were to become later, towns and town population could not possibly have grown as we know that they did. For growth and expansion was the hallmark of the age.

(4) *The moving frontiers*

1

The expanding and professionalised trade also had obvious geographical and political implications. Indeed, the economic geography of medieval trade and its involvement with international politics have been studied more fully and are understood better than almost any other aspect of the subject. For, unlike the other aspects of the history of trade, the story of moving frontiers and of emerging trade routes is compounded of war, politics and exploration, and has therefore been well illuminated by fully documented events. No wonder historians of trade have given them so much attention.

The attention, however, has been by no means unwarranted, for the political and geographical features of medieval commerce were not only conspicuous but also important. As trade increased and declined and as new regions were opened and old ones decayed, the whole balance of power in Northern Europe altered. Nothing indeed proves more the essential function of inter-regional commerce in medieval life than the part it played in the rise and fall of European principalities or in their political, military and naval power.

The purely political implications of economic geography are perhaps most obvious in the opening phase of medieval trade. The one geographical feature of North European trade in the Merovingian and early Carolingian period which historians take more or less for granted is its withdrawal from the world economy of the Roman Empire. The fall of Rome meant that in the sixth century Gaul, Brittany, and Rhineland no longer stood in the same relation to each other and to the rest of the world as three centuries previously. The economic links with Italy and the Mediterranean were not altogether severed, but the trade was undoubtedly becoming more localised. At the height of imperial prosperity, i.e. in the second century, the Empire formed an economic system dominated by the needs and policy of metropolitan Italy. Needless to say, there were exchanges between the provinces and within each province taken separately, and it is a mistake to think that even at the height of the imperial era all roads led to Rome. Yet, broadly speaking, the main currents of Roman trade formed a co-ordinated system, to which each province made a distinct and sometimes a highly specialised contribution. This system began to disintegrate in the closing centuries of the Roman era and was all but gone in 473.[20] In the course of the fifth and sixth centuries, movements of inter-regional trade, such as there were, conformed ever more to the shifting needs and opportunities of the different northern regions and ceased to form part of an imperial network or to be dominated by imperial merchants.

Here are a few examples. In the third and fourth centuries Britain exported foodstuffs to feed the Roman legions on the Rhine. In the Merovingian age the exports to the lower Rhine did not cease – for all we know they may have grown – but they were dominated not by the needs of the Roman legions but by those of the population of the Rhineland and they now probably consisted of metals and cloth, both of which in the imperial times used to be taken elsewhere. Another example is the North Sea fisheries. At the height of the imperial era Roman merchants conducted from Utrecht an active fish trade between the delta of the Rhine and the more southerly provinces of the Empire. In the Merovingian times fish continued to be exported, but it now went in many other directions, including that of France and South Germany, and was carried by local merchants. Similarly, Flemish, Frisian and possibly English cloth, which may previously have been used to clothe the Roman legions, was now carried, among other places, to Scandinavia.[21]

2

This picture of northern trade, grown more local and directed away from the centres of the Empire, is wholly compatible with what we know of the activities of the Syrian merchants and the continued imports of oriental goods into Marseilles. What Syrian merchants and the port of Marseilles handled were probably the exotic goods of the orient. The trade which was now becoming local and separate was the trade in the bulky and essential goods which was the northern trade *par excellence*; and such network of inter-regional exchanges as was now emerging was woven, not by Syrian merchants, but by other and more local groups of intermediaries.

Of these intermediaries, the earliest and the most prominent were the

[20] See F. W. Walbank, 'Trade and Industry under the Later Roman Empire in the West' in *The Cambridge Economic History of Europe*, vol. II, ed. M. Postan (Cambridge, 1952), pp. 76–85.

[21] In Pirenne's view this orientation would not presumably take place until the eighth century. Cf. F. Vercauteren, *Civitates de la Belgique Seconde*, 451–2.

Frisians. They owed their importance to the geographical opportunities as well as to the geographical limitations of their land. Frisia stretched along the coast of the North Sea from the estuary of the Sincfal (now Zwin) to the estuary of the Weser. It was relatively infertile, but its network of navigable rivers opening into the sea, and its well-sheltered channels between islands, fitted it well for fishing, navigation and water-borne trade. Within it, the point which gathered to itself most of the commerce was Dorstad on the old estuary of the Rhine: a place of great renown, the 'city of forty churches'. Whether it in fact was a great city or merely a conglomeration of fishing and trading villages is a problem which archaeologists will have to decide, but irrespective of its topography, it was important enough to stamp itself upon most references to Frisian trade. Later, especially in the ninth century, it rapidly lost its importance, partly through its destruction by the Normans, but chiefly through the change in the bed of the river from its old arm to the Waal. When this happened, the town of Tiel on the Waal took Dorstad's place, though in the process some of Dorstad's trade and much of its political importance may have passed to Utrecht.

From these centres, and from the delta of the Rhine as a whole, an entire network of routes radiated in every direction: to England, to Gaul and Western Francia, to Scandinavia and the Baltic. When we read in a seventh-century sermon, such as Bede's, that London was an emporium of trade housing many foreign merchants, we have to think in the first instance of the Frisians, for Bede expressly mentions Frisian merchants in another place. In most references to foreign trade and foreign merchants in the eighth and ninth centuries the Frisians invariably figure. Liudger, a visiting Frankish ecclesiastic of the eighth century, mentions Frisian merchants in London, and so does Alcuin.

We know much more about their trade to the South. Their main point of entry into Western Francia was Quentovic (near modern Étaples), from which they visited Rouen, Amiens and the interior of Western France. Certain records of the first half of the eighth century show them active at the fair of St Denis, which was at that time the most important internal market in France. But most of their commerce to the South probably flowed along the Rhine. Down the Rhine they shipped corn and wine from Alsace; up the Rhine they took their cloth, fish and other goods to pay for the corn. They established settlements in the chief Rhenish towns, in Cologne, Duisburg, Xanten near Düsseldorf, Worms; but Mainz was probably their most important destination. The town was well placed at the junction of the Rhine route with the routes which came from the South and the South-east, and there the trade of the Danubian plain and the Black Sea region entered the commercial currents of Western Europe.

Even more ancient, if not more abundant, were their trade connections with Scandinavia. Archaeological and literary evidence points to the immemorial antiquity of Scandinavian trade. This trade was largely in the hands of Scandinavians themselves, but in one period some of it was in the hands of the Frisians. A ninth-century *Vita* of St Anscarius, a priest engaged in missionary work in Denmark and Sweden, reveals by a number of accidental details the commercial activities of the Frisians. Anscarius apparently travelled with Frisian merchants to Schleswig and from there to Birca, the Swedish trading centre in the Baltic.

Such was the territorial scope of Frisian trade. Yet the part the Frisians played in it must not be misunderstood. They were its chief inter-mediaries, but they did not dominate it. The commodities they imported did not all stay in Frisia and did not even necessarily pass through it. Nor were they alone to serve the trade routes on which we find them. Though very active in the Anglo-Saxon trade, they did not dominate it to the exclusion of English merchants. Similarly, Frisians seem to have traded very actively to Western Francia, but we know that there was also direct trade between the Franks and their neighbours, and that some of this trade was in the hands of native merchants.

3

Even more independent and more important was the part played in the northern trade by the Scandinavians. In the economic history of the ninth and tenth centuries Norsemen left, if anything, deeper trace than the Frisians had done in the preceding period. In doing so they, like the Frisians, were largely impelled by the necessities of their geography. Like the Frisians, they had to seek their livelihood on the high seas and in foreign lands for the simple reason that their own land was unable to feed them. Here and there, in Eastern Denmark, in Southern Sweden, in parts of Southern Norway, men were able all through the Middle Ages to lead lives little different from those of agricultural communities in other parts of Western Europe. But elsewhere in Scandinavia society was of necessity made up of part-time peasants – men who lived on their farms part of the year and roamed the seas or navigated distant rivers the rest of the year.

Some of them went to sea as fishermen, others as robbers, adventurers, colonists and conquerors, still others went as traders; in fact, most of them were fishermen, traders and conquerors in turn. It is very largely as Vikings, i.e. as sea robbers and conquerors, that they appear in history textbooks, but economic historians meet them as traders long before their Viking expeditions began and long after they had ceased.

The Viking expeditions began in the first quarter of the eighth century, but archaeological evidence shows that there had been some trade between Scandinavian countries and the rest of Western Europe since pre-historic times. Even in the worst period of the Viking wars there was a great deal of purely commercial intercourse not only between the Viking setlements, but between Scandinavia and non-Scandinavian lands. The journey of St Anscarius, already mentioned, took place shortly after the reputed burning of Dorstad by the Vikings. Yet he travelled in a Frisian boat, and in Schleswig he met Danes who were apparently in the habit of going to Dorstad with purely pacific aims.

We must not therefore allow the tumult of the Viking era to obscure the story of common trade done in the ordinary way. The fact that it was both common and commonplace explains why so many of the contemporary sources pass it in silence. Our chief evidence of the raids are the sagas, and sagas were heroic stories about heroic men. Yet even in the sagas we find references to trade in its peaceful and prosaic forms. They sometimes refer to people who were merchants pure and simple, and also mention expeditions undertaken without any predatory aims. We also know that the Scandinavians built and navigated not only the swift assault boats in which they carried out their raids, but also the slower and roomier cargo boats for commercial traffic. It is indeed probable that some parts of Scandinavia specialised in trade to the exclusion of raiding expeditions. Thus the Gotlanders who traded with all the countries of Northern Europe did not, as far as we know, send out any identifiable Viking expeditions, even though we find them occasionally engaged in Nordic wars.

Thus considered, Scandinavian trade formed part of that network of commercial connections which we saw taking shape in North-western Europe under the leadership of the Frisians. In some respects, however, its part in North-western commerce was different from that of the Frisians, the Anglo-Saxons or the Franks. In the first place, the Scandinavian trade reached its highest point after the Frisians had begun to decline. In the second place, it far transcended in its range the older limits of northern commerce. In their voyages the Norsemen penetrated to Greenland and the coast of North America in the West, to the Bosphorus in the East; and while their western expansion was not of very great importance to European commerce, their eastern voyages were to have the greatest political and economic consequences. They forged a link between North-western Europe and the Baltic, and in addition they established important land routes across the continent of Eastern Europe.

The Baltic and the lands round it were until the eleventh and twelfth centuries well outside the scope of western commerce, just as they were outside the range of Germano-Latin Christian civilisation. But they were well within the range of Scandinavian contacts. The Scandinavians crossed and recrossed the sea on their way to the Baltic islands and from there to the Baltic coasts of modern Mecklenburg, Pomerania, Prussia and Livonia, and apparently maintained an active commercial intercourse with the inhabitants of these shores, Slavonic and Ugro-Turkish.

We know very little about the trade and navigation of the Baltic before the tenth century. There is little doubt that the Slav tribes inhabiting the Baltic coast had navigated the sea routes and traded by them. Jumne, on the Isle of Wollin at the estuary of the Oder, was the site of a Slavonic centre, and legend has preserved the fame of an ancient Baltic seaport on the same or a nearby site, the Vineta of the Slavs, the 'nobilissima civitas' of the chronicles, the reputed residence of great merchants and the repository of fabulous riches. Like the other legendary seaports, Vineta is said to have been engulfed by the sea, and, like the other *villes englouties*, it was reputed to toll its submerged bells in times of ill omen. Whether Vineta was in fact a town in the western sense of the word we do not know. Other towns of the Western Slavs depicted in the chronicles – Oppeln or Heithabu – were, we are told, little more than haphazard huddles of cabins made of wattle and mud. Nor can it be said with any certainty that Vineta was ever regularly visited by Scandinavians. It is, however, certain that, on the very border of the Slavonic East, near Lübeck, the Scandinavians possessed a trading settlement known to the chronicles as Reric, and that another settlement, Truso, sprang up not far from modern Elbing in West Prussia. But of all the towns and settlements they established on the fringes of the Slavonic East, none was more famous or endured longer than Novgorod. Novgorod the Great, the ancient city on Lake Ilmen, guarding the western terminus of a trade route from the Baltic to the interior of Russia, had drawn Scandinavian traders to itself since very early times, possibly since the eighth century, and we know of a Scandinavian settlement there in the tenth century.[22]

Scandinavian penetration into Russia did not, however, end with Novgorod. Before the eighth century was out the Scandinavians under Rurik established themselves as rulers of the 'Russian' tribes. Both before and after their conquest of Russia they regularly crossed and recrossed the great Eurasian plain en route to the East. Starting from the Baltic they went up the Neva and the Great Lakes, recrossed the Central Russian watershed by dragging their boats after them, and then sailed south and south-east by the rivers flowing into the Black and Azov Seas. Byzantium was their goal, and there they served as mercenaries, traded

---

[22] N. Vogel in *Hansische Geschichtsblätter* (1935), 181; idem in *Festskrift* in honour of Professor Koht; cf. F. Rörig in *Hansische Geschichtsblätter* (1933), 22 ff.

as merchants, and at least once pillaged the great city itself. But Byzantium was probably not the only eastern land they touched. We do not
know whether they themselves penetrated into the trans-Oxian region of
Baktria or into the trans-Caspian provinces of Persia. But they must at
least have touched upon the fringes of the Asiatic steppes and traded with
the Khazars and the Bulgars of the middle and lower Volga.

In this way the Scandinavians provided an economic link between
Northern Europe and the lands farther east – a link which became more
important after the direct maritime connections with the orient had been
severed in the eighth century. And this part they continued to play for
several centuries. They were still active in the Russian, Polish, and
Livonian centres in the twelfth century, still visited Utrecht in the
second half of the same century and the east coast ports of England in
the thirteenth century. But by that time their trade had already been overshadowed by the commercial activity in other parts of Europe, and before
long it disappeared altogether under the weight of the rising German
tide.

4

The time when the Scandinavian fortunes began to sink and the German
flood rose to engulf them coincides with the beginning of the most rapid
phase in the expansion of European economy and trade. The story of the
expansion between the eleventh century and the thirteenth has already
been told. So has also been the role of the Italians in starting it and in
maintaining its momentum. Yet in spite of the Italian stimulus and the
part they were beginning to play in the internal trade and finance of most
continental countries, the two trading areas – the northern and the
southern – remained more or less distinct. The great and growing exchanges between them were sometimes in the hands of the Italian houses
with branches in England and France and the Low Countries. But most
were carried on, so to speak, on the frontiers of the two areas – the places
where the Italians met the merchants of the North-west and where the
goods of northern origin and the Italian imports changed hands.

One of these frontier regions, at which the two commercial spheres
touched, was the region of East-central France, and in the first place
Champagne. The story of the great Champagne fairs will be told elsewhere. Here it will suffice to note that the reasons why Champagne
emerged in the twelfth century as the point of junction were to a large
extent political. Under the rule of the Counts of Champagne and Blois,
their country was one of the earliest in Europe to benefit from the feudal
peace which in the eleventh century replaced the feudal anarchy of the
preceding epoch. Its population and production grew. As now appears

probable, it acquired very early in the period a flourishing cloth industry.
But what favoured most its development as an intermediary was its convenient position at the intersection of ancient land routes leading from the
Mediterranean to the North German frontier, and from Flanders to
Central and Eastern France. Its ancient towns, Troyes, Langres, Rheims
and Laon were well placed at the focal points of the transcontinental
traffic and therefore provided convenient meeting places for the merchants of Italy and Provence on the one hand and those of Germany
and the Low Countries on the other. It was at these meeting points that
the great Champagne fairs sprang up in the twelfth century and developed in the course of the thirteenth century into veritable nerve centres
of medieval trade.

What made the confluence of trade in Champagne so important is
that the commercial currents which flowed into it had in the meantime
swollen into broad rivers. It will be impossible in this chapter to
describe them all, and still less to follow in detail their manifold courses.
Thus the southern stream – that which flowed from the Mediterranean
countries – was the most important of all, but its story is outside the
territorial scope of this essay. The western current, which issued from
the central and western regions of France, may be part of this essay's
subject, but it has been little studied and may at first sight appear to be
hardly worth studying. For it may be argued that so well-provided were
each of the main regions of Northern and Western France that they
were able to cover their needs from their own production and were not
dependent on foreign supplies or markets. This notion of international
trade as an occupation in which only poor countries need engage must
not, however, be taken too literally or indeed too seriously. The richer
provinces of France, perhaps because they were rich, had important
surpluses to dispose of. There was grain to spare in Picardy and Normandy, wine to sell in almost every province of Central and Western
France, wool in the uplands of Auvergne and the Cevennes, flax in the
north-west, and other specialised products of agriculture elsewhere. As
medieval countries go, France was a thicky populated country, and
early in her history cities of Roman pedigree as well as towns of more
recent origin began to attract large numbers of migrants from the
country. By the thirteenth century, Paris, with its 30,000 inhabitants, was
one of Europe's most important cities, and between the tenth century
and the thirteenth urban centres of more than local importance sprang up
everywhere – some of them, like Amiens and Orléans, were commercial
capitals of large provinces; others, like Rouen and Bordeaux, great river
ports or sea ports; others still, like Lille, Chartres, and Bourges, were
seats of textile and metallurgical industry; others, like Paris herself, were
all these things together.

A country so furnished could not remain a mere *congérie* of self-sufficient arcadias. That it in fact did not, is shown by such evidence of French trade as we have. The documents show foreigners visiting the fairs of Northern France – St Denis, Boulogne, Chartres, Compiègne – long before the fairs of Champagne rose to their fame. The ports of Northern France, Étaples (Quentovic) in the seventh and eighth centuries, Havre, Rouen, Barfleur and others in the eleventh and twelfth centuries, and countless other ports of call in the later centuries, figure prominently in the surviving records. In the English records the merchants of Amiens and Corbie importing woad are to be found among the earliest foreign visitors to London.

If, nevertheless, in the records of the Champagne fairs, the French current appears to be relatively unimportant, the reason for that is that by the end of the thirteenth century, when documents became abundant, commodities of other more highly commercialised regions (English wool, Flemish cloth) dominated the scene while France's economic connections with the outside world were beginning to suffer from the territorial conquests of Capetian kings and from the consequent industrial conflicts, war taxation and military operations.

By comparison, more abundant and better illustrated was the stream which issued from the North and the North-east. It was fed from a multitude of tributaries and, of the latter, one issued from a region which was itself destined to succeed Champagne as a meeting point of north and south.

This region was Flanders. Flanders, like Champagne, was unusually fortunate in its political beginnings. In the course of the Dark Ages different political fortunes befell the two halves of the Roman Belgica Secunda. The southern part, that of the lower Seine and the Marne, plunged into feudal anarchy early in the Carolingian era and was just emerging from it as it fell under the domination of the rising power of the French Capetians. The economic prosperity it enjoyed at the turn of the eleventh century under the French kings proved ephemeral, for as a border country on the very front line of the Capetian expansion, it was not too well suited for active industry or trade. Not so the northern part of the Belgica Secunda. By a fortunate accident the feudal fiefs and baronies of the South-western Low Countries were early in the tenth century assembled into a strong principality of the Counts of Flanders. Under their rule a large portion of the Low Countries, from Arras to Ghent, came to enjoy peace and order in advance of most other parts of Europe. And in the shelter of the Count's peace, arts could flourish, trade could prosper and towns could grow.

The geographical situation of the country was equally favourable. The country lay on the coast of the North Sea, open to sea-borne trade from almost every quarter; it was also cut across by navigable rivers, more especially the Scheldt, and was well provided with sheltered estuaries for harbours. Yet Flanders owes its industry as much to its geographical limitations as to its geographical facilities. While, under the shelter of Flemish peace, population grew, the yield of the land remained relatively small. The Flemings carried out a great work of internal colonisation, added polder to polder, erected dykes all along the coast and along the main water-courses. By the middle of the twelfth century they had acquired all over Europe a reputation as experts in land drainage, and their qualities – the Flemish system of reclamation, the Flemish freedom and the Flemish experience in organising new settlements – they carried with them at the invitation of German princes into the new lands beyond the Elbe. Yet neither internal colonisation nor emigration could solve their population problem, and the solution was found where such solutions normally lie, i.e. in industrialisation.

By the middle of the twelfth century Flanders became the foremost – and possibly the only – predominantly industrial country in Northern Europe. The chief centres of its cloth industry, Ypres, Ghent, Douai, came to rank among the most important towns of Northern Europe. Together with the commercial port of Bruges which served them, they formed by the end of the century the four members – the Four *Leden* – of Flanders, which began to rival the political power of the Counts in the thirteenth century and were to challenge it in the fourteenth.

Flanders also possessed certain other industries and trades. But until the end of the fourteenth century none of the other occupations compared in importance with cloth, and cloth was also the mainstay of Flemish commerce. Cloth was also the magnet which drew to Flanders the merchants of the world and gradually helped to develop in Bruges another international mart, rival and eventual successor to the fairs of Champagne. Bruges' greatness was probably rooted in the function it fulfilled at the turn of the twelfth and the thirteenth centuries as the point of entry of English wool and of English merchants. Before long the Italians came there in search of English wool and English custom, but by the end of the thirteenth century the Germans had established themselves in Bruges as the chief exporters of Flemish cloth, the principal buyers of Italian imports and the chief providers of Eastern European foodstuffs and raw materials.

5

By that time the Germans had come to dominate the international economy of Northern Europe. The thirteenth was indeed their century, but their pre-eminence in the economy of continental Europe had begun to reveal itself at least a whole century earlier.

Eventually the range of predominantly German trade, like the area of predominantly German speech and culture, stretched from the eastern borders of North Holland and Lorraine to the heart of Central and later also Eastern, Europe. But its focus, especially at its beginning, was in the Rhineland and its capital. For in the course of the twelfth and the thirteenth centuries all the trade routes and all the cultural influences which radiated from the Rhineland – its architecture, its crafts and its mystic art – came to centre upon one town, and that town was Cologne.

The early history of Cologne is shrouded in a certain amount of controversy. There is no doubt that its urban nucleus had survived from the Roman era and that as an administrative centre and as an episcopal residence Cologne preserved some semblance of urban life throughout the Dark Ages. It may also have preserved its economic function, for it could boast of an annual fair in the tenth century and housed merchants and artisans much earlier. By the end of the eleventh century Cologne had already become an emporium of trade and industry. Its two fairs – one at Easter and the other in August – were already well established, and so also was its fame for wealth and power. Writing early in the twelfth century Otto of Freising could assert that there was not a town in contemporary Germany or Gaul as rich as Cologne; and Cesarius of Heisterbach, a Cistercian compiler of miraculous stories, spoke of Cologne in somewhat the same way in which New York used to be spoken of in European books. There was something in the very air of Cologne that made men rich.

Some of Cologne's wealth was derived from industrial products: textiles, mainly linen, cloth and thread, and especially metal goods. Its bells were famous in thirteenth-century Europe, and so were other products of its copper-beating crafts. One of Cologne's masters, Frederick of St Pantaleon, ranks among the greatest metal workers of all ages. Still, it is in commerce and not in industries that the mainsprings of Cologne's wealth will be found. Its main field was the Rhine valley itself. Owing mainly to the growth of the hinterland, the estuary, once the focus of European trade, now ceased to occupy this position. Most of the delta's trade now passed through Cologne and, in the end, came to be handled by Cologne merchants. At the beginning of the period the merchants of Utrecht appear to have traded along the Rhine on their own account, but eventually Cologne ousted its competitors and succeeded in appropriating to itself the bulk of the valley's trade. In the twelfth century we find its merchants active as far south as Austria and Carinthia and also in Augsburg and Regensburg – the latter a town which gathered into itself the economic threads of the Danubian region.

Needless to say, the lands along the Rhine valley itself were not the only region to which Cologne's commercial connections extended; just as the Rhineland with Cologne was not the only area to play its part in the commercial development of the continent. Another such area was Flanders itself. Much of Flemish trade was with England, France and Southern Europe, and in the early phase of their commercial expansion, and especially in the twelfth century, the Flemings appear to have frequented the markets of Cologne and also the upper Rhine and Saxony as far east as the Elbe. But in the course of the thirteenth century as the active trade of the Flemings died out, the Cologners gradually became the chief intermediaries between Flanders on the one hand and Central and Southern Germany on the other. For a time in the thirteenth century they even succeeded in penetrating into the Anglo-Flemish wool trade and interposing themselves between the English wool growers and the Flemish cloth makers.

Another similar area lay to the west of the Rhine, between the Rhine and the Maas. The trade of this region, which the Germans usually describe as Maasland, was founded on the industries of its towns: Huy, Namur, Liège and Dinant. Huy and Liège produced some cloth for export, but their chief industry was metals, and Dinant was especially famous for its metal goods.

Almost equally important was the activity and greater still the future potentialities of the regions to the East of the Rhine. The territory between the Rhine and the Weser, usually described as Westphalia, was a valuable source of agricultural exports and of metal ores mined in the south-east of the region. Yet it was not in the export of domestic produce and not in Western Germany that the historical destiny of Westphalia lay. Ever since Frankish times the region had served as a corridor to the lands farther east. Several important east-to-west routes crossed it, and none were more important than the famous *Hellweg* which began at Duisburg, went between the Ruhr and Lippe and passed the towns of Dortmund and Soest before crossing the Weser into Saxony. On this route were to be found the Westphalian towns which were to lead in the commercial development of Eastern Europe: and it was thanks to the men of these towns that Eastern European trade before long fell into German hands.

The eastern specialisation of Westphalia was largely Cologne's own fault. Faced in the west with the barrier of Cologne's power, the rising towns of Westphalia naturally turned to the as yet virgin fields farther east. And although the merchants of Cologne were as active in the east as the men of any other German town, they could not claim there that position of overwhelming economic privilege which they enjoyed elsewhere. It is therefore no wonder to find the Westphalian towns taking a leading part in the exploratory period of eastern trade and forming the earliest trading stations in the east. We find them also acquiring a lion's share in the work as well as in the profits of urban colonisation and town-building all over North-eastern Europe from Lübeck to Riga.

Some of what has been said about Westphalia applies also to the region immediately to its east, i.e. Saxony. Saxony, as the documents reveal it in the twelfth century, had for more than four centuries been part of the Holy Roman Empire and was now an integral part of the German homeland. Like Westphalia, it owed its first entry into the commercial system of Europe to its mineral resources, for by the late twelfth and thirteenth centuries the Harz mountains were rapidly becoming the principal mining area of continental Europe, the main source of copper and lead, as well as of precious metals. The industry was centred round Goslar, and the fame of Goslar as the capital of the mining industry outlasted, even if it did not outshine, its fame as the residence of the Saxon and Hohenstaufen Emperors. Yet Goslar was not the principal commercial town of the country, for the simple reason that in Saxony, as in Westphalia, the most flourishing commercial activities were those which led its merchants to the east. To this activity Saxony and its towns were especially suited. In the early Middle Ages, i.e. before it was wholly assimilated to the Empire, it lay across the German route to the east like a barrier. Now the barrier had become a corridor. Whereas in the opening centuries of our period – eleventh and early twelfth – the regular overland traffic stopped at the Elbe crossings – chiefly at Bardowiek, but also at Magdeburg and at a few smaller places – at the end of the twelfth and all through the thirteenth century the frontiers of German trade moved eastwards, and men from the border towns of Saxony took part in the movement and greatly benefited from it.

6

The eastward spread was indeed the most characteristic trend of the epoch. Its beginning can be traced as far back as the Frankish era. From about the sixth century onwards the civilisation of the Latino-German West began to expand into the continental interior of Central Europe; and, in consequence, the entire economic balance of the continent gradually shifted to the east. In the early Merovingian times the focus of the Frankish state and society was in Gaul, but in the sixth and seventh centuries it moved from the left bank of the Rhine to the right. In the centuries between the fifth and eleventh the lands between the Rhine and the Weser were being fast reclaimed and settled by the overflow of their own population, and by the time Charlemagne became Emperor, the eastern and more purely Germanic parts of his kingdom were able to supply him with the bulk of his power and of his armies. But no sooner was this transference completed than a still further move to the east began, and the Saxon lands beyond the Weser were laid open to Frankish conquest and assimilation. It has been argued that to the Franks the acquisition of Saxony was a military and a political necessity, for they had to subjugate the Saxons if they were themselves to be saved from being submerged by the next wave of Germanic invasions. Whether in fact Charlemagne's Saxon expeditions were nothing more than preventive wars we do not know, but we know that the Saxon lands had been an object of attraction long before they could possibly have become a source of danger. Their military conquest was well prepared by missionary activity and was itself preceded and followed by commercial ventures and trading settlements. Before long Saxony was wholly absorbed in the trading area of Western Europe, and by the beginning of the eleventh century it had itself become the starting point for a further leap in the same direction. This time it was the turn of the Baltic and of the Wendish lands east of the Elbe.

This final phase of the process was also its most important one. It began with the conquest of Slavonic lands which was led largely by princes, and it continued as a great enterprise in settlement and colonisation. And long before the work of colonisation ended it brought fundamental change into European, and, more especially, German commerce. Urban colonisation by merchants and for commercial motives accompanied, and in some places even preceded, rural colonisation by knights and peasants. Not all the Westphalian merchants in search of Slavonic markets and sources of supply stopped at the line of the Elbe. As often as not they themselves ventured into the interior of the Wendish lands, and now and again penetrated into the Baltic region. With the permission of the Slavonic princes they began establishing trading stations all along the main routes leading to Novgorod and Smolensk, which were the two main points of entry into medieval Russia. In Schleswig, the starting point of the Scandinavian sea-route to the Eastern Baltic, Westphalian merchants possessed something in the nature of a factory in the early twelfth century. At the next stage of the same sea-route, at Wisby on the island of Gotland, they established themselves at about the same time. But from the point of view of subsequent history, the most significant of their trading factories was the one they apparently built up very early in the twelfth century, or even at the end of the eleventh century, at the Slavonic town of Lübeck. Profiting by the liberality of the Wendish prince, they formed there a permanent settlement at least as early as the twenties of the twelfth century. But in the late thirties Adolph of Holstein conquered the land and burned the city, and in 1143 the new Lübeck, this time a purely German town, was founded.

Lübeck was to be followed by other new towns. In the extreme north-east the German merchants founded at the very beginning of the thirteenth century the town of Riga, henceforth the centre of their trade in Livonia. By the end of the twelfth century the trading settlement in Wisby grew to turn the entire town into a German port and strong-point, and at the opening of the thirteenth century the town of Hamburg rose to match Lübeck at the eastern foot of the Jutland peninsula.

Of this first generation of new German towns none could rival Lübeck. It soon drew to itself the trade which had previously gone overland to Bardowiek, replaced Schleswig as the chief starting point for sea journeying across the Eastern Baltic, established itself in the fisheries of Southern Scandinavia and of the island of Rügen, and in the rising trade with Bergen and the interior of Sweden. By degrees the old overland routes as well as the old Scandinavian sea routes fell into desuetude, and the bulk of the trade with the east was forced into the channel which ran along the south coast of the Baltic and across the foot of the Jutland peninsula – the channel which Lübeck served and dominated.

This first generation of new German towns was soon followed by another and a larger crop of secondary formations. Lübeck, the first daughter town of the Westphalian cities, in itself became a generation or two later the 'mother' of other eastern towns. Immediately to the east, as to the south-east, it helped to found the towns of Schwerin, Wismar and Rostock, and a number of smaller towns. At the farthest east there sprang up Riga's sister towns of Dorpat and Reval and the chief towns of Prussia (but not yet Danzig). The whole chain of German towns sponsored by the Westphalian towns and Lübeck was practically completed by the end of the thirteenth century.

These new towns had a double function to perform. In the first instance they connected the lands of the west with the sources of Slavonic goods: furs, honey, pitch, tar, timber and rye. This was essentially a Baltic trade, and Russia was its chief source and market. The second function was to serve as an outlet for the goods of the newly colonised lands. Bremen and, above all, Hamburg collected corn from the regions of the Weser and the Elbe, and exported it to the west. Lübeck and Hamburg became the centres of the fishing industry of the Western Baltic, the salt trade of the Elbe, and the forest goods of Brandenburg. Somewhat later the Prussian towns of Marienburg, Elbing, Thorn and Königsberg, and later still Danzig, became the outlets for the corn and timber trade of Prussia, Lithuania and Western Poland.

7

To Northern Europe as a whole, and to the German lands in particular, the rise of the eastern towns and of the great route on which they stood was of profound, almost of revolutionary, importance. It transformed the whole composition and direction of northern trade. The industrial nations of the north-west and especially Flanders were now offered markets and new and very abundant sources of essential supplies. England, hitherto dependent on Scandinavian timber, began to import large and ever-growing quantities of Baltic wood. She also began to buy, sometimes for her own use, sometimes for re-export, quantities of Baltic grain. Other sylvan products – pitch, tar, potash, as well as furs and wax – now came from Eastern Germany, or from the Slavonic lands tapped by the Germans. Flanders, hitherto fed by the corn supplies from Northern France and Southern Germany, was now beginning to be supplied by Baltic grain. The Germans were also able to take food to Scandinavian countries previously dependent on imports from Britain.

All this brought wealth and power to the East German towns and marked the final stage in Germany's commercial rise. Their hold over East European markets, foodstuffs, and raw materials, also made them welcome and even indispensable all over Northern Europe. They won predominant power in Scandinavia, great economic influence in the Low Countries, important privileges in England. Before long, economic power was buttressed by a political organisation, and the German towns combined into the great naval, military and political union of the Hanse.

With the formal establishment of the Hanse the eastern expansion of North European trade can be said to have been completed, and a new and a different chapter in its history began. For, paradoxically enough, the official founding of the Hanse in the sixties of the fourteenth century was not so much a further step in German expansion as a manifestation of an entirely new phase in the history of European trade and of German power. It marks the end of eastward expansion – indeed of all expansion – and a new period in the economic history of Europe.

III.   THE AGE OF CONTRACTION

(1)   *The depression*

1

The great commercial expansion did not continue into the late Middle Ages and was not destined to merge without a break into the ascending economic movements of the sixteenth century. In some parts of Europe it slowed down; in others it ceased altogether. Historians will therefore be justified in regarding the two closing centuries of the Middle Ages, the fourteenth and the fifteenth, and more especially the second half of the former and the first half of the latter, as a period of arrested development, and even in speaking of a 'secular' depression succeeding the 'secular' expansion of the earlier centuries.

The contraction, like the expansion which preceded it, is easier to diagnose than to measure. Reliable figures capable of forming comprehensive statistical series are almost as rare in the records of the later Middle Ages as they are in the records of the twelfth and the thirteenth centuries. In England alone were national customs accounts kept in the later Middle Ages, and enough of them have survived to provide a broad statistical background to the history of English foreign trade. But even the English customs accounts are more complete and more reliable for some periods than for others. The figures for the fourteenth century are less comprehensive than those of the fifteenth and are not available in consecutive or comparable series except for wine, wool and cloth. The latter have been tabulated by Professor Gray in annual averages for two-yearly periods at intervals of about a decade. The fifteenth-century figures have been fully analysed elsewhere. The two series are shown in Tables 4.2 and 4.3:

TABLE 4·2   *Exports of wool and cloth from England in the second half of the fourteenth century (annual averages)*[23]

Years	Wool (sacks)	Broadcloths‡
1353–5	—	3,040
1355–7	—	7,485
1357–60	35,840*	9,346
1366–8	26,634†	14,593
1377–80	21,627	15,449
1392–5	19,359	43,072

* 1357–9 – 2 years.
† 1367–9.
‡ The figures in this column slightly underestimate the total and slightly exaggerate the rate of increase, for they do not include worsteds and other cheap cloths of the same kind which were relatively more important in the early period.

The figures tell their own tale. The only exceptions to the record of decline were the short-lived boom in the value of miscellaneous exports and imports in the mid-thirties of the fifteenth century which probably reflected the high cost of imports during an acute economic conflict with the Hanseatic League; and above all the high level of cloth exports throughout the period. The latter were rising throughout the second half of the fourteenth century and mounted with exceptional rapidity between

23 These figures have recently been corrected and supplemented in E. Carus Wilson, 'Trends in the Export of English Woollens in the Fourteenth Century', *Economic Hist. Rev.* III, no. 2, 1950, but the general trend they exhibit is the same.

1380 and 1395; but from the high point they then reached they soon descended to an average of about 30,000 broadcloths, round which they fluctuated for some 25 years. In the two decades of active trade with Central and Eastern Europe following the, so-called, Vorrath treaty with the Hanse in 1437, the exports of cloth rose well above the average and exceeded 50,000 cloths, but in 1448 they fell again to their pre-1437 level and remained there until the last quarter of the century. (Table 4.3.)

TABLE 4.3 *Exports and imports of dutiable commodities in England, 1399–1482 (annual averages in 3-year periods)**

Years	Exports of wool (sacks)	Exports of broadcloth	Imports of wine (tuns)	Exports and imports of miscellaneous merchandise paying poundage (values in £)†
1399–1402	15,023	27,760	—	—
1402–5	10,864	24,502	6,237	60,887
1405–8	14,221	29,315	6,220	187,439
1408–11	14,393	30,718	13,696	150,368
1411–14	14,447	25,108	12,113	124,313
1414–17	14,131	29,488	17,063	136,683
1417–20	14,778	28,366	10,975	145,192
1420–3	13,893	36,359	5,168	135,994
1423–6	13,959	42,665	3,591	109,049
1426–9	15,437	38,417	6,821	129,420
1429–32	9,749	40,641	8,940	119,691
1432–5	8,294	39,693	9,950	146,754
1435–8	2,353	40,814	6,097	113,275
1438–41	9,101	56,097	10,509	127,221
1441–4	9,776	55,976	11,748	130,452
1444–6	9,279	52,482	12,275	106,168
1446–8	7,654	53,699	11,000	121,795
1448–50	8,412	35,078	9,432	91,456
1450–3	7,660	38,928	7,424	91,001
1453–6	9,290	37,738	6,826	82,533
1456–9	7,664	35,059	4,072	59,089
1459–62	4,976	31,933	4,190	65,503
1462–5	7,044	25,855	7,074	57,449
1465–9	9,316	39,664	5,942	93,942
1469–71	7,811	27,610	3,411	53,421
1471–6	9,091	43,129	4,729	115,475
1476–9	7,502	51,889	6,887	120,333
1479–82	9,784	62,586	6,927	179,340

* 1444–6, 1446–8, 1448–50, and 1469–71 are computed in 2-year periods; 1465–9 is a 4-year period, and 1471–6 a 5-year period.

† The figures do not include miscellaneous exports by Hansards.

For other parts of Europe there is little statistical evidence beyond a few figures of local imports and exports or occasional series of measurements reflecting the movements of the more important trades. The best known of the former are probably the returns of the Hanseatic *Pfundzoll*, a tax on sea-borne trade levied by the principal Hanseatic towns in the second half of the fourteenth and in the fifteenth centuries. Unfortunately, the returns have not survived in a series sufficiently consecutive to reveal a convincing trend; and with the exception of the Lübeck figures for 1368–9, they have not yet been presented to historians in a wholly usable form. The longest of the series so far available, that of Hamburg, suggests that the sea-borne exports and imports rose from 250,000 Lübeck marks in 1362 to 374,000 in 1371, and then dropped to 336,000 in 1400.[24] But the figures may well exaggerate the rise and underestimate the fall in Hamburg's trade, for the *Pfundzoll* was frequently imposed in times of strained international relations and sea war when a great deal of traffic, which would otherwise have gone through the Sound, sought the greater security of the overland route through Hamburg.

On the other hand, the evidence of individual trades covers a range of commodities and places so wide as to make up for the paucity of more general measurements. And though little of it is statistical in the narrow sense of the term it is sufficiently full and varied to reveal the main economic trend.

2

The trend and the facts from which it emerges may appear to be primarily concerned with agriculture and industrial production rather than with trade. But the distinction must not be pressed too hard. In an earlier section heavy emphasis was laid on the predominance in North European trade of products of European industry and agriculture. Where facts make it appear very probable that Europe's production declined, or at least ceased to grow, there is every justification for concluding that commercial exchanges must also have slowed down or stagnated.

Naturally enough, the evidence of agricultural production is most copious, though also most difficult to interpret. Superficial signs of agricultural crises abound in the records of the fourteenth and fifteenth centuries. Wars were more frequent and more continuous than at any other time since the tenth century; great pestilences visited Europe in 1348–9 and at least twice again in the second half of the century. Crops, buildings, equipment, as well as the agricultural calendar, were bound to suffer, and production was bound to decline. In addition, rural economy was undergoing a process of readjustment which may, for a time, have reduced the level of both agricultural production and of trade.

Arable cultivation contracted everywhere, but on large units, and

[24] W. Stieda, *Revaler Zollbeicher*, lvii ff.

especially on 'demesne' farms of great estates, the contraction was most rapid. Such demesnes as still functioned in the fourteenth century in various parts of France were wound up in the course of the late fourteenth and fifteenth centuries. In England, where the demesne farming had survived to a far greater extent than anywhere else in Europe, the transformation was most radical.

The contracting acreages of the demesnes must not of course be used as an accurate index of agricultural decline. Yet even if corrected and heavily discounted, they still bear witness to a general recession. By no means all the lands lost to the demesnes were acquired by tenants; and there is every sign of poorer lands, whether on the demesnes or on lands anciently in the possession of tenants, gradually going out of cultivation. Theoretically, as areas contracted the yield per acre or per man should have risen; but even if this happened in the fifteenth century (and there is no evidence to show that it did) the total output was bound to decline.

What is more, a smaller proportion of the output was now drawn into the main stream of inter-regional trade. The dwindling of demesne farming signified also the decline of commercial production. No doubt, in this country, some large-scale units continued to be run by substantial tenant farmers, but in general peasant tenancies increased and multiplied at the expense of large units of commercialised agriculture; and peasant landholders must have consumed a far greater proportion of their produce than the quasi-capitalist owners of the demesne farms.

Thus on the thirty-two manors of the bishopric of Winchester at the beginning of the thirteenth century some 1750 quarters of wheat were sold, nearly all outside the manors. This amounted to 48 per cent of the gross output and 82 per cent of the 'net' output (after deduction of seed). When a century later the yields, i.e. the 'net' output in relation to seed sown, became considerably higher, the proportion of sales to gross output also rose to 70 per cent. On the six Wiltshire manors of the Duchy of Lancaster at the very beginning of the fourteenth century, the 'net' output of grain of all kinds (including some 75 quarters bought but excluding some 525 quarters of seed) was about 1330 quarters, while the sales amounted to 1208 quarters: indeed the output was so large that it must have included a carry-over of old grain. On the Wiltshire estates of Lord Hungerford, on which demesnes functioned until the middle of the fifteenth century, sales of grain reached similar proportions. On the Hungerford estate of Winterbourne-Stoke in 1448, 97 quarters out of the 'net' output of 112 were sold.

No such sales could be expected from peasant units, however commercialised some of them were. A little calculation, indeed mere common sense, will show that at a time when on the holdings of the peasants of the top rank – the virgaters – the area under corn in any year averaged about 15 acres per household (in Cambridgeshire at the time of the Hundred Rolls of 1273 the area sown annually by an average peasant above the rank of cottar was 7 acres) and when the yield of wheat, allowing for seed, was no more than eight bushels per acre, the marketable surpluses of an average peasant household were small. So even if the extent of cultivated land had remained the same, the change-over to peasant agriculture would inevitably have reduced the amount of grain available for sale, and with it the total volume of grain trade.

Hence also the reduced scale of inter-regional traffic in grain. The evidence of urban food supplies leaves the impression of a trade shrinking in volume and sometimes restricted in its range. We are told that in the late Middle Ages London was drawing its supplies from a much smaller area than earlier and had become more or less dependent upon the agricultural surpluses in the Home Counties. There is also some evidence to suggest that the grain supplies of other important English towns were becoming not only smaller (this could also result from decline in the town population), but sometimes also more local. Hence the growing preoccupation of towns with their food supplies and with the grain stocks: a preoccupation which overshadows the urban policies of most of the greater towns on the continent.

At first sight, no such shrinkage could be observed in the grain trade of the Low Countries, where the sea-borne supplies from the distant Baltic appeared to assume an even greater importance. Yet a shrinkage there must have been. It is quite possible that Baltic imports into the Low Countries grew in importance merely because the French sources of corn supplies had been running dry. The exports from the valleys of the Somme and the lower Seine, though by no means exhausted, were not, and could not be, as abundant as they had been in the middle of the fourteenth century. Anglo-French war, the English occupation of Normandy and Picardy, the choking up of river traffic by tolls, were bound to interrupt the flow; and there were also other signs of a more general agricultural depression. It was not therefore an accident that in some years in the fifteenth century we find the Norman towns importing grain from the Baltic; and the records have preserved an accidental report of a whole Hanseatic grain fleet arriving in the estuary of the Seine in 1450.

In some of these examples Eastern Germany and the other Baltic regions figure as the only examples of unfailing bounty. Did then the grain production and the grain trade of Eastern Europe escape the depression that prevailed elsewhere? To some extent they probably did, since they still continued to yield marketable surpluses large enough to feed Holland and Norway and to keep the great east-to-west trade flowing. But even if the flow never ceased it was probably not as full as it had been in the middle of the fourteenth century. Comprehensive statistics of the Hanseatic grain trade do not exist; such figures as we have are largely confined to the evidence of the grain deals of the Prussian Order, which are both incomplete and misleading. But all indirect evidence points to a slump in the fortunes of German agriculture throughout the greater part of the fifteenth century. An interval of at least a century separated the high-water mark of agricultural expansion in Eastern Germany in the fourteenth century from the outburst of large-scale commercial agriculture on the *Rittergüter* in the sixteenth century. During that interval, the map of Brandenburg, Pomerania, Mecklenburg and Prussia became covered with abandoned holdings, deserted households and depopulated villages, all pointing to the economic tribulations of peasant agriculture. But large-scale units of production were also going through a period of economic difficulty, for labour was getting scarce and dear, and grain was falling in price. Before the century was out landlords sought and found a remedy in *Bauernlegen* – a policy whereby peasants were deprived of land and forced to work on the estates. But the movement did not get under way until the very turn of the fifteenth and sixteenth centuries. From 1400 to 1475 – these are approximate dates – the landlords found their old prosperity going and the new prosperity not yet arrived. Would it therefore be too fanciful to conclude that if in that century Baltic supplies in the West still appeared as abundant as ever it was not because supplies had grown but merely because the demand had shrunk?

For there is little doubt that the demand for grain in the main consuming areas was shrinking. On some of the main inter-regional markets, those of the greater towns and of the principal industrial areas of Northern Europe, the numbers of inhabitants declined. The process was of course more complex in detail than it may appear on a broader view. Yet for all its complexity, it leaves little room for doubt about its effect on the grain market. The demand for grain apparently receded in the main consuming areas, and it must also have receded on the innumerable local markets throughout the length and breadth of Europe.

The importance of the local demand must not be underestimated. In chapters dealing with the earlier centuries attention was drawn to the large proportion of marketable foodstuffs which went to feed the villagers, manorial servants and artisans who did not possess enough land to cover their needs out of their own production. This class included agricultural labourers, rural artisans and smallholders of every type and size, and was always to be found in the countryside. It was, however, more numerous at some times than at others, and in most countries – certainly in Germany and England – this class contracted in the later Middle Ages. What with the steep decline of rural population and with the new opportunities for larger holdings on the lords' land and elsewhere, the numbers of landless or all-but-landless labourers in English villages fell out of proportion to the general decline of population. And as the numbers of wage-earners and smallholders sank, sales for local consumption must have dwindled.

It is because demand declined that the reduced production and smaller sales did not result in a chronic, still less a mounting, scarcity of food. Over the later Middle Ages as a whole, bread grains appeared more abundant than ever before. They were especially plentiful in the second quarter of the fourteenth century when prices fell more than 20 per cent below their level in the first quarter. Soon afterwards came the succession of bad harvests and low yields following on the great mortality of 1348–9; but this again was followed in England and abroad by the 'good seventies'. According to several continental chronicles, the harvest of 1375 was the best for fourteen years, and was followed by four years so good that according to an Alsatian chronicle, people were 'fatigued by the abundance'. In 1377 the prices of bread in England touched their lowest point for thirty years, and in 1395 in Strasbourg grain became so plentiful and so cheap that bakers replaced the 'standard' penny loaf with a halfpenny one. Bread was never to be quite so plentiful again, but periods of relative abundance occurred in various parts of Europe throughout the fifteenth century at intervals frequent enough to justify historians in regarding the whole period as an age of low agricultural prices. Above all, the first and third quarters of the fifteenth century in Western Germany, in the Low Countries, and in some parts of France and England, were times when supplies, relative to demand, were near their peak.

The recurrent phases of plenty raise problems closely linked with those of prices and will therefore be discussed again later; but they should be mentioned here if only in order to record a warning against a possible *non sequitur*. The decline of the grain trade and of arable agriculture could be accompanied by signs of abundance and must not be judged by them. On the other hand, in other branches of agricultural production the declining or stagnating output was not always matched by the decline in demand, and signs of abundance may be absent. Thus, for reasons which have not been fully accounted for, the supplies of foodstuffs of animal origin, and especially butter, were smaller in relation to demand than were the supplies of grain; and their values fell more slowly or even rose. Therein, however, lies a tale which properly belongs to another section of this chapter.

3

The category of animal products here discussed does not of course include

Europe's most important industrial material – wool. English customs figures make it clear that international trade in wool was on the wane. The tables 4.2 and 4.3 above will show that English exports, by far the most important in Western Europe and solely responsible for high quality wool imported into Flanders, Holland and Italy, declined from about 35,000 sacks per annum in the first half of the fourteenth century to about 8000 sacks in the second half of the fifteenth century. It would of course be wrong to ascribe the entire deficiency to falling production, for it is now well understood that in the meantime England had greatly increased her own cloth industry and consumed a greater proportion of her clip. Indeed so marked was the shift from foreign users to the English cloth-makers that until recently historians have used the figures of de-clining wool exports as evidence of England's rising cloth production. This argument, however, no longer holds good. H. L. Gray and others have shown that, at its highest, England's cloth production could not possibly have accounted for all the difference between the high level of wool exports in the middle of the fourteenth century and their low level in the late fifteenth.

TABLE 4.4 *Exports of wine from Bordeaux in the fourteenth century*[25]
(annual averages)

Years	Tuns
1305–7	95,650
1308–9	102,724
1310–11	51,351
1328–30	81,366
1335–7	45,315
1348–50	9,675
1352–8	19,681 (five years only)
1363–70	22,111 (six years only)
1372–3	14,373
1374–9	13,297
1379–81	7,842

Declining supply, as well as other difficulties of trade, also accounts for the confused and broken pattern of the wine trade. We know little about the fortunes of the wine exports of the upper Rhineland or of the Moselle, and hardly more about those of La Rochelle, but much more is known about the conditions in the southern and by far the most important wine area, that of Gascony. The region experienced not only the general economic difficulties of the age, but also the direct effects of military operations of the Anglo-French wars. At times only Bordeaux and its

[25] The figures of fourteenth-century wine imports have been derived from an article by Miss M. K. James, *Econ. Hist. Rev.*, n.s. IV (1951).

immediate surroundings escaped wholesale devastation. The toll of ruined vineyards has found faithful reflection in the statistics of four-teenth-century exports. The decline, interrupted for a while in the last decade of the fourteenth century, was resumed in the fifteenth. During the middle decades of the century, French occupation of Gascony led to a complete interruption of trade to England and all but deprived Gascony of its most important customer; and exports to England sank from the average of about 12,000 tuns in the thirties and forties (it was more than that at the beginning of the century) to less than 7000 in the fifties and sixties. It was not before the eighties of the fifteenth century that English merchants appeared again in force on the wine-market of Bordeaux and British imports of Gascon wine reached and passed their fourteenth-century volumes.

It is of course possible that the irregular and probably dwindling supplies of wine were in some parts of Europe compensated by increas-ing supplies of beer; for beer made with hops was the product of the Middle Ages in decline. From the middle of the fourteenth century on-wards it was brewed in ever-increasing quantities in most of the North German towns, above all in Hamburg, and also in towns of the Northern Netherlands. Historians do not, however, know enough about medieval consumption in different places and at different social levels to be able to judge to what extent wine and beer were true substitutes, and how far was beer merely ousting ales and other drinks of a humbler kind.

The light which the surviving records throw on the other branches of the victualling trade is equally uncertain and on the whole equally sub-dued. Enough is known about the salt trade of the Bay of Bourgneuf to suggest that here at least output and trade were growing in the fifteenth century. The documents, however, are not sufficiently continuous to report the effect of piracy and war in the forties and fifties, nor do we know enough about salt exports from other areas, e.g. Lüneburg, Zealand or South Germany, to be able to set the buoyancy of the Bay trade against the possible decline elsewhere. The evidence from the English salt areas suggests that there production was, to say the least, stagnating. The feudal farm of the main salt-making centres in Nantwich, North-wich and Middlewich, which was largely, though not wholly, made up of revenues of the salt-pans, fell from £168 in 1301 to £130 in 1347 and £90 in 1368. Indirect evidence – figures are lacking – suggests that production remained low for at least another century.[26]

A more general, even if an indirect, indication of a probable decline in international salt industry will be found in the vicissitudes of its chief customer – the herring trade. The great fishing industry of Skania was still active in the fifteenth century and was not to enter upon its final

[26] H. J. Hewitt, *Medieval Cheshire*, 118–19.

decline for another century or century and a half; but it was no longer expanding and was frequently depressed by war and by bad catches. In the good years at the turn of the fifteenth and sixteenth centuries as much was caught and salted as ever before. In Falsterbö, where most of the Skania fishing was then concentrated, at least 100,000 tuns (about 10,000 long tons) were salted in 1537, which was only about 20,000 tuns less than may have been salted in the same place in 1368. But in some years during the intervening period the catches and the trade fell to a mere fraction of the volumes of 1368 and 1537. The recurrent wars between the Hanseatic League and the Scandinavian kings and political friction with Flanders and England repeatedly interfered with both fishing and export. Possibly the fishing grounds themselves were beginning to show signs of wear, for there were complaints of bad catches in 1411, 1412, 1416, and 1425. In the late twenties, war, in interrupting both fishing and trade, proved to be a blessing in disguise, for with the return of peace yields recovered to reach their highest levels between 1432 and the midforties. In the middle of the century, however, complaints of poor catches became frequent again and continued at intervals throughout the period.[27]

This record of the fishing trade, if true, bears a striking resemblance to what was apparently happening in the great extracting industries of the time. More especially, the mining areas were now going through a phase which the old-fashioned economist would have described as one of rapidly diminishing returns. The symptoms were all local, and the complaint did not turn out to be permanent; but for the time being most branches of European mining were, so to speak, 'due' for a recession irrespective of what was happening at the same time in industry and trade in general. Sooner or later they were bound to pay the penalty for the rapid and cumulative expansion of the previous century and a half. For most of them the fourteenth and fifteenth centuries were their time of reckoning. By then seams became exhausted, or else had to be worked under conditions which were raising technical problems beyond the powers of medieval technology to solve.

From this point of view the most characteristic is the history of European silver mining. Exhaustion appears to have come over all silver-mining regions, secondary as well as primary. Derbyshire and Devonshire in England, Poitou and the Massif Central in France, and probably Sardinia in Italy petered out in the later Middle Ages; but far more striking and much more important was the decline of silver mining in its main centres, in Central and South-eastern Europe. The silver mines of Hungary had been exploited since the eighth century and reached full development in the twelfth and thirteenth centuries. The mining industry

[27] D. Schäfer, *Das Buch des lübeckschen Vogts auf Schonen*, xxxix ff.

of Saxony and especially that of Rammelsberg by Goslar, which since
the tenth century had been the principal source of European silver and
copper, passed the peak of its output and prosperity by the thirteenth
century. The highly important mining industry of Freiberg had risen in
the twelfth century and reached the furthest limit of its development by
the beginning of the fourteenth century; the development of the silver
mines at Meissen, in Tyrol, in Carinthia, and especially of the rich Transylvanian deposits and of the Bohemian mines of Iglau and Altenberg
was roughly contemporary; that of Silesia and perhaps Moravia somewhat later. But by the middle of the fourteenth century in nearly all
these regions the mining industry plunged into a depression from which
it did not climb out until the second half of the fifteenth century.
Water was the great enemy. The underground workings now reached the
strata exposed to the danger of flooding, and in spite of all the experiments and abortive attempts to deal with the underground water it was
not until about the late fifties that the experiments of Martin Claus of
Gotha solved the problem, and Saxon mining could be resumed on a
scale approaching that of the pre-crisis years.[28]

The vicissitudes of silver mining have been well recorded and well
studied. On supplies of silver the entire currency of medieval Europe
depended, and with them the price level was inextricably involved.
Historians therefore know more about silver than about any other branch
of medieval mining. It appears, however, probable that with the exception of iron most other medieval mining and metal trades went
through the same experiences as silver. Copper was mined in Saxony and
Hungary as a bye-product of silver and suffered a similar fate. The
copper production of Sweden, which was of more recent origin and had
developed relatively slowly, may have had a more even career. On the
other hand, the tin industry of England – probably the most ancient of all
the mining industries of Europe – contracted in the late fourteenth and
fifteenth centuries. At least once before the industry had been faced with
a similar prospect. In the early thirteenth century its ancient deposits
in Devonshire had been showing signs of exhaustion and the industry had
to move farther west to Cornwall. In the fourteenth century it was the
turn of the Cornish tin centres to suffer. The output fell from about 1328
thousand weights per annum in the thirties of the fourteenth century to
under 500 thousand weights in the mid-fifties. It recovered for a while

[28] See J. U. Nef, 'Mining and Metallurgy in Medieval Civilisation' in *The
Cambridge Economic History of Europe*, vol. II, p. 457; Bernhard Neumarn,
Die Metalle, Geschichte, Vorkommen, etc. *passim*; E. Reyer, *Zinn*, 6 ff.;
L. Lewis, *Stannaries*, 33 ff.; C. Neuburg, *Goslars Berghau bis 1552*, 55 ff., 78,
106; Ludwig Beck's *Geschichte des Eisens* is utterly unconcerned with quantities,
but the medieval section of vol. I (pp. 643 ff.) strongly supports the impression
of a general advance in the use of iron and steel in the later Middle Ages.

at the end of the century when it reached a very high peak of 1600 thousand weights per annum, but eventually it slumped again and stayed low – mostly below 900 thousand weights – for much of the fifteenth century. The output was not to reach and pass the figures of the pre-Black Death decades until well into the sixteenth century. The decline was not so clearly marked and did not appear to continue for a period equally long in the other important tin area, that of Zinnwald and Altenberg in the Bohemian mountains, but there too the rising trend was interrupted in the first half of the fifteenth century (the Hussite wars were mainly responsible), and production could not wholly recover until the seventies.[29]

The iron industry alone appeared to have escaped the depression. For one thing, it was more dispersed and more dependent on local conditions than other branches of mining. And it is also possible that the very disorders and wars of the time, which did so much to disturb industrial development elsewhere, stimulated the making of guns, cannon and miscellaneous weapons, and created what appears to be a mild war boom in the main iron-making regions. For in at least two main European sources of high-quality iron – that of Sweden and that of Bayonne-Bilbao – output continued at a level which did not sufficiently differ from that of the previous centuries to attract the attention of contemporary commentators. In most of the other important centres of the iron industry on the continent – even on the Lorraine deposits of the low-grade ore – the industry underwent in the second half of the fifteenth century a technical development – higher and better smelting ovens, greater use of water to work bellows and hammers – which suggests that the industry was expanding. How recent and how general this expansion was and how much it owed to war demand – all these are questions still awaiting an answer.

This catalogue of industries, sinking or just afloat, cannot be concluded without some reference to the most important of the medieval industries, that of cloth. This is not of course the right place in which to unravel its involved pattern in the later Middle Ages. If Europe is viewed as a whole, the later Middle Ages will appear as the time when cloth production both rose and fell. While it declined in Flanders and probably in France, it prospered in other places. In the fourteenth century the cloth industry of Brabant drew to itself some of the prosperity which seemed to be departing from Flanders. In the middle of the fourteenth century the English cloth industry made a sudden leap forward which brought it to its peak at the turn of the fourteenth and fifteenth centuries; in the fifteenth century the cloth industry of Holland, especially that of

[29] See Nef, op. cit., pp. 456–8.

Leiden, got under way. We are told that a number of smaller centres of cloth production came to the fore at that time. However, nothing less than a statistical inquiry could show whether the industrial activity in the new areas was sufficient to match the declining production of Flanders; and comprehensive figures are lacking. But judging from the falling supplies of raw materials, the cloth industry, and more especially the output of the high quality cloth for export, must also have declined. In Flanders, Brabant and Holland, by far the most important source of high quality wool was England, and English wool exports were declining.

4

The story of the cloth industry epitomises the entire history of commerce and industry in the later Middle Ages. The contemporary record of most other trades was equally broken and confused by local and contradictory movements. Regarded as a whole, European economy had its irregular rises and falls – what the economists call short-term fluctuations – which broke the continuity of the falling trends. Above all, the last quarter of the fourteenth century and the second quarter of the fifteenth were marked both in this country and abroad by signs of economic revival, however sudden and short-lived. Yet, on a broad view, European trade passed in the later Middle Ages through a trough long enough – sometimes longer than a century – to justify the diagnosis of a 'secular' slump.

There is now a broad agreement about the facts of the slump, but there is still much uncertainty about its explanation. Was the depression sufficiently 'general', i.e. common to a range of occupations sufficiently wide, to justify the assumption of a common factor? Some of the causes were undoubtedly accidental and contingent: misfortunes, local and temporary, which will be found in the record of every major industry and trade. The Hussite wars had their effect on Bohemian mines; Gascon campaigns disturbed the wine trade; Scandinavian wars interrupted the fishing and the curing of Skania herring; the Wars of the Roses may have interfered with English exports; and urban revolutions had their obvious effect on the Flemish cloth trade. All these were, so to speak, 'events': fortuitous happenings which sometimes coincided but were not deeply related. Some historians might therefore be forgiven for their reluctance to treat them as anything more than a series of accidents and coincidences.

Accidents and coincidences they doubtless were. Yet some of them, even if regarded in isolation, might on second thoughts appear to be not wholly fortuitous. It will not be too far-fetched to believe that the military and political conflict between the Hanse and the Danish kings was in fact due to the remarkable expansion of the Hanseatic interests in Skania fisheries and in Scandinavia in general during the previous century, or that the social war in Flanders was prepared by the previous century of industrial growth. Even less accidental and more obviously rooted in the expansion of the previous age were the seemingly un-related experiences of miners struggling in different parts of Europe against the difficulties of deep workings and against the mounting dangers of water. And in a field less purely economic, it is possible to interpret the gradual clogging up of important trade routes, described elsewhere, as a more or less inevitable consequence of the political regime which had gradually evolved in the later Middle Ages in the territories of France and the Holy Roman Empire: the solidifying of local custom in the former, the withering of central authority in the latter.

It is not, however, on these considerations alone that the hypothesis of a common cause rests. Much more important is the manifestation of cer-tain deep-seated factors similar to those which were responsible for the ascending movement of the earlier centuries. In the first place, there were prices. Just as the expansion of the twelfth and thirteenth centuries was accompanied by steep price rises all over Europe, so was the decline of the fourteenth and fifteenth centuries accompanied by price changes no less continuous, though possibly less spectacular. Some of these move-ments have already been mentioned; here they must be considered somewhat more closely. The series most easily available to the historian and most generally studied, that of grain, shows prices expressed in terms of stable exchange medium either falling or stagnating all over Europe. The 20-year means of English wheat prices collected by Lord Beveridge and his team of price historians moved in the manner shown in Table 4.5.

TABLE 4.5 *Annual wheat prices in the Low Countries*[30]

Years	Wheat prices in shillings (per qr)	Wheat prices in grains of silver
1300–19	7.01	1734
1320–39	6.27	1547
1340–59	6.31	1372
1360–79	7.55	1508
1380–99	5.57	1113
1400–19	6.37	1188
1420–39	6.65	1107
1440–59	5.56	926
1460–79	6.02	812
1480–99	6.40	852
1500–19	6.91	920

Thus, apart from the high prices of 1360–79, which were influenced by a succession of bad harvests, the current prices sagged with a tendency to fall, while silver prices fell with hardly a break. Comparable foreign prices are not available for periods as early and in samples equally representative. The two collections most commonly used – Hanauer's for Alsace and d'Avenel's for France – do not lend themselves to close analysis and will not by themselves support any reliable historical conclusion. All that the two series can be made to yield is a vague and general impression.

Yet general impressions are not to be spurned, especially if they happen to agree with other and more reliable evidence; and the impression is that the continental prices, in terms of silver, exhibit the English trend to a greatly exaggerated degree. The exaggeration was obviously due to the currency troubles of the times, for whereas English coinage remained comparatively stable (the silver content of the shilling stood at about 246 grains troy until 1344, and was thereafter reduced by slow steps till it fell to 133.20 grains troy in 1461) that of France and of most other continental countries was greatly debased throughout the fourteenth and fifteenth centuries. So fast and so continuous was the debasement that, however much the current prices rose, they never kept pace with it. According to recent authorities the Counts of Flanders at one time purposely manipulated their currency in the hope that the cost of living and wages would lag behind international prices.

TABLE 4.6 *Annual wheat prices in the Low Countries*[30]

(Index number: 1375–99 = 100)

Years	Current prices
1375–99	100
1400–24	104
1425–49	138
1450–74	109

Yet, however exaggerated the trend of the French and Alsatian prices, they moved in the same direction as the trends of other and more reliable series. Among the latter should perhaps be included the price series for Flanders since 1375, which has also been assembled by the International Price Committee. It shows the 'current' wheat prices fairly

30 I owe the Flemish prices to Lord Beveridge's courtesy. They are derived from printed sources, mostly from H. Van Houtte's *Documents pour servir à l'Histoire des Prix*. The Königsberg prices (Table 4.7) come from an anonymous mid-nineteenth-century summary of grain prices in the records of the Prussian Order, quoted in W. Abel, *Agrarkrisen und Agrarkonjunktur*, 32–3.

stable between 1375 and 1425 and then, after a brief and sharp rise in the first quarter of the fifteenth century, falling rather steeply for another twenty-five years. By the end of the third quarter of the fifteenth century they stood barely 9 per cent above the price in 1375 and barely 5 per cent above the price in 1400. In the same period prices measured in silver declined. (Table 4.6.)

The importance of the figures in Flanders lies in their relation to the world prices. The Low Countries were heavy importers of grain which they drew from more than one distant source and commonly from the Baltic. They were thus more sensitive to the general trends in European production and commerce than were the prices of such comparatively self-sufficient countries as England. From this point of view, also worth quoting is the little evidence we possess of the movement of prices in the principal source of grain exports in the same period, i.e. in the Eastern Baltic. In an anonymous mid-nineteenth century compilation based on the Königsberg records of the Prussian order, the price of rye expressed in units of silver is shown to behave in a manner strikingly similar to that of grain prices in the west. The prices for rye in Königsberg in the fifteenth century moved as in Table 4.7:

TABLE 4.7   *Prices of rye in Königsberg*
(Index number: 1399 = 100)

Years	Prices (silver)
1399	100
1405	89.29
1432	85.32
1448	79.81
1494	49.84
1508	36.48

Owing to the heavy debasement of local currency in the fifteenth century 'current' prices may actually have risen, but the rise was probably gentle compared to the heavy depreciation of the mark.

A movement of prices so continuous must have had an obvious effect on economic life. The falling or sagging prices for agricultural products happened to be accompanied by steeply-rising costs of labour and must therefore have depressed the profits of demesne farming and discouraged commercial production for the market everywhere. In the absence of clear statistical evidence about trade in luxuries and semi-luxuries, it is difficult to say to what extent it was affected. Did the purchasing power of the upper classes and their demand for goods decline with the falling profits of industry and agriculture?

On general grounds some such correlation could be expected, but whether the effect of prices went further than that, i.e. whether it was also responsible for the slump in the major industries, depends on a number of other considerations. It depends, in the first place, on the extent to which price changes were general, i.e. common to the entire range of medieval commodities. It depends also on the susceptibility of medieval producers to price stimuli; above all on the susceptibility of those agricultural producers, who did not depend on 'cash' crops for their income.

On the whole the evidence on both points will not support the hypothesis of prices as the main, and still less as the sole, cause of the slump. Our knowledge of medieval prices is largely confined to grain, but in so far as other series are available they suggest that the fall in prices was highly departmentalised. Thus it does not appear that prices for cloth or those for iron, or indeed those for other commodities, fell at all or fell in the same proportion as prices for agricultural products. Heterogeneous and difficult to collate as are the figures in Thorold Rogers's great collection, they nevertheless leave a strong impression that industrial prices did not in any way synchronise with those of grain. Prices for building materials were rising till the middle of the fourteenth century, were more or less stable from 1370 to 1425, and thereafter fell at a somewhat slower pace than grain. The prices of textiles (the least reliable in the collection) appear to fall from 1375 to 1440 and to rise thereafter. Prices for iron were rising fast in the second half of the fourteenth century and falling gently in the fifteenth, finishing in 1475 about 4 per cent above their level in 1350. Expressed in bushels of wheat the index of iron prices in the second half of the century rose without a break from 100 in the first half of the century to 159 in the decade of 1351 to 1360, and to 352 in 1389 to 1400.

Thus the prices for separate commodities did not move together. Even the different agricultural products depreciated and appreciated at times and at rates somewhat different from those of wheat. As far as it is possible to judge from the variegated collection of prices for animals and animal products assembled by Thorold Rogers, the relation between their prices and those for wheat was not at all close. (Table 4.8.)

The prices are here expressed in silver, and therefore somewhat exaggerate the fall in prices, but they reveal very clearly the difference between the two series. The prices for animal products in current coinage actually rose and were considerably higher in the period of 1401 to 1425 than in that of 1351 to 1375 and were not much lower in 1451 to 1475 than they had been a century earlier. Indeed, expressed in current prices, the series after 1351 continues the rising trend of the previous two centuries for at least another 125 years. Hanauer's figures for Alsace, however exiguous, and d'Avenel's collection for France, however heterogeneous, are nevertheless sufficient to suggest that in other parts of Western Europe the two series were at least as divergent as in England. Taking Hanauer's silver prices for 1351 to 1375 as 100, we find that in 1400–25 the grain prices fell to 64 while the prices for animal products stood at 87. Hanauer's silver prices, but not his current ones, broke thereafter, but while the index of his silver prices for grain fell between 1351 and 1450 from 100 to 71, that of his prices for animal products stayed at 100. In the subsequent collapse of food prices, largely reflecting the debasement of French coinage, the index of grain prices sank by the end of the century to as low a level as 40, but prices for animal products still stood at some 40 per cent higher at 54 to 56.

TABLE 4.8   *English prices of animal products and wheat*
(Index number: 1351–75＝100)

Years	Wheat	Animal products and cattle
1351–75	100	100
1376–1400	71	88
1401–25	70	99
1426–50	70	89
1451–75	55	76
1476–1500	53	68

Similar – no more reliable but equally significant – evidence about most animal products could be quoted from almost every continental country, but none of these prices are more significant or have been better studied than those of butter. Trade in butter may appear to the uninitiated too small to provide a foundation for any argument, especially one about medieval economy as a whole. Yet in spite of being cast on a small scale, it has turned out to be an important index of wider movements. For butter was a merchandise circulating over great distances and command-ing an international price; and what is even more important is that it happened to be a semi-luxury entering into popular consumption. When we are told that in this period a Prussian labourer earned the equivalent of 30 kilogrammes of rye per day, it is not necessary to know what Alfred Marshall said about the elasticity of the demand for bread in order to conclude that agricultural labourers were now better able to indulge in a little butter, however expensive. The price of butter was therefore highly responsive to changes in demand and supply, and was more sensitive as a barometer of markets than prices of more indispensable foods. It is therefore very significant that the price of butter and the price of grain diverged more widely than the prices of any other commodities. In the fourteenth and fifteenth centuries the butter prices rose very steeply, in both current coinage and in silver, in all the main sources of supplies, with the possible exception of Holland – in Sweden, in Norway, in Western Poland. Steepest of all was the rise in Norway. There, after about seventy or eighty years of relatively stable prices, butter suddenly rose by about 10 per cent in the sixties of the fourteenth century and by about 33 per cent by 1400. In the course of the fifteenth century the prices continued to soar; and by 1457 reached a level 200 per cent above that of 1400, dropping to about 100 per cent above that of 1400 in the next decade. On the other hand, the prices for rye imported from the Baltic moved relatively little, and if anything sagged. A similar discrepancy between the prices of rye and butter developed in Sweden and in Prussia, and above all in the Polish hinterland from where Prussian seaports drew most of their butter. In Cracow the index of prices for rye between 1398 and 1450 sank from 33 to 10, but at the same time the prices of butter rose from 10 to 33 or more than threefold.[31]

From the present point of view, the precise cause underlying the behaviour of butter prices is less important than the fact that they behaved differently from grain prices, and that they bear out more fully than any other price series the danger of generalising from a price trend which was apparently confined to grain. Indeed, even in the grain trade the influence of prices is not very obviously related to changes in production and trade. While in most European countries prices expressed in silver were falling, current prices in local coinage were rising; and in regions as self-supporting as most provinces of France and Central Germany it was the current prices that mattered most, for it was in relation to current prices that the cost of living, the rate of wages, and the profits of agriculture fluctuated. In England the break in the prices in the second quarter of the fourteenth century was unmistakable, but the downward trend was neither continuous nor very marked – certainly less continuous and less marked than the earlier rise. The line representing the long-term trend of English prices and based, say, in moving 25-year averages, is all but horizontal; the prices of 1500 being actually 10 per cent higher than those of the first quarter of the fourteenth century. The lowest prices of the period – those from 1450 to 1475 – were only 20 per cent below those of 1300 to 1325. Expressed in silver, the English prices fell rather more steeply; yet even they did not fall more than about 25 per cent: from 1372 to 1107 grains of silver per quarter of wheat in the century between 1340 and 1440. And it was in that century that English agriculture contracted most and its organisation changed most profoundly.

The economic and more especially the commercial trends of the time

---

[31] Julian Pelc, *Ceny w Krakowie w latach 1369–1600*, 127 ff.; for other butter prices see J. Schreiner, *Pest og Prisfall in Senmiddelalderen*, 82.

were thus out of scale with the movements of grain prices. Is that surprising? The only way in which changes in grain prices could influence production and trade was by calling forth greater or smaller supplies of marketable products. But earlier in this chapter it has already been emphasised that in agriculture prices were by no means the sole, or the main, conductor of economic stimuli. Peasant producers were far too self-sufficient to order their production and to regulate their marketable surpluses in direct response to commercial considerations; and in the later Middle Ages this element of self-sufficiency increased rather than diminished, or, what is the same thing, the proportion of agricultural producers sensitive to prices was smaller than before. There is thus even less reason for seeking in grain prices the main cause of the falling trends of the later Middle Ages than there is for seeking in them an explanation of the rising trends in the earlier centuries.

The doubts are reinforced by the uncertainty of the monetary factor. One of the reasons why prices offer such an obvious and tempting explanation is that at first sight they can easily be fitted into what is known of the contemporary changes in the supply of precious metals. The supplies of silver from the European silver mines gradually gave out, as silver mines entered upon their decline. The supplies from the Goslar region dwindled in the thirteenth century, those from the other mining areas of Central and Eastern Europe declined or ceased altogether in the fourteenth or early fifteenth centuries. There is also evidence of local scarcities of silver. Indeed, such re-minting as the English Crown undertook in the fourteenth and fifteenth centuries, in 1344, 1346, 1351, 1412 and 1461, had for its object to bring the silver content of the English coins into line with the shorter supply and the higher price of silver.

This now appears to be the generally accepted view. Its relevance to the problem of falling prices, however, is not as clear as it might at first sight appear. In the first place, there is a purely historical difficulty of dates and places. The movements of prices cannot easily be synchronised with the dates at which the mining of silver is known to have declined, nor can they be put into geographical relation with areas in which silver was mined. Whereas the Goslar mining was already depressed in the thirteenth century, and silver mining elsewhere reached its lowest depths by the middle of the fourteenth century, the fall in prices did not begin till some time in the first half of the fourteenth century and did not become general till much later. Silver began to flow again from the Saxon mines in the fifties of the fifteenth century, yet, expressed in terms of silver, prices stayed low and, in England at least, continued to fall till 1480. Moreover, the price changes occurred no earlier and were no more spectacular in the regions nearest to the sources of new silver than they were elsewhere; and it is difficult to read into the regional differences between the price series in Cracow, Alsace, Holland and Norway the familiar sequence of concentric ripples by which falling investment and employment in the mining areas could normally be expected to transmit the effects of a mining slump over the entire face of Europe.

There are also the more general arguments some of which have already been mentioned in the discussion of the thirteenth-century rises. To begin with, the annual increments of new silver at their highest were not as great as other changes in silver supplies could be and, in fact, were. By 1300 or 1320, the dates at which supplies of silver from continental mines began markedly to fall off, the total stock of silver in Europe, in relation to annual output, must have been truly enormous, for it had been amassed in at least two centuries, and probably three, of large and steadily mounting output. And when the total stock was thus two hundred to five hundred times that of its annual accretions, the international price of silver was influenced more by the manner in which it was employed than by the current flow from the mines. The falling investment in industry and agriculture as a result of the low level of profits, the changing financial technique, the diversion of currency into the hands of the Crown and its soldiers, the greater demand for silver for buckles and buttons: each of these phenomena could and should have had at least as great an effect on the value of silver as the changes in the supply of new bullion.

What makes the hypothesis of silver supplies all the more difficult to accept is that, even if the flow of new metal from the mines affected international supplies of silver, it did not in the same degree, or indeed in any degree, determine the supplies to individual countries. Individual countries received the bullion by means of international trade, and such was the structure of foreign trade in the later Middle Ages that while some countries earned vast balances, others did not; and that the changes in trade balances did not synchronise with the ups and downs of silver mining. On the roughest calculation, England's favourable balance on the visible trading account oscillated in the course of the fifteenth century between £50,000 and £150,000, and was on the average equal to about half the total value of English foreign trade and more than twice the value of coinage drawn in and out of the mint in the years of recoinage. And if, in the fourteenth and fifteenth centuries wool exports and grain exports declined, the deficiency was more than made up by the high taxes on wool, the development of English cloth exports, and the virtual cessation of Flemish cloth imports. There is thus every reason why silver should have continued to be imported, and there was nothing surprising or anachronistic in the verse of the fifteenth-century *Libel of English Policy*, in which its well-informed author describes the Prussians as importing

> plate of silver of weighes good and sure
> in great plenty which they bring and buy
> out of the lands of Bohemia and Hungary.

In times of reviving trade, such as the last quarter of the fourteenth century and the thirties and forties of the fifteenth, when the *Libel* was composed, the balance of trade and the imports of bullion may well have risen not only in relation to the total value of trade of those years but also in comparison with the trade balance of earlier centuries. True, that visible balance was apt to be eaten into by papal taxation and often frittered away in payments for war and garrisons abroad, but all this means is that the flow of silver in and out of this country was due to war and payments abroad, and not changes in silver output alone.[32]

5

Thus price movements there were, and from most of them important consequences followed; but they could not be entirely ascribed to monetary cause, and moreover they were not general. And price changes which are not 'general' but are mainly confined to grain, point to a factor which has already been shown to have operated in the opposite direction in the early centuries of the Middle Ages, i.e. population. On broad, and largely theoretical, grounds a fall in population would be compatible with all the phenomena which our evidence exhibits, and should raise none of the objections to which other general explanations are open. When population fell, some marginal lands would in all probability be abandoned and food would be produced on better land. Relative to the amount of land and labour engaged in food production and relative to the demand for food, supplies would then be more plentiful and therefore cheaper. There would thus be every reason to expect both smaller production and lower prices accompanied by the show of abundance which is so conspicuous in the late fourteenth and fifteenth centuries. A fall in population would also have, so to speak, a selective effect on prices, in that it would tend to lower the prices of

---

[32] The problem is further complicated by the use of gold. Most countries in Europe introduced gold coinage by the middle of the fourteenth century, and even before that happened, gold and gold coin of Italian and Byzantine origin was often used in settlement of international payments. The value of silver, or rather its local scarcities and superfluities, was therefore bound to be affected by the terms on which silver and gold coins were exchanged. And as commercial values of the two metals were often at variance with the 'official' or mint terms of exchange, flights to and from silver coinage were very frequent. When they happened they did at least as much to cause local scarcities and abundances of silver as any other changes in the supply of bullion.

agricultural products, which were previously being produced at high and ever-rising cost – or, to use the economist's terminology, under steeply diminishing returns – but would have little effect on commodities not greatly subject to diminishing returns, i.e. most industrial products. By increasing the proportions of silver per head it would counteract the effects of falling supplies from the mines, and might even counterbalance what economists would describe as 'deflationary changes in liquidity', but what historians would classify as greater tendency to hoarding. It would help to increase the 'effective demand' of large masses of population, i.e. stimulate their outlay on food and other goods, and thus lead to higher prices and greater supplies of semi-luxuries especially sensitive to fluctuations of demand.

All this is theory, and like all theories it may at first sight appear too simple to fit the infinite variety of medieval experience. But it so happens that this particular argument has emerged from evidence purely descriptive and from arguments largely empirical, and has in fact been first announced as a matter of historical fact by medievalists as innocent of population theory as only medievalists can be. To make this clear it may be worth marshalling some of the evidence even if this will mean transgressing the strict limits of this chapter's subject.

The most familiar evidence is that derived from the topographical record of depopulation, and, above all, from the evidence of vacant holdings and uncultivated fields in the later Middle Ages. In England neither the story of colonisation in the earlier centuries nor that of the depopulation in the later ones has been studied sufficiently closely to yield statistical estimates, but the historians who handled evidence abroad happened to be more quantitatively minded; and, if their results are to be trusted, the abandoned fields and holdings represented throughout the late Middle Ages a very considerable proportion of land erstwhile occupied. In South-western Germany the *Wüstungen* at the turn of the fourteenth and fifteenth centuries were so high as to account in some places for more than half of the holdings. Recent computation puts the proportion of vacant holdings in Scandinavian countries almost equally high.[33]

Needless to say, the evidence of abandoned holdings is apt to magnify the depopulation process it reflects. But allowing for fields abandoned for reasons other than shortage of population, allowing also for subsequent re-lets and re-occupation, there still remains a large balance of lands unoccupied and depopulated through shortage of manpower. Moreover

[33] Wilhelm Abel, *Die Wüstungen des Ausgehenden Mittelalters*, 1–13, 25–30; J. Schreiner, *Pest og Prisfall i Senmiddelalderen*, 58–63 and *passim*. For a detailed quantitative analysis of German *Wüstungen*, see Heinz Pohlendt, *Die Verbreitung der Mittelalterlichen Wüstungen in Deutschland*, ch. II and III, Göttingen, 1950.

the shortage was obviously general, i.e. not confined to agriculture alone. Contrary to what is sometimes assumed, the fall of population in the countryside was not the result of flight to towns, for population in towns was also dwindling. In this country the old corporate towns – Northampton, Lincoln – filled the air with protestations of poverty and with claims for reduction of royal taxes on grounds of depopulation. A German historian has computed that the population of North German cities declined in the course of the fourteenth and fifteenth centuries by at least 20 per cent. No such computation has been made for the towns of England or France, but those towns where the urban evidence has been studied at all closely – Bordeaux, Rouen, Arras – bear signs of contraction at least as great. The Flemish decline has already been noted.

Depopulation, both urban and rural, was of course, a complex process, mostly discontinuous and sometimes compensated by new growth; and indeed some of the new growth was so boisterous that in the absence of quantitative data it might well give the impression of a balance successfully redressed. Thus, while the population of most English towns fell after 1350, it may have remained more or less stationary in London, Bristol and Southampton and two or three other sea ports, and may for a time have grown in the cloth-making towns and villages of East Anglia, Yorkshire and the West Country. Similarly while the population in the towns of France, Flanders, Northern and Central Germany declined, that in North Netherlands (Holland) and in Southern and South-eastern Germany may have grown in the course of the fifteenth century.

This was a redress in some measure, but the measure must not be exaggerated. Judging from the amount of cloth produced – say 50,000 cloths per annum – the numbers engaged in English cloth industry at its height could not have been greater than 25,000 persons, if as great.[34] Abroad the cloth industry of Holland was not yet on a scale sufficient to make up for the decline of the industry elsewhere, just as her towns could not as yet have grown sufficiently to balance the fall of urban population in Flanders and France. Similarly, the development of Augsburg and Nuremberg was also too much in its infancy to counter-balance the ebbing fortunes of Hanseatic economy.

Further evidence of falling population will be found in the falling land values. In various parts of France payments for land continually fell, in spite of the rising wheat prices in current coinage. On the estates of St Germain-des-Prés near Paris rents fell without a break from 84*d* per *arpent* in the second half of the fourteenth century to 55*d* in the middle decades of the fifteenth century and to about 30*d* in the seventies and

---

[34] There are several ways of computing the figures. The simplest is to compute from the price on cloth and the costs of production. See M. Postan in *Economic History Review*, II (1950), 232.

eighties. In Sweden, Denmark and Norway land prices – both rents and capital values – were falling throughout the period, at a pace which appeared to outrun the fall in prices of grain.

Finally, there is the evidence of wages. For whereas prices of agricultural products fell, wages rose. Evidence of rising wages will be found all over Europe, but the most complete as well as the most reliable series of wages so far available is that of the wage rates on the manors of the bishopric of Winchester published by Lord Beveridge. That series reveals a twofold rise in real wages between 1300 and 1350: a rise strangely suggesting a scarcity of labour through falling population.

So unless and until new evidence to the contrary is produced, the commercial and industrial depression of the later Middle Ages must be accounted for by decline in numbers. There were fewer hands at work, and there were fewer mouths to feed. This need not have left individuals any worse off; indeed, there is every reason for believing that the working population of Northern Europe was now more prosperous than ever before. Yet collectively Europe became smaller and poorer, and the decline in her trade and industry was merely one manifestation of a contracting continent.

(2) *The regulated trade*

1

A long period of contracting trade left its mark on the men engaged in it. The economic status of the merchants, indeed their very behaviour, changed; and no change was more typical, more in tune with the times, than the passing of the great men. If the characteristic figure in commercial and industrial development of the early centuries was the adventurer-merchant depicted by Pirenne, the typical representative of the later Middle Ages was the sedate *bourgeois* of middle rank. Rich men were of course to be found in many large towns. Above all, the Anglo-French wars brought forth small groups of war financiers and speculators. But careers and fortunes like those of Jacques Cœur in fifteenth-century France remain isolated and shortlived; for this was no longer the time of the great speculators moving about the western world, founding cities, forcing open new trade routes, founding new commercial empires. Their race had all but died out and was not to be reborn until the very threshold of the Renaissance; the time when the Welsers and the Fuggers rose in the South of Germany, and a new generation of speculators appeared on the bourses of Antwerp and Amsterdam.

The fifteenth-century merchant new-style was a composite type made up of several elements of different antiquity. One of its components was

that of a merchant turned financier; and both the type itself and the
process by which he appeared on the scene were of course much older
than the later Middle Ages. Medieval merchants of all centuries were
prone to retire from active trade as soon as they had made their fortunes.
Having retired, the more substantial businessmen in England often
abandoned their towns and their urban associations altogether and established themselves in the country as gentlemen. On the continent, they
would more frequently choose to stay in the town as *rentiers*. They might
participate as sleeping partners in the active trade of others; they might
buy urban tenements and rents, take up municipal and other public
bonds and sometimes advance private loans.

The propensity to retire into a life of *rentier* is not difficult to account
for. The physical hazards of active trade abroad were not always
matched by opportunities for enrichment, and the opportunity grew
poorer as the foreign markets grew smaller. At the same time it is
probable that capital was still sufficiently scarce to command a high rate
of interest. As far as it is possible to judge (and the problem has not been
investigated as fully as it deserves), the return expected on the investment
of sleeping partners in fifteenth-century England was on the average well
in excess of 10 per cent per annum. The later Middle Ages also offered
new and ever-growing opportunities for financing needy municipalities
and kings at rates nearly as high.

There is therefore nothing incomprehensible or in any way mystical
about that process of financial degeneration which seems to have come
over a number of wealthy cities in the Middle Ages. When we find in
the middle of the thirteenth century the ruling class of Arras made up
largely of financiers advancing money to towns and princes all over
Northern Europe, we cannot explain this otherwise than by concluding
that many of the families, which in the late eleventh and twelfth centuries
had pioneered in European cloth industry and in long-distance trade, had
now 'made their pile' and sought in money-lending a quieter mode of
life and a less adventurous occupation. Other cities might also, like Arras,
pass out of the plane of active trade into mere money-lending. It so
happens that the rise of Arras to the position of a banker city to the rest
of Northern Europe occurred very early (for Arras's industrial career had
also begun very early) and has been well studied; but a historian with a
practised eye will find no difficulty in detecting in the later Middle Ages
the same process in most of the towns of Northern Europe which had
gone through a period of expansion and enrichment in the previous
century or century and a half. Much of the mystery of the otherwise
inexplicable withering away of the active trade of Flemish merchants
might be found in the growth of the *rentier* class. The men, who would in
an earlier age have acted as traders to foreign lands or even as employer-

clothiers, were now tending to withdraw into quieter occupations: into brokerage and hostel-keeping in Bruges, into passive investment elsewhere.

In the later Middle Ages this process became more general, more, so to speak, disseminated, but it did not account for the entire change in mercantile society. It accounted only for one component of the new *bourgeoisie*, and there were other components as well. Above all, there were the men who looked for and found security not outside but within occupations still largely commercial. They did so by trading in a smaller way, within well-organised and protected markets.

The typical figures of Northern European commerce in most towns in the late Middle Ages were a humbler lot of men than the merchants of some other times and places. Historians have always noticed the social differences which distinguished the commerce of the great Italian cities from that of the Hanseatic towns. Whereas the bulk of Italy's foreign commerce and finance in the later Middle Ages was in the hands of great commercial and banking houses, the Frescobaldi, the Bardi, the Peruzzi, the Medici, the Datini, the trade of the Hanseatic towns was in the hands of a greater number of smaller people. The difference, however, was not so much geographical as chronological. The records of the earlier centuries, the time when the great Hanseatic cities were being founded, are filled with the acts of great families attempting great things. In a few cities like Cologne it is still possible to find in the later Middle Ages great traders and speculators, like Tidman of Limbourg who financed Edward III, or Gerard von Wesel who tried in the middle of the fifteenth century to lead Cologne's break-away from the Hanse. Elsewhere in the German North, men of this stamp were no longer to be found. It is not that the great families wholly died out, for there were still Castorps and Warendorps all over Hanseatic regions. What happened was that they no longer occupied the position in the Hanseatic trade which had been theirs when they were blazing its trails in the newly opened lands beyond the Elbe.

The bulk of the trade was now in the hands of men of middling substance. And being middling they looked for safety and found it in co-operation, in combination and, more generally, in numbers. It was for their benefit that the Hanseatic League maintained in most foreign centres within its influence their great factories or *Kontors* with large bodies of resident agents or factors. It was their cargoes that were marshalled in convoys to the Bay of Bourgneuf, to the east coast of England, to Bruges. And it was their trade that was looked after by corporate organisations within the German towns – the *Bergenfahrers* and *Schönenfahrers* of Lübeck, the *Englandfahrers* of Cologne.

The English development was even more remarkable in that the dividing line was drawn more sharply. The early years of Edward III, coinciding as they did with the opening phases of the Hundred Years War and Edward's great fiscal operations, forced into bloom all the capitalist or quasi-capitalist elements in English life. Men like the brothers de la Pole, representing the upper rank of the English merchant classes, now rose to great wealth gained in supplying the armies, in arranging and transmitting payments abroad, in managing the king's taxes and levies on wool. Their economic power as well as their hold over the English wool trade reached their highest point in the thirties and forties when, having formed several syndicates, they were able to finance the Crown and to monopolise the entire British export trade in wool. But Edward's insolvency in the fifties brought about their collapse; and their collapse meant also the demise of a whole social order. When in the last quarter of the century the Staple of Calais finally took shape it was made up of a larger number of smaller men – men who in the fifteenth century came to be represented by the three generations of Celys: respectable, prosperous traders who, though in the highest rank of the wool trade, could not claim more than one fiftieth or even a hundredth share of England's wool exports. Needless to say, individuals of out-standing wealth did not wholly disappear from English trade and finance. The wars of Richard II called forth Brember and Lyon; the trade of Bristol could boast of Robert Cheddar and William Canning. And in fifteenth-century London, there was Dick Whittington. Yet in a curious way none of these men was as typical of the fifteenth century as the great London dynasties were of the thirteenth. They were probably not quite so rich; they were certainly less numerous. Above, all, they no longer dominated the trade of the country. The economic and financial power of the wool trade in its relations with the Crown and with the outside world now rested not on the wealth or influence of individuals but on the power of the corporate organisation – the Company of the Merchants of the Staple of Calais.

The Company of the Staple was not alone. The 'general' traders of England, who specialised in importing and exporting miscellaneous merchandise other than wool, now for the first time appeared in records as the Company of Merchant Adventurers. By then the name was out of date. The time when English general merchants adventured farthest into distant lands and seas was the turn of the fourteenth and fifteenth centuries and preceded by at least two or three generations the establish-ment of a company claiming the title of Merchant Adventurers. It was in the fifteenth century, when the expansion of English trade both in area and in quantity was over, and when the erstwhile opportunities for commercial adventure had fallen away, that the merchants arrogated to themselves the name to which they were no longer entitled. Their company was coming into ever-greater prominence as the century drew to its close, and made up in collective power and influence for the more modest substance of its members.

2

Corporate trade was indeed the typical feature of the later Middle Ages. Mediocre men combined to do what greater ones might have done in isolation. In later centuries, the late sixteenth and the seventeenth, corporate trade could be made to serve the ends of great speculative business. Similar corporations may also have existed in the earlier centuries of the Middle Ages. Did not the great Flemish capitalists of the thirteenth century operate in London through the Hanse of the Flemish towns, and did not the magnates of Cologne establish themselves in England at the time through a similar Hanse? In the later Middle Ages, however, corporate action and corporate support became the mainstay of mediocre firms. With their support large numbers could share in the trade of Northern Europe, and without it no merchant from Northern Europe could successfully operate. Corporations both protected and circumscribed the trade they controlled; and they did not confer collective power on their members without acquiring collective authority over them. By virtue of this authority, they were now able to regulate the scale and the methods of individual enterprise and to lay down rigid rules for prices and credit, for terms of sales, for relations with agents, and for the latters' residence and conduct.

As the scope of individual enterprises contracted and their reliance upon corporate organisation grew, so their methods and organisation changed. This is not the place to deal with all the facts of medieval business technique. One fact, however, is strictly relevant here. The modest scope of individual enterprises, as well as their large numbers, forced upon them a method of trade which in at least one respect differed from the methods of the great houses of Italy and South Germany. They were less, so to speak, self-contained. An individual English firm trading abroad, or a Hanseatic firm trading in England, or a Dutch firm trading in Antwerp and Bruges, did not as a rule trade through channels entirely and exclusively its own. Whereas a great Italian firm might be served by bodies of servants and partners, a typical Hanseatic or English firm, being too small to maintain a large body of permanent servants, would try and avail itself of the services of more or less independent agents and brokers. The difference must not of course be driven too far. Most English firms trading in Flanders sent out for shorter or longer periods representatives of their own, and there were Italian merchants in Bergen, London and elsewhere ready to act for any client in Italy. But on the whole the North European machinery of factories and corporate companies as well as the smaller scale of individual enterprise favoured a far greater development of resident agencies and of a specialised profession of foreign factors.

The corporate tendency manifested itself, however, not only abroad and in dealings with foreign countries but also at home and in matters of local trade. The municipal governments at home began to take an ever-greater interest in the commercial activities of their burgesses, and the age was one of mounting urban regulations and of accumulating urban legislation. The right to participate in the trade of the local markets and in the staple branches of foreign trade was being defined and circumscribed, the entry into them was being limited. Monopoly was indeed the prime object and the pre-requisite condition of urban regulations and became the guiding object of town policy. It was only the power of the king, as in England and France, or the political links with other towns, as in North Germany, that prevented the whole of Europe breaking up into a loose assembly of small but economically independent territories, each dominated by a monopolistic town. And even in England and France and the Hanseatic North, the monopolistic and corporate interests came to the fore in most towns.

Urban economy was indeed beginning to approximate to the textbook fiction of a medieval town: a diminutive region forming with its rural belt a self-sufficient unit, within which trade and industry were partitioned into equal shares and regulated by law. The reason why historians have so often been led to accept this fiction as a representative sample of medieval economy is that they know much more about regulated economy of the corporate town than they do about trade in its freer and less regulated aspects. For it is in the nature of regulation and control to breed documentary evidence and thus to perpetuate itself in history out of proportion to its real importance in historical development.

The corporate and monopolistic features of fourteenth- and fifteenth-century towns have thus shielded from view the meagrely documented activities of freer trades and freer towns. There were 'open' towns, and 'open' trades within them, even in the later Middle Ages. For we know that the great fair towns of Northern Europe – Bruges, Antwerp, Bergen-op-Zoom – were free ports where strangers were allowed to enter and where trade with strangers was more or less unrestricted by any law, except perhaps the law of residence and brokerage. Greater or smaller elements of freer trade might also be found in great metropolitan centres like London, in seafaring communities like Middelburg. Yet, on the whole, it was not these towns that typified the new order, but Danzig, which ended by excluding even the other Hanseatics from its local trade; Bergen, where the German merchants who dominated it established a close and highly-regulated monopoly over its trade; Rouen and Paris, where local companies watched and fought jealously over their fields of operations; and countless other smaller towns in France and Germany, which now sank into that well-regulated stupor from which they were not to awake until the French revolution and Napoleon's conquests.

The monopolistic and regulated economy of medieval municipalities was of course related to the political as well as to the social changes within the towns. In the political struggles, which mark the history of the North European towns in the fourteenth century, the rising parties were the craft gilds, which voiced the interests of the smaller men rooted primarily in the local markets. In many German towns, in Wismar, in Rostock, in Bremen, indeed in Lübeck itself, craft gilds rose in the second half of the fourteenth century or the beginning of the fifteenth to sweep out of office the descendants of the patrician families entrenched in town government. Similar revolts took place elsewhere – the Flemish risings of the fourteenth century indeed belong to the mainstream of the politics and diplomacy of the age. Except in Flanders, most of the movements of revolt failed; in towns, in which the democratic governments established themselves, they were as a rule ousted from office after a few years and replaced again by representatives of the patrician families. Yet, even at times and in places at which the counter-revolutions succeeded what they re-established was the political ascendancy of illustrious families and not the conditions which had once upon a time helped them to acquire their lustre. As has already been said, the great families themselves were no longer the same. They were mainly landowners, *rentiers*, public servants, or else traders differing only in name and personal descent from the middling men around them. The time for capitalists was over or not yet.

(3) *The Hanse*

1

The commercial depression, which for all its local variations, affected the whole of Northern Europe, and which, for all its discontinuity, lasted for a century and more, was bound to influence the political history of European trade. More especially it was bound to influence the economic policies in regions which happened to be most exposed to the action of commercial change.

North Germany was thus exposed to an extent greater than other parts of Europe. It would be natural to expect that, at the time when both population and commerce ceased to grow, the territorial scope of German trade should have ceased to expand and its outer frontiers should have ceased to move. Danzig was the last great foundation of the German town builders. After the beginning of the fourteenth century no other towns of importance and no new commercial positions were founded in the Slavonic East. The newest and easternmost Germanic settlements – beyond the Oder and the upper Danube – were destined to remain isolated oases amidst a culture which they failed to assimilate and within an economy which they never wholly subdued or integrated with their own.

It is therefore not as paradoxical as it may seem that the age which saw the end of German expansion should also have given birth to the most important political formation in German history of the late Middle Ages – the Hanseatic League. At first sight the League was a step so novel and so forward that it may be difficult to see in it signs of decline. Yet viewed from the point of view of economic and geographical facts, it represented in the field of transcontinental trade the all-prevailing trend towards collective protection. In the second half of the four-teenth century German commerce had all but reached the limits of its territorial expansion. From then onwards the German towns were more anxious to keep the positions they possessed than able to acquire new positions farther afield. This indeed became the purpose of the Hanseatic League, and from this point of view the League was little more than a federation which the German towns established among themselves to maintain by political action that place in European trade which they had won for themselves in the course of the economic changes of the preceding epoch.

The rise of the League was thus essentially a political event; and its early development was largely a constitutional process. Its starting points were the unions of German merchants abroad. The organisations of German merchants in Wisby and London were the earliest unions of this kind. Indeed it was in England that the very term 'Hansa' was used for the first time to designate the right of merchants to form trading associations. By the beginning of the thirteenth century the word ceased to be applied to the burgesses of English towns and was confined to the organisations of foreign merchants in London.[35] Thus a number of Flemish towns headed by Bruges formed in the thirteenth century a London 'Hansa', which represented them before English authorities and acted on their behalf in defence of their interests and privileges. Another such organisation was the Cologne 'Hansa', which was eventually to grow into the Hanse of the Steelyard comprising all, or nearly all, the German merchants trading in London.[36] The Great

[35] For a closely argued discussion of the evolution of the term, see R. Doehaerd, 'À propos du mot "hanse" ', *Review du Nord*, xxxiii, no. 129 (1951).

[36] It has been suggested, but not definitely proved, that there were originally two German *Hansae*, that of Cologne and that of the Easterlings, which later fused into one: see M. Weinbaum: 'Stalhof und Deutsche Gildhalle zu London' in *Hansische Geschichtsblätter*, Jahrgang 1928 (Lübeck, 1929).

Charter of 1303, which greatly extended the privileges of German merchants in England and which in later centuries came to be claimed by the Germans as the constitutional foundation of their privileged status in this country, dealt with the North German merchants as a single body. Since then the English merchants knew only of the *mercatores alemanniae*, and in this way the London Hanse of the Cologners became the London Hanse of the Germans. Under the Great Charter the Hanseatic merchants acquired valuable exemptions from customs, which put them in a more favourable position than other aliens, or indeed the native merchants of England. Their corporate organisation of the Steelyard received extensive powers of self-government and jurisdiction and a share in municipal authority in London. All in all, the Hanseatic rights in England established the Germans in a position of privilege and autonomy comparable to the 'capitulations' of a later age.

England, however, was not the only place where the merchants from North Germany came to have a corporate organisation and a privileged status. There was hardly an important commercial centre in Northern Europe, in which some German towns did not at one time or another receive grants of commercial liberties and did not organise into communal bodies of very much the same type as the German Hanse in London. Of these communal organisations the most important were the German 'factories' at the two termini of the great route: in Bruges and Novgorod.

The German factory, or *Kontor*, in Bruges was not as old as their London Hanse, but in the course of time it became their chief trading station abroad. At the time when the *Kontor* was established, Bruges was about to enter upon the most illustrious stage of its history. With the rise of the *Kontor* the active commerce of the Flemings themselves gradually declined; but, strange as it may seem, the importance of Bruges grew as the active trade of its burgesses dwindled. At the height of Flemish industrial and commercial development in the thirteenth and the early fourteenth centuries Bruges had been one of the economic centres of Flanders, one of its four *Leden*, but unlike the other three it was from the very beginning more important commercially than industrially. Its cloth industry was far behind that of Ghent, Ypres and Douai; nor did it possess any other important industries. Even in commerce Bruges had at first fulfilled a highly specialised function. Its geographical situation was inconvenient for internal trade: off the main artery of the Scheldt and on the periphery of the main internal land routes. But it proved very convenient as a port for commercial traffic between the Low Countries and England, and its trade expanded as the cloth industry of Flanders became more and more dependent on English supplies of wool.

Apparently it was this connection with England that attracted the Germans to Bruges in the first instance. There has been a certain amount of argument among German historians on this point, but on the whole it appears that the Germans had been in the habit of going to England long before they established themselves in Flanders. It was because Bruges had been the centre of Anglo-Flemish trade that it also became the centre of German-Flemish trade. But with the Germans there it soon developed into something more than an Anglo-Flemish trade junction and before long acquired many features of an international emporium. Bruges, the sea port and the seat of a great fair where the Germans and the English had been in the habit of going, now became also the port and the fair where the Bretons, the Normans, the Spaniards and later the Italians came to do their buying and selling. And as Bruges rose in importance, the Hanseatic *Kontor* drew to itself an ever-greater proportion of German trade. In the course of time its privileges, its federal organisation and its hold over the Hanseatic trade became the standing, not to say the burning, issue of the inter-urban politics of the German Hanse.

The third important centre of German foreign trade where the merchants from northern and eastern towns enjoyed important privileges and a communal organisation was the 'Petershof' of Novgorod. Novgorod was the eastern terminus of the great route and the chief centre of German trade in Russia. In the early Middle Ages the Scandinavians, and especially the Gotlanders, who were probably the first to establish a commercial factory in Novgorod, possessed there a 'Hof', i.e. a 'yard', with hostels and warehouses. But eventually the 'Hof' passed into the hands of the Germans and became the seat of a communal organisation of German merchants trading to Novgorod protected by treaties with Russian princes and enjoying liberties roughly of the same kind as those possessed by their factories elsewhere.

In addition to the three main corporations of Bruges, London and Novgorod, the merchants of the Hanseatic towns also possessed outposts in smaller places like the English 'treaty ports' of Lynn, Boston, Hull and Bristol, or the distant factory – 'Fondacho dei Tedeschi' – in Venice, and a more permanent stake in the municipal institutions of most Norwegian and Swedish towns, and more especially of Bergen. In addition, improvised corporate organisations were sometimes set up in the towns of the Low Countries to which German traders happened to transfer their activities in times of trouble. Thus a network of commercial stations enjoying exceptional treaty rights and valuable commercial privileges and often connected by routes completely dominated by German merchants, formed a commercial system as close and, by all appearances, as tightly knit as any Europe had ever seen.

This system in its main outlines was already in existence at the beginning of the fourteenth century, but at that time the system, like the 'informal' empires of a later age, owed its cohesion and unity to economic facts rather than to political ties. For, in theory, the corporate organisations in foreign places still led separate and independent existences and, so to speak, 'belonged' to the merchants trading in them. Viewed politically and juridically, the rise of the Hanseatic League in the closing decades of the thirteenth and the first half of the fourteenth centuries was nothing else than a gradual transformation of the informal system into a formal one, and a merger of the separate *Hansae* of German merchants into a single union of the towns themselves. How this transformation occurred is more or less clear and does not need much explaining. Equally clear is the process by which the union of the towns acquired a permanent organisation. Sporadic meetings of the 'home' towns to discuss matters raised by their merchants abroad could be, and were, held several times in the middle of the fourteenth century. All that was necessary to bring them together more or less permanently was a suitable occasion and a determined leadership. Both came in the second half of the century, at the time when trouble was brewing in Flanders and a growing tension in relations with Denmark led up to the first great Hanseatic war.

At the very outset of the conflict, in 1367, the towns met in Cologne to form a confederation which was this time to be provided with the rudiments of a permanent constitution and a common purse. The League survived the war, and the peace of Stralsund of 1370 which concluded the conflict is therefore regarded as the birthday of the Hanse. Furthermore, in both these conflicts, and particularly in the conflict with Denmark, Lübeck came forward as the leader of the towns and the spearhead of their attack. From that time onwards it came to be regarded, both within the Hanse and outside it, as the guardian of Hanseatic unity and as the sponsor of its policies.

This concludes the political and constitutional story of the rise of the Hanseatic League. But the most significant part of the story was neither political nor constitutional. It was economic, and the economic processes behind the constitutional evolution of the League were not those of rising unity and strength. On the contrary, the necessity which drove the towns to unite sprang from the recent, and on the whole dangerous, deterioration in their commercial position.

2

The changes in the internal relations of the Hanse might conveniently be considered first. No sooner had the Hanse emerged fully fledged from the war with Denmark than fundamental disunity began to reveal itself

in the affairs of the newly born League. In the past the economic basis
of Hanseatic unity had been their common interests in the monopoly of
the great route and in the common privileges which they had won for
themselves in foreign markets. They exercised their monopoly and enjoyed
their privileges as economic confederates rather than competitors, and
in this non-competitive combination Lübeck was the cementing agent
– a role for which it was well fitted both by its history and its geography.
German urban colonisation owed much to Lübeck's enterprise, and many
of the towns to the east of the Elbe had arisen more or less as Lübeck's
colonies. Throughout that early period they continued to be bound to it
by social and personal ties. Lübeck also exercised a strong economic
influence by virtue of its peculiar position on the route from the Baltic
to the North Sea. As long as navigation went along the sea coast and
internal waterways, goods from and to Prussia had to be discharged for
carriage by land across the Jutland Peninsula and thus had to pass through
Lübeck. However rapidly the trade of the Prussian and Livonian towns
grew, Lübeck stood to benefit by it; and as long as Lübeck continued to
be indispensable, none of the other towns was likely to object to its
exalted part in eastern trade.

This position could not last for ever. By the second half of the fourteenth
century Lübeck was losing, even if it had not yet wholly lost, most of its
special advantages. In the first place its social ties with the other towns
grew weaker. The colonisation movement had spent itself before the end
of the fourteenth century, and, after that, Lübeck all but ceased to send
out settlers to the newer towns. In Prussia alone the towns continued to
grow, but they appear to have drawn their population from Prussia itself.
So, while Lübeck still remembered that it was the mother of the Baltic
towns, the other towns were beginning to forget that they were Lübeck's
daughters. In the second place, Lübeck was ceasing to be an unavoidable
entrepôt on the east-to-west route. In the second half of the fourteenth
century, the men of Zuider Zee – of Campen, Deventer and Zwolle –
popularised the direct sea route to the east round Jutland, the so-called
Umlandfahrt; and their example was soon followed by the Prussians going
west, and by the English and Dutch going east. Among the Prussian towns
Danzig grew in the forties and fifties to become the chief city of Prussia;
and the Danzigers from the very beginning preferred to trade to Flanders
and to England by the direct sea route. Finally, Lübeck was losing its
predominant share in the trade of Prussia and Livonia. By the second
half of the fourteenth century the towns of Prussia and Livonia were
not only learning to trade to the west without the assistance of Lübeck,
but were also acquiring an ever-growing share in the exploitation of
their own hinterlands. The time was not distant when they would begin
to look upon their respective regions as fields exclusively their own. The

towns of Prussia would then begin to claim a monopoly of the trade of the Vistula as against the other members of the Hanse; Riga and Reval would lay the same claims to the trade of the Dvina.

The economic exclusiveness of the Livonian and Prussian groups of towns was a symptom of a *malaise* the effects of which were to be felt by all the Hanseatic towns and not by Lübeck alone. The local policies of separate territorial groups asserted themselves with ever-growing vigour. They were most vigorous of all in Prussia where they derived not only from the local economic interests of the towns but also from the peculiar position of the Teutonic Order. The Teutonic Knights were both the makers and the rulers of Prussia, for they had organised its conquest and ruled it as its sovereign princes. But unlike most other territorial rulers of Germany, the Order was very efficient: its administration was highly centralised and well organised, and its towns never assumed the same degree of independence as they did in other parts of Germany. So when the Hanse emerged it had to accept as a participant not only the towns of Prussia, but the whole of the Prussian state, that is to say, the Teutonic Order and its High Master.

The affiliation of the Order was undoubtedly a source of political strength to the League, for the High Master possessed a standing in international politics which was not to be trifled with, and his membership gave the Hanse a formal position in the world of territorial states. In the constitutional parlance of the time, the High Master was the *Beschermer*, the protector, of the League; something like a prince of the Hanseatic empire. At the same time the insistent particularism of the Order was a source of weakness. And nowhere did the particularism manifest itself more clearly than in the Order's commercial enterprises. It traded on a very large scale in corn, amber and other commodities. It possessed an elaborate commercial organisation with central offices (*Schäffereien*) in Marienburg and Königsberg, with a whole fleet of commercial boats and agents in Prussia and other large centres of Europe. In all this trade the Order acted very much as a competitor of the Hanseatic towns and even of its own towns. What is more, it made use of its political power to regulate internal trade in a way most suitable for its own commercial interests.

So much for the separate attitude of Prussia. The other group with very strong separate interests was the western wing of the Hanse, especially the Rhenish towns with Cologne. The latter continued to find its chief fields of activity in the Netherlands and in England. Whenever the Hanse had to undertake any measure against England and Holland, the merchants of Cologne disobeyed and circumvented it and were ready to give up the membership of the Hanse rather than suffer a loss in any of their own trade in the west.

The only towns whose interest and policy seemed to be directed all through the fifteenth century towards the maintenance of Hanseatic unity were those of the central groups of the Hanse, and especially the so-called Wendish towns with Lübeck at their head. But even here Lübeck's particular interests asserted themselves. It was determined to maintain its position as a barrier and an indispensable intermediary on the east-to-west route, and it strove for Hanseatic unity largely because that unity was the only means to maintain the *status quo*. Hence its constant attempts to prevent the direct connections between the Eastern Baltic and the North Sea. Hence also its bellicosity in all the conflicts with Holland and later also with England, the two countries which made the widest use of the direct sea route through the Sound. In other words, what Lübeck strove to maintain was not the Hanse *per se*, but the particular version of the Hanse which pivoted upon its port: an attitude which the other towns understood very well and frequently resisted.

3

In this way the close of the fourteenth and the fifteenth centuries witnessed the ever-widening divergencies of policy among the main constituent groups of towns within the Hanse. The divergencies were largely due to the differences of regional interests which have already been described. But, behind the regional particularism of urban groups like the Prussian, the Livonian or the Rhenish, it is also possible to discover signs of an economic contraction and reaction – the latter in the literal sense of a recoil from a new and unfavourable situation.

Some of the symptoms of the recoil will be found in the growing urban exclusiveness. Its general spread in the fourteenth and fifteenth centuries has already been described, but nowhere was the change-over towards local protectionism more clearly marked than in Northern Germany. In the centuries of German growth and expansion there was relatively speaking very little of what might be called a protective or exclusive tendency in municipal policy. Germans were expanding their trade with great confidence and seemed to fear no competitors. In their early treaties with Russia and England foreigners were given liberties of trade in German regions, and the Baltic was treated as an open sea. The internal government of the towns matched the liberal spirit of their trade. It was largely in the hands of patrician 'founder' families: an expansionist and adventurous race of men who cared comparatively little for the internal trade of their towns, and, as a rule, allowed foreigners to trade and to settle among them.

By the time of the Stralsund Peace of 1370 this liberal period was over.

The gilds of artisans and traders were becoming very powerful. The democratic revolts in a number of towns have already been mentioned. When the epidemic of petty-bourgeois movements subsided, the municipal governments, even where they were in the hands of the old families, found it easy to meet the wishes of the local gilds and to exclude the foreigner from the town markets and the surrounding rural regions. And some towns began applying anti-alien laws even against the Hanseatics.

The social changes in Hanseatic towns were of course a local reflection of an ageing process through which the whole of Europe was then passing. But at the same time they also reflected a change which was more economic than social, and as such peculiar to the Hanse. The reason why the towns now turned to their own regional trade and tried to protect their local markets is that their opportunities elsewhere had either dwindled or were seriously threatened. For since the middle of the fourteenth century the international position in Northern Europe had been continually changing to the detriment of German trade.

4

It has already been said that the immediate occasion for the formation of a permanent Hanseatic League was a threat to the Hanseatic interests in Scandinavia. The threat was not economic in origin. It sprang from a political movement in the Scandinavian kingdoms and did not threaten to raise up a rival economic power. Yet it was sufficiently characteristic of the difficulties which the Hanseatics were henceforth to encounter all over Northern Europe, and above all in Scandinavia, to be worth looking at more closely.

In the late twelfth and the thirteenth centuries the Scandinavian countries were, so to speak, an economic vacuum. The native merchant class had either disappeared or had not yet risen, while the rulers were too anxious to attract whatever trade they could and, besides, were too weak to resist the outright exploitation of their countries by the Germans. The Hanseatics first appeared in Scandinavia quite early in the Middle Ages, and the merchants of Cologne traded there in the thirteenth and probably in the twelfth century. But it was only when the Germans began to import their corn surpluses that they were able to appropriate to themselves the entire commerce of the region and to acquire there a position of overwhelming power. Towards the middle of the fourteenth century the Germans came to dominate the economic life of the three countries, supplanted the native commerce and shipping, and, with the single exception of the English, had no rivals or competitors to fear.

In Sweden they controlled the chief source of her riches – the mines. So great was their power in that country that by the beginning of the fifteenth century they appointed from among themselves one half of all the municipal governments. Equally deep was their penetration of Norway. The Norwegians were still actively engaged in commerce and navigation in the thirteenth century, but towards the end of the century the Germans made rapid inroads into their trade. We find them extending their hold over the towns of Oslo, Tunsberg, Trondjem, and especially Bergen. Bergen was the Norwegian staple town for the trade in the products of Iceland and other Norwegian islands and of the northern provinces, and it was from these regions that the most valuable products of Norwegian export came – stockfish and fish oil. And in Bergen, more than in any other Scandinavian town, the Germans were a kingdom within a kingdom, with their own laws and jurisdiction.

Their power in Denmark was somewhat more localised. Germans were settled in every Danish town, and German law replaced the Danish in national courts. But the chief point of their activity was the north shore of the Sound, the coastlands of Skania with its famous fishing grounds. For a time – a century and a half – Skania was a focal point of North European fish trade, and the periodic confluence of merchants at Skania made it also an important centre of exchange in other commodities. No wonder that the East Germans regarded Skania as an economic possession of great, not to say crucial, importance.

In the second half of the fourteenth century this position, so valuable, above all so powerful, suddenly deteriorated. Waldemar Atterdag, who rose to the throne of Denmark in 1340, not only set out to unify the Scandinavian kingdoms and thus to fill that political void in which the German towns had built their power, but, by his taxation, he also directly encroached on the Hanseatic privileges. The Germans were compelled to fight the immediate threat of taxation as well as the further danger of a united Scandinavia. The result of the struggle was a victory enshrined in the Peace of Stralsund of 1370, which was followed by the formal establishment of the Hanse.

The debut of the League was thus very successful. As a political weapon it proved itself equally successful in the struggles which it was to wage in the subsequent hundred or hundred and fifty years. The Treaty of Utrecht of 1474, which concluded a somewhat similar conflict with England a century later, still found the League in full possession of its foreign privileges and as triumphant over its enemies as it had been in 1370. Yet, successful as the League was in direct political action, it failed, as it was bound to fail, in its attempt to arrest the march of economic and political forces which continued to shape the evolution of trade in Northern Europe. It was unable to defend its position in Novgorod in the face of the rising power of the Tsars; unable to maintain its old position in Flanders in opposition to the new centres of northern trade which were rising under different auspices in Brabant and Holland; unable to maintain its monopoly of eastern routes; in fact unable to maintain the route itself, which came in the end to be rivalled and replaced by other routes crossing the continent farther south. Above all it was incapable of preventing the rise of the two great rivals who were destined in the sixteenth and seventeenth centuries to supplant the Hanse in the economic leadership of Northern Europe – England and Holland.

(4) *The English challenge*

1

The expansion of the Western Powers into regions hitherto monopolised by the Germans began to make headway in the second half of the fourteenth century. At first it was with the English threat that the Hanseatics appeared to be concerned most. English commercial activity in the north had been gathering strength all through the fourteenth century, and came to a head in its closing years. Yet what requires an explanation is not that that challenge should have come so early but that it should not have come earlier still. For throughout the Middle Ages England formed an essential part of the north-western trading area, and throughout the Middle Ages English merchants were themselves active on the trade routes to and from their country.

England's economic geography fitted her well to play an important part in the trade of North-western Europe. The shores of England were easily accessible across the narrow seas, and it will be recalled that in the Middle Ages as in the modern era sea routes were on the whole more efficient and cheaper than land routes. What is more, the English coast was not only easy to reach but was also worth reaching. Throughout the greater part of the Middle Ages England supplied the more highly specialised regions of Europe with the food and raw materials which some of them lacked. In this sense England's economy in the Middle Ages could be represented, as it often has been, as 'colonial'.

Like colonial countries of more recent times England may in some respects have lagged behind the neighbouring continental countries, but what justifies the appellation most is that the goods she exported were of the kind that would now be described as 'primary produce'. Some manufactured commodities were of course made in England and sold to foreigners throughout English history, and in the later Middle Ages wholly or partly manufactured cloth was to become the mainstay of English trade. But until the second half of the fourteenth century it was minerals, wool and foodstuffs that sustained England's trade and made the

English connection so indispensable in the economic life of Europe. At the very dawn of European history England supplied the rest of Europe with rare minerals, mostly tin. There is also every reason for believing that until the very end of the thirteenth century England was an important source of foodstuffs, grain and animal products which made her valuable to the Low Countries and indispensable to Scandinavia. Above all, it was the wool of her grasslands that made it possible for the highly specialised cloth-producing economies of the Low Countries and Italy to develop. Not until the late fourteenth century did England's part in European trade cease to be mainly that of a supplier of raw materials. But as long as she played that part she was bound to attract foreign trade and foreign investment in a larger measure than many other regions of Europe and to figure prominently in the commercial fortunes of the Western world.

It is thus not surprising that the history of commercial voyages to and from England should have reached to the very dawn of history. Phoenicians may or may not have paid regular visits to the West Country in search of tin, but it seems highly probable that in the Bronze Age bronze articles, manufactured from indigenous metals in Ireland and England, were exported or perhaps re-exported to the continent.[37] Even before they occupied the country the Romans may have imported minerals mined in Britain: Strabo mentions gold, silver and iron. There is also a strong presumption that Southern England became a source of grain supplies to neighbouring provinces of Gaul. Strabo mentions wheat exported from Britain in pre-Roman times, and centuries later Roman writers speak of wheat shipped from Britain to Rhineland. And although one writer, Ammianus Marcellinus, describes the shipments as a wheat tax (*annona*), the probability is that England had a large exportable wheat surplus.[38]

What happened during the long interruption of the Anglo-Saxon invasions, indeed how long it lasted and how complete it was, we do not know. But no sooner does the darkness lift and the documentary evidence become available than references to England's commercial relations with the continent reappear. Miscellaneous Anglo-Saxon sources bear testimony to the wide range of Anglo-Saxon imports and exports and so do other surviving facts of Anglo-Saxon archaeology. King Æthelred's enactment about the tolls of London reveals that at the time of the tenth and eleventh centuries London was frequented by merchants of Flanders, Normandy and North Europe in general; men from Francia

[37] S. Pigott, 'The Early Bronze Age in Wessex', *Proc. Prehist. Soc.* (1938).
[38] In the view of R. G. Collingwood and J. N. L. Myres, *Roman Britain and the English Settlement* (Oxford, 1937), 243, the exports were *annona* on a large scale; but was large *annona* exported from provinces not normally producing exportable surpluses?

and the German Empire are explicitly mentioned.[39] England was then
obviously within the trading area of Central and Northern Europe.
From Britain came foodstuffs, raw materials, and, for a time, slaves, and
the famous letter of Charlemagne to King Offa complaining of the deterioration in the quality of English cloths bears witness to the existence
of a well-established cloth trade. Some historians have gone so far as to
suggest that the so-called Frisian cloth, to which there are numerous
references in continental sources, was nothing else than Anglo-Saxon
cloth distributed by Frisian merchants.[40]

Whether this particular hypothesis is right or wrong there is no doubt
that the Frisians played an important part in Anglo-Saxon trade of the
time. Bede mentions Frisian merchants settled in York and London, and
there are other, less indirect, indications of Frisian participation. But the
Frisians were not alone. In the first place there were also the Scandinavians. In English political history contacts with the Norsemen were
mostly those of war, migration and conquest. There is, however, little
doubt that both before and during the age of the Danish invasion
Scandinavians were in the habit of trading to the British Isles, and the
Norsemen continued to trade even after they had established their
reputation as marauders and invaders. We find Danes settled in London,
in York and Exeter, and there is widely scattered evidence of Scandinavians trading with Anglo-Saxon England not only from Scandinavia
proper but also from Scandinavian settlements in Ireland and Iceland.[41]

The Norman conquest did not break the commercial ties with Europe,
but, if anything, added to them. The trade to Norway apparently continued uninterrupted and was very active in the twelfth century. In the
Sverrir's Saga, King Sverrir is shown commending in a speech the trade
of the English who brought wheat and honey, fine flour and cloth. The
date of the speech in the Saga is 1186, but its sentiments might with
equal justice have applied to the English trade a hundred years earlier
or a hundred years later. There are continuous references throughout the
thirteenth and the early fourteenth centuries to commercial shipments
from Norway to the harbours of East Anglia, mostly to Lynn and the ports
of the Humber,[42] laden with typical products of the North: timber, fish
and fish-oil. But in addition connections with Flanders were now develop

[39] Brit. Mus., Cotton, Titus A, fo. 140, cited here from text in *Hans. Urkundenbuch*, I, no 2.
[40] C. J. Klumker, 'Der friesische Tuchhandel zur Zeit Karls des Grossen u. sein
Verhältnis zur Weberei jener Zeit', *Jahrbuch d. Gesellschaft f. bildene Kunst
etc. zu Emden*, XIII, 1899.
[41] A. Bugge, *Die Wikinger*, 130–1. Cf. also idem, *Den Norske Traelasthandels
Historie* (1925), 47–8.
[42] *The Great Red Book of Lynn*, *passim*; *Diplomatarium Norwegicum*, IX, nos.
102, 159, 201, etc.; cf. A. Bugge, *Den Norske Traelasthandels Historie*, 138–
186.

ing very fast and the economic partnership between this country and the Low Countries, so characteristic of the European economy in the Middle Ages, was taking shape.[43]

That partnership was founded upon wool. English pastures with their persistent moisture and permanent grass, with their chalk subsoil or their salt-laden air, were ideally suited to the pastoral economy and more especially to the grazing of sheep. Pastoral pursuits therefore dominated the life on this island throughout the Celtic and the early Saxon ages. Livestock was then the mainstay of agricultural wealth, the standard unit of value and form of capital. Throughout the Middle Ages pasture continued to play an indispensable part in the processes of internal colonisation as well as in the routine of settled agriculture. England's marginal lands were mainly used for grazing, and even in the boulder clay valleys, mostly heavily wooded, herds of swine were pastured. As population grew in the twelfth and thirteenth centuries and more land was put under plough, some of England's natural pastures, such as the uplands in the Cotswolds, the high grounds of the South Downs, the Lincolnshire wolds, or the marshes of Somerset, might be put under plough and made to yield grain, mostly oats. But no sooner did population recede than the marginal arable was again turned into pasture whenever suitable. And there were also areas, such as the downlands of Hampshire and Wiltshire, the uplands of Yorkshire and Lancashire, the wet grasslands of Cheshire, the Welsh borders in Shropshire and Herefordshire, where pasture remained inviolate through the Middle Ages and where flocks and herds suffered little from expanding settlement. Cattle and more especially sheep were also to be found in the purely champion parts of England, where they played an essential part in the prevailing economy of mixed farming. They manured the soil and they supplemented the income from arable farming; indeed, the entire routine of the common field system was adjusted to suit the needs of village herds and flocks.

It is therefore natural that in spite of the inroads which the plough occasionally made into grassland, English wool production should have been growing throughout the earlier centuries of the Middle Ages. How much this growth owed to large-scale commercial investment and how much its quality improved by selective breeding, we do not know for certain. There is clear evidence that in the twelfth and thirteenth centuries Flemish and Italian financiers (and they were the only ones who happen to have left behind them written records) made long-term loans

---

[43] For a view that commercial connections between England and Flanders in the Merovingian and Carolingian periods were negligible, see P. Grierson, 'The Relations between England and Flanders before the Norman Conquest', *Trans. Royal Hist. Soc.* 4th ser., XXIII (1941).

to wool-growers. But by then English wool production was already at a very high level and its pre-eminence in Europe was already well established. As for breeding, there is every evidence to show that sheep-farmers in the Middle Ages understood the hereditary factor. They took care to mate the better animals *pro stauro meliorando*; they imported rams of good breeds, such as the Lindsey.[44] Whether as a result of breeding the quality of English wool as a whole was improving throughout the early Middle Ages is more difficult to tell. By the beginning of the fourteenth century wools of certain areas established their reputation for quality. The highest prices were paid for the fine and short wool of the scanty pastures on the Welsh marches, the home of the Ryeland sheep; and for the fine long wools of the Cotswolds, and of the wold and marshland of Lindsey and of Kesteven in Lincolnshire, the home of the 'old Lincolns'.

Wool exports grew with wool production. Wool merchants from abroad figure in almost every early document in which commercial dealings are mentioned. At the turn of the twelfth and thirteenth centuries we find Flemings buying wool in large quantities and involved on that account in complicated transactions with kings and landlords. One of them, William Cade, a Fleming active in the middle of the twelfth century, left a brief but very illuminating record of his commercial and financial transactions; but he was obviously not alone. It has already been mentioned that by the beginning of the thirteenth century the merchants of the Flemish towns formed in London something in the nature of a corporate organisation, the Flemish Hanse, which represented the Flemish merchants and presumably provided them with a common residence and essential commercial services. Some of the greater Flemish merchants of that age, Boinebroke, or Pied d'Argent, left almost as clear a mark in the English records as they did on the history of their native towns. They were capitalists of the purest water, speculators on a large scale, employers of large numbers of their countrymen, lenders of large sums to English monasteries and magnates, traders in cloth.[45]

Important as the Flemings were, they were not alone, and in the end they were not even the most important, among the foreign merchants drawn to England by her wool. In the second half of the thirteenth century the German merchants – the Cologners at first and later the Hanseatics – became active among the foreigners trading to England and exporting English wool, but the lion's share of the trade was eventually acquired by the Italians. How and why the Italian merchants first came

---

[44] H. Hall (ed.), *The Pipe Roll of the Bishopric of Winchester* (1903), 8, 40, 76.

[45] H. Pirenne, 'La Hanse Flamande de Londres', *Bulletins de l'Académie royale . . . de Belgique* (1899); Georges Espinas, *Sire Jehan Boinebroke* (Lille, 1933); G. Dept, 'Les Marchands flamand et le roi d'Angleterre, 1147–1216', *Revue de Nord*, XII (1926).

to England is a somewhat controversial question. As the twelfth century was advancing to its close Italians appeared all over Western Europe, in France as well as in England, and there is no telling why individual adventurers from Lombardy and Central Italy should have decided to try their luck in England. But there is little doubt that some of them were drawn to England and above all to English wool by the financial business with which they happened to be charged. Many of the Italian merchants from Central Italy, who came to this country in the late twelfth and thirteenth centuries, were active in the first instance primarily as collectors of papal taxation, not as traders or as money-lenders. In the financial dealings between individuals and in the loans to the Crown, it was still the Jews and not the Italians who were most active (indeed finance was the only occupation of English Jews at that time). Such were, however, the economics of papal taxation that the Italian tax collectors were bound to be drawn into wool trade and into private and royal finance. The proceeds of taxes had to be remitted, and wool was the most obvious form which the remittance could take. Some of the ecclesiastical taxpayers would indeed pay their tax in kind even though the transaction might be clothed in monetary form. And in the process of their wool business the Italian merchant bankers were bound to come very close – as it proved, too close – to the royal exchequer. Export licences, exemptions from duties and miscellaneous royal favours had to be negotiated and paid for. Above all, the sums of money and of goods which passed through the hands of the Italian bankers and tax-collectors were so large as to attract the greedy eye of the needy kings. Some of the papal taxes in Henry III's reign were in fact levied for the benefit of the English Crown and found their way into the royal coffer not as loans but as outright gifts.[46]

In this way wool trade and royal finance became inextricably mixed, and the mixture proved sufficiently potent to raise the Italians at the end of the thirteenth century to a dominant position in the English wool trade. At the turn of the thirteenth and fourteenth centuries, the great Italian houses of the Ricardi, the Frescobaldi, the Bardi and the Peruzzi, dominated the English wool exports and in some years exercised a total monopoly of exports and entire control of the royal customs.

From this position the Italians were eventually ousted by syndicates of native merchants and finally by the English Company of the Staple. In the last century of English trade in the Middle Ages English merchants

[46] W. E. Rhodes, 'The Italian Bankers in England and their loans to Edward I and Edward II'. *Historical Essays of Owens College Manchester*, ed. T. F. Tout and J. Tait (Manchester, 1907). C. Johnson, 'An Italian Financial House in the XIV Century', *Trans. St Albans and Hertfordshire Archt. and Archaeolog. Soc.* n.s. 1 (St Albans, 1903). A. Sapori, 'La Compagnia dei Frescobaldi en Inghilterra', *Studi di Storia Economica Medievale* (Florence, 1949).

controlled the bulk of the wool trade as well as a large share of other exports and imports. To a historian anxious to record the evolution of national power this *dénouement* might indeed appear as an act of fulfilment, and it was represented as such by Archdeacon Cunningham and other writers of the same generation. They saw the English merchants slowly and continually graduating to a position of pre-eminence in English trade. The early initiative and leadership belonged to foreign merchants, to Flemings, Hanseatics and Italians, but the English were good, if slow, learners, and by the middle of the fourteenth century they had acquired all the arts of commerce. Now at last, the moor who had done his duty could be dismissed – it was Edward III who did the dismissing – and English merchants were at last able to establish and enjoy the leadership for which they were now fully qualified.

This story, however, no longer appears as credible as it did once upon a time. The very notion of trade as a social art acquired by men at the end of their progressive ascent through history may have come natural to a generation which not only believed in continuous progress, but valued the commerce of their own day as the highest manifestation and fulfilment of their culture. Present-day historians, rubbing shoulders as they do with anthropologists and sociologists, find it more difficult to treat trade as a characteristic attribute of a sophisticated civilisation. The processes of trade itself were sufficiently simple to be practised by medieval man at all stages of medieval development. What determined the exact place which trade was to occupy in their daily lives and in their development was the historical setting taken as a whole – their laws and customs, their distribution of wealth, their access to circulating capital, as well as the political circumstances of the time. And it so happened that neither the institutions nor the provision of capital in medieval England were so deficient as to prevent English merchants from taking an active part in English trade.

The first references to English or Anglo-Saxon merchants are probably as old as references to any merchants in England. We heard about Saxon, which is commonly taken to mean Anglo-Saxon, merchants visiting the Merovingian fair of Saint-Denis, the fairs of Rouen and Troyes in Charlemagne's time, and resident in Marseilles early in the eighth century. In his letter to King Offa, Charlemagne promises protection to English merchants 'in accordance with ancient customs of trade'.[47] It is possible that the Saxons among the foreign merchants resident in Rome in the ninth century were also Anglo-Saxon, but, in general, references to English trade and English merchants in the ninth century are few,

---

[47] Haddon and Stubbs, *Councils*, III, 496. Cf. also G. Jacobs, *Der nordisch-baltische Handel der Araber* (1887), 112; A. Dopsch, *Die Wirtschafts-Entwicklung der Karolingerzeit*, Part II, 194–5.

for this was a disturbed period both in England and on the continent. References to Englishmen abroad become more frequent in the tenth and the eleventh centuries, and one of them suggests that in 1050 Englishmen sailed to the Baltic. The evidence of Anglo-Saxon towns reveals the existence of native merchants throughout the last two or three centuries of the Anglo-Saxon era.

That the native merchants were not all hucksters serving the local market is perhaps indicated by the accidental survival of the life story of a merchant whose career bestrides the end of the Anglo-Saxon and the beginning of the Norman period, St Godric of Fincham, whose *vita* has been so tellingly exploited by Pirenne. The English merchants who visited Utrecht at the end of the twelfth century were probably wool traders. The Anglo-Norman documents repeatedly mention English wool merchants, and their numbers increase as the records of English trade accumulate. In 1273 the hostilities with Flanders led to a royal embargo on wool exports, and that in its turn led to the institution of licences for export; the surviving collection of licences reveals the existence of a very large body of native merchants engaged in wool trade.[48]

In general, the surviving evidence of English trade and finance of the thirteenth and fourteenth centuries abounds with names of great merchants who were either English born or permanently settled in England and who played a great part in every branch of English trade: acted as king's merchants, or on occasions helped to finance the king and to serve him in various financial and commercial capacities, administered his war chests, organised the remittance of funds abroad, purveyed goods for his household and armed forces, or merely supplied him with large quantities of imported commodities. In the twelfth century and the thirteenth there were de Waleys, de Haverhills, Finks, Fitz Alans, de Cornhills, Basings, Blands, Buckerels, de Rokesleys, Aswyks, de Ludlows: a small but powerful class which was fast acquiring the character of a hereditary caste dominating the civic councils of London, active in every important branch of English trade, and holding large investments in landed property and mortgages (Gregory de Rokesley at one time held a mortgage over the lands of no less a person than the Bishop of Ely). The class merges imperceptibly into the financial oligarchy of the mid-fourteenth century – the de la Poles and their associates.

True enough, it was not until the middle of the fourteenth century that English merchants succeeded in establishing themselves in full control of the wool trade and in a position of predominance in English trade as a whole. This development, however, did not come about by a gradual process of apprenticeship and graduation, but through a series of

[48] A. Schaube, 'Die Wollausfuhr Englands vom Jahre 1273', *Viertelj. f. Sozial u. Wirtschaftsg.* VI (1908).

political and economic events of a kind that would have given English merchants an equivalent position at any time in English history. The effective cause was the financial crisis in the affairs of the Crown in the early phases of the Hundred Years War.

That wool trade and wool traders should have become enmeshed in the tangled skein of fourteenth-century finance is not at all surprising. The annual wool crops may not have represented half of the nation's wealth as a petition in Parliament would have it; but they undoubtedly represented a very large proportion of the nation's marketable produce or of what now would be described as the country's main 'cash crop'. The wool trade therefore had an obvious attraction for kings on the look out for money or for goods capable of yielding quick cash. Wool was bound to become an obvious object of royal finance. Taxes on wool grew throughout the fourteenth and fifteenth centuries. In addition to the 'old Custom' of 7*s* 6*d* per sack fixed in 1275, 'new custom' of 3*s* 4*d* was levied on foreigners since 1303. In the course of the fourteenth century the king repeatedly tried to force out of the reluctant Parliaments grants of high subsidies on wool. By the end of the century grants of wool subsidies became regular, and, with this addition total taxation on wool rose to 40*s* per sack exported by Englishmen and 53*s* 4*d* per sack exported by foreigners. This new tax was not, however, established without a previous deal with the Commons over the control and the management of the wool trade.[49]

The wool trade was also involved with royal debt. The wealth represented by the annual wool crop was frequently raided by the Crown for short-term loans. Richard I's ransom had been paid out of a loan raised by the proceeds of English wool sales abroad, and loans raised in such fashion became common at the end of the thirteenth and the early fourteenth centuries. In 1297 Edward I financed his Flemish expedition by pre-empting in England and then selling abroad 8000 sacks of wool. This device was later employed by Edward III on a much larger scale and with less regard for the interests of wool traders and wool growers.

In this way the wool trade was inevitably drawn into the machinations which mark the history of Edward III's war finance. With each successive crisis the conduct of the wool trade had to be reorganised, and each reorganisation brought it a step nearer to the monopoly of the Staple. The first and most important crisis led to the destruction of the Italian interests. The Italian commitments in the wool trade and in royal finance reached the highest point under Edward III. For the first thirteen or fifteen years of his reign, and more especially in the years of hectic war finance between 1337 and 1340, the Florentine house of the Bardi

---

[49] E. Power, *The Wool Trade in English Medieval History* (Oxford, 1941), pp. 63–103.

and from 1336 onwards also the great Florentine house of Peruzzi lent the king vast sums generally on the security of taxes, mostly the wool customs. In the end, however, their operations in England and elsewhere over-strained their resources. As long as they were still able to add loan to loan they remained in possession of their privileges in English wool trade. But as soon as their liquid resources began to give out, as they did in 1343, the king inevitably defaulted. By 1346, the whole of the English business of the two houses was reduced to a vanishing point, and for a time the Florentine bankers had to withdraw not only from the English wool trade but from the English scene altogether.

The place of the Italians was at first taken by a consortium of the wealthier English wool traders and financiers. The consortia, made up of more or less the same group of commercial magnates and as a rule led by William de la Pole and his associates, were formed or re-formed on three or four occasions after 1345. They helped to finance the siege of Calais and the Crécy campaign by a series of large loans (up to £100,000) on the security of the wool customs. In return they received the virtual monopoly of the English wool exports. On several occasions all exports of wool were prohibited except under licence, and only the members of the consortia were allowed to export.

By 1349 the syndicates suffered the same fate as the Bardi and the Peruzzi, and the royal default led not only to the temporary eclipse of de la Pole's circle but also to a change of system. The king had now to turn to a larger body of wool merchants, and to do this at a time when he badly needed parliamentary consent for higher subsidies on wool. In the end he was able to obtain both the subsidies and the loans in ex-change for important concessions. The parliament of 1351 granted the wool subsidies for three years in exchange for abolition of all mono-polies, but in the end monopolies were not so much abolished as widened by being vested in the English Company of the Staple. That Company became the main source of regular loans on the security of wool and wool customs.

The device of the Staple was by no means new. A staple of sorts was already in existence in the last quarter of the thirteenth century when, in order to operate his forced loan on wool of 1294–97, Edward I directed his own wool and that of the wool merchants at first to Dordrecht and then to Antwerp: both towns situated near the places where he needed funds for his war. But this was not yet a full-fledged staple. It was per-missive and not compulsory and it did not create a monopolistic Com-pany of the Staple. An attempt to make it compulsory was made in 1313 when it was fixed at St Omer, but even then the system was as yet very fluid and experimental. Between 1316 and 1326 the Staple was moved from one foreign town to another; between 1326 and 1337 it twice crossed the Channel to selected English ports, and for a brief interval the trade was altogether free. But after 1337 and more especially after 1350 the organisation of the trade rapidly moved towards the monopoly of the English Company of the Staple.

The process began with a full swing away from monopolies of any kind. It has already been shown that in 1351 Parliament stipulated, as a *quid pro quo* for the grant of wool subsidies, that all monopolies should be abolished. In accordance with this stipulation the Ordinances of the Staple enacted in 1353 left the aliens free to buy and export wool as much as they liked, and no Englishman was allowed to engage in exports. This arrangement could not last. It was profitable to wool growers entrenched in Parliament, but too unfavourable to the English merchants and consequently also to their ability to lend money. The system began to break down in 1357. By 1361 the English Company of the Staple was in possession of a virtual monopoly of wool exports to Northern Europe; by 1399 it was safely and permanently launched in Calais. Even then Italians were able to export some wool under royal licence on condition that they took it to Italy and did not sell it in competition with the staplers on the wool markets of the Low Countries. But on the latter the English monopoly was now unchallenged.

The monopoly suited the bulk of the English wool merchants who now formed the Company of the Staple; it suited the rising interest of the clothmakers for it created wide discrepancies between wool prices at home and abroad. Above all, it suited the king. The custom and subsidy on the export of wool was the best possible security which he could offer, and a chartered company enjoying the monopoly of the trade was a much safer source of loans than the series of firms and syndicates which had, one by one, gone bankrupt in the early years of the Hundred Years War. The link with the Crown was further reinforced by the Act of Retainer of 1446, by which the Company farmed the whole of the custom and the subsidy on wool, and undertook in return to pay the wages of the garrison at Calais and certain other fixed charges, repay itself for its past loans and deliver any surplus over and above a fixed sum into the Exchequer. The only interest which suffered was that of the wool growers; and this may have been one of the reasons why the production of wool declined.

The English predominance in the wool trade was thus a product of political and fiscal causes. It was not a manifestation of English trade 'come of age', still less a stage in the economic growth of English trade and economy. It was brought about by successive acts of royal policy and as a result of a bargain between the king and merchants. Moreover it did not result in any increase in the volume of the wool trade handled by English merchants. If we are to trust the figures of the royal export licences of 1273 which have already been mentioned,[50] the English share in the wool exports of the time, though not more than one-third of the total, represented some 11,500 sacks, shared by some 280 exporters. By the middle of the fifteenth century about the same number of staplers exported eight to ten thousand sacks. The English predominance had grown, while the wool trade had shrunk.

2

More relevant to the story of English economic growth was the development of the cloth trade and the wine trade. English wine trade was in some respects one of the oldest branches of English commerce, and also one in which English merchants were predominant from the outset. Evidence of English imports of foreign wine – mostly French – go back to the early years of the Norman rule and beyond. Under the Angevins England found itself politically linked to Gascony, the main wine-producing area of Europe, and the connection thus established stimulated Gascon viticulture and also opened before English merchants a great and ever-expanding field of enterprise. Large, and for a time growing, quantities of wine were imported from Gascony, and most of the imports came to be handled by English merchants, mainly those of Bristol. In return Gascony had to be supplied with foodstuffs, cloth and other miscellaneous goods, which came from England or via England, and were mostly brought by English merchants and on English ships. The trade reached its highest point at the beginning of the fourteenth century, when in some years as much as 90,000 tuns of wine were imported into England.

The most spectacular event in the history of English trade in the late Middle Ages – an event which did more than anything else to conjure up the spectre of the English challenge in the Baltic – came as a result of English cloth exports. Manufacture of marketable cloth was indigenous in this country, and some cloth was always exported. Exports of cloth to France in the seventh and eighth centuries have already been mentioned. A Norwegian saga mentions English cloth among imports to Iceland at the end of the tenth century.[51] English cloths of various kinds, sometimes described by the parts of England from which they came, continue to be mentioned in the records of the twelfth and thirteenth centuries. But although active, the trade was rather small: very much smaller than the Flemish cloth trade and the wool and wine trades of England. In the second half of the fourteenth century, however, the industry suddenly grew to rival and finally to overshadow all other branches of English industry and trade.

[50] See above, p. 208.   [51] A. Bugge, *Die Wikinger* (Halle, 1906), p. 132.

The factors behind the growth have been described elsewhere. Cloth manufacture was establishng itself outside the bounds of corporate towns and was thus better able to keep its labour costs low and to employ mechanical devices, mostly water power. The disorder in Flanders and emigration of artisans from there brought an addition of skilled labour to the English industry. Some protection to more expensive brands of cloth resulted from the prohibition of Flemish imports. But from the point of view of this essay most significant of all is the connection which undoubtedly existed between the growth of the cloth industry and the financial vicissitudes of the wool trade. Continuous interruptions and disorganisation of wool exports hit the rival cloth industries. Above all an export tax of some £2 10s per sack greatly lowered the costs of production at home by comparison with foreign cloth, and it is also possible that English wool monopoly also helped to raise the price of wool to the foreign clothmakers. Thus assisted, the English cloth manufacture forged ahead until by the 1490s the English exports at times exceeded the high figure of 50,000 cloths or an equivalent of some 10,000 to 12,000 sacks of wool and about twice that in value.

With English cloth exports so great, the whole character of English foreign trade and the behaviour of English foreign traders were bound to be transformed. As long as English exports consisted mainly of wool, there was no need for English merchants to go far afield in search for markets and customers. Wool was a raw material of industry; its customers were foreign cloth manufacturers; and the only important cloth manufacturing centres were not only highly localised but also situated near at hand, mainly in the Low Countries. On the other hand, finished cloth had to be sold to potential consumers and in the main centres of potential consumption, or in other words, to men and women all over continental Europe and beyond. It is therefore no wonder that whereas the wool staplers were able to transact their business in Calais and had no need to venture beyond Bruges, English cloth exporters had to push out in every direction, and, in the first place, into East European markets where Flemish cloth had previously been sold. We find fleeting references to Englishmen in Stralsund and Danzig in the eighties of the fourteenth century. In Danzig they were well established by the nineties and possessed a settlement and a factory by the end of the first quarter of the fifteenth century. By that time there was also an English company in the Norwegian trading port of Bergen, where, in exchange for English cloth and other miscellaneous goods, goods of Norwegian and Icelandic origin, mostly fish, could be bought. It is quite possible that there was also an English component in the international mart at the fishing centres of Skania.[52]

[52] For these and most of the subsequent facts of Anglo-Hanseatic relations, see

3

The English appearance in the Baltic brought home to the Hanseatics the dangers of the English challenge. Unfortunately for Anglo-Hanseatic relations and for peace in the Baltic, the English penetration into the northern markets began in earnest at a time when conditions for it were least propitious. English merchants began to frequent the east-to-west route at the very moment when foreign competition appeared to threaten the foundations of Hanseatic prosperity and unity. They tried to establish themselves in Danzig at the very time when the protection of the local market and regional monopoly was becoming the fundamental purpose of municipal policy. Their appearance in the Hanseatic system would have produced a considerable conflict in any case but, in the conditions of the late fourteenth and early fifteenth centuries, it was bound to result in a bitter and desperate struggle.

To begin with, the struggle was developing in English favour: mainly because for the time being the English drive was well backed at home, whereas the German opposition was not. In the English towns the relatively small and specialised groups of men trading to the Baltic found support from the main body of urban opinion which was strongly anti-Hanseatic. Left to themselves the towns could always be relied upon to act against all foreigners, the Venetians, the Genoese, the Flemings as well as the Hanseatics; but the Hanseatics offered the best and the easiest targets. Their exceptional fiscal privileges and their proud position in the city of London – a city within a city – were bound to draw on them the greater share of urban xenophobia. The anti-Hanseatic movement combined the demands of merchants threatened with exclusion from the trade of Prussian towns with the appetites of merchants anxious to exclude the Hanseatics from the trade of English towns. The common enemy produced a sense of common interest and ranged the mass of English urban classes behind the agitation.

At first this movement also enjoyed the full support of the government. In the conditions of the early fifteenth century the government, and more especially the Commons, found it very easy to respond to the pressure of anti-Hanseatic interests and to understand their motives and their language. The temper of the age, fed by accidents of the Hundred Years War, was charged with nationalist pride; the social changes of the times were helping to draw together the official class in English government and the upper ranks of the merchant class. In addi-

M. Postan, 'The Economic and Political Relations of England and the Hanse', E. Power and M. Postan (eds.), *Studies in English Trade in the Fifteenth Century* (London, 1933), reprinted as chapter 5 below.

tion the City of London had evolved in the fifteenth century an efficient 'lobby' in Parliament, and even the provincial towns sometimes elected special deputations 'to make suit in Parliament against Hanseatic privileges'. No wonder the Hanseatics came to regard Parliament as their chief adversary and never expected from it any favour or concession.

The policy of the Lords and of the King's Council was somewhat less definite, for individual lords and prelates sometimes shielded the merchants of the Hanse from enmity and vindictiveness of the Commons and were often referred to in Hanseatic correspondence as their only friends in England. Yet as long as the Council was capable of comprehending and obeying the *raison d'État*, the underlying assumptions of its policy towards the Hanse was little different from those of the merchant classes. On those occasions when personal and party interests of magnates were not much involved, and when conciliatory attitudes to the Hanse were not dictated by the military and political events in Flanders and France, the Council did its best to back the native merchants over their demands in the Baltic.

Thus backed (and as long as it was thus backed) the English mercantile offensive appeared to be very formidable and was indeed scoring success after success. A conflict in the eighties of the fourteenth century ended somewhat to the advantage of the English merchants, and the treaty of 1388 which wound it up recognised for the English their 'old rights' and their freedom to come to the lands of the Hanse and Prussia and to settle there and to traffic freely and undisturbed. A similar conflict in the first decade of the fifteenth century ended by another treaty, in which the English were confirmed in their right to come to Prussia and there *mercari, ibidemque morari et exiende ad lares et domicilia propria redire*. Under the cover of this treaty the English merchants established a flourishing factory in Danzig with a communal organisation, a communal house and a governor with disciplinary powers over its members. When difficulties again arose in the thirties, mostly over the position and privileges of the English company in Danzig, the treaty of 1437 conceded to the English merchants not only their old rights of entry, trade and residence, but also fiscal exemptions as exceptional as those the Hanseatics possessed in England. The English traders were to be free of all taxes imposed in the course of the previous hundred years or more.

On each of these occasions the English merchants benefited from the fundamental disunity in the ranks of the Hanseatic towns. Even though the Danzigers were bitterly opposed to the English merchants in their midst, the Prussian Order and even some interests within Danzig itself set great store by their trade to England and were among the first to seek an end to the successive conflicts. Similarly, the western wing of the Hanse, especially Cologne, had no part in the quarrel of the English position in the Baltic and was always willing to compromise. Even the position of Lübeck was not as yet very consistent and she could be found on occasions counselling moderation and concession to the English claims.

Thus aided, the English prospects appeared very bright indeed. To some Hanseatics the English danger appeared in a light curiously prophetic. Viewed in this light the English threat appeared greater than it actually was, more urgent and more threatening than that of the Dutch. This alone would be sufficient to explain why the strength of Hanseatic opposition stiffened in the middle of the century and why Lübeck swung in support of the anti-English policy. It was badly hit by English piracy, it had grown to fear the effect of great maritime links between Prussia and the west, and in general it was now adopting a belligerent attitude in defence of the Hanseatic hold of the great route. At the same time the English pressure was weakening. This was not altogether due to factors purely or mainly economic. The export of English cloth declined in the middle decades, but the decline was in itself due to failure of the English commercial offensive. The reason why the latter failed is more likely to be found in the political disorders of the middle decades of the century.

With the War of the Roses approaching, the Council became a mere instrument of the rival baronial parties and was no longer able to give support to the English claims against the Hanseatics. It is not that the economic policy of the late Lancastrian and the early Yorkist governments was inspired by any new and different principles. Its worst failing was that it ceased to be inspired by any principles whatsoever. The private interest of ruling magnates in and out of King's Council was allowed free licence, and matters of state policy were made to serve the predatory aims of powerful men. Not only were the merchants unable to rely on the latent power of English arms, but that power itself became a mere instrument of predatory sea-war and piracy. There were easy and substantial gains to be derived from attacks on Hanseatic shipping, and the Council not only did nothing to stop piracy on the high seas but itself directly and indirectly contributed to its extension. It was largely under the auspices of influential members of the Council that the first great attack on Hanseatic shipping in the Bay took place in 1449, and the second great attack in 1458 was led by no other person than Warwick. The outburst of piracy helped to consolidate Lübeck's anti-English policy and to cement the unity of the Hanseatic League and led to a naval war which threw the entire trade and navigation on the North Sea into chaos. At the same time, in spite of the raging naval war, the parties in the Council were not averse from making use of the Hanseatic assistance in their domestic struggles.

In the end a private deal between Edward IV and the Hanseatic

League put an end to all English chances in the conflict with the Hanse. Under that deal the Hanseatics helped Edward to equip the expedition which brought him back to England, and in exchange they received back, in 1474, unaltered and unimpinged, their old privileges without having to concede any rights to the Englishmen in the Baltic towns. They immediately stepped into the place they had occupied in English economic life in the first half of the century, and this place they were to preserve until well into the Tudor era. Their share in English foreign trade soon passed the highest point it had reached before. While they exported on the average about 6000 cloths annually between 1406 and 1427, and about 10,000 annually between 1438 and 1459, their exports rose to well above 13,500 between 1479 and 1482.

The English merchants derived whatever profit and comfort there was to be derived from the restoration of peace and the resumption of Hanseatic trade. But their attempts at direct relations with the markets of Central and Eastern Europe suffered a set-back from which they were not to recover until the age of Elizabeth. Their chances of establishing themselves there were further reduced by political changes in Prussia. Danzig, now under the sovereignty of Polish kings, enjoyed almost a complete *Landeshoheit*, involving full autonomy in matters of government and economic policy. In confirming the treaty with England it postulated that the English were to be treated as all other foreigners. The English merchants themselves ceased to press for parity in the old and full sense of the term, since by now the Baltic trade was no longer vitally important to them. Whether as a result of the continued friction with Denmark and consequent closing of the Sund, or as a result of the war-time re-arrangements in the organisation of English trade, the direct trade of English merchants to Danzig was dwindling very fast. Whereas on several occasions in the first half of the century there were over thirty English boats anchored in the port of Danzig, only twelve boats arrived from England during the three years following the cessation of hostilities, and in 1497, when the registers of the Sund tolls begin, not a single English boat passed the Sund. As late as 1503 there were only twenty-one English boats passing the Sund and it was not until 1547 that the English shipping to the Baltic could again stand comparison with that of the Dutch.

4

The effects of the English defeat reached further than the mere failure to establish a factory in Danzig. Its net result was to interrupt for nearly two generations the expansion of English trade into the outlying European markets and to canalise all English commerce into the single current which led to the Low Countries. The traffic in Baltic goods was taken out of English hands; some of it proceeded indirectly by way of Brabantine fairs, some of it was carried on by the Dutch and the Hanseatics. And with the end of the Baltic trade there also came the end of the Baltic trader. Not until the rebirth of direct Baltic connections in the middle of the sixteenth century and the rise of the Eastland Company did the Baltic 'interest' establish itself again among English merchants.

The loss of the Prussian connection happened to coincide with the lopping off of most other outlying branches of the English trade. In Norway the Hanseatics had since the beginning of the fifteenth century tightened their hold over the trade of Bergen and defeated all the attempts of the English merchants to restore that position. The cessation of the Bergen trade at first sent the English merchants directly to Iceland, but this new enterprise, however important in itself, only completed the ruin of the English trade in Scandinavia. It plunged England into a state of chronic conflict with Denmark, and in the second half of the century it finally shut the Dano-Norwegian waters to English trade and navigation. Even more damaging, though less enduring, was the interruption of English trade to Gascony. This connection, so old and so important in the economic life of the country, was to be disturbed and finally broken during the concluding phases of the Hundred Years War. The French reoccupation of Gascony put an end to the flourishing English exports of cloth and all but interrupted English imports of wine. For a time even the clarets of Gascony were not obtainable except through neutral markets in the Low Countries.

Thus, having lost the more distant markets on the periphery of their trading area, the English merchants were compelled to restrict their maritime and commercial ventures in Northern Europe to the Low Countries; and the 'Merchant Adventurers', a corporation of merchants trading to Flanders and Holland, absorbed the bulk of English trade and the mass of English traders.

The effects of this concentration reached even further than commerce. The historians of the English cloth industry may also find a connection between concentration of English trade to the Netherlands and concentration of English production on undyed and unfinished cloth. There is no doubt that the bulk of English cloth exports in the late fourteenth century and beginning of the fifteenth century consisted of fully dyed and fully finished cloth. But, when with the falling off of the outlying markets the English exporters lost direct contact with the main body of consumers, they had to adjust themselves to a trade on a market still largely dominated by local cloth industries. A *modus vivendi* was found in increasing the exports of undyed and unfinished cloth and selling it to the dyers and finishers from Flanders and Holland. These were essentially the terms on which the great expansion of English cloth exports under the Tudors was made possible, and the old symbiosis in England and the Low Countries was re-established.

(5) *The rise of Holland*

1

Compared with the English challenge that of the Dutch matured relatively late, but its late inconspicuous beginnings turned out, from the Dutch point of view, to be a blessing in disguise. It was very largely because the English attack opened rapidly and successfully that the Hanseatics, and especially the Prussians, read into it the dangers which it did not in fact spell. It had received strong backing from the English government in the first half of the fifteenth century, and thus added further weight to the German alarm. For, after all, at the beginning of the fifteenth century England was a first-class military power with a long record of successful aggression, and in the estimation of the Prussians it had already revealed some of its congenital propensities for empire-building. Did not the Danzigers argue in 1410 that if the English were allowed to settle and to trade in Prussia they would soon annex the country as they had annexed Bordeaux and Gascony? It was because the English danger loomed so large that the Prussians at first and the whole of the Hanse in the end opposed it with remarkable vigour.

The strength of the Dutch position was that their rise owed little to political action and that it was purely economic throughout its early history. They had insinuated themselves into the Baltic trade before the Hanse as a whole woke up to their menace; and so firmly was their power grounded in economic and geographical facts – and eventually in naval prowess – that it could not easily be countered by the political and naval measures at the disposal of the Hanse. Hence the paradox of their challenge: it turned out to be so strong in the end because it appeared so weak at the beginning.

One of the reasons why the so-called commercial rise of Holland in the later Middle Ages was so inconspicuous is that it was a product of local rather than of national development. The country which we know as the Netherlands consisted of at least four geographical regions, each with an economic history of its own: Zealand, Friesland, South Holland and North Holland. In the so-called Dark Ages the delta of the Rhine was the centre of northern commerce. Later, during the Middle Ages, the region of the delta, with Utrecht at its head, was still important as a centre of trade in corn, fish and wine. At the end of the same period,

South Holland with Dordrecht was also showing signs of considerable commercial activity, and so did also the northernmost end of the Netherlands: Campen, Deventer, Zwolle, Gröningen. These towns stood in a loose connection with the Hanse which seems to have paid them very well. But in the fourteenth century important centres of commerce began to appear in parts of the Netherlands hitherto relatively backward, i.e. in Zealand and in North Holland. It is this development of North Holland that is usually meant when the rise of the Dutch is discussed, and it was this development that hit the Hanseatic trade most.

The exact circumstances of the development are somewhat obscure. Dutch historians sometimes connect the rise of Amsterdam, and with it of the rest of North Holland, with the German transit trade through the waterways of Holland *en route* to Flanders and England. According to this view the new dykes obstructed the northern entrance into the Dutch system of rivers and made it necessary to transfer the goods into smaller boats. Amsterdam sprang up at the northern entrance to the dyke system, and Rotterdam at the southern, but other Dutch towns also began to take a hand in this traffic, and by the end of the fourteenth century Holland could already stand on her own feet and was able to enter into a competition with the Hanse. On a somewhat broader view the trade of North Holland grew partly out of the internal trade of the country and partly out of the sea-borne trade between some of its towns and other countries. Like the rest of the Netherlands, North Holland and South Zealand possessed ships and engaged in trade from time immemorial. They were forced to it both by the abundance of their waterways and by the one-sided economic development of the surrounding regions which necessitated a constant movement of foodstuffs. But, whereas in the earlier centuries the distant journeys of Hollanders were probably confined to England and Flanders, in the late fourteenth century they turned to the Baltic. One of the reasons why Hollanders went eastwards was probably the introduction of the *Umlandfahrt* round Jutland. But the chief cause was that the Dutch economy was expanding at the time when opportunities for sea-borne trade in other directions were limited.

Their economic expansion, though two or three centuries old, was gathering speed in the fifteenth century. The thirteenth century saw the Dutch completing the dyking system which protected them from the invasion of the sea. The following century saw a great development of agriculture and cattle-breeding and industry, and the fifteenth was marked by a sudden efflorescence of the old cloth industry. When at the close of the fourteenth century Flanders succumbed to a deep depression, Holland, together with England, rose to the leadership of the continental cloth production. By the middle of the fifteenth century Leiden became one of the foremost cloth centres in the world. Simultaneously with the cloth manufacture there developed also other industries, and especially beer brewing and fishing. In the course of the fifteenth century Holland was also becoming an important source of herring for Western Europe, and its salted fish was carried as far south as Bâle. In addition, both the industry and the trade benefited by the unification of the Netherlands in the fifteenth century by Philip of Burgundy and by the long spell of peace under his rule.

It was largely because their economy grew so gradually that their appearance in the Baltic passed almost unnoticed by their contemporaries. Apparently they entered the Hanseatics' preserves chiefly as carriers, and until the very end of the Middle Ages they were active in the Baltic as sailors at least as much as traders. On some routes they carried Hanseatic goods and were therefore very useful to those towns which had large quantities of bulky goods to carry, such as Riga, Reval or Danzig. By the same token they were most unwelcome to Lübeck. Lübeck was consequently the first to rise in opposition to the Dutch, and throughout the fifteenth century Lübeck was at the back of all the anti-Dutch activities of the Hanse. And for exactly the same reasons Prussia was unwilling to quarrel with the Dutch and on several occasions did its best to thwart Lübeck's plans against Holland.

The story of the Dutch penetration and of their successful combat with the Hanse cannot be told here with all the detail it deserves. By the end of the second decade of the fifteenth century, Dutch progress in the east had grown far enough to have drawn to itself the alarmed attention of the Hanseatic politicians and to have produced the first serious conflict. The issue was raised in 1417 by Lübeck and the other Wendish towns which managed to get through a Hanseatic diet some limitations of the Dutch trade, but were unable to carry with them the Prussian towns in further attempts to close the Baltic to the Dutch altogether. This, however, was only the first of the many Dutch–Wendish clashes to come. By degrees friction became chronic and, for many years, peace was with difficulty maintained by temporary truces. In 1437 the truce was not renewed and a formal state of war lasted from 1438 to 1441. It was during that war that the Dutch revealed to the outside world how much their economic power had grown in the preceding fifty years. In the end the Hanse had to give way in spite of a whole succession of what seemed to have been political triumphs and to conclude the peace treaty of 1441 recognising the freedom of the Dutch trade in the Baltic.

The strength of the Dutch resistance during the war was something of a revelation to the German towns. But the defeat of the Hanse was clinched not so much by the power of Holland as by that conflict of interests within the Hanse, which appeared every time the Wendish towns tried to do anything against the Dutch. Prussia would not support Lübeck against Holland, and in addition the western wing of the Hanse, and especially the towns of the Zuider Zee, Campen, Zwolle and Deventer, vacillated between their loyalty to the Hanse and their commercial interests in Holland. In the end, some of them concluded separate agreements with the Dutch and thus broke the ring of the Hanseatic blockade. With slight variations the same story repeated itself each time the Wendish towns proposed action against Holland, and all the active measures of the Hanse against the Dutch remained ineffective.

2

What made the Dutch especially difficult to combat was that very often the Hanse could not help handicapping itself by the aggressive policy it adopted towards other foreign powers. In their endeavours to arrest the course of economic change the Hanseatics repeatedly took measures which, whatever their avowed object, in the end merely contributed to the increase of Dutch trade. There were several such measures in the fifteenth century. In the fifties the Dutch trade received a great stimulus from a Hanseatic blockade of Flanders, when a great deal of Hanseatic trade passed to the South Germans and the Dutch. In the sixties and the seventies the blundering Hanseatic politicians offered the Dutch the greatest of all their opportunities by their short-sighted and aggressive defence of their Bruges 'staple'. The circumstances of this staple policy are indeed sufficiently interesting in themselves to be worth describing in greater detail.

As a result of the process already explained, Bruges had become by the first half of the fifteenth century the most valuable of Hanseatic markets abroad. It was the centre of German cloth trade and the terminus of the great Hanseatic east-to-west route – the point where this route tapped the channels that led to the French, the Italian and the Iberian South. But in the course of the fifteenth century Bruges began to lose its advantageous position. There were political complications in Flanders itself and there were also economic causes. In the first instance the Zwin, the waterway connecting Bruges with the sea, was silting up and no amount of dredging and dyking could stop the process. Secondly, in the course of the fifteenth century the Flemish industries migrated in directions unfavourable to Bruges. Partly as a result of Brabantine policy, but partly as a result of decline of South-west Flanders, economic leadership passed to the regions in the north-east, especially to Brabant. And, according as the trade and industry of Brabant grew, the old ports of Brabant, Antwerp, with its satellite market of Bergen-op-Zoom, began to rival Bruges as centres of cloth and wool trade. Before long they also began to rival it in other fields. In the same way as Bruges had grown to become the all-important western terminus of the great Hanseatic route to the Baltic, Antwerp now grew to become the terminus of more recent and rival routes: one to the south via Lorraine and one to Eastern Europe via the Rhine valley, Frankfurt-am-Main, and Frankfurt-am-Oder. The alternative routes appeared in response to a number of incentives, but they probably owed much of their prosperity to the initiative of the Dutch and of the merchants of the South German towns seeking a way round the Hanseatic monopoly. And the tighter the Hanseatic hold over the northern trade, the more determined became the endeavours of the outsiders to develop alternative routes.

To Lübeck the old route was of greater significance than to anybody else. Lübeck was the town of the Hanse most interested in maintaining the old Hanseatic lines of communication, and in addition it was also the town most closely linked with the Bruges *Kontor* by a network of interests woven together in the course of a hundred years. But the measures it adopted in defence of Bruges were doomed to failure. They were not supported by other parts of the Hanse and, what is more, they still further undermined the economic position of Bruges. This is especially true of the so-called 'staple' rules. In order to restore Bruges to its old position in the Hanseatic trade, the Hanse laid down in the middle of the fifteenth century a series of rules by which costly goods and goods which con-stituted the monopoly of the Hanse, i.e. wax, furs, metals, Skania herring, had to be imported to Bruges before they could be sold elsewhere in Flanders or the Low Countries. In addition, all cloth, whether it was pro-duced in Flanders or in Holland, had to brought to Bruges before it could be exported to the east. At one time an attempt was even made to exclude Dutch cloth altogether, and to force every German boat carrying staple goods to call at Bruges even if the goods were directed to England or to the towns of the western Hanse. Needless to say this staple policy defeated its own ends. Hanseatic trade could not at one and the same time maintain its volume and be tied down to a decaying place. What happened was that the rules of the staple were evaded in spite of their energetic enforce-ment; and that in so far as they were obeyed they depressed the Hanseatic trade and stimulated the trade of the South German and the Dutch towns. The Hanseatics themselves began to call in ever-increasing numbers at Antwerp and the towns of Holland – Amsterdam, Middelburg, Haarlem, Delft and Vere – and to stay away from Bruges. Even the Flemings began to send their cloth to Bergen-op-Zoom and Antwerp, from whence the Dutch carried it to Amsterdam, which was now a very important centre of cloth trade.

In 1477 the Hanseatic Diet revoked the staple rules, but it was already too late, for they had done all the harm they could. By the end of the century Bruges was beginning to take on the aspect of 'Bruges le mort',

Antwerp with Bergen became the chief mart of Northern Europe, and the Dutch were in an impregnable position. They now traded as far east as Breslau and Cracow, and the towns of Prussia themselves began to look with dismay at the Dutch entering Poland. For 1495 we possess the earliest returns of the toll-stations at the Sound, the famous *Sundtolls,* and in that year the Dutch vessels formed the bulk of all the shipping bound for the Baltic.

BIBLIOGRAPHY

I. PRINTED SOURCES

Fagniez, G. *Documents relatifs à l'histoire de l'industrie et du commerce en France (au moyen âge).* 2 vols. Paris, 1898, 1900.

Gregory of Tours. *The History of the Franks,* I and II (transl. by O. M. Dalton). Oxford, 1927.

Hölbaum, K., Kunze, K. and Stein, W. *Hansisches Urkundenbuch.* Verein für Hansische Geschichte. Halle and Leipzig, 1876–1907.

Koppmann, K. *Die Recesse und Andere Akten der Hansetäge von* 1236–1340, I–VIII. Die Historische Kommission bei der Königl. Akad. der Wissenschaften. Leipzig, 1870–97.

Kunze, K. *Hanseakten aus England,* 1275 *bis* 1412. *Hansische Geschichtsquellen,* VI. Verein für Hansische Geschichte. Halle, 1891.

Kuske, B. *Quellen zur Geschichte des Kölner Handels und Verkehrs im Mittelalter.* 3 vols. Gesellschaft für Rheinische Geschichtskunde. Bonn, 1918–23.

Lange, C. C. A., Unger, C. R. and others. *Diplomatarium Norvegicum,* vols. I ff. Oslo, 1847, etc.

Lappo-Danilevsky, N. *Recueil des documents relatifs à l'histoire de la Neva.* Petrograd, 1916. (Edition of the Imperial Academy of Sciences.)

Lechner, G. *Die Hansischen Pfundzollisten des Jahres* 1368. Quellen z. Hansisch. Gesch., N.F. vol. x. Lübeck, 1935.

Neale, E. W. W. *The Great Red Book of Bristol.* Text (pt. I). Bristol Record Society's Publications, vol. IV, 1937.

Poelman, H. A. *Bronnen tot de Geschiedenis van den Oostzeehandel,* I. Rijks Geschiedenkundige Publicatiën. The Hague, 1917.

Posthumus, N. W. *Bronnen tot de Geschiedenis van de Leidsche Textielnijverheid,* 1333–1795. Rijks Geschiedenkundige Publicatiën. The Hague, 1910–22.

Ropp, G. von der. *Hanserecesse* 1431–76. Zweite Abteilung, I–VII. Verein für Hansische Geschichte. Leipzig, 1876–92.

Severen, L. Gilliodts-van (ed.). *Cartulaire de l'ancienne Estaple de Bruges.* 4 vols. Société d'Emulation, Bruges, 1904–6.

Smit, H. J. *Bronnen tot de Geschiedenis van den handel met Engeland, Schotland en Ierland,* 1150–1485. Rijks Geschiedenkundige Publicatiën. The Hague, 1928.

Sneller, Z. W. and Unger, W. S. *Bronnen tot de Geschiedenis van den handel met Frankrijk*, I Rijks Geschiedenkundige Publicatiën. The Hague, 1930.

Thomas, A. H. *Calendar of Early Mayor's Court Rolls of the City of London, 1298–1307.* Cambridge, 1924.

— *Calendar of Plea and Memoranda Rolls of the City of London.* 2 vols., 1323–64, 1364–81. Cambridge, 1926, 1929.

— *Calendar of Select Pleas and Memoranda of the City of London, 1381–1412.* Cambridge, 1932.

Unger, W. S. *De Tol van Iersekeroord: documenten en rekeningen, 1321–1572.* The Hague, 1939.

— *Bronnen tot de Geschiedenis van Meddelburg in het landsheerlijken tijd.* Rijks Geschiedenkundige Publicatiën. The Hague, 1923.

Warner, G. (ed.). *The Libelle of Englyshe Polycye.* Oxford, 1926.

II. SECONDARY AUTHORITIES

Abel, W. 'Bevölkerungsgang und Landwirtschaft im Ausgehenden Mittelalter in Lichte de Preis- und Lohnbewegung.' *Schmoller's Jahrbücher*, 58 Jahrg., 1934.

— *Agrarkrisen und Agrarkonjunktur im Mitteleuropa.* Berlin, 1935.

— *Die Wüstungen des ausgehenden Mittelalters.* Jena, 1943.

Agats, A. *Der Hansische Baienhandel.* Heidelberg, 1904.

Arens, Franz. 'Wilhelm Servat von Cahors zu London.' *Vierteljahrsch. für Sozial- und Wirtschaftsgesch.* 1904.

Arup, E. *Studier i Engelsk og Tysk Handel's Histoire, etc.* 1350–1850. Copenhagen, 1907.

Avenel, G. de. *Histoire économique de la propriété, des salaires, des denrées et de tous les prix.* 6 vols. Paris, 1886–1920.

Bächtold, H. *Der Norddeutsche Handel im 12. und beginnenden 13. Jahrhundert.* Abhandlungen zur mittleren und neuen Geschichte, hrsg. von G. v. Below, H. Finke und F. Meinecke, Heft. 21. Berlin and Leipzig, 1910.

Bahr, C. *Handel und Verkehr der deutschen Hanse in Flandern während des vierzehnten Jahrhunderts.* Leipzig, 1911.

Baker, J. L. N. *Medieval Trade Routes.* Historical Association Pamphlet, no. III. 1938.

Beardwood, Alice. *Alien Merchants in England 1350–1377. Their Legal and Economic Position.* Cambridge (Mass.), 1931.

Beck, L. *Die Geschichte des Eisens.* 4 vols. Brunswick, 1891–9.

Beloch, J. 'Die Bevölkerung Europas im Mittelalter.' *Zeitschrift für Sozial- und Wirtschaftsgesch.* III, 405. Freiburg i. B., 1894.

Below, G. von. *Aus Sozial- und Wirtschaftsgeschichte.* Stuttgart, 1928.

— *Probleme der Wirtschaftsgeschichte.* Tübingen, 1920.

Bens, G. *Der deutsche Warenfernhandel im Mittelalter.* Breslau, 1926.

Beveridge, W. 'Wages in the Winchester Manors.' *Econ. Hist. Rev.* (1936), VII, no. 1.

— 'Yield and Price of Corn in the Middle Ages.' *Economic History* (Suppl. to *Econ. Journ.*), no. 2 (1927).

Bigwood, G. 'Les Financiers d'Arras.' *Revue Belge de Philologie et d'Histoire,* 1924.

Bigwood, G. 'La Politique de la Laine en France sous les règnes de Phillipe le Bel et de ses fils.' *Revue Belge de Philologie et d'Histoire*, 1936.

Bloch, M. 'Le Problème de l'Or au Moyen Age.' *Annales d'Histoire Sociale et Economique*, 1933.

Blockmans, Fr. *Her Gentsche Stadspatriciaat tot Omstreeks* 1302. Antwerp, 1938.

Bouquelot, G. *Les foires de Champagne*. 2 vols. Mémoires d'Academie des Sciences et Belles Lettres. Paris, 1938.

Boutruche, R. *La Crise d'une Société: Seigneurs et Paysans du Bordelais pendant la Guerre de Cent Ans*. Paris, 1947.

Bouvier, R. *Un Financier Colonial au XV Siècle. Jacques Cœur*. 1928.

Boyer, H. *Histoire de l'industrie et du commerce à Bourges*. Bourges, 1884.

Bruns, F. (ed.). *Die Lübecker Bergenfahrer und ihre Chronistik*. Hansische Geschichtsquellen, N.F., Bd. II. Verein für Hansische Geschichte. Berlin, 1900.

Bücher, K. *Die Entstehung der Volkwirtschaft*. 2 vols. Leipzig, 1920.

Bugge, A. *Den Norske Traelasthandels Histoire*, 1. Skien, 1925.

— 'Handelen mellum England og Norge indtil Begyndelsen af det 15de Aarhundrede.' *Historisk Tidskrift*, Raekke III, Bind 4, pp. 1–149. Oslo, 1898.

— 'Die nordeuropäischen Verkehrswege im früheren Mittelalter.' *Vierteljahrsch. f. Sozial- u. Wirtschaftsgesch.* IV (1906).

— 'Der Untergang der Norwegischen Seeschiffahrt.' *Vierteljahrsch. f. Sozial- u. Wirtschaftsgesch.* 1904.

Carus-Wilson, E. M. (ed.). *The Overseas Trade of Bristol in the later Middle Ages*. Bristol Record Society's Publications, VII (1936).

Carus-Wilson, E. M. 'Trends in the Export of English Woollens in the Fourteenth Century.' *Econ. Hist, Rev.* III, 1950

Daenell, E. R. *Die Blütezeit der deutschen Hanse. Hansische Geschichte von der zweiten Hälfte des XIV, bis zum letzten Viertel des XV. Jahrhunderts*. 2 vols. Berlin, 1905–6.

Deroisy, Armand. 'Les Routes Terrestres de laines Anglais vers la Lombardie.' *Revue du Nord*, XXV (1939).

Desmarez, G. *Etudes sur la Propriété Foncière dans les villes du Moyen Age et spécialement au Flandre*. Université de Grand. Recueil des travaux publiés par la Faculté de Philosophie et Lettres, 1898.

Dion, R. 'Orléans et l'ancienne navigation de la Loire.' *Annales de Géographie*, XLVII, 1938.

Dopsch, A. *Economic and Social Foundations of European Civilisation*. (Transl.) London, 1937.

— *Die Wirtschaftsentwicklung der Karolinger Zeit*. 2 vols., 2nd ed. Weimar, 1922.

Ebel, W. 'Das Rostocker Transportgewerbe.' *Vierteljahrsch. für Sozial- und Wirtschaftsgesch.* 1938.

Eck, A. *Le Moyen Age Russe*. Paris, 1933.

Espinas, G. *La Vie Urbaine de Douai au Moyen-Age*, I-IV. Paris, 1914

— *Les Origines du Capitalisme*. 2 vols. Lille, 1933, 1936.

Feaveryear, A. E. *The Pound Sterling*. Oxford, 1931.

Flower, C. T. *Public Works in Medieval Law*, I and II. Selden Society Publications, 1923.

de Freville. *Mémoires sur la commerce maritime de Rouen.* 2 vols. Rouen and Paris, 1857.

Gilliard, Ch. 'L'Ouverture du St Gothard.' *Annales d'Histoire Economique et Sociale*, 1929.

Giry, A. *Histoire de la Ville de Saint-Omer*. Paris, 1877.

Goetz, L. K. *Deutsch-Russische Handelsgeschichte des Mittelalters*. Hansische Geschichtsquellen, N.F., Bd. v. Lübeck, 1922.

Gras, N. S. B. *The English Customs System*. Cambridge (Mass.), 1918.

— *The Evolution of the English Corn Market*. Cambridge (Mass.), 1915.

Gray, H. L. 'The Production and Exportation of English Woollens in the Fourteenth Century.' *Eng. Hist. Rev.* XXXIX (1924), 13–35.

Grierson, P. 'The Relations between England and Flanders before the Norman Conquest.' *Trans. Roy. Hist. Soc.*, 4th ser., XXIII (1941).

Guiraud, L. *Recherches et conclusions nouvelles sur le prétendu rôle de Jacques Cœur*. Paris, 1900.

Hänselman, L. 'Braunschweig in seinen Beziehungen zu den Harz- und Seegebieten.' *Hansische Geschichtsblätter*, 1873.

Höpke, R. *Brugges Entwicklung zum Mittelalterlichen Weltmarkt*. D. Schaffer's Abhandlungen zur Verkehrs- und Seegeschichte, no. 1. Berlin, 1908.

— *Der Deutsche Kaufmann in Neiderlanden*. Hansische Pfingsblätter, no. 7. Lübeck, 1911.

— *Der Untergang der Hanse*. Lubeck, 1923.

Hartwich, C. *Die menschlichen Genussmittel*. Leipzig, 1911.

Hayem, J. *Mémoires et Documents pour servir à l'Histoire du Commerce et de l'Industrie en France*. Paris, 1922.

Henaux, F. *Fabrique d'armes de Liège*. Liège, 1858.

Hewitt, H. J. *Medieval Cheshire*. Manchester, 1929.

Hirsch, T. *Danzigs Handels- und Gewerbsgeschichte unter der Herrschaft des deutschen Ordens*. Leipzig, 1858.

Hoopt, C. G. 't. *Het ontstaan van Amsterdam*. Amsterdam, 1917.

Huvelin, P. *Essai historique sur le droit des marchés et des foires*. Paris, 1897.

Imbertin, F. 'Les Routes Mediévales.' *Annales d'Histoire Economique et Sociale*, 1939.

Inama-Sternegg, K. T. von. *Deutsche Wirtschaftsgeschichte*. 3 vols. Leipzig, 1899.

Jastrow, Ignaz. 'Über Welthandelstrassen in d. Geschichte d. Abendlandes.' *Volkswirtschaftliche Gesellschaft. Volkswirtschaftl. Fragen*, Jahrg. VIII Berlin, 1887.

Jenkinson, H. 'A Money-lender's Bonds of the Twelfth Century.' Lane Poole, *Essays in History*, 1927.

Johnsen, O. Albert. *Norgesveldets Undergang, et Utsyn og et Opgjør Nedgangstiden*. Oslo, 1924.

Jullian, C. *Histoire de Bordeaux depuis les origines jusqu'en* 1895. Bordeaux, 1895.

Kendrick, T. D. *A History of the Vikings*. London, 1930.

Ketner, F. *Handel en Scheepvaart van Amsterdam in de Vijftiende Eeuw*. The Hague, 1936.

Keyser, E. 'Der bürgerliche Grundbesitz der Rechtsstadr Danzig im 14. Jahrhundert.' *Zeitschrift d. Westpreussischen Geschichtsverein*, Heft LVIII (1918).

Kesselbach, G. A. 'Schleswig als Vermittlerin des Handels zwischen Nordsee und Ostsee vom 9. bis in das 13. Jahrhundert.' *Zeitschrift für Schleswig-Holsteinischen Lauenburgische Gesch.* 1907.

Klettler, P. *Nordwesteuropas Verkehr, Handel und Gewerbe im frühen Mittel-alter*, Deutsches Kultur, Historische Reihe, geleitet von A. Dopsch. Vienna, 1924.

Köster, G. 'Die Entwicklung der nordostdeutschen Verkehrstrassen bis 1800.' *Forschungen zur Brandenburgischen und Preussischen Gesch.* Bd. 48 (1936).

Koster, A. *Schiffahrt und Handelsverkehr des Östlichen Mittelmeeres.* Leipzig, 1924.

Kowalewsky, M. *Die ökonomische Entwicklung Europas bis zum Beginn der kapitalistschen Wirtschaftsform.* 8 vols. Berlin, 1901–14.

Krocker, E. *Handelsgeschichte der Stadt Leipzig. Die Entwicklung des Leipziger Handels und der Leipziger Messen.* Vol. VII of von Schulte's and Hoffmann's *Beiträge zur Stadtgeschichte.*

Kulischer, J. *Allgemeine Wirtschaftsgeschichte.* Berlin, 1928.

— *Russische Wirtschaftsgeschichte.* 1. Jena, 1925.

Lamprecht, K. *Beiträge zur Geschichte des Französischen Wirtschaftslebens im XI. Jahrhundert.* Leipzig, 1878.

Lapsley, G. T. 'The Account Roll of a Fifteenth-Century Iron Master.' *Eng. Hist. Rev.* XIV, 1899.

Lauffer, V. 'Danzigs Schiffs- und Waarenverkehr.' *Zeitschr. d. Westpreussischen Geschichtsvereins*, Heft XXXIII. Danzig, 1894.

Laurent, H. *Un grand commerce d'exportation au moyen âge: La draperie des Pays Bas en France et dans les Pays Mediterranéens, XII-XVe siècle.* Paris, 1935.

— *Choix de documents inédits pour servir à l'histoire de l'expansion commerciale des Pays-Bas en France au Moyen Age* (XIIe–XVe siècle). Brussels, 1934.

— 'Marchands du palais et marchands d'abbayes.' *Revue Historique*, CLXXXIII, 1938.

Lestocquoy, J. *Les Dynasties Bourgeoises d'Arras du XIe au XVe siècle* (*Patriciens du Moyen-âge*). Arras, 1945.

— 'Les Etapes du développement urbain d'Arras.' *Revue Belge de Philologie et d'Histoire*, 1944.

Levasseur, E. *Histoire du commerce de la France*, I. Paris, 1910. *Histoire des classes ouvrières et de l'industrie en France avant* 1789. 2nd ed. Paris, 1901.

— *Histoire de la population française avant* 1789 ... 3 vols. Paris, 1889–92.

Lewis, G. R. *The Stannaries, a study of the English tin mines.* Cambridge (Mass.), 1908.

Lombard, M. 'L'Or Musalman du VIIe au XIe siècle.' *Annales: Economies, Sociétés, Civilisations*, no. 2 (1947).

Lot, F. *L'état des paroisses et des feux de* 1328. Paris, 1929.

Lot, F. and Fawtier, R. *Le premier budget de la monarchie française* (1202). Paris, 1932.

Lunt, W. E. *Financial Relations of the Papacy with England to* 1327. Cambridge (Mass.), 1939.

Luzatto, G. *Storia del Commerzio.* Florence, 1914.

Magnusen, F. 'Om de Engelskes Handel og Foerd paa island i det 15de Aarhundrede.' *Nordisk Tidskrift for Oldkyndighed*, II. Copenhagen,1833.

Malowist, M. 'Le développement des rapports économiques entre la Flandre, la Pologne et les Pays Limitrophes du XIIIe au XIVe siècle.' *Revue Belge de Philologie et d'Histoire.* X, 1931.

Marquant, R. *La vie économique à Lille sous Philippe le Bon*. Paris, 1940.

Mickwitz, G. *Die Kartellfunktionen der Zünfte*. Helsingfors, 1936.

Moerman, H. J. 'Bijdragen tot de Economische Geschiedenis van Kampen in de Middeleuwen.' *Economisch Historisch Jaarboek*, 1920.

Naude, W. *Getreidehandelspolitik der europäischen Staaten, XIII.-XVIII. Jahr.* Berlin, 1901.

Nef, J. U. 'Silver Production in Central Europe, 1450–1618.' *Journal of Political Econ*. XLIX, 1941.

Netta, Gheron. *Die Handelsbeziehungen zwischen Leipzig und Ost- und Südosteuropa bis zum Verfall Warenmessen*. Zurich, 1920.

Neuburg, C. *Goslars Bergbau bis 1552*. Hanover, 1872.

Neumann, G. *Heinrich Castorp*. Lübeck, 1932.

Niermeyer, J. F. *De Wording van onze Volkshuishouding*. The Hague, 1946.

Nöe, Albert. *De Handel van Noord-Nederland op Engeland in de XIIIe Eeuw*. Haarlem, 1918.

Ochenkowski, W. von. *Englands wirtschaftliche Entwickelung im Ausgange des Mittelalters*, Jena, 1879.

Pigeonneau, H. *Histoire du Commerce de la France*. I. Paris, 1885.

Pirenne, H. *Histoire de Belgique*, vol. I, 5th ed. Brussels, 1929 and vol. II, 3rd ed., Brussels, 1922.

— *Medieval Cities. Their Origins and the Revival of Trade*. Princeton, 1925.

— *Mahomet et Charlemagne*. Paris, 1937.

— 'Un Contraste économique: Mérovingiens et Carolingiens.' *Revue Belge de Philologie et d'Histoire*, II (1923).

— 'Les Périodes de l'histoire sociale du capitalisme.' *Bulletins d'Académie Royale de Belgique*, no. 5 (1914).

Posthumus, N. W. *De Geschiedenis van de Leidsche Lakenindustrie*, I. The Hague, 1908.

Power, E. E. 'The English Wool Trade in the reign of Edward IV.' *Camb. Hist. Journ*. II. Cambridge, 1926.

— *The Wool Trade in English Medieval History*. Oxford, 1941.

Power, E. E. and Postan, M. M. *Studies in English Trade in the Fifteenth Century*. London, 1933.

Püschel, A. *Das Anwachsen der deutschen Städte in der Zeit der mittelalterlichen Kolonialbewegung*. Berlin, 1910.

Renouard, Yves. *Les Hommes d'Affaires Italiens du Moyen Age*. Paris, 1949.

Reyer, E. *Zinn: eine geologisch-montanistisch-historische Monographie*. Berlin, 1881.

Reynolds, R. L. 'The Market for Northern Textiles in Genoa, 1179–1200.' *Revue Belge de Philologie et d'Histoire*, VIII (1929).

— 'Merchants of Arras and the Overland Trade with Genoa, XIIth Century.' Ibid. IX (1930).

Rhodes, W. E. *The Italian bankers in England and their loans to Edward I and Edward II*. In Owens College Essays (eds. T. F. Tout and J. Tait). Manchester, 1902.

Rogers, J. E. Thorold. *A History of Agriculture and Prices in England*. Oxford, 1866–1902.

Rörig, F. *Hansische Beiträge zur Deutschen Wirtschaftsgeschichte*, Breslau, 1928.

Rörig, F. *Der Markt von Lübeck. Topographisch-statistiche Untersuchung zur deutschen Sozial- und Wirtschaftsgeschichte.* Leipzig, 1922.

— *Mittelalterliche Weltwirtschaft.* Jena, 1933.

Ruding, R. *Annals of the Coinage of Great Britain.* London, 1840.

Ruinen J. *De Oudste Handelsbetrekkingen van Holland en Zeeland met Engeland.* (*Dissertation.*) Amsterdam, 1919.

Russell, J. C. *British Medieval Population.* Albuquerque, 1948.

Rutkowski, J. *Histoire économique de la Pologne avant les partages.* Paris, 1927.

Sabbe, E. 'L'importation des tissus orientaux.' *Revue Belge de Philologie et d'Histoire,* 1935.

Salzman, L. F. *English Trade in the Middle Ages.* Oxford, 1931.

Sapori, A. *Studi di Storia Economica Medievale.* Florence, 1947.

— *La Crisi delle Compagnie Mercantili dei Bardi e dei Peruzzi,* Florence, 1926.

Schäfer, D. *Die Hanse.* Monographien zur Weltgeschichte, no. XIX. Bielefeld and Leipzig, 1903.

— *Das Buch des Lübeckschen Vogts auf* Schonen. Hansische Geschichtsquellen, IV. Halle, 1887.

Schanz, G. *Englische Handelspolitik gegen Ende des Mittelalters, mit besonderer Berücksichtigung des Zeitalters der beiden ersten Tudors, Heinrich VII und Heinrich VIII.* 2 vols. Leipzig, 1881.

Scheffel, P. H. *Verkehrsgeschichte der Alpen,* 2 vols. Berlin, 1908–1914.

Schreiner, J. *Pest og Prisfall i Senmiddelalderen.* Oslo, 1948.

Schulte, A. *Geschichte der grossen Ravensburger Handelsgesellschaft,* 3 vols. Stuttgart and Berlin, 1923.

Schulz, F. *Die Hanse und England von Edwards III bis auf Heinrichs VIII Zeit.* Abhandlungen zur Verkehrs- und Seegeschichte, v. (Ed. D. Schäfer.) Berlin, 1911.

Sée, H. 'Peut-on évaluer la population de l'ancienne France?' *Revue d'économie politique.* Paris, 1924.

Seeger, H.-J. *Westfalens Handel und Gewerbe.* Studien zur Geschichte de Wirtschaft und Geisteskultur. Bd. 1. Berlin, 1926.

Smit, H. J. 'De betekenis van den Noordnederlandschen in 't bijzonders van den Hollandschen en Zeeuwschen handel in de laatste helft der 14er eeuw.' *Bijdragen en Mededeelingen van het Historisch Genootschap.* Utrecht, 1930.

— 'Handel en Scheepvaart in het Noordzeegebied gedurende de 13ᵉ eeuw.' *Bijdragen voor Vaderlandsche Geschiedenis en Oudheidkunde* (1928).

Sneller, Z. W. 'De Hollandsche Korenhandel in het Sommegebied in de 15e eeuw.' *Bijdragen en Mededeelingen van het Historisch Genootschap,* 1925.

— 'De entwikkeling van den handel tusschen Noord-Nederland en Frankrijk tot het midden der vijfteinden eeuw.' *Bijdragen en Mededeelingen van het Historisch Genootschap,* 1922.

— 'Wijnvaart en wijnhandel tusschen Frankrijk en de Noordelijke Nederlanden in de tweede helft der 15e eeuw.' *Bijdragen en Mededeelingen van het Historisch Genootschap,* 1922.

Söderberg, T. *Storra Kopparberget ander Medeltiden.* Stockholm, 1932.

— 'Det Svenska Bergsbrukets uppkomst.' *Historisk Tidskrift,* 1936

Sombart, W. *Der moderne Kapitalismus,* 3rd ed., 1. Munich and Leipzig, 1913.

Stein, W. 'Die Hanse und England beim Ausgang des hundert-jährigen Krieges.' *Hansische Geschichtsblätter,* Bd. XXVI (1921), 27–126.

Steinhausen, G. *Der Kaufmann in der deutschen Vergangenheit.* Jena, 1912.

Sterck, J. F. M. 'De opkomst van Aemstelredam godsdienstig en economik.' *Tijdschrift voor Geschiedenis,* 1926.

Stieda, W. *Hildebrand Veckinchusen.* Leipzig, 1921.

— 'Über die Quellen der Handelsstatistik im Mittelalter.' *Abhandlungen d. Königl. Preussischen Akad. der Wissenschaften,* 1903.

Sturler, J. de. *Les Relations politiques et les échanges commerciaux entre le Duché de Brabant et l'Angleterre au moyen âge.* Paris, 1936.

Swank, J. M. *History of the Manufacture of Iron in All Ages.* Philadelphia, 1892.

Tyler, J. E. *The Alpine Passes.* Oxford, 1930.

Unger, W. S. 'De Hollandsche graanhandel en graanhandelspolitik in de middeleeuwen.' *De Economist* (1916).

Unwin, G. (ed.). *Finance and Trade under Edward III.* Manchester, 1918.

— *The Gilds and Companies of London.* The Antiquary's Books, ed. J. C. Cox, 1908.

— *Studies in Economic History* (Collected Papers), 1927.

Usher, A. P. *The History of the Grain Trade in France,* Cambridge (Mass.), 1913.

Vercauteren, F. *Etude sur les Civitates de la Belgique Seconde.* Brussels, 1934.

Vogel, W. *Geschichte der deutschen Seeschiffarht,* I. *Von der Urzeit bis zum Ende des XV. Jahrhunderts.* Berlin, 1915.

— 'Ein seefahrender Kaufmann um 1100.' *Hansische Geschichtsblätter,* 1912.

Vollbehr, F. *Die Holländer und die deutsche Hanse.* Jena, 1930.

Walsh, A. *Scandinavian Relations with Ireland during the Viking Period.* Dublin and London, 1922.

Werveke, H. van. 'Der Flandrische Eigenhandel in Mittelalter.' *Hansische Geschichtsblätter,* 1935.

— 'Monnaie, lingots et marchandises.' *Annales d'Histoire Economique et Sociale,* 1932.

— 'Currency Manipulation in the Middle Ages: The Case of Louis de Male, Count of Flanders.' *Trans. Roy. Hist. Soc.* ser. 4, XXXI (1949).

— 'Essor et décline de la Flandre.' *Studi in onore di Gino Luzzatto.* Milan, 1949.

Willard, J. F. *Parliamentary Taxes on personal property* 1290–1334.' Cambridge (Mass.), 1934.

— 'Inland Transportation in England during the Fourteenth Century.' *Speculum,* I. 1926.

Zycha, A. *Das Recht des ältesten deutschen Bergbaues bis ins 13. Jahrhundert,* Berlin, 1899.

5

THE ECONOMIC AND POLITICAL RELATIONS OF ENGLAND AND THE HANSE FROM 1400 TO 1475*

Abbreviations used in this paper

C.C.R.	Calendar of Close Rolls
C.P.R.	Calendar of Patent Rolls
Dipl. Norv.	Diplomatarium Norvegicum, ed. A. Bugge, C. C. A. Lange, and C. R. Unger
E.H.R.	English Historical Review
G.R.B.	The Great Red Book (Bristol)
Hans. Gbl.	Hansische Geschichtsblätter
H.R.	Hansische Recessanbücher
Journal	Journals of the Proceedings of the Court of Common Council (London)
K.R.	King's Remembrancer (of the Exchequer)
L. Bk.	Letter Books
L.T.R.	Lord Treasurer's Remembrancer (of the Exchequer)
Proc. and Ord. P.C.	Proceedings and Ordinances of the Privy Council of England, ed. Sir H. Nicolas
R.S.	Rolls Series
Rot. Parl.	Rotuli Parliamentorum
Stat.	Statutes of the Realm
U.B.	Hansisches Urkundenbuch, ed. K. Höhlbaum, K. Kunze and W. Stein
V.S.W.G.	Vierteljahrschrift für Social- und Wirtschaftsgeschichte

I. THE RIVALRY

The subject of Anglo-Hanseatic relations is something more than just one chapter in the history of English expansion. All through the Middle Ages the activities and policies of the Hanseatic towns dominated the economic configuration of Northern Europe, and thus affected every-thing the English did, or failed to do, in the Baltic and the North Sea.

* This paper first appeared in E. Power and M. Postan, eds, *Studies in English trade in the fifteenth century*, Routledge, London, 1933.

The Hanse formed a background to English commercial development, as inevitable and sometimes as unaccountable as the weather itself.[1]

Over the greater part of the Middle Ages that background was far from favourable to English commercial development. Every attempt of English merchants to expand their trade with the other countries of Northern Europe was bound to bring them into conflict with the economic system established and guarded by the Hanse. The main currents of northern trade in the later Middle Ages ran from east to west, between the recently opened markets and sources of raw materials in Eastern Europe, and the older countries in the west. It was to their position on this current that the towns of the German Hanse owed their greatness. The two poles, Novgorod in the extreme east and Bruges in the west, were just outside the racial and political limits of German expansion, but all along the intervening route there grew up a chain of purely German towns, each commanding an important halt in the route or a junction with a contributory stream of traffic. In the centre there were the great cities of Lübeck and Hamburg, both situated at points where the coastal shipping going east or west struck the projecting coast of Jutland, and goods had to be unloaded for transportation by land across the peninsula. Like their Saxon and 'Wendish' neighbours (Bremen, Wismar, and Rostock) they were also natural foci of the northward and southward traffic: northward to the fishing centres of Skania on the Sund, and the principal ports of Scandinavia, and southward to the cornlands of Eastern Saxony, Brandenburg, and Mecklenburg. The western section of the route was served by the towns of Westphalia, the Zuider Zee and the Rhine, and dominated by the ancient and proud city of Cologne. It was the function of Cologne to connect the great transcontinental current with reservoirs traditionally her own – the Rhine valley, England, and the Netherlands. To the east of the Lübeck–Hamburg combination there were the towns of Prussia clustering round the new and rapidly growing port of Danzig. These formed the next stage in the journey through Livonia to Russia, and tapped the interior of Prussia and Poland. In the extreme north-east were the towns of Livonia guarding the approaches to Novgorod and the intermediate regions of westernmost Russia.[2]

These towns lived on and by the great route. They exploited it not only directly, but also indirectly: by the power it gave them in foreign fields. The industrial centres of Western Europe were badly in need of the East

---

[1] The references to the Hanse in section 1 are, when not otherwise stated, based on the accounts in E. R. Daenell, *Die Blütezeit der deutschen Hanse*, W. Vogel, *Geschichte der deutschen Seeschiffahrt*, and D. Schäfer, *Die Hanse*.

[2] W. Stein, 'Die Hansestädte', in *Hans. Gbl.* (1913–15), Jahrgang, 1913: Erstes Heft, pp. 233–94, Zweites Heft, pp. 519–60; Jahrgang, 1914: Erstes Heft, pp. 257–89; Jahrgang, 1915: Erstes Heft, pp. 119–78.

European markets; the industrial, wool-growing and fishing regions of the west were badly in need of east German corn and of the sylvan products of Poland and Russia. As long as the north German towns dominated the route to the Baltic east they possessed a virtual monopoly of trade to the east, and as long as they possessed that monopoly their merchants were welcome and indispensable in more than one foreign country. In England the merchants of north German towns acquired, by the end of the thirteenth century, liberties and privileges, which in some matters placed them well above all other foreigners, and even above the English merchants themselves. In Flanders they formed, from the middle of the thirteenth century, a privileged body of merchants occupying an exceptional place in the commerce of Bruges and well protected by treaties with the Dukes and the 'four members' of Flanders. In Novgorod they succeeded a generation earlier in ousting their Scandinavian predecessors and establishing a monopoly in Russian trade. But nowhere was their power greater than in Scandinavia. In the course of the late thirteenth and early fourteenth centuries they acquired a hold over the mineral wealth of Sweden, the fisheries of Skania, and the fish and fur trade of Norway, established their domination in the municipal government and law of Sweden and Denmark, and came very near to ousting the Norwegian merchants from their own port of Bergen. The four great German factories: the 'Steelyard' in London, the Hanseatic 'commonalty' in Bruges, the Court of St Peter in Novgorod, and the German Bridge in Bergen, were outlying termini of a commercial system spreading, in centipede formation, all along the great route and all over Northern Europe.[3]

An economic domination so thorough over a territory so vast was bound to be inimical to the maritime and commercial enterprise of outsiders, English, Dutch or Scandinavian. But at no time was its enmity more pronounced than at the end of the fourteenth and the beginning of the fifteenth centuries. The very emergence of the Hanseatic League as a political organisation in the middle of the fourteenth century was symptomatic. Their war against Denmark in 1367 was the first of the great trade wars which the Hanseatic towns were to wage in defence of their economic position in northern trade, and it was also the first official debut of the Hanse as a political and military league. Throughout its subsequent

---

[3] C. Bahr, *Handel und Verkehr der deutschen Hanse in Flandern*, pp. 57–111; L. K. Goetz, 'Deutsch-Russische Handelsgeschichte des Mittelalters' (*Hans. Geschichtsquellen*, Neue Folge, Band v; Ver. f. *Hans. Geschichte*; Lübeck, 1922), pp. 30–74; F. Schulz, *Die Hanse und England*, pp. 9–12; A. Schück, 'Die deutsche Einwanderung in das mittelalterliche Schweden und ihre kommerziellen und sozialen Folgen', in *Hans. Bbl.*, Jahrgang, 1930 (1931), pp. 78–9; Bugge, 'Der Untergang der Norwegischen Seeschiffahrt' (*V.S.W.G.*, 1904); *Die Lübecker Bergenfahrer*, ed. Bruns (1900), pp. iii–vii.

career the League remained true to the objects of 1367. It existed in order to defend the economic foundation of the Hanseatic monopoly; its object was to organise military and political action against possible economic change and commercial competition. This policy of political resistance to economic change was forced upon the Hanseatic towns by the whole trend of contemporary developments. In the late fourteenth and the fifteenth centuries the economic positions which the Hanseatic towns had won for themselves in the course of the preceding century were rapidly changing and could not endure without constant political protection. The changes were manifold. Some of them affected the international situation in Northern Europe, others occurred in the inner structure and mutual relations of the Hanseatic towns. But whether external or internal, they undermined the very foundation of Hanseatic prosperity, and forced upon the league a policy of rigorous and jealous protection.

In the first place, the situation in Northern Europe as a whole was no longer the same as in the first half of the fourteenth century. In the west the Flemish cloth industry was being rapidly overtaken by the English, and in the fifteenth century also by the Dutch industries. The day was not distant when the Hanseatic colony in Bruges would be unable to control the flow of western produce to the east. Further east and north the Dutch were showing the first signs of commercial activity. By the beginning of the fourteenth century Holland had completed the main part of her defensive work against the sea and was entering upon a period of rapid economic development. Their shipping which had always been very active in the North Sea was now steadily penetrating into the Baltic, and towns like Amsterdam and Rotterdam were beginning to claim a far greater share in the east to west trade than the most vital interest of the Hanse would permit. Further east and north the Scandinavian countries were undergoing an experiment in unification which threatened to emancipate them from the Hanseatic tutelage. Queen Margaret was able to rule unhampered by the Hanseatic towns, thanks rather to her good sense than to Hanseatic indifference, but her predecessor and successor had been led into a conflict with Hanseatic interests in the fisheries of Skania and the domestic trade of Denmark and Norway.[4] Lastly, as will be shown further, England made her appearance as a serious rival in the Baltic..

The changing international situation was in itself bound to make the

---

4 'Aussenpolitische und innerpolitische Wandlungen in der Hanse nach dem Stralsunder Frieden', pp. 149, 144–6, and 'Die Hanse und die nordischen Länder', in F. Rörig, *Hansische Beiträge zur deutschen Wirtschaftsgeschichte* (Breslau, 1928); E. Daenell, 'Holland und die Hanse im 15. 'Jahrhundert' in *Hans. Gbl.*, Jahrgang, 1903 (1904), pp. 3–41; H. J. Smit, *De Opkomst van den handel van Amsterdam. Onderzoekingen naar de economische ontwikkeling der stad tot 1441.* (Amsterdam, 1914.)

Hanseatic towns fearful for their future. But their fears were made greater still by the fact that by the beginning of the fifteenth century they were already losing their mutual cohesion and sense of harmony. The towns composing the Hanse formed from the geographical and the economic point of view at least three distinct groups: the central body and the two wings. The western wing, comprising the towns of Zuider Zee, Westphalia, and the Rhine, was chiefly concerned with the trade of Western Germany, England and the Low Countries. The eastern section, formed by the towns of Prussia and Livonia, was economically bound up with the markets of Prussia, Poland, and Russia. It was the central group, the Saxon and Wendish towns, and above all Lübeck, that gave cohesion and unity to the system. Lübeck's position was central in more than one respect. Its site on the Jutland peninsula formed a geographical link between the eastern and western wings, and its position as a link enabled its merchants to assume the economic function of intermediaries, as carriers and traders, to the different regions of Hanseatic territory. It is therefore no wonder that Lübeck became the 'head' of the Hanse, the builder and defender of its unity. As long as it kept its position of intermediary it stood to benefit by the economic development of the other sections, and could easily reconcile their interests with its own. The integrity of the Hanse was Lübeck's interest and therefore became Lübeck's policy.

Unfortunately for the Hanse the relations between Lübeck and the other parts had begun to change towards the end of the fourteenth century. In the second half of the century the Zuider Zee towns established direct connections with the Baltic by sea, and this *Umlandfahrt* was becoming more and more popular according as the English and the Dutch were finding their way into the Baltic. This new route gave a stimulus to Dutch and English enterprise in the Baltic, but, what was equally important, deprived Lübeck's position on the Jutland peninsula of its old importance. It was the chief sufferer from the new route, and its own interests forced it to take a lead against the foreign penetration. On the other hand the towns of Prussia, with their bulky goods, availed themselves readily of the new opportunities for direct shipping to the west and of the competitive services of foreign, above all Dutch, carriers. Different, again, was the attitude of the western towns. Some of them had initiated the *Umlandfahrt*, all of them were closely bound up with Dutch trade, and Lübeck could expect no support from them for its conservative and anti-Dutch policy. The harmony of Hanseatic interests was thus rapidly becoming a thing of the past.[5]

This cleavage, or rather the threat of a cleavage, contributed greatly to the anti-foreign policies in the Hanseatic councils. Itself a product of

[5] F. Rörig, *Die Hanse und die nordischen Länder*, op. cit., pp. 162–5.

economic and geographical change, the cleavage justified and intensified Lübeck's resistance to what was the most conspicuous feature of the change: the rise of rivals in the west. The sacred name of unity could now be invoked on behalf of the *status quo*. The recurrent separatism of Cologne or Prussia not only impeded and weakened Hanseatic action, but also raised fears and forebodings, which in the end only strengthened Lübeck's policy of rigid protection and conservation.

The spirit of monopoly and exclusiveness, so strong in the councils of the Hanse as a whole, was also finding its way into the internal policies of the individual Hanseatic towns. The middle of the fourteenth century saw the end of the pioneering era in Eastern Europe, during which the rest of the east German towns had been founded and settled. But the passing of the pioneering age meant also the passing of the pioneers. The earlier period in the history of the German towns was a time of constant expansion and adventure; its main figures were men of expansive and adventurous type. The leaders of the urban policies of the thirteenth century, the typical east-going families of Westphalian and Saxon origin, had no need to be exclusive in the local markets of their towns. Their interests were flung far and wide, all along the Hanseatic route, in Northern Europe and beyond. Their prosperity was based on their ever-growing foreign trade; and foreign trade, especially when it is growing, invariably favours free trade. But in the late fourteenth and the fifteenth centuries the influence of these men on urban policies was fast declining. With the Hanseatic expansion at the point of saturation, the interests and the policies of individual towns were turned more and more upon the local markets. The considerations of local trade began to predominate over those of foreign trade, and the voice of men whose connections and horizons were local, began to predominate in the councils of the towns. In some of the Hanseatic towns a series of democratic revolts in the second half of the fourteenth century, and especially at the very beginning of the fifteenth, for a short time delivered the power into the hands of the petty bourgeoisie. But even in those towns and in those times, in which the government of the patriciate remained uninterrupted, the prejudices and interests of the democracy dictated the commercial policy. The exclusion of the outsider, and above all the alien, from the local trade became the settled object of municipal policy. And this new policy was bound to make the Hanseatic system in the late fourteenth and fifteenth centuries even more inimical to foreign penetration than it would otherwise have been.[6]

---

[6] F. Rörig, *Aussenpolitische und innerpolitische Wandlungen*, op. cit., pp. 150–153; W. Stein, 'Über die ältesten Privilegien der deutschen Hanse in Flandern und die ältere Handelspolitik Lübecks', pp. 113–22, in *Hans. Gbl.*, Jahrgang, 1902, pp. 51–133 (1903).

Unfortunately for the future of Anglo-Hanseatic relations, it was in the late fourteenth and fifteenth centuries that the English penetration into northern markets began in earnest. The causes of this spurt in English commercial activity are fairly obvious. In the second half of the fourteenth century large quantities of cloth began to be produced in England for export. The English merchants, some of whom were themselves cloth manufacturers, possessed those local connections and contacts with production which foreign exporters lacked. They were also assisted by a mildly protective customs tariff. Thus favoured, they early acquired a large share in the new branch of the export trade, and the larger their share the greater was their need of foreign markets and their power of penetration.[7]

The penetration proceeded along each of the traditional channels of English trade. The main line of traffic led to the great fair towns of Flanders, Zealand, and Brabant, the chief intermediaries in the trade with the continental interior and the Mediterranean South. Two other channels led directly to the markets of Southern Europe by way of the ports of Aquitaine and Iberia, and to the markets of Scandinavia and Central Europe by the way of the Baltic and the North Sea. In this last direction the English penetration had begun very early. Of English trade with Scandinavia there are traces in Anglo-Saxon evidence; the connections were not interrupted in the twelfth and the thirteenth centuries, and were still active in the fourteenth century. On the great herring mart of Skania – the threshold of the Baltic – they may have been active as early as the late thirteenth century. That they traded there in the sixties and the early seventies of the fourteenth century is shown by the Hanseatic measures directed against them at the time. On the whole, the trade of the English there seems to have been fitful and irregular. Although they continued trading in the late fourteenth and early fifteenth centuries, they never acquired a footing as permanent and valuable as that of the principal Hanseatic towns or even as that of the Dutch. But their trade to Prussia, though more recent, seemed to become more and more important according as the production of cloth was providing them with an incentive and an opportunity. Prussia supplied the most important English imports – corn, timber, pitch, tar, and ashes; Prussia was the chief distributor of English cloth in Poland and Western Russia. It was, therefore, towards Prussia that the English directed their *Drang nach Osten*. In the second half of the thirteenth and the beginning of the fourteenth centuries we find them occasionally in different Baltic ports, but in the second half of the century they planted themselves in

---

[7] For the growth of the English cloth exports in the fourteenth century, see H. L. Gray, *The Production and Exportation of English Woollens in the Fourteenth Century.*

Danzig. By the end of the century they formed a numerous and influential foreign colony, trafficked with Danzigers and foreigners, sold wholesale and retail, owned houses and warehouses, and possessed something in the nature of a corporate organisation.[8]

Unfortunately this penetration, rapid and thorough as it was, was certainly ill-timed. The English were entering into the Baltic at the very moment that the direct connections between west and east were beginning to threaten the foundations of Hanseatic prosperity and unity. They tried to establish themselves in the trade of Danzig at that very time when the protection of the local market and regional monopoly was becoming the fundamental principle of municipal policy. Their penetration into the Hanseatic system would have produced a considerable conflict at any time, but under the conditions of the late fourteenth and early fifteenth centuries it was bound to result in a bitter and desperate struggle.

The struggle was further complicated and embittered by its connection with the question of Hanseatic privileges in England. Ever since their first appearance in England the merchants of north German towns enjoyed a position of exceptional favour. The merchants of Cologne and Westphalia first, the merchants of the more eastern towns later, were allowed to form in London a corporate body, a Hanse, similar and parallel to the older Hanse of Flemish merchants. This corporate organisation was soon transformed into the permanent communal settlement of the Steelyard.[9] It held property in the City and undertook certain communal obligations in a manner which made it a partner in the municipal defence and government. Ancient custom and royal grants invested it with rights of jurisdiction over its members and valuable privileges as to the conduct of their suits with Englishmen. Its members also claimed, and over the greater part of the Middle Ages possessed, the right to trade with foreigners and sell retail. And then, to crown all, a series of Royal charters, and especially Edward III's *carta mercatoria*, conferred upon the Hanseatic merchants valuable exemption from the system of customs tariffs which the government was at that

---

[8] A. Bugge, *Handelen mellem England og Norge*; idem, *Den Norske Traelasthandels Historie*, pp. 165–6; *H.R.*, I, viii, nos. 1167 and 1168; Schulz, op. cit. pp. 13–14; D. Schäfer, 'Das Buch des Lübeckischen Vogts auf Schonen', *Hansische Geschichtsquellen*, vol. IV (Halle a. S., 1887), p. 93, par. 58; *H.R.* I, i, no. 51, par. 11 (p. 470), no. 522, par. 7; *U.B.* ii, no. 206 (Stralsund, 1312), iii, no. 507; T. Hirsch, *Danzigs Handels- und Gewerbsgeschichte*, pp. 98–100. In 1385, the goods of at least eighty-five English merchants were arrested in Danzig: *H.R.*, iii, no. 404 A, par. 1 (cf. list in B, par. 1).

[9] According to Dr M. Weinbaum, 'Stalhof und Deutsche Gildhalle zu London', in *Hans, Gbl.*, Jahrgang, 1928 (Lübeck, 1929), pp. 45–65, there were originally two separate settlements in London, that of Cologne and that of the other North German towns.

time building up. Under the provisions of these charters the Hanseatics were exempt from all the subsequent increases in the tariffs, so that by the beginning of the fifteenth century they paid even less than the native merchants on their cloth exported from this country, and were not liable to the payment of the additional subsidy of poundage and tunnage.[10]

The privileged position of Hanseatic merchants was bound to provoke an attack from commercial interests at home. Between this attack and the general anti-foreign movement in the English towns there was an obvious connection. But the connection was often implemented, and sometimes even overshadowed, by issues peculiarly Hanseatic. The towns endeavoured to exclude the foreign merchants from direct contact with consumers and with agricultural producers by limiting the duration of their residence and regulating the scope and the manner of their dealings. These endeavours were directed against all foreigners alike, the Venetians, the Genoese, the Flemings, as well as the Hanseatics, but the Hanseatics provided the best and the easiest target. It was only natural to expect that their commercial connections in England, their exceptional fiscal privileges and their proud position in the city would draw upon them the greater share of the urban xenophobia. But what gave to the anti-Hanseatic movement a character peculiarly its own was the strength and the inspiration which it drew from the conflict with the Hanse overseas and from the rather specialised body of anti-foreign feeling among the English merchants trading to the Baltic.

It is this combination of issues, some arising from competition at home, and others from rivalry overseas, that made the Anglo-Hanseatic clashes more frequent and much stronger than they would otherwise have been. Dangerous as are speculations in the 'might-have-beens' of history, one can safely say that the single issue of English trade in Prussia would never have produced a strong movement at home. The merchants habitually trading to Prussia were a limited group of men. They may have carried great weight in some of the ports on the east coast and in the neighbouring industrial centres, Lynn, Hull, York, and Norwich, but they were hardly represented in the flourishing midland towns or in the great seaports of the south and west coast. In London their mainstay was the fishmongers; and, powerful as the London fishmongers were, they seldom carried with them the main body of the London patriciate. During the greater part of the fourteenth and the fifteenth centuries the city and its government were led by men whose interests were in the distributive trade of London, or in the commerce with Flanders and Brabant.[11] At the same time the merchants of the Hanse were consider-

---

[10] See below, sections 2 and 3. The customs rates on cloth were: 1s 2d per cloth (English), 12d (Hanse), and 2s 4d (other aliens).

[11] *H.R.* 2, iii, no. 669; *K.R. Cust. Accts., passim*; cf. the lists in *H.R.* 1, iii,

ably more popular with influential opinion in England than the merchants of most other countries. They had friends and defenders among the nobility, the cloth workers and the lower classes; even the jingo author of the *Libelle of Englyshe Polycye* had a few nice things to say about them. Their goods were all essential commodities, not luxuries, and were sold 'well cheap'. Thus an agitation on the issue of Baltic trade would have provoked the opposition of the consumers' interests, without at the same time enlisting any active support from the bulk of the English merchant class. A situation of this kind apparently did arise once in the fifteenth century, when the Genoese nipped in the bud the English attempt of 1412 to trade in the Mediterranean. On that occasion the government organised reprisals against the Genoese, but in the absence of any strong pressure from influential merchant opinion, the whole conflict degenerated into a mere question of compensations, the anti-Genoese measures were revoked and the English kept away from the Mediterranean for another fifty years.[12] What made the anti-Hanseatic agitation so persistent and so effective was the fact that at one and the same time it represented the grievances of merchants excluded from the trade of Prussian towns, and the appetites of merchants anxious to exclude the Hanseatics from the trade of English towns. A common enemy produced a sense of common interest, and a sense of common interest ranged the mass of the English commercial classes behind the agitation.

This combination of interests found its natural expression in the 'programme of reciprocity'. By the end of the fourteenth century the English demands finally crystallised into a formula irresistible in its logic and simplicity. As an English petition put it, all that the English demanded was that they should be given the same treatment in Prussian and other Hanseatic centres as the Hanseatics enjoyed in England, and that, as long as the Hanseatics refused to concede the English demand, their privileges in England should be revoked.[13] This demand of 'parity' eventually became the constant theme of English petitions and complaints. The official spokesmen of English merchants used it with great effect whenever they felt a need to be convincing; the Hanseatics found it very hard to parry; it became a battle-cry of the anti-Hanseatic party in Parliament and the King's Council, and the bugbear of the Prussians.

no. 404 A, par. 1, and B, par. 1. Among the London Aldermen in the fifteenth century there were thirteen fishmongers as against forty-one mercers, thirty-three drapers, thirty-one grocers, sixteen goldsmiths, thirteen skinners, seven ironmongers, and three vintners; in the fourteenth century there were forty fishmongers. A. B. Beaven, *The Aldermen of the City of London*, vol. 1, pp. 329–30.

[12] *Libelle*, ed. Warner, line 420; the Hanseatic trade 'is encrese ful grete unto thys londe'. *Cotton MSS., Nero*, 27.

[13] A statement of the claim to reciprocity was already contained in the English complaints of 1379; *H.R.*, 1, ii, no. 212, par. 1.

But it was not in logic alone that the strength of this programme lay. Essentially an 'omnibus' programme, it imposed a tactical unity upon fundamental differences of aim. The merchants trading to Prussia were not prepared to accept a rebuff there, even if it resulted in a revocation of Hanseatic privileges in England; nor were the bulk of the London retailers likely to agree to the continuance of the Hanseatic privileges in England, even if they were accompanied by similar privileges for the Englishmen in Danzig. But as long as the claims of the former and the grievances of the latter were still unsatisfied, the demand for reciprocity provided a convenient formula for a temporary unity of front.

This unity of front added to the strength of the English attack in the same measure in which want of unity in the Hanseatic ranks weakened the effect of their opposition. On no other point of Hanseatic policy did the variance between the component parts of the Hanse manifest itself more fully than in the conflict with the English. The merchants of the western wing, i.e. the towns of Westphalia, the Zuider Zee towns, and above all Cologne, were very active in the English export trade. The distribution of English cloth became in the fifteenth century one of the principal branches of Cologne's commerce; the Cologne *Englandfahrer* formed a very influential body of merchants in their city as well as the most numerous section in the London Steelyard. At the same time they were not concerned with the dangers of the English competition in Prussia and not over anxious to lose their privileges in England for the sake of Lübeck's or Danzig's safety. As a result, the leaders of the Hanseatic policy had always to reckon with possible separate action on the part of the western towns. In the second half of the century, at a most critical period in the Anglo-Hanseatic relations, Cologne formally repudiated the official policy of the Hanse and very nearly destroyed the whole Hanseatic system in the west. The attitude of the western wing had its counterpart in the independent attitudes of Prussia and Danzig. In its policy towards England Danzig was torn between two mutually exclusive objects. It wanted to keep the English out of the local market and at the same time it was anxious to maintain the highly important commercial connections with England. Thus while Danzig's local monopoly provoked conflicts with England, Danzig's interest in the English trade prevented it from decisive action. On more than one occasion it shirked violent measures advocated by Lübeck, and on more than one occasion it was the first to break a Hanseatic blockade of England and seek separate ways out of a struggle which it had itself begun. The Prussian attitude was further complicated by the independent policy of the Prussian Order. For although the Order was formally a member and a protector of the Hanse, it often embarked on separate policies towards the other powers of Northern Europe.

In these circumstances it is no wonder that out of the several clashes in the late fourteenth and the early fifteenth centuries the English merchants emerged undefeated. Every time the Hanseatic charters came up for confirmation the whole question of Hanseatic privileges in England and of the position of the English in the Baltic was raised, and every time it was raised the pressure of mercantile interests was sufficiently strong to force the programme of reciprocity upon the Council and the Parliament. The Hanse, divided against itself, could not offer an effective opposition. More than once the English negotiators very nearly managed to detach both Prussia and Cologne from the League, and not until 1468 was the Hanse able to organise a war or a successful blockade against England. To an informed observer in the late thirties of the fifteenth century the English position would have appeared full of promise: they seemed bound to win.

As we know now they did not win. Before the third quarter of the century was over the English merchants had been definitely shut out of the Baltic, and it was left to the Dutch to fight out the problems of Hanseatic monopoly on the northern seas. The English settlements in Prussia and Scandinavia had either disappeared or ceased to play an important part in the direction and organisation of English trade. The Hanseatics returned to London in full possession of their ancient privileges and extended their share of the English cloth exports far beyond the point it had reached in the first half of the century. It was much later, in the sixteenth century, that the English penetration of the Baltic was resumed, and it was not until then that the attack against the Hanseatics in London produced the first important curtailment of their privileges.

The causes of this defeat were too many and too various to be summarised in a single phrase. They formed a chain of unforeseen occurrences of the kind that make up the story of history and upset all schemes of cause and effect. The only generalisation which the facts permit is the rough statement that the chain of occurrences was of a political and not an economic order, and was due more to the vicissitudes of government than to the action or inaction of merchants. It is not that the government was unfriendly to the merchants, ignorant of the situation, or indifferent to the needs of English trade. It never was definitely pro-Hanseatic or anti-merchant. On the contrary, as long as the fifteenth-century government functioned as government, and as long as it could define its attitude to the Hanse undisturbed by other political considerations, it adopted an economic policy favourable to the interests and opinions of the merchant classes. The iconoclastic researches of Professor Unwin have cast a doubt over the whole question of the economic policy of the English crown in the later Middle Ages. Economic historians, he thought, antedated the birth of the mercantilist and protectionist policy. Cunningham was too simple in asserting that a medieval king like Edward III was capable of a consistent course of economic action towards objectives definitely national and nationalistic. Such a king lived from hand to mouth; most of his economic measures were produced in response to the exigencies of the moment; they had purely fiscal ends in view, were always personal or dynastic in motive and were unrelated to any underlying economic principle.[14] These views of Edward's policy are now generally accepted, and it is not the object of this essay to revise them. But at the same time they must not be allowed – and Unwin himself does not allow them – to decide our estimate of the economic policies of the late fourteenth and fifteenth centuries. In the first place, we know very little, much less than historians often assume, about the medieval conceptions of state and nationality; and until we know more all the discussions of economic nationalism are bound to be somewhat unsubstantial. Then, secondly, we must guard ourselves against too rigid a test of what constitutes an economic policy. 'Continuous unity of purpose' is not the only test, and the motives, however hypocritical, which a government professes, must not be excluded from the discussion of its policy. Throughout the greater part of history, even in our own time, the legislative and the administrative record of a government is often a joint product of wish and necessity, of conscious policies and of the exigencies of the moment. And inconsistencies in the record of a government are as much a measure of its want of policy as they are that of the strength of the needs of the moment.

A conflict of this nature between the economic *desiderata* of the fifteenth-century governments and their actual record provides the key to the Hanseatic riddle. Their *desiderata* fully reflected the nationalist bias of the times. No student of the period can fail to observe its insistent and conscious Englishry. The demarcation of things English and foreign was grounded well enough to be taken for granted in the popular parlance, literature and political utterances of the time. And the nationalism of the age was bound to reflect upon the prevalent notions of state policy in general and economic policy in particular. The *Libelle of Englyshe Polycye* was saturated with it, but the *Libelle* did not stand alone. We find its sentiments echoed in diplomatic and commercial correspondence, in parliamentary petitions, and let us add, in the preambles of acts of Parliament. Sarcastic as historians are apt to be about the motives alleged in such preambles, it must not be forgotten that the object of a preamble was to justify the act by relating it to those moral and political principles which could command a general acceptance; the more hypocritical they were the more conclusive they are as evidence of the spirit of the times. The author of the memorandum on the war aims of 1449 was abreast

[14] *Finance and Trade under Edward III*, ed. G. Unwin, *Introduction*.

and not ahead of his time when, among the principal objects of the war in France, he included the destruction of Breton and Norman shipping, 'in order that the English merchants may have the shipping of the seas'. So also was the anonymous author of the rhymed memorandum on English commercial policy with his insistence on the wealth of England and his motto: *Anglia, propter tuas naves et lanas omnia regna te salutare deberent.* These sentiments were unquestionably accepted by the draftsmen of Richard's navigation acts, the Lancastrian bills in restriction of imports from Flanders, and the bullionist acts of the fourteenth and the fifteenth century. A student of the century could find many more instances of similar mentality and phraseology, all revealing the strength of the precocious 'mercantilism' of the later Middle Ages.[15]

This being the temper of the age, it was easy for the government to respond to the pressure of the anti-Hanseatic interests, and to understand their motives and language. Naturally enough the different elements of the fifteenth-century government could not be expected to be more united on the Hanseatic question than they were on other diplomatic and political problems of the day. But the difference of emphasis and tactics often concealed a common attitude which was almost identical with that of the merchant community. The House of Commons was constantly prepared to voice the point of view of the urban middle classes, and its middle class bias was repeatedly exploited in the commercial interests of the merchants. The City of London had evolved in the fifteenth century an efficient machinery for propaganda in Parliament; the provincial

---

[15] *Letters and Papers Illustrative of the Wars of the English in France*, ed. J. Stevenson (R.S.), vol. II, part 2, p. 724, par. 7; *Johannis Capgrave Liber de Illustribus Henricis*, ed. F. C. Hingeston (R.S., 1858), p. 155; *Libelle*, ed. Warner, lines 6–7: 'Cherysche marchandyse, kepe thamiralté, that we be maysteres of the narowe see'; *Political Poems and Songs relating to English History* (R.S., 2 vols., 1859–61), vol. I, part 2, pp. 282–7. The policy underlying the phraseology of legislation in the late fourteenth and fifteenth centuries is too vast a subject to be treated *en passant*. But a few things may be noted. To begin with, economic legislation is commonly justified by reference to the 'bien universelle' of the kingdom (e.g. *Stat.* 14 Hen. VI, c. 2). That the notion of 'common wealth' could have an economic meaning is shown by the constant reference to 'profit', 'l'encrece', 'la prosperité', 'encrece de riches', 'grande richesse' as the subject of legislation. It is also clear that the underlying concept of the 'roialme' was national: 'Engleterre', 'cest terre' (e.g. *Stat.* 4 Edw. IV, c. 2); Englishmen rather than king's lieges, 'natifs engloys' contrasted to the 'persones dautri lange et destranges terres et nacions' (*Stats.* 18 Hen. VI, c. 1, 3 Ric. II, c. 3). It is also clear that the concept of national 'wealth' was sometimes linked up with the abundance and prosperity of merchants ('lors esteantz plusours en nombre et de grande richesse', *Stat.* 27 Hen. VI, c. 2), the accumulation of treasure and, above all, the growth of the navy (*Stats.* 3 Ric. II, c. 3, 4 Hen. V, 2, c. 7. 14 Hen. VI, c. 8, 15 Hen. VI, c. 2–c. 4, 18 Hen. VI, c. 2). In other words, the mercantilism of the fifteenth century, however tongue-tied, knew its text: 'the navie and merchandises of this realm' (*Rot. Parl.*, vol. v, p. 31).

towns sometimes elected special commissions to 'make suit in Parliament against the Hanseatic privileges'. Their combined pressure seldom failed to carry the Commons, and the Hanseatics justly regarded Parliament as their chief adversary and never expected from it any favour or concession.[16]

This attitude of the Commons was reinforced by the activities of the civil servants in charge of Hanseatic policy. There is no other subject in the constitutional and administrative history of the fifteenth century more obscure and at the same time more important for the understanding of foreign and economic policies than the functions, power, and personnel of the chief clerical offices in the government. In the limited field of Hanseatic policy the influence of the clerks of the Council responsible for the official correspondence and negotiations was much greater than a superficial view of events would suggest. Men like Russell, Hatcliff, and above all, Thomas Kent, represented definite policies towards the Hanse, and those policies were, during the greater part of the fifteenth century, fashioned on definitely nationalistic lines. Thomas Kent was apparently the moving spirit behind the negotiations with the Hanse in the middle decades of the century; his memoranda and speeches contained the clearest exposition of the programme of parity and reciprocity, and it is not surprising that the Hanseatics regarded him as their arch-enemy in England.[17]

Less obvious and certainly less definite was the policy of the Lords and of the King's Council. The 'lords and prelates' sometimes shielded the merchants of the Hanse from the enmity and vindictiveness of the Commons, and were often referred to in the correspondence of the Hanse as its only friends in England. It will also be shown further that in the end the triumph of personal and mercenary interests in the Council, and the conflicting claims of the foreign and military policies which it tried to pursue, prepared the way for the Hanseatic victory. Yet as long as the Council was capable of comprehending and obeying the *raison d'état*, the underlying assumptions of its policy towards the Hanse were little different from those of the merchant classes. The German historians of the Hanse have tried to explain the vacillations of the Council by the influence of the 'consumers' interests'. The nobility of England were producers of wool and consumers of imported goods and their representatives on the Council were led by the interests of their class to oppose the monopolistic attempts of the English merchants to exclude foreigners

---

[16] *H.R.* I, vii, no. 594, 2 v, no. 173, 2, ii, no. 65, 2, iii, no. 283, 2, v, nos. 206 and 263 par. 7; *U.B.* viii, no. 285.

[17] The career of Thomas Kent will, it is hoped, soon form the subject of another study; cf. W. Stein, *Die Hanse und England*, pp. 83–4. Hatcliff began to play a very conspicuous part in the Anglo-Hanseatic relations after the 'verdict' of 1468, see below, pp. 280–2 and n. 75.

from immediate contact with the English consumers and agricultural producers. Yet the importance of these consumers' influences can easily be exaggerated. The Lancastrian and Yorkist councils contained members with interests and investments in trade and shipping: men like Lord Hastings, Lord Roos, Lord Buckingham, the Bastard of Fauconberg, Lord Say, the Duke of Suffolk, and Cardinal Beaufort.[18] But to assume that the policy of the Council was dictated by the interests of the noble 'merchants' would be as crude a simplification of the facts as to assume that it was dictated by the interests of the noble 'consumers'. The Gloucester party, and presumably the Yorkist party in its early years, courted the favours of the merchants and defended their point of view; while Cardinal Beaufort, in spite of his commercial activities, resisted the anti-Hanseatic irreconcilables in Parliament and Council. In time of war the Council as a whole was more anxious to placate the Hanse than in time of peace, while during the anarchy immediately preceding the civil war the lords of the Council were anti-Hanseatic for the mere reason that the Hanseatic sheep were fat, and the baronial wolves were hungry. The attitude of the Council constantly fluctuated, and the fluctuations were due to a variety of causes: the struggle of baronial parties, the relations with Parliament, the military and the diplomatic situation. But on those occasions when the personal and party interests of the magnates were not involved, and the military and political situation was favourable, it was the considerations of English trade and the interests of English merchants that determined the policy of the King and his Council. These occasions were quite frequent in the first forty and in the last twenty years of the century. Whenever they occurred the Hanseatics were as bitter about the opposition of the Council as they were about that of the Commons.[19] But they were not frequent enough to provide the English merchants with that constant and uninterrupted political and military backing which their programme of monopoly and penetration demanded. Over

[18] *H.R.* 2, ii, no. 65: 'dat de oversten herren namlik de prelaten dis landes nicht willen des dutschen copmans ut dem lande entberen'; ibid., 2, v, nos. 206 and 263 par. 7, contain a clear indication of the council's attempts to circumvent the anti-Hanseatic policy of the Commons. For commercial activities of nobles see *L.T.R. Cust. Accts., passim.* Beaufort: Sir J. H. Ramsay, *Lancaster and York* (Oxford, 1892), vol. ii, p. 34, Hall's Chronicle (1809): 'he standing the chief merchant of wools' (Gloucester's allegation); Suffolk: W. J. Haward, *Economic Aspects of the Wars of the Roses in East Anglia, passim;* Buckingham: *H.R.* 2, iv, no. 25; the Yorkist nobles: C. L. Scofield, *The Life and Reign of Edward the Fourth,* vol. ii, pp. 417–20. Not all the noble recipients of export licences necessarily traded on their own account, yet Warwick, Fauconberg, Howard, Northumberland, and Hastings took a hand in trade. Cf. the Hanseatic allegations in *H.R.* 2, vi, no. 97.

[19] *H.R.* 2, i, no. 147 (p. 99), 2, iii, no. 283: 'wy hebben weynich vrende manck den heren unde der gemenheyt'; *Proc. and Ord. P.C.,* vol. v, pp. 167, 170, 177, 228, 233.

and over again in the course of the century considerations of war on the continent led the Council into a conflict with the objects of its Hanseatic policy. The objects were completely neglected in the middle decades of the century, when the violent outbreak of party struggles overshadowed all other issues, Hanseatic and non-Hanseatic alike. And during that interval a foundation was laid for the Hanseatic triumph of the seventies.[20]

It is in this sense that the 'vicissitudes of government' are to be considered responsible for the failure of the English offensive. It is not that the government did not possess or was incapable of conceiving an economic policy, or that the policy was inconsistent with the programme of the merchants. What happened was that a policy, nationalist in origin and objects, was partly neutralised by a political and military situation on the continent, and partly destroyed through the destruction of all policy and all government in the War of the Roses. In this light the story of Anglo-Hanseatic relations becomes one of a frustrated development, of an economic process defeated by a play of political accidents. To this story we shall now pass.

2. THE THREE SUCCESSES (1400 TO 1437)

The year 1400 found Anglo-Hanseatic relations broken and confused by a conflict several years old. This troubled opening of the century was something of a forecast, but it was also something of an epitome, for it was in the preceding twenty-five years that the issues of 1400 had matured and the main groupings of interest formed. The first signs of an organised agitation against the Hanse appear in 1375, when the English merchants addressed a petition to the King complaining against unfair treatment at the hands of the Hanse. The petition was probably provoked by the arrival of the Hanseatic delegation in 1375 and its attempts to obtain for the Hanse an exemption from the subsidy of tunnage and poundage. Nevertheless the grievances of the English eastgoing merchants were real enough. In the seventies of the fourteenth century English cloth had penetrated far into the heart of the Hanseatic *Verkehrsgebiet*, and at the same time the economic policy of the Hanseatic, and especially the Prussian, towns had become definitely protectionist and anti-foreign. When in the years 1377–8 the accession of Richard II provided the English merchants with another opportunity for an anti-Hanseatic agitation, they could point to a whole series of 'injustices' inflicted upon them in Danzig, Skania, and Norway.[21] Their

---

[20] Cf. Stein, op. cit., p. 32.
[21] *H.R.* i, iii, nos. 317, 318 (Norway), 319 (Skania); *U.B.* iv, no. 600; *H.R.* i, ii, nos. 210, 211, 212, iii, nos. 102, 103.

grievances were now substantial enough to force the problem of English trade in the east to the forefront of the negotiations, and for the first time in English history the commercial monopoly at home and the English penetration abroad were exhibited as complementary parts of one and the same programme. Both were incorporated in the 'four points' of the English demands. According to these demands the Hanseatics were, first, to admit the English to trade in Hanseatic regions (including 'Revele, Pernowe et Cyflandia') as freely as the Hanseatics traded in England under the royal charters of privileges; secondly, to give them similar rights in Skania; thirdly, to relieve them of collective responsibility; and finally, to specify the names of the towns composing the Hanse. These four points contained the first clear statement of that programme of reciprocity which was to dominate the Anglo-Hanseatic policies in the subsequent hundred years.[22]

It is the emergence of this programme that gives importance to the negotiations. Their immediate and practical outcome was a minor victory for the English point of view. The sponsors of the anti-Hanseatic petition, led by the merchants of London, exploited well the pro-London and anti-foreign turn of national policy at the beginning of the reign. The new government, however unlikely to revoke for good all the privileges of the Hanse, behaved as if it indeed understood and supported the principle of reciprocity. It made the continuation of the Hanseatic privileges contingent on similar privileges to the English in the Hanse towns, and in the meantime suspended the Hanseatic charters. And although a year later a Hanseatic delegation to England managed to obtain letters of protection for a year, the Government continued to insist on its condition. It was only in 1380, after the Hanseatics had formally recognised the right of Englishmen to trade in its territories, that Richard's government gave way and confirmed the charter.[23]

This outcome was not sufficiently decisive to establish anything in the nature of a durable arrangement. It merely defined the issues instead of settling them, and, with the issues clarified, a serious clash was bound to occur sooner or later. The restoration of Hanseatic privilege in 1380 did not put an end to the agitation in England or to the friction abroad. Prussia persevered in her animosity to the English, and used the pretext of English piracies to put off her acceptance of the treaty. The English on their part continued their agitation against Hanseatic trade in England. In the absence of a definite arrangement as to the principles of Anglo-Hanseatic trade, the English authorities, both national and municipal,

---

[22] *H.R.* I, ii, no. 212.
[23] *H.R.* I, ii, nos. 102, 210, 211; *U.B.*, iv, nos. 645, 647, 674; *H.R.* I, nos. 224, 225 (1380), not 1381?), cf. F. Schulz, op. cit., p. 33.

interpreted the provisions of the charter in a way which did away with many of the fiscal liberties of the Hanse. The Hanseatic merchants were made to pay the subsidies of tunnage and poundage, additional customs on cloth and even the subsidies of the fifteenth and tenth – all payments from which they would have been exempt if their privileges under the charter had been faithfully and loyally observed.[24]

An additional cause for mutual recriminations was provided by the activities of pirates. Piracy on the high seas in the Middle Ages was as constant and as inevitable a feature of the shipper's routine as inclement weather or bribes at the ports. But at times of international friction, with its opportunities for reprisals and counter-reprisals, its accumulating ill-feeling and its unemployment among shippers, piracy could easily assume the dimensions and do the harm of a naval war. Piratical activity of this kind went on in the seventies, and culminated in 1385 in the capture of a Hanseatic fleet off Swyn. With this capture the crisis came to a head. A series of reprisals, at first in Prussia and later in other towns of the Hanse, as well as of counter-reprisals in England, completely interrupted the trade between the two countries. In Prussia all imports from England and all exports of Baltic goods to England were prohibited. The English merchants moved out of Danzig to Stralsund, and the English government prohibited all journeys to Baltic lands.[25]

The crisis was now very acute, but its very acuteness made for its healing. The Prussians had for some time felt themselves isolated in their opposition to the English 'four points'. In 1381 the Wendish towns demanded that the English should be allowed and tolerated in the country. They were not subject to the competition of English traders and were consequently satisfied with an agreement embodying the English claims to parity. The friction was above all an Anglo-Prussian one, and the Prussians had to rely solely upon their own determination. Unfortunately, even their determination proved unreliable. In this, as in all the subsequent Anglo-Prussian conflicts, the merchants of Danzig found themselves torn between their fear of English competition and their need of English trade. In the end it was their need of English trade that prevailed. So that when the events of 1385 resulted in the virtual cessation of intercourse, the Prussian resistance gave out and the main obstacle to an agreement on the lines of the proposals of 1380 disappeared. The agreement of 1388 reaffirmed all the Hanseatic freedom and privilege in England, and at the same time recognised for the English their

---

[24] Ibid., pp. 34–5; *H.R.* I, ii, no. 236; iii, nos. 142, 143; *U.B.* iv, nos. 753, 759, 761, 762, 806, 835, 910, 1054; *Hanseakten aus England, 1275 bis 1412*, ed. K. Kunze, no. 327 pars. 1–2.
[25] *H.R.* I, iii, no. 204, § 3, ii, nos. 309, 329,; iii, nos. 197, 404; *U.B.* iv, nos. 849, 850, 888, 933, 934; *C.C.R.*, 1385–9, p. 535.

'old rights' and their freedom to come to the lands of the Hanse and Prussia, to settle there and traffic freely and undisturbed.[26]

Thus ended the first serious clash. It is its place in the evolution of issues, rather than its effect on the respective positions of England and the Hanse, that gives it importance. The treaty of 1388 produced no immediate and definite change in the position of the English in the Hanseatic regions. They continued to trade in Danzig after 1388 in very much the same manner as they had done before the troubles of the seventies broke out. Altogether the wording of the clause dealing with English 'rights' was too vague and too general to stand comparison with the very definite provisions of the Hanseatic charter in England. But vague and shadowy as the English gains were, they marked the conclusion of an epoch and the beginning of a new one. The troubled period of 1375–90 provided the English with an opportunity for formulating the principles on which their subsequent claims were to be based. It also compelled every one of the protagonists – the Hanse as a whole, the Prussian towns, the English government, the English merchants – to define and announce their attitudes. For another sixty years the successive stages of the Anglo-Hanseatic rivalry were all enacted round the same issues, and evoked the same responses. They were all variations on the themes of 1380 and 1388.

It is in the midst of one of these variations that the story of the fifteenth century begins. The nineties of the fourteenth century and the opening years of the fifteenth century witnessed a revival of friction and a second outbreak of the Anglo-Hanseatic conflict. As at the time of the first clash, the friction began simultaneously in London and Prussia. The grant of the subsidy of tunnage and poundage in the Parliament of 1381 definitely included the Hanseatic imports and exports, and provoked an immediate outcry from the Steelyard. These difficulties in England had their counterpart in the accumulating difficulties in Danzig. With the settlement in 1388 the English resumed their penetration of Prussia. The English 'liggers' (i.e. resident representatives of English firms) took up what seemed to be a permanent residence in Danzig. Some of them brought over their families and acquired houses and shops. They dominated the trade in English cloth and also took part in some of the local trades. Their commerce and mutual relations were regulated by a cor-

---

[26] *H.R.* I, ii, no. 236; *U.B.* iv, no. 888. The negotiations took place in Prussia. *H.R.* I, ii, nos. 402–6: 'quod ligei mercatores Anglie quicumque liberam habeant facultatem se applicandi cum navibus bonis etc., ad quemcunque partem terre Prussie . . . transferendi ibique cum quaecumque persona libere contrahere et mercari, sicut antiquitus et ab antiquo extitit usitatum; quod quidem in omnibus et per omnia Pruthenis concessum est in Anglia.' The rest of the treaty is devoted to the subjects of claims and jurisdiction bearing directly on the immediate causes of the conflict.

porate organisation, which they seem to have possessed in the nineties, presumably with a communal house, periodical assemblies and elected officials. To this growth of trade the Prussians could hardly remain indifferent, and they struck out against it as soon as relations with the English were showing the first signs of strain.[27]

With this feeling in the air, it is no wonder that the centre of friction, which was in the first place the English fiscal measures, was soon transferred to Prussia. Regarded from the point of view of the Hanse as a whole, the events in England did not justify anything in the nature of violent retaliation, especially as Henry IV confirmed the Hanseatic privileges within a few months of his accession. The Hanse as a whole seemed consequently unwilling to quarrel with England. The only group clamouring for retaliation was the one which would have welcomed any opportunity for a quarrel, the Prussians, and the measure of retaliation upon which they decided was the one which they would have taken in any case: the curtailment of English trade in Danzig. In February, 1398, Prussia officially terminated the treaty with England; in 1396 the diet of Prussian towns had decided to restrict the English rights of residence; and in 1402, when the conflict passed into an acute stage, the rules against the English settling with 'wife and children' and trading with foreigners, or in the interior of Prussia, were singled out for immediate enforcement.[28] The Prussian towns also tried for years to organise a boycott of English cloth. At first these attempts failed through the indifference of the other parts of the Hanse, but in the end the other towns were won over. It was English piracies that decided the attitude of the non-Prussian towns. The prevailing tension provided a good incentive for mutual attacks on the high seas, and the English did not confine their exploits to Prussian shipping alone. By 1405 the successive acts of piracy had raised the whole of the Hanse against the English; and in March, 1405, the Hanseatic diet at Lübeck prohibited both the trade in English cloth and the export of Baltic goods to England.[29]

---

[27] *H.R.* I, iv, nos. 124 par. 2, 192 par. 3; ibid., nos. 360 par. 4 ('dat se alle lande mit erem wande vorvullen'), 397 par. 8 (retailing cloth in fairs), v, no. 101 pars. 2 and 3; Daenell, op. cit., vol. I, p. 64; ibid., n. 1; *H.R.* I, iv, no. 5: the corporate organisation in 1391. The right was not provided in the treaty in spite of the English demands: *H.R.* I, iii, no. 403 par. 4, cf. F. Schulz, op. cit., p. 51, n. 1; *H.R.* I, iv, nos. 397 par. 8, 537 pars. 3–6, 100 par. 4, 101 pars. 2 and 3; *Hanseakten*, ed. Kunze, no. 322 par. 9; F. Schulz, op. cit., p. 45, n. 2 (J. Beby, Governor of the English in 1391).

[28] *U.B.* v, nos. 386, 387, 391; *H.R.* I, iv, nos. 433, 345 par. 2, v, no. 101 pars. 2, 3.

[29] *H.R.* I, iv, nos. 397, par. 19, 413 par. 7, 503 par. 11, 539 par. 6, 541 par. 23, 559 par. 11 ('blihet steende czu gutir geduld'); ibid., v, nos. 74 par. 2, 83; *Hanseakten*, ed. Kunze, nos. 317, 326, 329, 334–7, 345, 357, 359, 361; *H.R.* I, nos. 100 par. 1, 130; *C.C.R.*, 1402–5, pp. 101, 337, 419; *U.B.* v, nos. 542, 569, 570, 597, 603, 615, 618, 620, 621, 633, 634; *H.R.* I, v. nos. 211, 212, 225 pars. 3–5, 15.

It looked as if the conflict might pass into a formal war; and if a war at this point did not break out, it was entirely due to the fact that the hostilities on the high seas had carried the dispute much farther than the real interests of both Prussia and England permitted. Whatever their respective interests had been at the time of the first skirmishes in the late nineties, they were far from warlike in 1405. The embargo on English trade was not sufficiently complete to have any immediate political effect in England, but it was sufficiently complete to produce economic difficulties in Prussia. The other parts of the Hanse evaded the prohibition of trade; and even some of the Danzig men imported English cloth from Holland and Skania and shipped Baltic goods to the west. Now, as in 1388 and again several times later, the whole purpose of Danzig's measures was defeated by the inner contradictions of its economic interests, and the determined policy of its anti-English majority was checked by the separate interests of the merchants trading to England. Within a few months of the Lübeck decision, the Prussian towns themselves began to consider the possibility of revising it. At a diet in Falsterbo they proposed the raising of the embargo and threw the trade open at the first opportunity. It was in vain that the Hanseatic factory in Bruges exhorted the Hanse to hold out 'because the Hanse can do without the English cloth much better than the English can do without Hanseatic goods'. For, judging by the frequency of evasions, it was Prussia and not England that found the cessation of trade in 1405 difficult to bear. As a Prussian ambassador to England had himself to acknowledge some time later, the Prussians 'der Engelschen nicht entbehren mögen'.[30]

Important changes had also occurred in the English position. England was in conflict with Burgundy, and John, Duke of Burgundy, had been trying to draw the Hanse into an anti-English alliance. An alliance of this kind, apart from its political and military danger, also threatened to close to England that channel of Flemish and Dutch trade, which was then the only alternative in Western Europe to the troubled Hanseatic routes.[31] In the circumstances there is no wonder that the English government appeared more anxious than before to proceed with the negotiations which had been lazily dragging on since the beginning of the century. In 1405, an English delegation arrived in Prussia, and in October of the same year a draft treaty was ready for confirmation. Before the confirmation could take place – and the English were still somewhat dilatory – a new complication was created by an English capture

---

[30] *H.R.* I, v, nos. 274, 302 pars. 1–15, 308 pars. 1–10, 20, 24, 25, 27, 311 par. 12, 255 par. 5, 262, 275, 659. But the same factory wrote in 1405 that the imports of Hanseatic goods into England and the Low Countries was, in spite of the embargo, so abundant that no shortage was felt ('neyn ghebrek en is'); *H.R.* I, v, no. 274.

[31] *H.R.* I, v, nos. 255 par. 8, 256, 257, 271, 272, 390, 392, 404.

of five Hanseatic boats on their way to Spain.[32] But Prussia was now too anxious for peace to be put off by a piratical attack. The negotiations for the renewal of trade continued much to England's advantage; the English negotiators succeeded in reducing the Hanseatic demands for damages to a relatively small sum, and they even managed to create a serious cleavage in the Hanseatic ranks. Lübeck and the Wendish towns, when drawn into conflict, had none of Danzig's economic motives for anti-English action; now that the problem of peace was under discussion they had none of Danzig's economic motives for hurry and impatience. The consideration which in the first place decided their attitude to the English was the English piracies, and they consequently saw no reason now for concluding peace without adequate compensation for their losses at the hands of the pirates. Moreover, the Hanseatic factory in Bruges, with its interests in the Flemish cloth trade, was more perturbed by the prospects of peace than by the possible losses and dangers of war. It advised the Hanseatic towns to hold out against the English, and to force them to submission by tightening up the blockade.[33]

It was in spite of this advice, and in the face of the opposition of the Wendish and Saxon towns, that Prussia in the end concluded peace with England. And it was against the settled policy of Danzig that the treaty, which was finally concluded between Prussia and England, embodied a general recognition of the principle of 'reciprocity'.[34] The English were confirmed in their right to come to Prussia, and there to *conversari, libere more mercatorio tam cum Prutensis quam aliis, cuiuscumque nacionis vel ritus fuerint, mercari, ibidemque morari et exiende ad lares et domicilia propria redire.*

Thus ended the second important clash, the first in the fifteenth century. It occurred over the same issues and brought out the same alignment of interests as the preceding clash of the fourteenth century. Like the preceding clash it ended in favour of the English, and the English gains were made more real still by the political situation in the years immediately following the conclusion of the treaty. A series of democratic revolutions in the Wendish towns in 1408 and 1410 disabled for a time the central section of the Hanse, and deprived the league as a whole of any effective leadership. At about the same time the Teutonic Order was overwhelmed by a disastrous war with Poland, and after the defeat of Tannenberg (1410) was not in the mood or in the position to enforce the

---

[32] *H.R.* I, v, nos. 265–9, 276 par. 4, 296 par. 7, 339 pars. 16–17, 343, 348, 350, 351.

[33] *H.R.* I, v, nos. 484, 525, 526, 537; cf. no. 319. That the English tried to sow dissent from the very beginning is clear from *H.R.* I, viii, no. 1061. The attitude of the Bruges factory was the same all through the period; *H.R.* I, v, nos. 313, 392 par. 6, 659.

[34] *U.B.* v, no. 830; *H.R.* I, v, nos. 525, 633.

execution of England's obligations to Prussia. The English government made use of the opportunity to withhold the further instalments of the sum due to the Hanse under the treaty; delegation after delegation failed to extract full payment from England, and most of the sum was still unpaid in the thirties. In Prussia itself the High Master of the time, Henry of Plauen, who was no friend of Danzig's, helped the English to protect and consolidate the positions they had won in 1408. Thus favoured, the English developed their trade in Danzig to a remarkable extent. The English custom accounts record large and regular shipments to and from Prussia. In Danzig the English body of residents was taking a firm root.[35]

Yet, advantageous as the issue of this second clash was, the settlement was by no means permanent or secure. After a few years, events in England and Prussia began to move again towards another impasse, and the subsequent conflict was not to be settled till 1437. The treaty of 1408 itself contained the roots of the revived strife. From the English point of view it was at least as good as that of 1388, but not as good as the one for which they had clamoured. The general formula of reciprocity could not confer privileges as tangible and as valuable as those which the Hanseatics enjoyed under their charter in England. As long as full parity and reciprocity remained unrealised, the English programme could not satisfy English merchants in Prussia nor arrest the agitation of English merchants in England. It was not enough that they could come to Danzig, settle there, and trade wholesale and retail with Danzigers and foreigners. They also wanted to be admitted to the Livonian and West Russian markets and to be given fiscal exemptions equivalent to those which the Hanseatics claimed in England; above all, they wanted an official permission to form a corporate body with a communal seat, a 'Hanse' of their own. We have already seen them insisting upon their 'right to a society' after the treaty of 1388, and the very fact that the treaty of 1408 contained no provision for a 'society' made the English demand for one even more insistent than before. In some of their later petitions the English merchants justified their insistence by considerations of practical, and largely of social, convenience. The society was wanted, they argued, in order to keep their members out of taverns and the company of loose women. But the real value of a 'society' lay elsewhere. The existence of a corporate body involved the right of jurisdiction over its members, and the power to enforce its own rules and regulations, or, in other words, the opportunity for escaping the jurisdiction of Danzig's courts and the rules and regulations of Danzig's municipality. A common

---

[35] Both sides were influenced by the bad harvest and the high prices for corn in England in 1409: *H.R.* 1, v, nos. 547, 548, 643; Daenell, op. cit., vol. i, pp. 162–8, 174; *H.R.* 1, v, no. 620; vi, nos. 24, 114, 195, 304, 500. *K.R. Cust. Accts., passim.*

'house' combined with English-owned lodgings and shops meant a virtual exemption from that oversight and control, which Danzig, like most medieval municipalities, exercised over its foreign residents through the machinery of licensed hosts and hostelries. The 'society' was meant to be the English counterpart of the German Steelyard in London, an institutional embodiment and a guarantee of the exceptional position of the English in Danzig. Without the 'society' the parity provided by the treaty was incomplete and unreal.[36]

The treaty was equally unsatisfactory to the Danzigers. The formula of the English 'rights' was too vague to give complete satisfaction to the English, but it was sufficiently vague to alarm the Prussians. They were afraid that it might, after all, be construed into a body of privileges as extensive as those of the Steelyard in London. But what they feared most was the attempt to read into the treaty the 'right to a society'. They feared it for the same reasons for which the English wanted it. In some of their memoranda to the English government they tried to justify their opposition by the assertion that the English had used their communal house as a 'prison'. On other occasions they alleged political motives. The English, they feared, were congenital empire-builders; if allowed to settle and trade in Danzig, they would soon annex the country of Prussia, as they had annexed Bordeaux and Gascony.[37] But behind all these official motives, however genuine, there was the determination to prevent the English from developing their trade outside the control and jurisdiction of the town, and thus making the *Gastenrecht* impossible to enforce.

With both the English and the Prussians in this mood, the struggle was bound to break out anew, and in the thirties all the issues were again in the melting-pot. As on the previous two occasions the crisis followed after a long period of steadily accumulating friction; and friction began to accumulate before the ink was dry on the treaty. Some of that friction was undoubtedly due to the English refusal to honour the financial obligations of the treaty. Much ill-feeling was created by piracy and mutual commercial reprisals. Attacks on the high seas were more or less inevitable in the international commerce of the time, but the period between 1417 and 1430 received more than its rightful share of naval perturbations. Most of these were due to the war between Denmark and the Hanse in 1427, in the course of which the Hanse was compelled to close the Sund, and the English suffered equally from King Eric's agents and from the Hanseatic privateers.[38] But it was the revived dispute over

[36] *H.R.* 2, ii, nos. 169 par. 3, 318 par. 3.
[37] *H.R.* 1, vii, nos. 708, 649, 821; viii, nos. 454, 668; *H.R.* 2, ii, no. 76 par. 25; *H.R.* 1, vii, no. 708 pars. 2–6.
[38] The attempt of the Hanse to enlist the support of the Emperor Sigismund at the Council of Constance ended in a fiasco: *H.R.* 1, vi, nos. 186, 187, 381, 446

the English position in Prussia and the Hanseatic position in England, that provided the main source of conflict.

The dispute revived first of all in Prussia. The Danzigers, who had never accepted the English interpretation of the treaty, tried to assert their point of view as early as 1410, when, according to an English complaint, the burgomaster proclaimed that the English should no longer traffic with foreigners and sell their goods retail or possess a corporate organisation. Fortunately for the English, Henry of Plauen was then the High Master of the Order, and through his intervention the English merchants obtained the revocation of the measure. But within a year of his intervention Henry of Plauen was deposed by a revolution, and his successors were not inclined to fight Danzig on behalf of the English. For another three years the position of the English apparently remained unchanged, until, in 1414, the municipality of Danzig again re-enacted its order regarding English trade, which the High Master had overriden in 1410.[39] But even this action had little immediate effect upon the trade and economic position of the English merchants, for the English trade to Danzig continued to flourish all through the second decade of the century. It is in 1418, after the failure of the Hanseatic appeal to the Emperor, that we observe the first signs of the English counter-agitation. In that year we find Henry V addressing to the High Master a complaint against the maltreatment of the English merchants in Danzig, reminding him of the maxim that 'the English should be treated in the Hanse even as the Hanseatics are treated in England'. This reminder was accompanied by an anti-Hanseatic offensive in London. In January, 1418, the merchants of the Steelyard complained before the Mayor's Court of the exactions of certain local dues, from which they considered themselves exempt under the terms of their charter. On this occasion the Mayor's Court decided for the Hanseatics, but two years later the sheriffs of London proclaimed their determination to collect the dues from the merchants of the Hanse, and the King's Council overruled the verdict of the Mayor's Court. London's official attitude was underlined by the refusal of the Mayor and Corporation in 1419 to

pars. 7–10. Having engineered the appeal to the Emperor, the Bruges contor found it almost impossible to extract from the towns a definite statement of grievances against England: ibid., nos. 400 par. 21, 450, 451; *U.B.* vi, nos. 661, 694, 712; *H.R.* 1, viii, nos. 218, 240 par. 3, 414, 507, 508 A, 775, 777, 784, 794, 1167; *H.R.* 2, i, nos. 53, 105. Until the outbreak of the Dano-Wendish war in 1427, the mutual attacks and arrests were not as frequent or important as alleged in the English and Hanseatic complaints at the time, e.g. *U.B.* vi, nos. 187, 418, 447, 635, 934. The most important were: the arrest of the Hanseatic boats in 1417 (*H.R.* 1, vi, no. 451, where it is much exaggerated) and the arrest of the English in Greifswald in a dispute twenty years old: *H.R.* 1, vi, nos. 556 A par. 57, 581, 582, vii, no. 592 par. 7.

[39] *H.R.* 1, v, nos. 655, 674; vii, nos. 592 pars. 1–6, 593; viii, no. 452 pars. 1–2; ibid., 2, ii, nos. 76 par. 20, 169 pars. 2–3.

appoint an English alderman to the Steelyard: a refusal which went against an explicit provision in the Hanseatic charter and an established practice of the City. If we are to believe a later petition of the Steelyard of 1423, the fiscal 'oppression' of the preceding few years had been prompted by the English merchants and above all by the merchants of London. Their agitation redoubled its vigour on the death of Henry V in 1422. With the accession of a new king the Hanseatic charter came up again for confirmation, and the whole machinery of organised pressure was now brought into play to prevent the renewal of the 'privileges'. The records of Lynn have preserved an illuminating account of a meeting of merchants, at which an impost was levied for the costs of the anti-Hanseatic campaign in Parliament; and the merchants of Lynn were no doubt well supported by merchants of other towns. A formal case against the Hanse was provided in the petition of merchants trading to Prussia, enumerating all their grievances against Prussia and Danzig. Within a few weeks of the petition, and while the question of the charter was still under consideration, the government granted the Hanseatic merchants protection for a year. But during the same year a decision of the Council made the Hanseatics liable to the subsidy of tunnage and poundage, and the Steelyard had a grievous tale of 'oppression', actual and threatened, to report to the Hanseatic towns.[40]

In the Hanseatic towns the events in England produced an immediate, though not a very violent, repercussion. The Danzig municipality continued that policy of curtailment of English rights which it had begun in 1414. It tried to prevent the permanent settlement of the English in the town, to stop their retail trade, and their intercourse with 'foreigners'. It was in vain that the English merchants complained at what they considered a breach of their rights and pressed their demands for an organisation in a series of petitions and deputations to the High Master of the Order, for both their complaints and their demands remained unsatisfied. But at the same time the Order and the municipality of Danzig carefully avoided the violent courses advocated by others. When in 1423 the Hanseatic diet at Lübeck recommended that the English merchants resident in the Hanseatic towns should be imprisoned and their goods confiscated, as reprisals for the recent events in England, the Order and the Prussian towns refused to carry out the decision, and the English trade to Prussia continued uninterrupted.[41]

This moderation was temporarily successful, for neither party was at

[40] *H.R.* i, vii, nos. 87, 88; *U.B.* vi, no. 238; *H.R.* i, vii, nos. 592–4; *U.B.* vi, no. 528, and *Entry Book*, ii, f. 3 (Archives of the Corporation of King's Lynn); *U.B.* vi, nos. 474, 475, 479, 482, 613, 643, 611, 612, 651, 504, *Proc. and Ord. P.C.* vol. iii, pp. 110–11; *H.R.* i, vii, nos. 609 par. 6, 671.

[41] *H.R.* i, vii, nos. 461 pars. 1 and 19, 708, 746, 773 pars. 7–8, 800, 821; ibid., nos. 609 par. 6, 611, 623, 624 par. 5.

the time prepared to court the danger of a formal rupture. The English trade had been badly hit by the Dano–Wendish war and the closing of the Sund, and was threatened by the renewal of Flemish measures against the English cloth in 1428. Prussians, in their turn, were not over-anxious to bring about a complete cessation of their English trade. It is therefore no wonder that the counsel of moderation for a time prevailed on both sides, and during the four years between 1426 and 1430 the brewing trouble was somewhat allayed by a number of conciliatory measures. In February, 1426, the government, in response to a Hanseatic petition, appointed an English alderman to the Steelyard, thus overriding the decision taken by the City of London seven years before. For a few months the City tried to resist, but a repeated royal order in January, 1427, broke its opposition. Direct negotiations between the Steelyard and the City led to a general compromise, by virtue of which the City sanctioned the appointment of the English alderman. The same compromise also settled the outstanding question of municipal dues, and the merchants of the Hanse were exempt from the payment of most of the local imposts. As their part of the compromise, the merchants of the Steelyard undertook to intercede with the High Master and the town of Danzig on behalf of the English merchants there. When, a year later, the English merchants in Danzig tried again to draw attention to their unsatisfactory position in Prussia, the Steelyard addressed a carefully worded request to Danzig to respect the old customs of the English in Danzig for the sake of the position of the Hanse in England. Whether as a result of this intercession or for other reasons, the Order and the towns seemed for a time to modify their attitude to the English demands. In its reply to the Steelyard, Danzig expatiated on the exceptional favours which the English, in spite of their complaints, continued to enjoy there. At the same time, the Englishmen in Danzig obtained their first important concession on the question of corporate organisation. In December, 1428, the High Master, while still refusing to recognise the formal claim of the English to exceptional treatment, conceded to them the right to have an elected governor to lead and rule over their members. In 1429 a Prussian delegation visited England to exact the payment of further instalments under the treaty of 1409 and to settle the outstanding differences. In its financial mission the delegation fared no better than the previous delegations, but it apparently obtained from the government a confirmation of the Hanseatic freedom from all taxation not specified in the charter; and the trade showed signs of revival after the ominous slump of the year before.[42]

---

[42] *H.R.* I, viii, p. 358 n. 5; *U.B.* vi, no. 767, n. 1; Smit, *Bronnen*, vol. i, no. 1012, p. 627, n. 1; *U.B.* vi, nos. 533, 764, 767; cf. *H.R.* I, viii, nos. 451, 611, 777, 784, 794; *Rot. Parl.*, IV, p. 303 (27); *C.P.R.*, 1422–9, p. 346; *U.B.* vi, nos. 651,

Unfortunately, this spirit of moderation could not, and did not, endure for very long. The mutual concessions of the years 1426 to 1430 did a a great deal to relieve the growing tension, but they left the important issues unsolved, and therefore could not prevent another change for the worse. The English in Danzig, in spite of the High Master's concession in 1428, continued to clamour for full parity and to protest against recent taxation. The English merchants in London and other towns, in spite of the compromise with the Steelyard in 1427, were preparing to renew their agitation against Hanseatic privileges. The slightest pretext was likely to lead to an outbreak, and the pretext was found in the unsettled problem of Hanseatic liability to tunnage and poundage. When in 1431 the subsidy of tunnage and poundage was granted to Henry VI for two years, the merchants of the Steelyard were made to put up sureties for the payment of an additional 'increment of' 6d for each pound worth of goods and 3s for a tun of sweet wine, imposed upon foreigners. As might be expected, the imposition raised a storm in the Hanseatic towns, and the threat of reprisals in Prussia forced the English government to suspend the collection of the additional 'increment', pending the decision of Parliament and Council. But by that time the damage had already been done, the agitation on both sides had been resumed and was not to be stopped. The Prussians began to behave as if the day of reckoning had come at last. They forced the English merchants in Prussia to produce sureties to the sum of 1200 nobles, to be forfeited if the 'increment' were exacted in England. For his own part, the High Master resuscitated all his ancient financial claims, satisfied some of them by seizing English goods, and threatened to settle the others in a similar fashion. For a time, the position of the English became so difficult that it seemed as if they would have to leave the country altogether. Their deputation to the High Master did not help much, nor did the somewhat half-hearted intercession of the Steelyard. If anything the anti-English movement grew. In June, 1434, a Hanseatic diet in Lübeck elaborated a plan of action against the English; a delegation from the diet to the High Master extracted from him a promise to expel them from Prussia; and in fulfilment of his promise, he sent a letter to Henry VI, which was worded as a complaint, but conceived as an ultimatum. The extension of the campaign was probably due to simultaneous events in England. In spite of the fact that in December, 1433, the government extended the protection to the Hanseatics for another year, the goods of Wendish towns appear to have been arrested. This, and the new regulations as to

658; *L. Bk. K.*, f. 33 (MS); *U.B.* vi, no. 723; *H.R.* i, viii, nos. 32, 433 par. 10, 453 par. 2, 546 par. 7; *U.B.* vi, no. 888; cf. the Danzig account of the active trade and privileged position of the English in Prussia; *H.R.* i, viii, nos. 454, 668.

the manner of valuation of goods for customs purposes, threatened to stop the entire flow of Hanseatic trade to England.[43] The breach was now as wide as it had ever been before; correspondence and mutual re-criminations obviously could not heal it; and if a commercial war or, what was practically the same, ruinous reprisals on the high seas, were to be averted, the whole problem of Anglo-Hanseatic relations had to be resubmitted, as in 1388 and 1408, to a complete revision by a fully authorised peace conference.

It is doubtful whether a conference of this nature was intended when the Hanse sent out its great delegation of 1434–6. But the seriousness of the situation, the comprehensive scope of Hanseatic claims and grievances and the English insistence on maters of justice and right, were bound to focus the negotiations on fundamental principles. The head of the dele-gation, Henrich Vorrath, the Burgomaster of Danzig and probably the greatest statesman among contemporary leaders of the Hanse, soon realised the position and was prepared to go considerably beyond his limited terms of reference. In the end, the negotiations, however small their practical consequences proved to be, struck a balance of the events of the preceding twenty-five years and wound up the third successive clash in the history of Anglo-Hanseatic relations.

Yet the debut of the delegation in England was far from auspicious. The Hanseatic memorandum contained an enormous claim for com-pensation, and the English were as yet in no haste to consider it. More-over, the international situation on the eve of the conference of Arras was still too uncertain, and the English attitude to the Hanse could not be defined while war and peace hung in the balance in Flanders and Northern France. The Hanseatic address elicited from the government 'vele soter wort na older Engelschen gewonheit', but beyond 'sweet words' nothing of importance was done or said and the negotiations were adjourned, to be resumed in Flanders in the following spring. But even in the following spring the negotiations did not produce any material results. The peace conference with France and Burgundy was yet to take place, and the English delegates were probably relieved to find that the instructions of the Hanseatic delegates prevented them from the discus-sion of those subjects in which the English were most concerned, and in the first place the situation at Danzig. The negotiations were postponed again, and the delegation had to try to accelerate matters by pressure. In order to force England to immediate negotiations and to safeguard the Steelyard from possible reprisals, the delegation ordered a formal

---

[43] *Rot. Parl.* iv, pp. 366, 389, 426, 503; *U.B.* vi, nos. 942, 991, 992, 1005, 1011, 1021, 1046, 1061; *H.R.* 2, nos. 146, 147, 168, 319; *U.B.* vi, no. 1065; *H.R.* 2, i, nos. 146, 147, 168, 319; *U.B.* vi, no. 1065; *H.R.* 2, i, nos. 169, 241, 192, 321 pars. 1–3, 324, 355 pars. 1–7, 356, 357; *U.B.* vi, no. 1099; *H.R.* 2, i, nos. 319, 320; *Rot. Parl.*, vol. vi, p. 493.

cessation of trade with England. It commanded the Hanseatic merchants to leave England, warned them to avoid English waters and urged the towns to expel English merchants. In the meantime the Hanseatic towns were preparing materials, lists of grievances and instructions to ambassadors for the coming negotiations.[44]

As these grievances and instructions show, the expectation of Prussian towns had run very high. Their representatives were to demand payment of all the old debts and damages for the attacks of pirates and breaches of privileges; they were to insist on the full and unequivocal restoration of the charter, and at the same time to refuse to concede to the English any definite privileges in Prussia. But even before the negotiations were due to begin the political and economic situation made the Prussian programme impossible to carry out. The political situation after the conference of Arras, with its formal breach with Burgundy, made the English anxious to restore economic relations with the Hanse and weakened their position in the negotiations. But it also weakened the position of the Hanse and Prussia, for their relations with Flanders were almost as uncertain as their relation with England. When the news of the possible outbreak of war between England and Flanders reached Danzig, a letter went to Vorrath urging him to arrange a truce with England as soon as possible, and at any rate before the hostilities with Flanders began, so that at least one avenue of trade with England should remain open. Even more unfavourable was the economic position. The very measures Vorrath had taken and recommended in the spring rebounded against the Hanse. The embargo on English trade, like similar embargoes in the past, was impossible to enforce and merely revealed the economic disunion of the Hanse and its dependence on English trade. As on previous occasions it provided an opening for neutrals and intermediaries, and above all for the Dutch. But there were men and towns within the Hanse itself only too willing to break the injunction. The Cologners treated the whole dispute as no concern of theirs, continued their trade with England, and, to make their position secure, contemplated separate negotiations with the English government. The Zuider Zee towns, and especially Campen, whose allegiance to the Hanse had always been loose and somewhat wayward, acted now in complete independence of the rest of the Hanse. The Bergen factory, in spite of its connections with the Wendish towns, issued permissions of trade to England. In the circumstances it is no wonder that in the winter of 1436 we find the Steelyard still functioning in London, and entries of Hanseatic imports reappearing over and over again in the customs accounts. It is equally no wonder that the Prussians themselves found it impossible to observe the embargo. Prussian goods were carried by land to Flanders in spite of prohibition, and some Prussian goods

[44] *H.R.* 2, i, nos. 383–5, 406, 407, 421, 429–32, 435, 437.

belonging to merchants of Danzig were shipped directly to England. In April, 1436, the High Master for a certain sum of money (*gegen Entgelt*) allowed a group of English merchants to come to Prussia with 'six great ships'. In the circumstances, Danzig had to confess its inability to make the prohibition effective. 'We must let things go as best they can; we cannot do more than is in our power.'[45]

Danzig was now obviously hard pressed. In July, 1436, it furnished its delegates with another set of instructions much more moderate than those of 1435. The tone of the despatch was now distinctly troubled and anxious; Vorrath must use all the possible means to restore mutual traffic if the men and land of Prussia 'are not to lose their livelihood'. But moderate as the tone of the Hanseatic instructions now was, they were still impossible to carry out without wrecking the negotiations. They still withheld from Vorrath the power to treat about the English privileges in Danzig, which were the central issue and the stumbling-block of the negotiations. In the conversations of autumn and winter of 1436, Vorrath's position was very difficult, almost tragic. He knew that the negotiations could not succeed as long as he adhered to the Danzig instructions, and the failure of the negotiations might mean the break-up of the Hanse. The non-Prussian parts of the Hanse were loath to lose their hard-won privileges in England for the sake of Danzig's monopoly over its local market. Their spokesmen were careful to remind the Prussians that the towns had won the privileges for their merchants two hundred years previously, 'while the Prussians were still pagans'. Rather than suffer from Danzig's intransigence, the Wendish towns, the leaders of the Hanse, would sooner conclude a separate peace with England.[46] It was therefore obvious that if the old privileges and the unity of the Hanseatic policy were to be preserved, Vorrath would have to go beyond Danzig's instructions. After a great deal of hesitation he was forced to break his undertaking to his own town and negotiate about the position of the English in Danzig.

The concession made, Vorrath was able to report progress to the Hanseatic towns, and in the early winter of 1437 the treaty was in sight. The Hanseatics obtained the renewal of the privileges and the confirmation of their freedom from new taxation, including the tunnage and

---

[45] *H.R.* 2, i, no. 436, Ramsay, op. cit., vol. i, pp. i, pp. 475–80; *H.R.* 2, i, no. 522. The problem of English cloth trade in Flanders had become acute again in 1433 and 1434; *H.R.* 2, i, nos. 191, 192, 215, 268 par. 13, Smit, *Bronnen*, vol. ii, p. 668, footnote 2; *H.R.* 2, i, no. 567: 'up date men yo von hynnen eyne side vrii hadde to besoken', cf. Daenell, op. cit., vol. i, pp. 376–8; *H.R.* 2, i, nos. 501, 568, 563, 577; ii, nos. 4, 19, 25–8, 31, 37, 65, 70.

[46] *H.R.* 2, ii, no. 16, 4: 'Doch hadden de stede vor 200 jaren, eer dat lant to Prusen cristen was, 'in vel enden vryheit unde privileje von den kopman vorworven, de hope se wol to beholden, al moten se darumme lyden'; *H.R.* 2, ii, no. 53, and p. 14.

poundage. They also obtained from the English a promise to pay the outstanding instalments of the debt under the treaty of 1409. But they had to forgo all the financial claims of more recent date, and what was most important of all, had to include in the treaty a general clause defining and safeguarding the English position in the Hanseatic regions more exactly and fully than any similar formulas had done in the past. In addition to the general and conventional reciprocity clause restating the English right to enter Prussia, settle there (*morari*), and trade unrestricted with whomsoever they pleased, the treaty gave the English fiscal exemptions as exceptional as those of the Hanseatics in England, for they were to be free of all taxes imposed in the course of the last hundred years and more.

Even these concessions fell short of the *maximum* of English demands and might not have been accepted had it not been for the moderation of the lords and the open advocacy of Cardinal Beaufort. The English merchants tried to prevent the ratification of the treaty, or, as Vorrath believed, to postpone it so as to be first in the field with their cloth fleet.[47] Yet the treaty was an undoubted English triumph. It again demonstrated the strength of England's position, and it again concluded a period of violent disagreement by reasserting in favour of England those very principles about which England and the Hanse had in the first place disagreed. Vorrath tried to justify himself before the Hanse by insisting that his concessions did not involve a definite grant of privileges to the English. But the Danzigers themselves refused to accept his interpretation and regarded the treaty as a complete capitulation, while the English merchants, as soon as they reappeared in Danzig, spoke and behaved as if a charter of privilege had indeed been granted to them.

3. THE FAILURE (1437 TO 1475)

The treaty of 1437, though never confirmed by Prussia or recognised by Danzig, attained the furthest limit of Hanseatic concessions to England. For the third time the Prussian resistance to English demands was broken and for the third time the Hanseatic league had to sacrifice the interests and prejudices of the Danzig merchants in order to save its political unity and its trade to England. After half a century of agitation, the English merchants trading to Prussia and the Baltic acquired the substance, if not the form, of the 'privileges' which would serve as counterpart of the

---

[47] *H.R.* 2, ii, nos. 29, 46, 63, 65–8, 70, 73, 79, 84. According to the Hanseatic version, the opposition to the ratification was led by the merchants of the 'nortcost' anxious 'ere laken dar . . . bringen und allene den markt holden'; *H.R.* 2, ii, no. 71, also nos. 67 and 75. On Beaufort's action, see *H.R.* 2, ii, p. 15; *H.R.* 2, ii, nos. 220, 224, 226.

Hanseatic charter in England. Whether Vorrath actually delivered and sealed a grant of 'privileges' apart from and in addition to the treaty can well be doubted. No traces of a grant of this kind have come down to us, and in spite of the repeated challenge from the Hanseatics, the English negotiators in the second half of the century were unable to produce any documentary evidence of the grant. But whether a document of this kind was ever issued or not, both the English and the Prussians were convinced that the treaty of 1437 embodied a concession of 'full privileges'. On the strength of it the English merchants and official representatives in Prussia claimed full parity with the Hanse. They presented a formal statement to that effect to the High Master and the municipality of Danzig the moment they appeared again in Danzig, and repeated it over and over again in the negotiations which took place in the forties and the fifties. In these subsequent negotiations the English claims never went beyond the provisions of the treaty, and from 1437 till the end of our period their demands were all narrowed down to the contention that the treaty of 1437 be confirmed and observed. The treaty obviously gave a full, or at any rate the fullest possible, satisfaction to their fifty years' old claims, and marked the furthest point they had as yet attained in the offensive against the Hanse.[48]

This point was not to be passed or even reached again until the Tudor era. The English success of 1437 was the last success in the fifteenth century and marked the end of one epoch and the beginning of another. Hitherto every clash had ended to the advantage of the English merchants; with every successive peace treaty they were brought a step nearer to the coveted position of parity. But in the forties a reverse process set in. The same issues, interests, and ambitions continued to dominate the situation, and conflict broke out as frequently and as easily as before. But the results were no longer the same. The successive clashes brought the English merchants no advantage, real or fictitious; most of them were disastrous to English shipping and trade; and after thirty years of unrest they terminated in the Hanseatic triumph at the peace conference of Utrecht.

No single fact or group of facts will explain this reversal of fortune, but the student of the fifteenth century will find an easy and an obvious

---

[48] *H.R.* 2, ii, nos. 539 par. 2, 540 par. 1, 647 par. 1. The documentary evidence of a separate agreement regarding the status of the English in Prussia, if it existed, would have been seized by the 'Bergenfahrer' together with the other documents of the English delegation; *H.R.* 2, iii, no. 687. *The Antient Kalendars and Inventories of the Treasury of His Majesty's Exchequer*, ed. Sir F. Palgrave (1836), vol. II, pp. 213 and 221, refers to the original of the Anglo-Prussian *appunctamentum* in the hands of the delegation. Cf. the instructions to the English delegation to Utrecht in 1473: *H.R.* 2, vii, no. 22 par. 11.

connection between the English position in the Baltic and the general
political situation of England during the middle decades of the century.
The late thirties saw the beginning of that disastrous period of Henry VI's
reign which ended in the loss of Normandy and Aquitaine and the civil
war at home. Of this general decline of English fortunes, the defeat of
English ambitions in the Baltic was merely a part, and was due to the
same set of causes as the other defeats of the mid-century: the disintegra-
tion of the Lancastrian government. The very year, 1437, in which the
peace with the Hanse was concluded, witnessed the formal end of Henry's
minority, and a new turn in English government and policy. The government of Henry VI's minority, however venal and inefficient, had been
saved from complete subservience to a clique by the balance of parties on
the Council. But Henry's quasi-personal government established the
domination of a single baronial party, which was only more reckless and
selfish for being shielded by the saintly figure of the King. The ruin of
the government now proceeded by rapid and irretrievable steps. The
retirement of Beaufort from active politics in 1443 and his death in 1447,
the defeat of Gloucester in 1440 and his death in 1447, led to the brief
but disastrous ascendency of Suffolk. And then the assassination of
Suffolk in 1450 delivered the deranged King and the distracted country
into the incompetent hands of the Queen and the Beaufort litter.

The new regime was bound to affect the course of Anglo-Hanseatic
relations. Its foreign policy, or rather the absence of it, destroyed the
advantages of England's economic position. A great deal of England's
strength in the first phase of the struggle was due to the fact that her
direct commercial connections with the Hanse, however valuable, were
not indispensable. There was no need for English cloth to remain unsold
and for her imports of continental, or even Baltic, goods to cease, as long
as the markets of Flanders, Zealand, and Brabant remained open to
English merchants. These markets were kept open in the last quarter of
the fourteenth and the first quarter of the fifteenth century by the policy
of Burgundian alliance during the first phase of the Hundred Years War.
Unfortunately, after the conference of Arras the relations between
England and Burgundy were steadily getting worse. England's misman-
agement of the war and the French military successes, forced the shrewd
Duke Philip to withdraw from the unprofitable entanglement. But the
withdrawal would not have led to a definite breach or to war, had it not
been for the faults of the English government: its incapacity to see and
accept a reverse, its political inconsistency in relation to France and its
bellicosity against the Burgundian 'traitors'. To these standing causes of
friction there were added difficulties arising from Philip's protective
measures against English cloth, with the result that the two countries
were constantly at loggerheads, and English trade to the great marts of

Flanders, Zealand, and Brabant was repeatedly interrupted.[49] And whenever these interruptions occurred England had to maintain peace with the Hanse in order to keep at least one channel of North European trade open to her merchants. On these occasions the English government was forced into an attitude of anxious moderation, and was prepared to give in to the Hanse both in the question of privileges in England and in that of the English position in the Baltic.

But it was the political situation at home that affected most the course of Anglo-Hanseatic rivalry. It is not that the domestic policy of Henry VI's 'personal' government was inspired by any new and different principles. Its worst failing was that it ceased to be inspired by any principles whatsoever. The mercenary interests of the ruling magnates in, and out of, the King's Council were allowed full licence. Matters of state policy were made to serve the private gains of party chieftains. And as there were easy and substantial gains to be derived from attacks on the Hanseatic commerce, the anti-Hanseatic piracy developed with every successive stage in the disruption of the English government. Persons with grievances, real and imaginary, found it easy to obtain letters of marque against the Hanse. With these letters and without them, attacks on Hanseatic shipping became more frequent than at any other period in the fifteenth century. And for the first time in the fifteenth century the attacks proceeded not only without opposition, but also with the assistance of the government. The ordinance for the keeping of the seas of 1442 established an organised system of privateering, free from the cumbersome restrictions of the earlier laws as to safe conducts and truce on the high seas. Thus freed, the English privateers were able in a short time to revolutionise the relations of England and the Hanse, and lead, through the great privateering 'coups' of 1449 and 1465, to a naval war and to the Hanseatic triumph of the sixties and the early seventies.

The revolutionary effect of this privateering outburst is hard to overestimate. In the first half of the century piracy had been an accompanying feature of the Anglo-Hanseatic rivalry, disturbing and annoying, but never sufficiently important to overshadow the economic and political issues. Now from being a mere incident piracy grew to become, by its magnitude and blatancy, the central issue in the relations of England and the Hanse. It was now the main subject of Hanseatic grievances, the main cause of conflict, and the main topic of negotiations. And with the change of issue there came a change in the grouping and the attitudes of

---

[49] It is hardly possible to speak, as Professor Pirenne does, of the continued economic peace between England and Burgundy from 1439 onwards: H. Pirenne, *Histoire de Belgique* (Brussels, 1903), vol. II, p. 233. Yet it remains broadly true that from the mid-fifties onwards the English trade to Brabantine fairs and to Middelburgh was rarely interrupted. See below, footnotes 70, 72, 108.

the combatants. As long as the issues were predominantly economic and related to the English demand for equal treatment in Danzig, the quarrel was very largely confined to England and Prussia. Lübeck and the central section of the Hanse remained largely unaffected, and their indifference to the Prusisan point of view very largely explains the isolation and the defeat of Danzig in the successive clashes of the late fourteenth and early fifteenth centuries. But now that piracy was becoming the principal issue, Lübeck and the Wendish towns entered the fray, and eventually assumed the leadership against England. Lübeck was the principal victim of the successive attacks on the Hanseatic fleets, and was determined to wrest penalties and reparations. The very paucity of its direct trade to England, which explains its want of sympathy with Prussian intransigence in the first half of the century, enabled it now to adopt a radical policy. It had little to lose from the interruption of trade with England, and it might even benefit by a naval war involving the closing of the Sund and the diversion of all the west-to-east traffic to the old trans-Jutland route. If we are to believe a Prussian allegation, Lübeck's taste for naval war had been whetted by the conflict with Holland, when it diverted to itself the shipping and the profit of other towns.[50] Its action against England was thus bound to be more vigorous, and consequently more successful, than that of Prussia, and the vigour of this action, as well as the cohesion of the anti-English coalition, grew with every important capture of Hanseatic shipping. Under Lübeck's leadership the different groups in the Hanse, with the single exception of Cologne, succeeded in establishing a real unity of front against England, and found themselves in a position not only to wage a naval war, but also, for the first time, to enforce a really effective embargo on the direct trade between England and the Baltic.

Thus the combined effect of anarchy at home and slap-dash policy abroad was to weigh the scales heavily against England in her struggle with the Hanse. The whole situation, international and domestic, was unfavourable to the policy of expansion and reciprocity, but even on those few occasions on which the general situation happened to favour the English, unforeseen but inevitable events intervened against them. The clash of parties at home, the war abroad, and above all the piracies on the high seas, could always be relied upon to produce a catastrophic event of this kind and destroy again the revived hopes of success.

The first of these catastrophic events did not occur till the capture of the Bay fleet in 1449, but the twelve years which had elapsed since the conclusion of Vorrath's treaty were filled with rumblings of a gathering storm. Much of the unrest was due to the Prussian opposition to the

---

[50] *H.R.* 2, iii, nos. 647, 669: 'so schiffet man abir di gutir kyn lubeke, dormete krigen si di fart und gedeyen.'

Vorrath treaty, and more still to the agitation of the English merchants in Prussia. Yet the principal centre of disturbance was to be found not in Prussia, but in that confined world of English baronial politics from which most of the mid-century storms were to come.

The English complaints at the non-fulfilment of the treaty began almost as soon as the English merchants set foot again on Prussian soil. In 1439, they tried to obtain from the municipality of Danzig the recognition and concession of their rights under the treaty. In 1440 they approached the High Master with a similar request. In the same year, a petition was addressed to the English government complaining against the new taxation in Danzig and the imprisonment of the boats and goods of several English merchants. In 1441 the merchants of England were petitioning the King and Parliament that the High Master should be called upon to seal the Vorrath treaty on pain of forfeiture of Hanseatic privileges. In 1442 another petition with a comprehensive list of English grievances against the Hanse was submitted to Parliament.[51] Nevertheless, the real position of the English in Danzig and their prospects there would not in themselves have created any serious difficulties with the Hanse. For one thing the Danzigers were completely isolated in their opposition to the treaty. The rest of the Hanse, including Lübeck, not only confirmed it themselves, but were urging Danzig to do the same. The Steelyard in writing to Danzig had to admit the justice of some of the English complaints. Even the other Prussian towns differed from Danzig and were prepared to ratify the treaty. And the Danzigers themselves, in spite of all the show of obstinacy, were very anxious that the traffic with England should remain uninterrupted and undisturbed. They opposed the imposition of the pound-toll (*Pfundzoll*) by the High Master in 1442, on the plea that it kept the English merchants away. In reply to the English complaints of 1439, 1441, and 1442, they were careful to point out that the English enjoyed greater favours in Danzig and traded there more than other foreigners. The official representatives of the English merchants in Danzig swore an affidavit in 1422, repudiating all responsibility for the complaint of the previous years, and denying its allegations against Danzig. This affidavit was no doubt extracted from the English merchants by a great deal of pressure, but the statements which it contained, whether voluntary or not, were not all fictitious. In their petitions of 1439 the English merchants themselves claimed that they were frequenting Danzig more than any other nation, and they apparently extended their trade during the war between the Hanse and Holland in 1440. In 1440 the Livonian towns complained of the unusual abundance of English cloth in Novgorod and Livonia, some of which must have come via

---

[51] *H.R.* 2, ii, nos. 318, 346, 380, 539, 644; *Proc. and Ord. P.C.*, vol. v, pp. 167, 170, 177; *Rot. Parl.*, vol. v, pp. 64–5.

Danzig; and at the end of the decade, after the privateering coup of 1449, the Prussians were able to lay their hands on an amount of English merchandise which they themselves described as very plentiful and exceeding in value their very considerable claims for compensation. All through these years the English maintained in Prussia a corporate organisation which officially represented them in their negotiations with Prussia and Danzig.[52]

It was therefore not in Prussia that the real source of the unrest was to be sought. The real source was now in England, where a succession of events in the forties was slowly preparing the way for a rupture with the Hanse. The first harbinger of the coming trouble was the official revival of aggressive anti-foreign policy in the Parliament of Reading in 1440. By an act of that Parliament the foreign merchants in England were again subjected to the limitations and control of the municipal *Gastenrecht*. They were forced to reside in approved hostelries and to submit all their dealings to the registration and control of their hosts. Their freedom of trade was limited by the obligation to sell all their goods within a prescribed period of time, to employ all the proceeds on the purchase of English goods and confine their dealings to wholesale transactions with Englishmen. In short, the maximum of the anti-foreign demands of English towns, which had been checked and opposed by the early Lancastrian governments, was now carried into effect. Taken by itself this measure is somewhat hard to explain, but fitted into the political situation of the time it acquires its proper meaning as an attempt to draw the middle classes into the struggle of the baronial parties. In some of his previous clashes with Beaufort's party, such as that of 1426, Gloucester had been able to mobilise a certain amount of middle-class support, at any rate among the burgesses of London. Whether his middle-class party was still alive by 1440 we do not know. What we do know is that throughout the intervening years the Beaufort party persisted in those very same policies and actions which had originally brought it into conflict with London opinion. Thus even if we are not entitled to assume the survival in London of the active pro-Gloucester sympathies, we can safely assume the survival of the anti-Beaufort antipathies. And, according to private reports to Germany, these antipathies descended to Suffolk and the younger Beauforts together with the rest of the Cardinal's heirloom. In the circumstances, the anti-Council interests in the City, unless previously bribed and reconciled, could be expected to side with the Gloucester faction as soon as the conflict broke out anew. As the conflict broke out again with Gloucester's memorandum against Beaufort in 1440 and the counter-attack on Eleanor Cobham in 1441, it is natural to assume that

[52] *H.R.* 2, ii, nos. 314, 570 par. 2, 318 par. 3; 638, 639, 647, 655, 682; ibid., nos. 434 (date?), 458, 325, 329; ibid., iii, no. 536.

the anti-foreign legislation in the Parliament of 1440 was something in the nature of a bribe. That the coincidence of the two events was no mere accident is further suggested by the recurrence of a similar situation in 1447. And if it was not an accident, then what it meant was that the economic interests of the merchant class were being exploited by the ruling party for its political ends, and the issues of commercial policy made a mere pawn in the inter-baronial struggle.[53]

The Act was therefore bound to affect the future of Anglo-Hanseatic relations. The Hanseatic merchants were excluded from its provisions, but they could not be excluded from the changed atmosphere in Parliament and the City of London, or from the partisan manipulations of economic policy. It was the changed temper and the partisan politics at home rather than the position in Danzig that instigated the sequence of anti-Hanseatic petitions in 1440, 1441, and 1442, and determined the attitude of the Parliament of 1442. The petition, which the English merchants in Danzig were made to disclaim, apparently proceeded from individuals with personal grievances and claims against the Hanse. But at the Parliament of Westminster in January, 1442, a petition of the Commons demanded resolute action against Prussia; and, in accordance with the demand, an ultimatum was issued to the High Master threatening the annulment of privileges in England if the Vorrath treaty were not ratified before Martinmas.[54]

Equally ominous were some of the other measures of the Westminster Parliament, and none of them more so than the so-called act for the safe-keeping of the seas. The act provided for the equipment and maintenance of a fleet of twenty-eight ships for the protection of English shipping from attacks at sea. Judged by its face value it was a genuine measure for the policing of the seas, not unlike similar provisions repeatedly made in the first half of the century. But judged in the light of

---

[53] *Rot. Parl.*, vol. v, p. 24. Most of the English chronicles stress the anti-foreign legislation of the parliament. *Chronicles of London*, ed. C. L. Kingsford, p. 146; Caxton, *Polychronicon*, chap. 22. The chronicles abound with stray references to Gloucester's party in the City in connection with the disorders of 1425: *Incerti Scriptoris Chronicon Angliæ de Regnis Trium Regum Lancestrensium, Henrici IV, Henrici V, et Henrici VI*, ed. J. A. Giles (1848), p. 7, 'cives Londonie favebant parti ducis', *Chronicles of London*, op. cit., p. 76, 'to stande by the Duke of Gloucestre . . . and . . . agent the Byshop of Winchestre'; cf. also p. 83 (Gloucester organising military protection for himself in the City), and p. 81 (popular opposition to Beaufort). Direct evidence of the existence of a definite Gloucester party in the City at the time of the Cobham trial is lacking, yet the events of that year combined in a significant manner; cf. Caxton's assortment: Eleanor Cobham's trial, the affray between the Court and the men of London, the struggle of parties in the City, and the distribution of titles among Suffolk's followers.

[54] Of the sponsors of the petition of 1441 (*Proc. and Ord. P.C.*, vol. v, pp. 167, 170, 177), two at least, Thomas Kymberley and John Hatterby, had personal claims against the Hanse: *H.R.* 2, ii, nos. 539 par. 7 and 644 par. 42.

some of its special clauses, and in conjunction with the other acts of the same Parliament, it was itself a menace to peace, more likely to extend piracy than to suppress it. The fleet had to be provided by private individuals, mostly powerful men like Sir William Bonville, Sir Philip Courteney, Lord Pons, John Howard, John Church, Hugh Taverner, and others who, as the subsequent events showed, were closely related to certain members of the King's Council. The distribution of prizes was arranged in a manner extremely generous and profitable for the masters and owners of boats. Legal obstacles to captures at sea were raised by several acts limiting the validity of safe-conducts and virtually revoking the earlier law against the breaking of truce, under which the English privateers had found it very difficult to 'faire de guerre pur le sauf gard du mer'. But whether the act was a genuine measure of national policy or a piece of mercenary legislation, it became in the end a cloak for extensive privatering and a source of anarchy on the high seas. And what the official privateering under an act of Parliament left undone, private captures and reprisals completed.[55]

The troubles, thus begun, were slowly mounting in the subsequent years, until in 1446 the political situation of 1440 and 1442 was re-enacted, and a second decisive action agianst the Hanse was taken. Gloucester, defeated over the trial of Eleanor Cobham, could still be expected to oppose Suffolk in the matter of the royal marriage and the cession of Maine, and was now to be annihilated. The ground had been prepared for his impeachment, and at the end of 1446 a Parliament was called at Bury St Edmunds, 'away from his friends the Londoners', to accomplish his destruction. At the same time the much-prorogued Parliament of 1445–6 had shown its temper by refusing to vote new supplies until its final session in 1446. It was, therefore, not a mere co-incidence that at that last session, and only a few months before the writs for the anti-Gloucester Parliament were to be issued, the 1442 ultimatum to the High Master was recalled, and a similar ultimatum issued threatening the revocation of privileges if the treaty were not ratified.[56] As the Steelyard correctly observed, what the English wanted was not so much the confirmation of the treaty as the revocation of privileges and freedom of reprisals and piracy against the Hanse. All sorts of claimants were alleging damages and grievances as a pretext for letters of marque against Hanseatic shipping. The letters of the Steelyard to Lübeck, Cologne, and Danzig struck a note of real panic: there were no friends left in Parlia-

---

[55] *Rot. Parl.*, vol. v, p. 59. At the same time the Parliament definitely swept away the older legislation for the keeping of truce on the high seas: *Stats.* 2 Hen. V, 4 Hen. V, 14 Hen. VI, c. 8, 15 Hen. VI, c. 2–c. 4, 20 Hen. c. 11.

[56] Caxton, *Polychronicon*, chap. 24; *Rot. Parl.*, vol. v, p. 65. Cp. Suffolk's speech in *Proc. and Ord P.C.*, vol. vi, p. 33. 'language is sowen upon me in London'. *H.R.* 2, iii, p. 150, n. 1, nos. 265, 267, 283.

ment or Council. When in the summer of 1447 a Prussian delegation visited England, the government could not negotiate because the king and everybody else were 'away in the country for the summer vacation'. But in the opinion of the Steelyard the 'vacation' was merely a subtle pretext for prolonging the state of indecision until the last day of August when, under the terms of the ultimatum, the Hanseatic privileges would lapse and 'no end of letters of marque would be issued'.[57]

Most of these fears came true, though not immediately. The charter was made to lapse, but the anti-Hanseatic move in England was too insincere, and the Hanse too pacific, for an immediate and final rupture. In March, 1449, after a year of manœuvring, a conference between the Hanse and the English took place in Lübeck, which very nearly succeeded in postponing a crisis. The beginning of the conference was not very promising. The English delegates, with Thomas Kent at their head, were uncompromising. They took a stand by the treaty of 1437, and demanded the exclusion of Prussia from the conference as a preliminary condition of negotiations. The Prussians on their part were equally determined not to recognise the treaty and to remain at the conference. Yet both sides were unwilling to close all the roads to peace. A new conference was arranged for 1451, and in the meantime private and separate conversations between the English and the Prussian delegates led to mutual promises of truce and toleration.[58] Thus a path was still open to a compromise, and a compromise might well have been attained in 1451 if, within two months of the closing of the Lübeck conference, the misgovernment in England had not culminated in the 'great capture' of the Bay fleet. On 23 May 1449, a fleet of 110 vessels, Flemish, Dutch, and Hanseatic, on its way from the Bay of Bourgneuf, was attacked and captured by the English privateers under Robert Winnington. The boats were taken to the Isle of Wight, the vessels and the goods belonging to Flemish and Dutch merchants were released, but the bulk of the booty, which belonged to the Hanseatic merchants, was made a lawful prize of the privateers.[59]

The news of the capture burst upon the unsuspecting world like a bomb and provided a turning-point in the relations of England and the Hanse. The effect was only partly due to the great number of ships and

[57] *H.R.* 2, iii, nos. 283, 286, 287, 294, 295; ibid., p. 164, n. 1; ibid., nos. 479, 289, 317 par. 2.

[58] *H.R.* 2, iii, nos. 479, 460, 464; ibid., nos. 288, 289, 293, 308, 317–19, 353, 402; ibid., nos. 480–7; ibid., nos. 475, 488; ibid., 503–5; cf. Stein, op cit., pp. 27–37 and p. 37, n. 2.

[59] *H.R.* 2, iii, nos. 530, 531, 533, 535; *Paston Letters*, no. 68; Stein, op. cit., pp. 48–51. Winnington's commission for the guarding of the seas was dated 3.4.1449 (*Letters and Papers illustrative of the Wars of the English in France*, vol. i, p. 489), but his fleet was not a new venture but a direct descendant of the fleets equipped under the act of 1442.

the high value of goods captured. Its real importance lay elsewhere. To begin with, it was the first important attack on the Bay fleets. Ever since the opening of the Hanseatic navigation to the saltworks in the Bay of Bourgneuf, large fleets had passed within a few miles of the English coast. The safety of the Bay route must have weighed heavily with the Hanse in their dealings with England. In the words of the *Libelle of Englyshe Polycye*, the Hanseatics, who 'aventure full greatly into the Bay', were compelled to seek England's friendship, for 'if they would not our friends be, we might lightly stop them in the sea'. Now for the first time the peace of the Bay route was broken, and broken in a mere quest for booty, without direct cause or provocation. In the second place, the assailants were no mere pirates, outlaws of the sea, or merchants seeking revenge and compensation, but the king's privateers, a fleet maintained and equipped on the same vicious principles as that of 1442. What is more, its leaders were connected with an important party in the Council. At least some of Winnington's boats belonged to Thomas Daniell, an influential member of the Council, and it is quite probable that Winnington was merely Daniel's agent and representative at sea. Immediately on the capture of the fleet, Winnington wrote to John Trevelyan, a member of the Council and an active partisan of the Suffolk faction, informing him of the coup and asking for his good offices. The request obviously was not made in vain. Within a few days of the capture, the Steelyard had to report to the Hanse that the 'lords' were making it known that the booty would not be restored to its owners. The names of the members of the Council in league with pirates were no secret to anybody. The merchants of the Steelyard and the popular opinion in London imputed the guilt to the whole of the Suffolk clique in the Council, and above all to Lord Say, Thomas Daniell, and John Trevelyan.[60] Finally, the capture had an immediate and disastrous reaction upon the position of the English merchants. On the morrow of the attack on the Bay fleet the country was filled with rumours of further and better exploits to come. And if the narrow seas were not at once plunged into the anarchy of mutual and general piracy, it was probably due to the fact that the English merchants were made to bear the cost of the capture. The Hanseatics promptly arrested the English goods in their territories, and the Prussians noted with satisfaction that the English

---

[60] *Libelle*, ed. Warner, lines 326–7; cf. A. Agats, *Der hansische Baienhandel* (Heidelberg, 1904), pp. 25–6, 38; his assertion that Lübeck's trade was relatively unimportant is not borne out by the evidence; *H.R.* 2, iii, nos. 531, 638, 647, 669, 670. Very characteristically Hans Winter associates Thomas Kent with the party on the council accused of the capture. The same party, he thinks, was responsible for all the ills of the time. The king himself was not to blame, considering that he 'is very young and inexperienced and watched over as a Carthusian'; cf. Stein, op. cit., p. 47, n. 1.

merchandise in Danzig was sufficiently plentiful to cover all their losses. It goes without saying that the English government protested against the confiscations, and that the protest was not much more than a hollow formality. The Council threatened to compensate the English merchants out of Prussian and Lübeck goods in England, and the Steelyard was afraid that the English rulers might 'rob Peter to pay Paul'. Yet, in spite of the Steelyard's fears, Paul remained unpaid.[61]

It is in this abdication of all pretensions to state reasons that the real significance of the episode lay. By a single stroke the official policy divested itself of its connections with the interests or demands of the merchants. No sooner was the booty bagged than the government turned to the Hanseatic towns with pacific overtures. Its chieftains had had their fill, and it had every reason to feel friendly and satisfied.[62] Its concern for the merchants' programme and its bellicosity of 1449 were unsuited to the occasion, and quickly dropped. In their turn, the English merchants, deserted and betrayed by their fickle allies of 1442 and 1446, ceased to press for parity and reciprocity. They had suffered almost as much as the Hanse at the hands of the government. They saw the trade with the Hanse interrupted, and interrupted not for the sake of their economic demands, but for the private gains of well-connected adventurers. To them the present conflict was both senseless and unprofitable. It is, therefore, no wonder that a Prussian agent in London could report a short time after the capture that everybody was blaming the governing clique for the rupture with the Hanse, and that everybody wanted peace. One may or may not believe his report that the rebels of Kent had marched into London demanding the restoration of the Hanseatic trade and the punishment of the pirates. But it was no mere accident that the men whose lives the rebels demanded were in the first place those very 'statesmen' whom everybody thought responsible for the Bay capture.[63]

Equally striking were the repercussions in the Hanse. Only a few months previously at the conference of Lübeck, Prussia had, alone against the whole of the Hanse, resisted the English demands. But now a single stroke put Lübeck in Danzig's place as England's implacable foe. Lübeck

---

[61] *H.R.* 2, iii, nos. 531, 535 (postscript), 570, 626; ibid., nos. 533, 536, 555 par. 2, 557, 559. The English merchants in the Low Countries had to shoulder the responsibility for the capture of the Flemish and Dutch boats; *H.R.* 2, iii, no. 560; Caxton, *Polychronicon*, chapters 25 and 26.

[62] *H.R.* 2, iii, Nos. 591, 563, 569, 570, 572; iv, no. 103; *U.B.*, viii, no. 100. According to *H.R.* 2, iii, no. 569, the privileges were restored to the Hanse, though not in full, in the early autumn. The exclusion of Danzig, unlike that of Lübeck, from the grant proved to be a mere formality, as the subsequent negotiations with Prussia and the safe-conducts clearly indicate; cf. below, n. 68.

[63] *H.R.* 2, iii, nos. 658, 647, 669, 670. Winter was working hard to embroil Prussia with Lübeck and may well have been in the English pay. He himself constantly paraded his connections with high English functionaries.

was one of the chief sufferers in the attack of 1449, and Lübeck had always regarded itself as the guardian of the Hanseatic routes. But what counted most of all was the fact that unlike Danzig it had no English goods within its walls to cover its losses. As a result, the attitudes of Lübeck and of Prussia came to be completely reversed. Prussia, with all her losses made good, was not at all anxious to break with England. The High Master vetoed all the proposals for the cessation of English trade or prohibition of English cloth, refused to take any violent measures against the English and readily agreed to the English proposal of separate negotiations. The arrangements for a conference at Deventer, made before the Bay capture, were now cancelled, and an English delegation with Thomas Kent at its head was sent to Prussia, there to negotiate a separate settlement. But this arrangement only stiffened Lübeck's attitude. Anxious to recover its damages, and enraged at what it considered the Prussian betrayal, Lübeck merely redoubled its demands for strong measures against the English.[64]

Unfortunately for the future of Anglo-Hanseatic relations, events soon provided Lübeck with an opening for 'direct action'. The boat with the English ambassadors to Prussia was captured on 20 July 1450 by the Lübeck *Bergenfahrer* and brought to Lübeck together with a rich booty in cloth and no less a person than Thomas Kent on board. The goods were confiscated to cover Lübeck's losses, and the ambassadors put under arrest. Yet the capture, striking and profitable as it was, did not satisfy Lübeck's thirst for retaliation, and in the years immediately following Kent's imprisonment, accident and design combined to harden Lübeck's temper. To begin with, Thomas Kent, with some of the other prisoners, was let out on parole in order to go to England and obtain there compensations for Lübeck. But he broke the parole and stayed in England to resume there his work on the Council and to remain for another fifteen years in charge of English policy in Northern Europe, and probably in command of the anti-Hanseatic forces in England.[65] Then, partly in retaliation for the capture of the ambassadors, and partly through the continued state of anarchy on the high seas, the English pirates redoubled their atacks on Hanseatic shipping, and especially on that of the Wendish towns. Finally in 1458, at the very time when the epidemic of piracies seemed to have quieted down, there occurred the second capture of the Bay fleet, for which the Earl of Warwick himself was responsible. On the pretext that the Hanseatic boats refused to salute the

---

[64] *H.R.* 2, iii, no. 555, par. 1, alleges the pressure of 'other estates', but cf. the attitude of Prussian towns themselves in ibid., nos. 607, 574, 608, 651; cf. ibid., nos. 638, 647, 669, 670; Stein, op. cit., pp. 54–8.

[65] *Die Lübecker Bergenfahrer*, ed. Bruns, p. 352, par. 18; *H.R.* 2, iii, no. 638; *U.B.*, viii, nos. 1, 6. On Kent's and Stocker's flights, cf. Stein's version, Stein, op. cit., p. 76.

English arms, Warwick engaged them in a battle from which he emerged with easy honours and an immense booty.[66]

It is, therefore, no wonder that throughout these years Lübeck persevered in its anti-English attitude and refused to respond to the pacific invitations of England or the counsel of moderation from the rest of the Hanse. When in 1451 the English sent a delegation to a conference in Utrecht, Lübeck refused to negotiate with the head of the delegation, Thomas Kent, and the other 'escaped prisoners', and insisted on their return to captivity and the compensation for the Bay capture as a preliminary condition of negotiations. The expostulations of Prussia and Cologne were of no avail. Nor were the repressive measures against the Hanseatic merchants which the English government adopted a few months later. Lübeck meant war and prepared for it. By arrangement with Denmark it closed the Sund to English shipping and prohibited the passage of English cloth to the east.[67] Several times during the subsequent years, in 1452, 1453, and 1454, the English made attempts to arrange another conference and met with a willing response from every part of the Hanse, including Hamburg. But Lübeck still held out, kept the Sund closed to English shipping, and strained every effort, in the face of wholesale evasion on the part of Prussians and Cologners, to stop the trade in English cloth in Hanseatic regions.[68]

These relations between England and Lübeck were a direct result of a decade and more of misgovernment and piracy and the first step towards England's defeat in the late sixties and seventies. Yet during this first phase, in the fifties, the English position was far from hopeless. At times it even seemed as if, in spite of the political disorganisation at home and Lübeck's activities abroad, the clash might yet end again in a reaffirmation of England's claims in the Baltic. The English piracies had certainly succeeded in raising Lübeck's opposition, but the opposition was not formidable as long as Lübeck remained alone. And throughout this first phase of England's retreat Lübeck did remain alone. The other parts of the Hanse were showing every sign of an accommodating temper. The Prussians, ever since their abortive attempts at separate

---

[66] *U.B.*, viii, nos. 20, 21, 84 (especially pars. 1–50), 215, 780; *Three Fifteenth-century Chronicles*, ed. J. Gairdner (Camden Society, new series, 28, 1880), p. 71. See below, n. 70.

[67] *H.R.* 2, iii, no. 709, especially par. 8; *U.B.*, nos. viii, nos. 40, 47; *H.R.* 2, iii, nos. 636, 654; iv, nos. 19, 21, 41, 46; *U.B.*, viii, no. 87; ibid., no. 79; *H.R.* 2, iii, no. 662; ibid., no. 663; iv, nos. 14, 20, 23, 24, 51 par. 3, 80; *U.B.*, viii, nos. 261, 264.

[68] *H.R.* 2, iv, nos. 55, 78 par. 3, 100, 102, 114, 122, 135, 168, 176, 127, 196 par. 32; 235, 248 par. 8, 263, 304; *U.B.* viii, nos. 180, 280, 281 (p. 117) n. 1, 285; Stein, op. cit., pp. 79–89; *H.R.* 2, iv, nos. 69–71, 80, 87, 101, 105, 106, 159, 160, 174, 176, etc.; *U.B.*, viii, nos. 137, 140, 149, 171, 174, 178, 249, 261, 264, 305.

negotiations with England in 1451, were all tact and moderation. Danzig continued for a time to hug its old fears of English competition, but by 1453 even Danzig ceased to trouble about the English danger, for, as we have seen, the English seem to have dropped for the time being their old demands of parity and reciprocity. Under the protection of safe-conducts repeatedly issued to the English merchants during those years, the English trade to Prussia struggled on, and with Prussian assistance the English merchants sometimes succeeded in evading Lübeck's barrier across the Sund. Even for several years after the outbreak of war in Prussia between the Order and the Estates, the English merchants were still to be found in the Baltic East. The same is true in a still greater measure of the English trade with the western towns, and especially Cologne. There, Lübeck was powerless to interfere with the course of traffic, and the towns seldom considered themselves bound by the interests or decisions of the Hanse as a whole. But what must have completed the isolation of Lübeck was the attitude of Hamburg, its ancient ally and satellite, and now a determined advocate of peace with England. In the end, Lübeck was compelled to raise the embargo in 1454, and to give a grudging consent to a peace conference; and although the civil war in Prussia prevented the conference from taking place, the trade could continue under the eight years' truce proclaimed early in 1456.[69]

Thus from the English point of view the prospects of the mid-fifties were not all black, and what made them rosier still was the fact that throughout those years the ports and the fairs of the Low Countries were open to the English. The situation continued to be promising until 1458, when the second capture of the Bay fleet by Warwick raised new difficulties. Yet even this second capture did not alter the situation, or the issues, at all profoundly. Lübeck's interests and pride suffered again, and its wrath was as overwhelming now as it had been in 1449. But the other towns remained as anxious as ever to maintain the trade with England, and Danzig implored Lübeck not to do anything that might

---

[69] *H.R.* 2, iii, no. 693 par. 1: 694 par. 1: 695 par. 1: ibid., no. 694 par. 12: iv, nos. 16, 51 par. 3, 101, 133, 236, 354, 355; *U.B.*, viii, nos. 27, 46; *H.R.* 2, iii, nos. 567, 697; iv, nos. 235, 236, 238, 399, 400, 401, 450–2; *U.B.* viii, nos. 574, 754. The proclamation of truce (*H.R.* 2, iv, no. 452) did not involve the restoration of privileges but even the suspension of the privileges could not stop the Hanseatic merchants from coming to England: *U.B.*, viii, no. 100 (1451). On all these problems, cf. Stein, op. cit., pp. 89–90 and 109–25; his explanation of Lübeck's change of attitude is hard to check, and a different hypothesis is suggested by the evidence in *H.R.* and *U.B.*, e.g. *H.R.* 2, iv, nos. 101, 105, 106. The same applies to Stein's explanation of the Prussian attitude, which was Danzig's as well as the Order's (cf. above, n. 64). What counted a great deal with the Prussians was the fear, freely admitted, that they could not afford to quarrel with both Burgundy and England at the same time: *H.R.* 2, iv, nos. 693 pars. 2–3, 694 pars. 2–4.

prevent the prolongation of the eight years' truce, due to expire in 1459.[70]

The isolation of Lübeck and the consequent strength of England's position were made still greater by the arrival of the Yorkists. The change of dynasty reopened the question of Hanseatic privileges, and at the same time revived the hopes and ambitions of the middle-class party. The demands of the English merchants, forgotten and neglected during the preceding period, were again resuscitated. The Council and the Parliament were again, as twenty years earlier, snowed under by petitions and complaints recalling the Vorrath treaty, and reasserting anew the programme of reciprocity. London resumed its anti-Hanseatic offensive, organised pressure on the Council and Parliament and attempted to deprive the Steelyard of its constitutional position in the City. In deference to the pressure of the towns – and the Yorkist party apparently inherited the middle-class policy, genuine or false, from the Gloucester faction – Edward announced to the Hanse his intention to revise the whole question of Hanseatic privileges. The government renewed the privileges by a number of temporary grants of 1461, 1463, and 1465, but pressed for a more permanent arrangement every time the temporary extensions expired.[71] If it continued at all to extend the privileges in this way, it was partly because the relations with Burgundy were much too uncertain for a definite breach with the Hanse, and partly because every successive year emphasised the isolation of Lübeck and seemed to prepare the way to its defeat. An abortive Hanseatic conference in 1465, at which English delegates were present, must have demonstrated to the Wendish towns the utter hopelessness of their position. At last, in 1467, Lübeck seemed to give way. In a manner as yet guarded and careful, its leaders notified the other Hanseatic towns that it would be prepared to waive the preliminary conditions on which it had insisted ever since 1451, and to enter into negotiations with England. With Lübeck thus humbled, and the other parts of the Hanse anxious to maintain peace and preserve their privileges, it looked as if the story of English penetration and political success were going to be resumed.[72]

[70] The political truce of four years concluded in 1447, was not interrupted by Philip's measures against English cloth. It was very nearly broken by the Bay capture, but was saved by the payment of compensation and renewed in 1451. *H.R.* 2, iv, nos. 666–9; *U.B.*, viii, nos. 769, 780. Prussian attitude: Smit, *Bronnen*, vol. ii, pp. 849 n. 1, 883 (n. 1). The relations up to 1464; ibid., no. 1412, p. 903, n. 1, no. 1541, p. 981, n. 1. *H.R.* 2, iv, no. 670; *U.B.* viii, no. 772.

[71] *H.R.* 2, v, nos. 146, 117, 147, 173, 263 pars. 3, 10, and 32, 712 par. 8. The English programme went even beyond the treaty of 1437, and included the demand that the Hanseatics should not be allowed to import goods from the Bay and the Low Countries; *U.B.* viii, no. 1067; *H.R.* 2, v, nos. 161, 165, 167, 168, 169, 176–9, 206; *H.R.* 2, v, nos. 179, 263, 284, 537, 646, 647, 649, 655, 769, 770; *U.B.*, viii, nos. 1110, 1116, 1117; ix, nos. 71, 211, 212.

[72] *H.R.* 2, v, nos. 176, 177, 218, 285, 317, 318, 542, 543, 548, 568, 583, 643, 644.

It was at that moment that the arrests and the 'verdict' of 1468 shattered the prospects of a renewed English advance, and opened the second and final phase in the defeat of English expansion in northern seas. Already at the end of 1467, and the beginning of 1468, the Hanseatic observers began to notice a change in the Yorkist attitude to the Hanse. The truce for thirty years, which Edward concluded with Burgundy in the winter of 1467–8, secured for England one channel of trade to the continent and the Parliament became less anxious to maintain good relations with the Hanseatics. And when in June, 1468, an English fleet bound for the Baltic was captured by the King of Denmark off the Sund, the government seized the Hanseatic goods in London as compensation for the English losses. A quasi-judicial verdict of the Council confirmed the seizure on the ground that a few Danzig boats were at the time serving in the Royal Navy of Denmark, though neither the Hanse nor Danzig had any part in the capture or any previous knowledge of it. The Danish government insisted that it was alone responsible, and that it was acting in retaliation for the English malpractices in Iceland. But whatever was the real role of the Hanse in the affair, all the Council wanted was formal ground for the seizure of Hanseatic goods in London. 'They know that they cannot obtain any redress from the Danes, who do not trade to England, and have no goods in London and on the seas, and they have invented the accusation to cover their losses out of our possessions.' Such was the Hanseatic complaint and such was apparently the actual position.[73]

The light-heartedness with which the Council acted on this occasion was doubtless due to the friendship with Burgundy, but it was also to a great extent due to the personal influence of certain men on the Council. The Hanseatics in their protests against the verdict alleged that the several members of the Council were themselves an interested party in the case they were judging. The contention was apparently well-founded.

659–66, 693, 712 pars. 7, 9–12, and 36, 713–16, 719, 720, 731; *U.B.* ix, nos. 253, 387; *H.R.* 2, vi, nos. 53–5, 87; *U.B.* ix, nos. 415, 433. A good measure of Hanseatic anxiety is given in the letters of the Bruges factory and of Hamburg: *U.B.* viii, no. 1190, and *H.R.* 2, v, no. 719. Relations with Burgundy in 1464–5 were upset by the tightening up of the anti-English cloth regulation and the migration of the Merchant Adventurers to Utrecht: Stein, 'Die Merchant Adventurers in Utrecht', *Hans. Gbl.* 1899; Smit, *Bronnen*, vol. II, no. 1543; *U.B.*, ix, p. 91, n. 4. But the trade to the Low Countries was not really interrupted for more than nine months.

[73] *H.R.* 2, vi, no. 87, 'de sake nu kortes met deme selven heren konynge und deme heren hertogen van Burgundien in sunderlinges bestant und vruntschop gestalt syn und dagelik mer gestalt werden, so dat de Engelschen deshalven den copman van der hense des de myn achten sullen'; *Fœdera*, vol. XI, pp. 591–9; *H.R.* 2, vi, nos. 97, 99, 103, 111, 119, 162, 165, 185; *U.B.*, ix, no. 467, 482, 526, 527, 530; *H.R.* 2, vi, no. 111; *U.B.* ix, nos. 468, 471, 476, 521, 524, 570; *U.B.*, ix, no. 467 pars. 1–4.

It was only through that personal influence in the Council that the claims of the fifteen Englishmen who had suffered at the hands of the Danes were given preference over the views and desires of the bulk of public opinion, including that of the merchant class. The Archbishop of Canterbury was reputed to have warned the government of the folly of the verdict; the clothworkers of Gloucestershire, mobilised for the purpose by the Steelyard and its well-paid friend the town clerk of Bristol, intervened on behalf of the German merchants, and so did also the Merchant Adventurers in the Low Countries in the person of their governor, William Caxton. But public opinion at home was no more effective than the pressure of almost all the princes and political powers of Northern Europe. The Emperor, the Pope, the Bishop of Utrecht, the Duke of Burgundy, the towns of Flanders, the feudal rulers of the Low Countries and Western Germany wrote to England to advocate the cause of the Hanseatic prisoners. But the Council remained adamant, the relations of England and the Hanse were thrown into confusion again, and the possibility of a peaceful solution of the Anglo-Hanseatic conflict favourable to England and advocated by the merchants was thrown away for the second time since 1449.[74]

The only compensation the English merchants could derive from the episode was the definite separation between the Hanse and Cologne. The Cologne merchants were at the time of the capture passing through a period of estrangement from the rest of the Hanse. The Hanseatic policy in Flanders at the time and Lübeck's irreconcilable attitude to questions of English policy had raised in Cologne a great deal of opposition to the Hanse. At the time of the 'verdict' the separatist opinion dominated the town government in Cologne; the leader of the Cologners in London, Gerard von Wesel, was himself something of a separatist. So that when the verdict, however illegal and unjustified, made the goods of Cologne responsible for the reputed crimes of the other part of the Hanse, the Cologners decided to take the final step and break with the Hanse. The Council, where Thomas Kent was still active, did its best to help the split along, freed the arrested Cologners, exempted their goods from reprisals, and eventually reissued the privileges for the sole enjoyment of Cologne and the exclusion of the other towns.[75] The policy

[74] *H.R.* 2, vi, no. 97, gives the names of Warwick, Northumberland, Fogge, and the Archbishop of York among those involved in the Danish capture, and further investigation would reveal names of other nobles. Thus Richard Outlaw, the nominal owner of the *James* and the *Mary* of Lynn (*U.B.*, ix, no. 478) captured by the Danes, was closely connected with Howard: Haward, op. cit.; *U.B.*, ix, no. 478; ibid., nos. 431, 490, 497, 501–7, 511, 549, 554; ibid., no. 525 (clothworkers).

[75] *H.R.* 2, vi. nos. 114, 115, 164, 182, 222, 356 par. 74, 106, 114, 115, 358; *U.B.*, ix, nos. 479, 603, 698, 699. Cologne cultivated the friendship of the pro-Hanseatic party: the Bishop of York, the Privy Seal (the Bishop of Rochester),

of splitting the Hanse, pursued since the middle of the century, thus seemed to triumph at last.

This triumph, however, was more than offset by its reactions on the rest of the Hanse. From the point of view of the Hanse as a whole the events of 1468 merely completed the reorganisation of anti-English forces begun in 1449. If they succeeded in detaching Cologne from the Hanse, they also succeeded in restoring cohesion and unity among its other parts. Prior to 1449, Danzig had been alone and unaided in its opposition to England; between 1449 and 1468, Lübeck was similarly isolated in its struggle for compensations; but after the 'verdict' the struggle against England became a joint concern of all the Hanseatic towns from Westphalia to Livonia. The moderate counsel was discredited. Lübeck's intransigence stood vindicated; England indeed appeared the deadly foe and the menace to Hanseatic unity that Lübeck had made her out to be. The Danzigers now resuscitated their ancient anti-English attitude as suddenly as they had abandoned it in 1449, and events in Prussia facilitated their reconversion. The breach between the Prussian Estates and the Order had by now removed all extraneous restraints and moderating influences over Danzig's economic policy, while the continued state of civil war in Prussian territory made direct trade with England almost impossible. The Danzigers could now easily afford a naval war with England, for there was little that they could lose by a war of this kind that they had not already lost through the cessation of trade. The other Hanseatic towns merely followed the united lead of Danzig and Lübeck.

The immediate result of the new alignment was the outbreak of the naval war which Lübeck had vainly tried to organise since 1450, and the war continued until well in the seventies. The varying fortunes of the combatants, the complications introduced by France and Flanders, the stalemate eventually reached, have all been faithfully chronicled by the German historians of the Hanse, and need not be repeated here. What requires stressing is the fact that although the war undoubtedly prepared the way for the triumph of the Hanse in 1473, it was not immediately and directly responsible for it. The fortunes on the high seas constantly fluctuated, and not always to England's disadvantage. In the first phase of the war the English had the worst of the struggle. But in the end the losses suffered by neutral shipping at the hands

Master Lamport and Master Hatcliff. The latter was to play an important part in preparing the peace of 1474. Cf. *H.R.* 2, vi, nos. 219 and 592, 223; *U.B.*, ix, no. 699.

[76] *H.R.* 2, vi, nos. 161, 184 pars. 47–74, 185 pars, 11 and 22; 202, 221 pars. 21, 24, and 25, 283. Once the breach had become inevitable, it was to Danzig's interest to make the stoppage of trade as complete as possible. *H.R.* 2, vi, nos. 356 pars. 61, 62, 68, 72, 73; ibid., no. 360; ibid., nos. 418–20.

of Hanseatic and above all Danzig privateers provoked the hostility of
Flanders, while the entry of France into the struggle created a state of
triangular warfare equally damaging to the Hanse and to England. In
the end the Yorkist government managed to equip a strong fleet under
Howard's command and to inflict great losses on the Hanseatic shipping.
From this time onwards the contest was leading to a draw, with the odds
slightly in England's favour.[77]

If the war was, nevertheless, disastrous to the interests of English trade
and English merchants it was not through its unsuccessful issue on the
high seas, but from other and more general causes. To begin with, war
was disastrous because it was war; it preyed upon all shipping in the north
seas and thus intensified that state of anarchy which had prevailed there
ever since the late forties. In the second place, it perpetuated the political
relations and attitudes dangerous to the future of England's position and
peace on the northern seas. Lübeck and Danzig were now cementing their
friendship and unity, directed against England, while the separation of
Cologne was not producing the good results expected from it. True,
English cloth continued to be sold abroad throughout the war years.
Denied access to the old east to west channel, it went by the southern
route via Frankfurt, Nuremberg, and Breslau. The Prussians themselves
began to complain in 1471, as they had done in the previous blockades
of England, that an embargo on English cloth could not be enforced.
They were themselves accused of smuggling English cloth into the Hanseatic lands. It is also true that the cessation of direct traffic between
England and the Baltic did not result in a serious shortage of Baltic
goods in England. Timber, pitch, tar, ashes and furs, both from the
Baltic and from other parts of Europe, were obtainable in the neutral
markets of Zealand and Brabant, and from there the Cologners, the
Dutch and the English regularly shipped them to England. Yet the new
channels of cloth export and the new sources of Baltic goods were mere
makeshifts, and not very satisfactory ones at that. The cloth exports of
the Cologners after 1468, large as they now were, fell far behind the
combined exports of the Hanse as a whole in the preceding period, and
the decrease was not accompanied by a corresponding rise of the exports
of the English merchants themselves. The customs returns of the principal
cloth-exporting ports show a considerable decrease in the export of cloth
during the middle decades of the century. This decrease may well have
been exaggerated in the customs figures for it is not unlikely that the

---

[77] *H.R.* 2, vi, nos. 283, 321, 322–4, 316, 316a, 347; *U.B.*, ix, nos. 691, 692; *H.R.*
2, vi, nos. 317, 331 pars. 2–4; 352, 362, 371. It is interesting to note the
fluctuations of the Burgundian policy on the Anglo-Hanseatic issue with the ups
and downs of the Yorkist fortunes in England. *H.R.* 2, vi, nos. 418, 420, 434,
444, 509, 531. The naval war definitely turned to England's favour in the late
summer of 1472: *H.R.* 2, vi, no. 558; *U.B.*, x, p. 83; cf. Schulz, op. cit., p. 120.

collection of customs suffered during the years of anarchy, yet the decrease revealed by the figures is too regular to have been entirely due to the fault of the returns themselves. It must have been due to a variety of causes, of which the Anglo-Hanseatic war and the cessation of Hanseatic trade to this country was certainly one. An examination of the particular customs accounts of London, Lynn, Boston and Hull also reveals a decline in the importation of the Hanseatic commodities, while occasional references elsewhere would indicate a corresponding rise in their prices.[78] It is, therefore, no wonder that the country soon began to show signs of weariness and opposition to the struggle. The very 'cloth-workers of Gloucester', whose support the Cologners had mobilised in 1468, refused now to lend themselves to any further plans of Cologne against the Hanse. Apparently, the cloth producers and the general body of the consumers in the country had all lost from the cessation of Hanseatic trade more than they had gained from the separate arrangement with Cologne. If the merchants of London and the East Coast continued to support the war party, the rest of the country was now anxious for peace.[79]

Still it can be doubted whether the peace would have come when it did, and would have been bought, as it was, at the price of English surrender, had it not been for the accompanying political developments. In the first place, the War of the Roses was resumed in 1470 with the return of Margaret and the flight of Edward. The Hanse was drawn into the renewed struggle, and soon found itself in the position of *tertium gaudens*. Margaret, while planning her return, had aproached the Hanse with requests of assistance, promising in return to restore the privileges in full and redress all the Hanseatic grievances. On that occasion the

[78] *H.R.* 2, vi, nos. 547, 481 par. 1, 589. On the development of the southern route, see Daenell, op. cit., vol II, pp. 111, 112, 145. Prussian goods had been imported from Flanders during the previous conflicts: *H.R.* 2, ii, no. 4, *K.R. Cust. Acct.*, 73/25. For Prussian goods so imported, see *K.R. Cust. Accts.*, *passim*. *U.B.*, ix, no. 541 contains a Prussian complaint that at the time of the 1468 conflict there came to England 'eyn floet van schipen ut Selant mit onsen nacien gueder tegen onseen wyllen'. In the following year it was alleged that the English traded freely in the Low Countries 'und dar allerley ware glik hir bynnen landes kopen und vorkopen', *H.R.* 2, vi, no. 283; Smit, *Bronnen*, vol. II, no. 1628. Yet of Baltic goods thus brought in, there was bound to be 'a dearth and a shortage'; e.g. bowstaves, *Stat.* 4 Edw. IV, c. 2. A similar situation had arisen in 1450, when, during the interruption of trade following the capture of the Bay fleet, Prussian goods were imported from the Low Countries and rose in price: *H.R.* 2, iii, no. 670, cf. below, n. 109.

[79] *H.R.* 2, vi, nos. 547, 594. The English representatives in the preliminary peace negotiations of 1472, made it clear that on the question of peace 'sze in in Engelant in twen partien ryden': *H.R.* 2, vi, n. 550. In May, 1472, London was still against peace, but 'de anderen van den Engelschen begeren vrede': ibid., no. 547. A month later the report was that 'in Engelant begheren se al pays to hebben myt den Duitschen': ibid., no. 594. On the attitude of the towns, see ibid., vii, no. 103.

Hanse refused to commit itself, but when Edward in his turn began to plan an expedition to England, he was able to do so with the assistance of the Hanse. The Hanse may have acted on the advice of the Duke of Burgundy who sponsored Edward's enterprise, or it may itself have gauged the chances of the combatants and decided to back the winner. But whatever were its reasons, the fact remains that it was on Hanseatic boats and under Hanseatic escort that Edward sailed to England, there to resume the war and to emerge victorious on the battlefield of Barnet. For these services he promised to satisfy the Hanseatic complaints and demands, and these services were alleged as the official motive for the far-reaching concessions made to the Hanse at the conference of Utrecht.[80]

An unofficial liaison was established between the English and the Hanseatic agents in 1472 in Bruges, and in 1474 the Conference met at Utrecht. From the very first, difficulties arose on which the negotiations very nearly broke. The Hanseatics demanded complete restoration of their old privileges, unequivocal exemption from all taxation not specified there, compensation for the losses suffered by their shippers and merchants, annulment of the 'verdict' of 1468, and restoration of goods arrested on that occasion. They intended to obtain special guarantees from the principal towns as to the observation of the future treaty. Above all, they demanded the withdrawal of privileges from Cologne. The English negotiators took a stand against every one of these demands; on their part they recalled the Vorrath treaty and insisted on the principle of reciprocity. But in the end they had to give way. After two adjournments, the conference ended in a peace treaty embodying almost all the Hanseatic demands. A formula of reciprocity was included in the treaty recalling that of 1408, but less definite and extensive than that of 1437. It promised in a general manner that the English should enjoy in the Hanseatic lands their old rights, but it did not contain the provision for the exemption from taxes. The point on which the English negotiators were most un-yielding was that of Cologne's status, but even on this point they gave way in the end, and Cologne, deserted by the English and spurned by the Hanse, was deprived both of her privileges and of her position in the Hanse. It was only several years later that she was readmitted to the Hanse and the Steelyard.[81]

---

[80] *H.R.* 2, vi, nos. 315, 331 pars. 2–4, 434, p. 399, n. 1; ibid., vii, no. 22 par. 7, 'because divers persones of their nation and company have acquired themselves thankfully towards his highness at the time of his great business'. From the very beginning of his reign Edward tried to obtain political support from the Hanse in exchange for the confirmation of their privileges: *H.R.* 2, v, no. 147. To what extent Edward's attitude was affected by the fear of an understanding between the Hanse and France it is difficult to say; cf. Daenell, op. cit., vol. ii, p. 124.

[81] *H.R.* 2, vi, nos. 547, 548, 550, 592, 593, 595, 596, 608, 638, 639, 651. In these negotiations an outstanding part was played by William Hatcliff, who, accord-

In 1475 the Hanseatic merchants returned to England in full possession of their ancient privileges, armed with the additional guarantees of London, Lynn, Boston, and Hull, and with their financial claims secured on their customs payments to the sum of £10,000. They immediately stepped into the place they had occupied in English economic life in the first half of the century, and this place they were to preserve until well into the Tudor era. Their share in English foreign trade soon passed the highest point it had reached before. While they exported on the average about 6000 cloths annually between 1406 and 1427, and about 10,000 annually between 1438 and 1459, their exports rose to well above 13,500 between 1479 and 1482. Some of this rise may have been due to changes in the administration of the customs, yet it continued throughout the early Tudor reigns.[82]

The English derived whatever profit and comfort there was to be derived from the restoration of peace and the resumption of Hanseatic trade. But their attempts at direct relations with the markets of Central and Eastern Europe received a set-back from which they were not to recover until the age of Elizabeth. The formula of reciprocity would not have been of much avail to them now. Danzig under the sovereignty of Polish kings enjoyed almost a complete *Landeshoheit*, involving full autonomy in matters of government and economic policy. It refused to admit even the vague and shadowy claims to reciprocity in the new treaty. For some two years it refused to confirm the treaty, in spite of the expostulation of all the other towns. When, in the end, it decided to confirm it, it did so on the understanding that the English were to be treated as all other foreigners. The English merchants themselves ceased to press for parity in the old and full sense of the term. According to the report of the Hanseatic delegates to Utrecht, all the English meant by 'old rights' in Prussia were the 'rights' actually exercised there on the eve of the war. But even these claims, modest as they were, ceased to be of great importance to English trade. The whole Baltic trade was no longer vitally important. Whether as a result of the continued friction with Denmark and consequent closing of the Sund, or as a result of the war-time rearrangements in the organisation of English trade, the direct trade of English merchants to Danzig was dwindling very fast. While on several occasions in the first half of the century there were over thirty English boats anchored in the port of Danzig, only twelve boats arrived from England during the three years following the cessation of hostilities, and in 1497, when the registers of the Sund tolls begin, not a single English boat passed

ing to *H.R.* 2, vii, no. 259, 'der sake eyn procurator alle tiid gewest isz'; cf. n. 75, *H.R.* 2, vii, no. 103; *U.B.* x, no. 241; *H.R.* 2, vii, no. 22, 30, 34, 37, 43, 103, 105, 106, 259.

[82] *L.T.R. Cust. Accts.* (See App. iii); Schanz, op. cit., vol. ii, p. 28, n. 1.

the Sund. As late as 1503 there were only twenty-one English boats passing the Sund, and it was not until 1547 that the English shipping to the Baltic could again stand comparison with that of the Dutch.[83]

4. THE TRADE

To pass from the story of the Anglo-Hanseatic rivalry to an account of the trade itself, its commodities, business routine, and corporate forms, is to exchange the shifting scene of politics and war for the enduring scheme of economic needs and habitudes. The needs which the trade with the Hanse served, and the forms which it took, were seemingly unaffected by the Anglo-Hanseatic conflict. Its economic basis was provided by the economic development and structure of Northern Europe, and could be neither easily destroyed nor fundamentally altered by the course of the struggle. Nor could the prevailing methods of trade and forms of commercial organisation be affected, for these were determined by the transport, communications and social structure of the later Middle Ages. Yet this constancy of economic facts can easily be exaggerated. Within the traditional channels of exchange, and the enduring framework of commercial organisation, there was room for a certain number of variations, and some of these were undoubtedly due to the development of the Anglo-Hanseatic rivalry. It is not the object of this section to exhibit these variations to the exclusion of the other and the more static facts. But no student of the period will fail to note them, less in the account of the commodities and markets, more in the story of the business forms and the corporate organisations of the English merchants.

Occasional references in the previous sections must have made it clear that the bulk of the commodities exchanged between England and the Hanseatic regions consisted of Baltic goods and English cloth. It goes without saying that the Baltic goods were by no means the only article of Hanseatic import. In the first place, some Hanseatic merchants took part in the trade between England and the great markets of the Low Countries, whence they imported all the miscellaneous commodities of Europe. In the earlier centuries, and as late as the middle of the fourteenth century, the trade to and from Flanders was one of the main Hanseatic activities in England.[84] In the late fourteenth and the fifteenth century the over-

---

[83] *H.R.* 2, vii, nos. 63, 65, 66, 131, 132, 161, 188, 189, 288, 151, 325 par. 14. Lauffer 'Danzigs Schiffs- und Warenverkehr', in *Zeitschrift des Westpreussischen Geschichtsverein*, part xxxiii, tables i and iii; N. Ellinger Bang, *Tabeller over Skibsfart, etc.*, vol. i, pp. 1–50; *H.R.* 2, ii, no. 36, par. 26 (36 boats arrested in 1429).

[84] R. Häpke, 'Brügges Entwicklung zum Mittelalterlichen Weltmarke' (*Abhandlungen zur Verkehrs- und Seegeschichte. Band* i. Berlin, 1908), p. 63; A. Schaube, *Die Wollausfuhr Englands vom Jahre 1273*; *Hanseakten*, ed. Kunze, nos. 365–75; Bahr. op. cit., p. 134.

whelming bulk of that trade was already in English hands, yet even at this time there were to be found Hanseatic merchants, especially Cologners, who regularly exported cloth into the Low Countries and imported from there a most varied assortment of goods. In the second place, miscellaneous commodities other than those of Baltic origin were imported direct from the regions of the Hanse. Of these, canvas, linen, and linen yarn ('Cologne thread'), were probably the most important. Fish, chiefly the cured 'white' herring of Skania, and fish oils, were imported by merchants of almost every region in the Hanse. Beer produced by Bremen and Hamburg, madder of Westphalian origin, a certain amount of woad, as well as metal goods from Cologne, Westphalia, the Harz mountains and Hungary, have also left a trace on the records of Hanseatic imports.[85]

But compared with the goods of Baltic origin, all these commodities were of only secondary importance in the Anglo-Hanseatic trade. They could be, and in part were, imported into England from lands outside the Hanseatic regions. In the linen trade important sources of supply were situated in certain districts of South Germany, Northern France, and the Low Countries, and from these large quantities of linen were imported into England, both directly and through the great continental fairs. Some of the English demand for linen was met by Irish production. The same in a still greater measure applied to woad and metal goods, of which by far the most important sources were situated in France, Spain, and Italy. Even white herring could be, and often was, of Dutch origin, imported by English and Dutch merchants, and beer could also be brought from the recently established breweries of Holland. These commodities, therefore, would not have drawn the English merchants to the Hanseatic regions in the face of Hanseatic opposition, and would not have made the Hanseatic trade as important to England as it actually was.[86]

---

[85] *K.R. Cust. Accts.*, e.g. 76/17, 203/1, 194/19. Commodities: *K.R. Cust. Accts.*, e.g. 73/5, 73/10 (beer, madder), 76/11 (thread), 8/21 (fish). For their countries of origin, see J. B. Hurry, *The Woad Plant and its Dye*, pp. 120–1, 127–31; K. Hoyer, 'Das Bremer Brauereigewerbe', p. 194, in *Hans. Gbl.*, Jahrgang, 1913: Erstes Heft (1913), pp. 193–232; G. Bens, *Der deutsche Warenfernhandel im Mittelalter*, p. 63 (madder); Bahr, op. cit., pp. 135–6, *Das Buch des Lübeckischen Vogt auf Schonen*, ed. D. Schäfer, pp. xix–lv; B. Kuske, 'Der Kölner Fischhandel vom 14–17. Jahrhundert', pp. 230–2, in *Westdeutsche Zeitschrift, für Geschichte und Kunst*, Jahrgang 24, Drittes Heft (Treves, 1905), pp. 227–313; L. Beck, *Die Geschichte des Eisens in technischer und kulturgeschichtlicher Beziehung* (5 vols., Brunswick, 1884–1903), vol. I, pp. 829–30; *Handelsrechnungen des Deutschen Ordens*, ed. C. Sattler (Verein für die Geschichte von Ost- und Westpreussen, 1887), pp. 258, 321, 353 and *passim* (copper).

[86] *K.R. Cust. Accts., passim*. An early fifteenth-century account (51/39) enumerates among the imports the linen of Westphalia, Hainault, Brunswick, and Brabant; cf. A. Schulte, *Geschichte der grossen Ravensburger Gesellschaft*, vol. III, pp.

It was the goods of the Eastern Baltic that provided the basis of Hanseatic imports. One of these was corn. England's demand for corn considerably exceeded the immediate needs of her population. For the greater part of the century she had garrisons to feed in the marches of Calais, Guisnes, and Aquitane. She supplied corn to Gascony in exchange for wine, and sometimes exported cereals to Iceland in exchange for fish. In years of plenty England had a surplus sufficient to cover all these needs, but in years of scarcity she was badly in need of supplementary imports, not only to meet outside liabilities, but also to feed her own population. The easiest and the most obvious sources of these supplementary supplies were the cornlands of the 'colonial Germany' to the east of the Elbe and of Western Poland, with their natural geographical and commercial centre in Prussia. These Baltic sources were not directly tapped by industrial regions in their immediate vicinity, as were those of South Italy and Northern France, and they were above all plentiful and reliable. We consequently find the English turning to Prussia for supplies in years of dearth such as 1417 and 1439, and also carrying on a direct corn trade between Danzig and Gascony.[87]

Less urgent, but more regular and constant, was the demand for the sylvan products of the Baltic. The extent which the deforestation of England had reached by the fifteenth century is hard to estimate. But it is clear that already in the thirteenth and fourteenth centuries England depended on foreign and especially Norwegian supplies for the high-grade timber used in construction and ship-building. The opening up of Prussia in the fourteenth century introduced Western Europe to the untold reserves of forest possessed by the Baltic lands, Poland, and Russia; and from the beginning of the fifteenth century Prussia became the only important source of timber. The kinds most commonly imported were wainscot, bowstaves, masts, the so-called 'clapholt', and 'trenchours'. But timber was also imported in the shape of manufactured wooden articles – boxes, coffers, furniture (counters) and, above all, boats.[88] Danzig, with its unlimited supplies of all the raw materials employed in the construction of boats, developed an important ship-building industry, of which the English merchant made wise use, and for obvious reasons. The nature of the return cargoes to England very often

73–86. Hurry, op. cit., pp. 94–104, 176–82; *Libelle*, ed. Warner, p. 18; Kuske, op. cit., pp. 232 ff.; Smit, *Bronnen, passim*; J. G. van Dillen, *Het economisch Karakter der middeleeuwsche Stad*, (Amsterdam, 1914), pp. 190–3. Smit, *Bronnen, passim*.

[87] *H.R.* 2, iii, nos. 386, 390, 644 par. 9; *K.R. Cust. Accts., passim*, e.g. 76/32, 73/10; Sattler, op. cit., pp. 21, 77, 165 ff.; Hirsch, op. cit., pp. 116, 181, 186; *U.B.*, vi, no. 111; Caxton, *Polychronicon*, chap. 21; *H.R.* 2, vi, no. 26 para. 21; Bens, op. cit., pp. 15–16.

[88] *K.R. Cust. Accts*, e.g. 76/17, 62/4, 10/7 and 8; Bugge, *Den Norske Traelasthandels Historie*, p. 27; Hirsch, op. cit., p. 116.

necessitated the employment of additional shipping. The English imports, chiefly cloth, were compact and valuable, while the Prussian exports, corn and sylvan products, were bulky and cheap. Thus the English merchants required larger shipping space for the westward than for the eastward journeys. Some of this additional freightage they obtained by hire. But some of it they bought, and as a great deal of Prussian exports into England consisted of materials for naval construction, there was every commercial reason for the importation of these materials 'ready made up' into vessels. It is, therefore, no wonder that the Danzig ship-building industry attracted a great deal of English custom, and that the use the English made of it provoked alarm in the Hanseatic Councils. In 1428 we find the Hanseatic diet in Lübeck complaining that the sale of boats to the English and the Dutch was raising up harmful competition to Hanseatic shipping. One of the first measures of the municipality of Danzig against the English in Prussia was to prohibit the sale of boats to them. The frequent re-enactments of the prohibition suggest that it was by no means easy to enforce, but it automatically became effective with the general decline in the direct trade with England, to the great disadvantage and displeasure of the ship-building interests in Danzig.[89]

As important as timber, if not more so, were the other sylvan commodities: pitch, tar, and ashes. Ashes were one of the most important materials in the industrial chemistry of the Middle Ages, and were employed in England in the manufacture of cloth. Pitch and tar were chiefly used in ship-building. The same use was also served by some of the other commodities of East European origin, such as hemp and sail canvas. Two of the other typically Hanseatic commodities, wax and furs, were also of Russian and Polish origin; these, however, were also brought in by the merchants of other Hanseatic groups and from places other than Prussia. Hungarian copper, the high quality iron (osmund) of Sweden and local varieties of ordinary iron formed also quite an important category among Prussian imports.[90]

The importance of all these Baltic goods will more than explain the special value which the English put on the Hanseatic, and above all on the Prussian, trade. This importance was further enhanced by the extent and character of English cloth exports. Of course, cloth was not the only commodity habitually exported from England by the Hanseatics, or imported by the English into the lands of the Hanse. In the early part of the fourteenth century Hanseatic merchants had played an important part in the wool trade between England and the Low Countries, and wool

---

[89] Vogel, op. cit., pp. 538–9; E. Baasch, *Beiträge zur Geschichte des deutschen Seeschiffbaues und der Schiffbaupolitik* (Hamburg, 1899), pp. 5–7, 197–8; *H.R.* 2, ii, nos. 421, 434; *U.B.*, viii, no. 225.

[90] *K.R. Cust. Accts.*, e.g. 10/7 and 8, 96/37 (Reval wax), 62/4, 76/11; Hurry, op. cit., pp. 32, 177 nn.

formed the main basis of their exports.[91] But the consolidation of the staple system and the working of the preferential tariffs gave the English merchant the virtual monopoly of the wool trade to Northern Europe, and reduced the Hanseatic share in it almost to nothing. It is therefore only occasionally that we find Hanseatic merchants exporting small consignments of wool and wool-fells, chiefly of the kind that over the greater part of the century was exempt from the action of the Staple laws – thrums, shorlings, lamb-fells. Equally irregular were the exports of other foodstuffs and raw materials, cheese, rabbit skins, tallow, red herring, and sometimes mineral coal. Somewhat more important were the exports of metals and metal goods. Tin from the West Country and pewter vessels manufactured in London were bought in large quantities by Hanseatic merchants, chiefly Cologners, and figure constantly in customs accounts and in the records of the English dealings with the Hanse merchants. A scrivener's book of 1442 shows that, in the course of a year's trade, the purchases of a group of Hanseatic merchants included tin and pewter vessels valued at £300. The other purchases of the same merchants included in the same book were valued at about £4000.[92]

The English merchants trading to Prussia exported from England very much the same commodities; but in addition, they also brought into Prussia a certain amount of goods of foreign origin. The herring which they imported into Prussia was probably the red herring of Yarmouth, for it was salted and packed in England. But some of the other commodities undoubtedly came from those regions on the Atlantic seaboard of the Iberian Peninsula and France – especially Gascony – with which English merchants were in constant and close contact throughout the fourteenth and the greater part of the fifteenth century. We find them selling southern fruit ('figs and raisins') and Gascon wine in Danzig, and some of the salt sold by them may well have come from the Bay of Bourgneuf.[93]

Yet both in the export trade of the Hanseatic merchants and in that of Englishmen trading to Prussia, cloth was overwhelmingly the most important commodity. The annual averages of Hanseatic cloth exports, exclusive of worsteds, varied from 6000 in the years between 1406 and 1427, and 10,000 between 1438 and 1459, about equal to those of all the other foreigners and about half as large as those of English merchants. Compared with cloth, the other articles of Hanseatic exports fade almost to insignificance. Evaluated at the official rates adopted for the purposes of customs, the average annual value of the Hanseatic cloth

---

[91] See n. 84; Schaube, op. cit.; Häpke, op. cit., pp. 63–4.
[92] *K.R. Cust. Accts., passim*; *K.R. Var. Accts.*, 123/37.
[93] *H.R.* 1, viii, nos. 578 par. 3, 579, 583; ibid. 2, ii, nos. 318 par. 2, 644 paras. 14–15.

exports between 1438 and 1459 was well above £20,000, while the value of their other exports could not much have exceeded the sum of £1200.[94]

The cloth which the English themselves exported into the Hanseatic regions went almost invariably to the Baltic countries, and especially to Prussia. It has been shown that one of the motives of their penetration into the Hanseatic regions was their quest for Baltic goods. It was, there-fore, in Danzig that the focus of the English-borne cloth trade was to be found. At the end of the fourteenth, and the very beginning of the fifteenth centuries, the herring markets of Skania attracted some of the English merchants with their cloth. As long as the English maintained these commercial relations with Scandinavia, and especially Norway, they also took their cloth there. But after the beginning of the fifteenth century direct references to English trade to Skania disappear from the records. As for the English trade in Norway, its history in the fifteenth century, when it is written, will reveal little more than a series of fitful and irregular endeavours by English merchants to resume the position they had occupied there in the previous century and to penetrate into markets completely monopolised by the Hanseatics. In the second half of the century even these attempts came to an end, owing to the un-interrupted state of conflict with Denmark. Thus of all the regions of the Hanseatic *Verkehrsgebiet* Prussia stood out as the only important centre of the English-borne cloth trade.

On the other hand, the cloth exported by the Hanseatics was distributed on the continent through several channels. A small part of it, especially that carried by the merchants of Cologne and the Zuider Zee towns, was taken to the great international marts of Northern Europe – Bruges, Antwerp, Bergen-op-Zoom, and Middleburgh – to be sold there, partly for further manipulation by Flemish and Brabantine cloth workers, but chiefly for distribution in the different parts of the continent. The bulk of the exports, however, went directly without the intermediary agency of the great fairs to the regions of the Hanseatic *Verkehrsgebiet*. In this direct distribution of English cloth there was a certain amount of territorial specialisation between the different groups of Hanseatic merchants. The Cologners distributed the English cloth all along the valley of the Rhine. From there, through the market of Frankfort-on-Main, it penetrated into Southern Germany as far as the valley of the Danube and Galicia, with its great markets of Lemberg and Cracow. A certain amount of the cloth carried by the Cologners went east along the great Hanseatic route, but that was a secondary line of Cologne's trade, important only at the time when the other sections of the Hanse were prevented from direct trade with England. During the greater part of the late fourteenth and fifteenth centuries the Rhine valley drew to itself

[94] *L.T.R. Cust. Accts.*

the bulk of Cologne's trade, and Frankfort was the second seat of Cologne's *Englandfahrer* – the corporation of merchants trading to England.[95]

The merchants of Prussia, whose share in English exports was second only to that of the Cologners, distributed the bulk of their cloth in Prussia, Lithuania and Poland, and took it as far east as Western Russia, Hungary, Wallachia (modern Roumania), and the north coast of the Black Sea. For a short time an attempt was made to establish a Staple for cloth in Elbing, but the continued economic growth of Danzig and its political importance defeated the project of a Staple. By the end of the first decade of the fifteenth century Danzig was the central market for English cloth in Prussia, with Thorn as a secondary outpost on the way to Poland and Western Russia. It was also from Danzig and by Danzigers that a great deal of English cloth came to Livonia for distribution there and farther east in Novgorod. In the latter market the English cloth had become a serious competitor of the Flemish cloth in the first quarter of the century, and the local demand for it was strong enough to raise serious alarm among the Hanseatic groups with vested interests in Bruges and the Flemish cloth trade.[96]

The other sections of the Hanse carried English cloth all over the Hanseatic *Verkehrsgebiet*, including Livonia and the lands beyond. The Wendish towns – Lübeck, Bremen, Wismar, and Rostock – dominating as they did trade with the Scandinavian countries, easily arrogated to themselves the bulk of the trade in English cloth in Norway, Denmark, and Sweden. In connection with that trade the Wendish towns founded an important intermediary station at Boston. Their boats commonly called at Boston on their way to Bergen, sometimes discharged there goods for the English market, and sometimes did not, but invariably took on board English commodities for sale in Scandinavia, partly victuals, but mostly cloth.[97]

It will be seen that the bulk of English cloth exported by the Hanseatics,

---

[95] See n. 8. For Cologners in cloth fleets to the Low Countries, see *K.R. Cust. Accts.,.passim, H.R.* 2, i, no. 192. Cologners carrying cloth eastwards: *Quellen zur Geschichte des Kölner Handels und Verkehrs im Mittelalter*, ed. B. Kuske, vol. II, nos. 23, 24, 30, 69. The Cologners in Frankfurt: ibid., *passim; U.B.*, viii, nos. 87, 93; A. Dietz, *Frankfurter Handelsgeschichte* (4 vols. Frankfurt a. M., 1910–25), vol. I, pp. 60–1, vol. III, pp. 313–14; J. Müller, 'Geleitswesen und Güterverkehr zwischen Nürnberg und Frankfurt a. M. im 15. Jahrhundert', pp. 192–4, in *V.S.W.G.* Band 5, pp. 173–96 and 361–400. Stein, 'Die Hansebruderschaft der Kölner England-Fahrer', in *Hans. Gbl.*, Jahrg. 1908; Smit, *Bronnen*, vol. II, no. 1076.

[96] Schulz, op. cit., pp. 16, 46; Goetz, op. cit., p. 516; Hirsch, op. cit., pp. 165, 182, 186, 198; *H.R.* 2, ii, nos. 325 and 329 (Novgorod), *U.B.*, viii, no. 514 (Wilno).

[97] *Die Lübecker Bergenfahrer*, ed. Bruns, pp. xc, xl–lix, xi–xii, 302 ('Englandvarer von Bergen uth Norwegen to Busten vorkerende'); *H.R.* 2, ii, no. 354.

or by Englishmen trading to Hanseatic regions, was distributed among the 'ultimate' consumers of cloth. Most of the regions where the Hanseatics sold it belonged to the 'flax and linen' areas of Europe, and did not possess important cloth industries of their own. A certain amount of cloth was produced in different parts of Germany, especially in the Rhineland, Brunswick, and Silesia, but most of this production was purely local, employed local wool and served local needs. Even in its principal centres the market was served by cloth of Flemish and English origin. Unlike Flanders, Brabant or Holland, the regions of Hanseatic trade took and demanded not so much wool, yarn or unfinished cloth, as fabrics that could be sold directly to the consumers. Therefore the cloth imported there could be, and was, brought in a fully finished state, dyed, fulled, and shorn.[98]

The same fact emerges also from what we know of the English end of the trade. On the whole it will be true to say that the Hanseatic merchants drew their cloth from all the manufacturing regions in England, and exported all the varieties of cloth produced in this country. Although most of their shipping, and consequently the bulk of their trade, was concentrated in London and the ports on the East Coast – Ipswich, Boston, Lynn, Yarmouth, Hull, and Newcastle – they did not confine their dealings to the production of the eastern cloth-producing regions, Essex, East Anglia, and Yorkshire. We find them buying and exporting large quantities of cloth of the western and southern counties, the Southampton broads, the Western says, the Welsh friezes. In the fourteenth and fifteenth centuries England was more of an economic unit than it is fashionable to imagine. The main branches of her trade were as much inter-local and inter-regional, as they were to be at any time before the arrival of the canal and the railway. The Hanseatics found it possible to concentrate their shipping in the ports on the East Coast only because they were not compelled thereby to confine their activities to the production of the near-lying Colchester, Norwich, or York. We find them dealing with cloth merchants and cloth producers all over the country, and these dealings were greatly facilitated by the part played by London as a national market of the cloth trade.[99] If the Hanseatic merchants sometimes concentrated on certain branches of cloth export, the concentration was largely fortuitous, and due to the accident of medieval taxation more than to any other cause. At the end of the fourteenth century the so-called kerseys and straits, cheaper and narrower fabrics than the standard cloth of assize, were not yet subjected to the

[98] *K.R. Accts. Var.* 102/128/37. *Libelle*, ed. Warner, lines 321–3; *Quellen*, ed. Kuske, op. cit., vol. I, no. 1160; vol. II, nos. 264, 265; Schulte, op. cit., vol. III, p. 111; *Die Lübecker Bergenfahrer*, ed. Bruns, pp. 131, 150; cf. Bens, op. cit., p. 46; van Dillen, op. cit., pp. 77–8, 82–4.

[99] *Quellen*, ed. Kuske, op. cit., vol. II, no. 1160; Schulte, op. cit., vol. III, p. 111.

payment of the general cloth custom, and the Hanseatic merchants had every inducement for exporting them in large quantities. Apparently the same happened with worsteds. Judging by the indirect evidence in the customs accounts, worsted cloths of different varieties – cloths and beds, double, single, and semi-double – formed a greater share of Hanseatic cloth exports than they did of the cloth exports of other merchants, and the difference was apparently due to the fact that the Hanseatic exports of worsteds were taxed very lightly.[100] The only feature of the Hanseatic exports which cannot be put down to a fiscal cause, and which marked them off from the exports to the Low Countries at the end of the fifteenth, and in the sixteenth, century, was the fact that they were made up of finished cloth. This fact has already been stressed once, in the analysis of the cloth markets, and it will stand out again in its full significance in connection with the story of English commercial organisation.

The business organisation of the English trade to the Hanseatic lands and that of the Hanseatic trade to England possessed many features in common. Some of their similarity was doubtless due to the cosmopolitan origin and nature of merchant customs, for in Northern Europe conventions of merchant law, commercial terminology, and business routine differed comparatively little from country to country. But a great deal of the similarity was due to the economic character of the trade between England and the Hanse, and above all to the nature of the commodities exchanged. It has been shown that exchanges between England and the Hanse were very largely confined to English cloth and Baltic goods. These commodities had to be carried across long distances and disposed of in distant markets. The carriage and the disposal required longer and more continuous action than, to take an obvious example, the importation of onions from Flanders or the sale of pewter vessels to Italians in London. Then, at both ends of the trade, in the purchase of cloth in England and its sale in Prussia, or in the purchase of timber in Poland and its sale in England, the transactions were based on credit.[101] The use of credit, coupled with the 'reciprocal' character of the trade, called into being a complicated system of payments and assignments, and required constant and 'continuous' activity on the part of the merchant. Finally, the trade in cloth and in Baltic goods lent itself very easily to that combination of wholesale and retail trade which characterised big business in the Middle Ages. Recent discussions of the problem of wholesale trade in the medieval

---

[100] *L.T.R. Cust. Accts., passim; Hanseakten,* ed. Kunze, p. xxxix, *H.R.* i, viii. nos. 909, 921 par. 7; *U.B.,* iv, nos. 998, 1054, 1074; *Rot. Parl.,* vol. iii, pp. 272, 281, 294.

[101] *Chancery Brevia Regia or Files: Tower Series. G. (Statute Merchant and Statute Staple Certificates), passim; K.R. Accts. Var., passim;* M. Postan, *Credit in Medieval Trade.* For advances on corn and timber in Prussia and Poland, see Hirsch, op. cit., pp. 232–4.

towns have established beyond dispute the fact that wholesale trade, i.e. purchase and sale in bulk between merchant and merchant, was very common, but that at the same time it was generally combined with dealings in retail. This relation of wholesale and retail prevailed also in the business of the Hanseatic merchants in England and in that of the English merchants in Danzig. Cloth brought by the English merchants was often sold in bulk to local traders, but a great deal of it was retailed to consumers. It was this retail trade that provoked the opposition of the Danzigers, among whom cloth merchants (*Gewantschneider*) were very influential. And it was this retail trade which formed the main, and at times the most disputable, point of the English programme of reciprocity. On their part the Hanseatic merchants in London had engaged in retail trade since their first appearance in England. In the fifteenth century the English records of debts show them selling Baltic goods not only to merchant intermediaries, but also directly to consumers.[102]

Now, the essential feature of an import trade combining wholesale with retail transactions is its 'continuous' nature. The wholesale disposal of an imported cargo need not take more than a few days, or even a few hours, but its retail distribution is a matter of weeks and months. And if we remember that the Anglo-Hanseatic trade also involved a complicated machinery of payment and a difficult system of transport, we shall easily understand the comparative complexity of its commercial organisation. This organisation was even further removed from a 'primitive medieval' type than the organisation of some other branches of English trade. It can well be doubted whether the conventional picture of a vagrant trader, travelling with his goods to the foreign markets and bringing back his return cargo, ever represented the upper strata of the medieval merchant class. It certainly did not represent English merchants engaged in foreign trade in the fourteenth and fifteenth centuries. The buying and the preparing of goods in their country of origin, their transportation, their sale abroad and the management of credit and payments, were all activities of a 'continuous' character requiring the constant attention, and often the simultaneous presence, of several persons in different places. The Merchant Adventurer of the old-fashioned text-books, the artisan trader of Sombart's classification, a mere sea-going huckster, would have fared very badly in the trade between England and the Hanse. The trade was, and could only be, conducted by merchant firms, each employing a group of men, and each assisted by a well-developed system of commission trade.

It is not the object of this essay to describe the inner organisation of the medieval firm or to trace the development of medieval commission

---

[102] G. von Below, 'Grosshandel und Kleinhandel,' in his *Probleme der Wirtschaftsgeschichte*.

trade. The former has in part been done elsewhere in connection with the English wool-trade while the latter will have to be done by students specialising in the history of medieval partnerships. Both these subjects interest us here only in so far as they illustrate and explain some of the most significant features of Anglo-Hanseatic trade.

In theory, the 'integral' firm, i.e. the business unit continually employing several persons, and the system of commission trade, were two alternative ways of serving the same economic ends. But in practice, both were used by the same merchants at the same time. The 'integral' firm enabled the merchant to cope with the complexity of foreign trade by assigning the different members of his organisation to the different departments or geographical centres of his trade. This system of 'local branches' or 'agencies' was common both among the Hanseatic merchants trading to England and the English merchants trading to Prussia. A merchant like Robert Garr, habitually trading to Prussia, employed a resident 'servant' in Danzig and apparently several other men in England. But he could also make use of persons occupying a position intermediate between that of a permanent member of a merchant firm and an independent commission agent. The agents or factors of the English merchants representing them in the different localities, especially abroad, were sometimes their servants and sometimes their partners. In itself the distinction was not of great importance, for junior partners commonly described themselves as the 'servants' of their senior partners, while elements of partnership commonly entered into the ordinary contract of service. What is important is the fact that the designation of 'partner', 'factor', or 'attorney' could also represent the relations of independent agents to their habitual clients overseas. A person representing a merchant in a distant place need not be a real member of his firm, his partner or servant. His services to the merchant could be temporary and occasional; they could be enlisted for individual transactions and relate to single consignments of goods. The records of medieval trade abound with instances of partnerships and associations concluded for the duration of single deals. Most of these were *commenda*-like arrangements ('depository partnerships') by which merchants of Lynn or London could entrust their goods to merchants crossing over to Prussia for sale there. And from a *commenda*-like arrangement of this kind, it was only a short step to the equally common practice whereby merchants resident in England sent goods to merchants for the time being in Danzig with a request and instructions to sell. This practice was widely used by the Hanseatic merchants in their foreign or inter-urban trade, and received a separate recognition in German law and language under the name of *sendeve*. It was equally common, though it did not possess a separate name, among the English merchants trading to Prussia. The students of

English records will be familiar with the merchant sending his goods to persons in other towns or abroad, with instructions to do their 'best' to his 'use and avail'. And with these requests to do their 'best' we enter into the realm of commission trade pure and simple.[103]

There was thus no distinct demarcation between the association of persons within the framework of the 'integral' firm and the conduct of trade by means of commission agents. The majority of medieval business firms combined both methods. They maintained permanent associates – partners or servants – in important centres of their trade, and sold or bought their goods through 'commissionaires' in all those places where they did not at the time maintain agents of their own.

This organisation of trade explains a great deal of what is otherwise unintelligible in the history of the commercial settlements and factories abroad. Above all, it accounts for the conspicuous place which the problem of foreign factories occupied in the commercial policies of the time. The English settlement in Danzig and the Hanseatic settlement in England were largely composed of agents trading on behalf of merchant firms at home. These agents were – to use an expressive middle-German term – 'liggers'. They were resident factors spending most of their time in the foreign centres. Their commercial activities were vitally affected by the condition of their residence and their rights of trade; these, in their turn, depended upon the organisation and the status of the factory. Viewed in this light, the English and the Hanseatic claims on behalf of their respective settlements merely embodied the conditions required for the smooth functioning of the system of resident factors. It was because of that system that the commercial policies of the fifteenth century were so much concerned with the problems of corporate organisation and communal centres for the merchants abroad.

Of the actual organisation and routine of the factories we know relatively little, though, thanks to the work of Lappenberg, Weinbaum, and Engel, we know more of the German settlements in England than we do of the English settlement in Danzig. At one time there was a whole chain of Hanseatic factories in England; the evidence of the thirteenth, and the early fourteenth, centuries suggests the existence of over twelve branches. In the fifteenth century, however, only four seem to have functioned – London, Lynn, Ipswich, and Boston – and these settlements were the only ones concerned in the transactions and land-transfers carried out under the treaty of 1475. In origin, and to some extent in behaviour, the provincial factories were independent of the Steelyard, but in theory the Steelyard was regarded as the headquarters of the Hanse

---

[103] *H.R.* 2, ii, no. 644 pars. 27, 28, 45; *U.B.*, viii, nos. 122–3; W. Schmidt-Rimpler, *Geschichte des Kommissionsgeschäfts in Deutschland.* Band i. (Hall a. d. S., 1915), *passim* and pp. 57–61.

in England, and successive measures in the fifteenth century strengthened its control over the provincial factories. The latter were dominated by merchants of the central and the eastern towns, while in London, at any rate prior to 1475, the majority of the members and the leading part in the government belonged to Cologne. In the fifteenth century the membership of the Steelyard was, for the purposes of government, divided into three parts – the western with Cologne at its head, the Westphalian-Saxon, and the Prusso-Livonian. The division was designed to prevent the domination of any separate group of towns in the government of the factory, for each part was to be represented by the same number of members on the governing court. But the method of election, by which the part under-represented among the members could have its places at the court filled by the other towns, gave Cologne much more than her constitutional share in the government of the Steelyard.[104]

The functions of the Steelyard government were manifold. It had to manage the finances of the settlement, to impose and collect the 'schoss' payable into its treasury by the Hanseatic merchants trading to England, and to distribute the payments, both open and clandestine, to the national and municipal authorities in England. In the second place it represented the Hanseatic merchants in England before the English government and officials. This work of representation was done with the assistance of the English alderman of the Hanse, appointed to the government of the Steelyard under the Hanseatic Charter of 1303. The primary, though not the official, function of the English alderman was to serve as a liaison between the Steelyard and the English authorities, and in this he was assisted by a whole body of English intermediaries, mostly lawyers. But he also had extensive rights and powers in the exercise of jurisdiction in the mixed suits between the English and the Hanseatics, as well as the enforcement of internal discipline within the Steelyard. The maintenance of this discipline was the third important function of the government of the Steelyard. The Steelyard itself, with the houses rented in its immediate neighbourhood, formed the residential centre of the Hanseatic community. It was there that the goods were warehoused and the commercial transactions carried out and that the bachelor merchants (the junior partners and factors were unmarried) resided.[105] It is therefore no wonder that the Ordinances of the Steelyard are filled with regulations concerning the morals and manners, both commercial and private, of the resident members of the factory: regulations which were sufficiently minute and sufficiently strict to suggest to an ingenuous and bewildered historian the

---

[104] K. Engel, *Die Organisation der deutsch-hansischen Kaufleute in England im 14. und 15. Jahrhundert*, pp. 173–7, 199–212.
[105] Ibid., pp. 177–9, 192–6, 221–5.

theory that the Hanseatics in London were all knights of the Prussian order.[106]

Unfortunately no constitutional enactments comparable to the Ordinances of the Steelyard have survived for the English association in Prussia, and we are consequently not in a position to reconstruct fully or coherently its fifteenth-century organisation. Some of its features, however, emerge clearly enough. Its government consisted of a governor and aldermen, and during the greater part of the century the post of governor was held by important merchants, heads of English firms trading to Prussia. Their functions were chiefly those of representation before the authorities in Prussia and jurisdiction over matters arising between the English merchants themselves. When in 1428 the High Master finally gave his recognition to the corporate government of the English merchants, he did so 'in order that the governour should keep order and hold court among the English'. The scope of that jurisdiction we do not know, but at a certain period it must have been very extensive. One of Danzig's replies to the English grievances mentions the prison in the English house – a statement which the English did not expressly deny or disprove. It was also alleged that the English society levied an impost from its members comparable to the 'schoss'. But whatever the functions of the governing body, they certainly were less extensive than those of the government of the Steelyard. Unlike the Steelyard, the English factory in Danzig was not a communal settlement. Common residence was not enforced among the English in Danzig, nor is there any trace of common warehouses. Even at those times when the English possessed a 'common house', they also owned private lodgings and shops in the town, and the 'house' was apparently nothing more than a meeting-place and the seat of the corporate government.[107] Hence the absence of evidence as to the regulation of the lives of individual Englishmen comparable to the disciplinary regulations of the Steelyard. The social and the business needs of the merchants and the activities of the governor and aldermen required something in the nature of a communal centre, and explain the agitation for the right to possess one. But neither the absence of a communal centre during a considerable part of the century, nor the want of official recognition, could prevent the government of the factory from functioning. We find 'the governour and aldermen of the English merchants' addressed, or referred to, throughout the first half of the century

---

[106] Walford.

[107] Hirsch, op. cit., p. 100; *H.R.* 2, ii, no. 655 (taxation and jurisdiction); ibid., no. 655 ('prison'). *U.B.*, viii, no. 45; *H.R.* 2, iv, no. 25 (aldermen). Some kind of oath is implied in *U.B.*, viii, no. 76. *H.R.* 1, vii, no. 593 par. 4 presupposes the possession of a coat of arms and a 'bannere'. In 428, the English in Danzig describe themselves as a 'cumpenye': *U.B.*, viii, no. 451. 'Good stone houses.' *H.R.* 2, ii, nos. 380, 539 par. 2.

and in those years during the second half in which trade between England and Prussia was maintained. It is only in the late sixties and the seventies, which saw the general decadence of the Anglo-Prussian trade, that references to the 'governour and aldermen' became rare and cease altogether.

The eclipse of the society of the English merchants in Danzig throws a flood of light on the problem of the origin and the progress of the Merchant Adventurers. It is not the object of this essay to deal with this problem in its entirety. The early history of the Merchant Adventurers is closely related to certain important developments in the trading guilds at home, and should form the subject of a separate investigation. What interests us here is the connection which existed between that history, on the one hand, and the fortunes of the English in Prussia, on the other. The connection is clearly indicated in the very event with which historians commonly begin their accounts of the Merchant Adventurers in the fifteenth century. By a series of charters of between 1404 and 1408, a legal recognition and a corporate status were conferred upon three companies of English merchants trading abroad. One of these embraced merchants trading to the Low Countries, and the other two, merchants trading to Norway and the Baltic respectively. It was the Company of the merchants trading to the Low Countries that came in the end to be regarded and described as the Company of the Merchant Adventurers *par excellence*. The story of its origin is the story of its relative growth: the growth of one organisation at the expense of the other two. The problem, therefore, is not to discover how the English merchants trading abroad came to form a company (there is nothing strange or difficult in that), but how they came to form a *single* company. It is essentially not a problem of origin, but one of concentration.[108]

To this problem an answer, albeit an indirect one, has already been given. The rise of a single company of Merchant Adventurers was merely the converse of the eclipse of the company in Prussia. If at the beginning of the century we find several companies all functioning, it is because in the beginning of the century the several channels of English trade were all active. Of these channels the one leading to the Low Countries was

---

[108] *Foedera*, vol. IV, i, pp. 67, 107, 125; G.S. van Brakel, Gz., 'Die Entwicklung und Organisation der Merchant-Adventurers' in *V.S.W.G.*, Band V (1907), pp. 401–32; Edward III's charter of 1353 contains the earliest reference to an organisation of English merchants abroad (Cunningham, *Growth of English Industry and Commerce*, vol. I, p. 623), but the charter of 1407 is the first definite grant to an organisation in the Low Countries distinct from the Staple. The charter of 1462 is characteristically restricted to the Merchant Adventurers in the Low Countries, and a petition of 1497 refers to the Brabantine marts as the only important ones. The trade to Brabantine fairs suffered only one severe interruption, that of 1464–5; see above, notes 70, 72. For the earliest reference to the organisation in Prussia, see above, n. 27.

doubtless from the beginning the most important, but it was as yet not sufficiently important to embrace the overwhelming bulk of English trade and thus to overwhelm and overshadow the other channels and the other organisations. What happened between the beginning of the century and its last quarter was that trade in the Low Countries attracted to itself the bulk of English commercial enterprise. The English trade to the Low Countries was now the only branch of English foreign trade that mattered, and consequently the organisation of the English merchants there was the only organisation to function.

Why and how this happened we already know. The net result of the Anglo-Hanseatic rivalry was to interrupt the expansion of English trade in the east, and to sever its connections with the Scandinavian countries and Prussia. In Norway the Hanseatics had tightened their hold over the trade of Bergen and defeated all the attempts of the English merchants to restore their position. It was very largely the cessation of the Bergen trade that sent the English merchants to Iceland. But this new enterprise, however important in itself, only completed the ruin of the English trade in Scandinavia. It plunged England into a state of chronic conflict with Denmark and, in the second half of the century, definitely shut the Dano-Norwegian waters to English trade and navigation. Even more significant, and to the readers of this essay more familiar, was the English defeat in the Baltic. In the second half of the century the English trade there was much reduced by recurrent conflict with the Hanse, by the civil war in Prussia, by the triumphant protectionism of Danzig and by growing insecurity on the high seas. By the end of the eighties the direct trade to Prussia had been reduced to vanishing point. The traffic in Baltic goods had been taken out of English hands; some of it proceeded indirectly by way of the Brabantine fairs, and some of it was carried on by Dutch and Hanseatics. And with the end of the Baltic trade there came also the end of the Baltic trader. The English merchants were forced to restrict their maritime and commercial ventures in Northern Europe to the trade in the Low Countries, and the 'Merchant Adventurers' absorbed the bulk of English trade and the mass of English merchants.

The story of this absorption emerges very clearly from the records of English foreign trade. The municipal records of the East Coast towns contain a number of references, mostly indirect, to the existence of distinct groups of merchants trading to the Baltic, Scandinavia, and the Low Countries. But these distinctions almost disappear from the records in the sixties and the seventies, while the references to piracy in the North Sea in the same period begin to abound with the names of merchants once active in the trade with the Hanse. More direct and conclusive is the evidence of the 'particular' customs accounts. The customs accounts of London reveal the existence in the first half of the century of a specialisation among merchants trading to foreign countries. Throughout the early part of the century the accounts record the regular shipments of a large group of merchants, mostly drapers, grocers, and mercers, varying from 50 to 120 persons, exporting cloth to the Low Countries and importing miscellaneous commodities from the great fairs. These shipments are interspersed with those of a smaller group, which, judging by their cargoes and sometimes by their ships, must have traded with the Baltic lands. A few of the shippers in this group were grocers, mercers, or drapers, but most of them, and certainly those whose names recur most often together, are fishmongers and stockfishmongers. Similarly, some of them occasionally participate in the shipments of the Netherlands group, but the majority seem to keep away from the trade to the Low Countries. If there is any branch of trade which they combine with that to the Baltic lands, it is the trade to Spain and Portugal, or Gascony – a very natural combination, considering the connection between the Gascon wine trade and the Prussian corn trade, and the character of some of the staple commodities of Iberian and German trade (iron, bowstaves, etc.). But whatever the lines of specialisation in the southern trade, those in the English trade of Northern Europe ran clearly between the merchants trading to Prusia and the Baltic on the one hand, and the merchants trading to the Netherlands on the other. This differentiation, however, does not continue beyond the middle decades of the century. When at the beginning of Edward IV's reign a new and a very complete series of particular customs accounts begins, it has already lost almost all trace of the old demarcation. The shipments to the Low Countries are as regular as ever, but they now comprise the overwhelming bulk of English merchants active in the port of London. The shipments to Gascony follow an irregular curve corresponding to the fluctuations of peace and war with France. But the Baltic group has gone. Some of the erstwhile Baltic merchants have died in the meantime, some must have retired through old age or the cessation of the direct trade with Prussia, while others now ship regularly to the Low Countries together with the majority of English merchants. And, to accord with this tale of the exports, there is a remarkable change in the composition of the imports. The Baltic goods continue to be imported, but they are no longer brought by English merchants from Prussia. Some, especially after 1476, are imported by the Hanseatics. Most of them come in from the Low Countries as part of the general cargo from the great fairs.[109]

The predominance of the Netherlands group, i.e. of the Merchant Adventurers *par excellence*, and of their trade to the fairs, is merely the

[109] *K.R. Cust. Accts.*, *passim*, e.g. London, 76/11 (Barr, Pelican, Swan), 77/3. (Saxby, Coke, Church, etc.; the same to Portugal), 77/1 (Gervoys, Pelican, Green, Barry); Hull: 62/4 and 16.

other side of the English withdrawal from Prussia and the Baltic. In this light, the rise of the 'Company of the Merchant Adventurers' loses a great deal of its conventional glory. It was not a 'landmark in the history of English expansion', for it occurred at a time when English trade was temporarily contracting. It did not open to the English trade any new 'fields of enterprise', though it may have adjusted it to the loss of the old ones. In the last quarter of the century, and in the Tudor era the Company may have enabled the English merchants to extend their trade beyond the highest peak it had ever reached before the treaty of 1475, but Unwin has argued that such growth of the English cloth trade as took place in the sixteenth century proceeded independently of the Company of the Merchant Adventurers and in spite of its policy of restriction. Further research may add still more to Unwin's detractions. The historian of the wool-trade may find the Company helping to organise the premature demise of the wool-staple. The historian of the cloth industry may find a connection between the concentration of English trade in the Netherlands and the concentrations of English production on undyed and unfinished cloth. But even if the conventional story of the Merchant Adventurers in the sixteenth century survive the onslaught of historical criticism, the story of its rise in the fifteenth century will have to be revised. It will have to be interpreted not as a victory, but as the by-product of a defeat; not as a stage in an inexorable growth, but as a sign of temporary concentration and contraction.

6

ECONOMIC RELATIONS
BETWEEN EASTERN AND
WESTERN EUROPE*

The history of the economic relations of western and eastern Europe cannot be told as a simple or even a continuous story. These relations did not develop similarly and did not play the same role in the economic life of different parts of Europe and at different points of time in the Middle Ages. In general, trade between west European and east European territories affected economic life and social conditions more powerfully after the eleventh century than before. Furthermore, the economic effects went deeper in the north and centre of Europe than in its southern regions.

The chronological difference is something most historians would take for granted. It is generally, if uncritically, assumed that trade – all trade – grew in importance from century to century, and was therefore more abundant and had greater economic effect in the later Middle Ages than in the so-called Dark Ages. What is perhaps not so generally accepted is that the more southerly currents of east–west trade should have played a relatively subordinate part in the economic development of the continent as a whole and of its main regions taken separately. It is an accepted tradition of economic historiography to focus attention on the story of the Mediterranean or Levantine trade and to treat its development as the main theme of European commercial history. Its preferential treatment by modern historians is easily explained. It abounds with episodes familiar to the readers and writers of popular history and touches upon some of the best-known political and cultural landmarks in the Middle Ages, such as the rise and progress of the Italian commercial cities, their role in the crusades, the spread of Near Eastern manners, tastes and learning. The record of this trade is also strongly tinted with the romance which clings to all evidence of traffic with the Orient. For it was by the southern routes that men of western Europe were able

---

* *Eastern and Western Europe in the Middle Ages* © in 1970 Thames and Hudson. This article first appeared in *Eastern and Western Europe in the Middle Ages*, edited by Geoffrey Barraclough.

to come into personal, indeed physical, contact with the moslem East, north Africa and central Asia, and more indirectly with India and China.

Yet the purely economic and social importance of this trade was not so great as its romantic and picturesque appeal. The flow of commodities brought in or taken out by the southern trade currents washed over Europe without irrigating the main fields of economic activity outside the Mediterranean world itself and without greatly accelerating the motion of social change. Except for bullion, few of the incoming goods were in the nature of essential commodities catering for the necessities of life. They were mostly spices, exotic fruits, silks, brocades and a few other costly artifacts of oriental workmanship, and they served the demand for luxuries of the rich and the powerful: princes, ecclesiastical institutions and dignitaries and feudal chieftains. To this extent the southern trade was, so to speak, outside the mainstream of economic activity serving the needs of the medieval population *en masse* and the medieval economy as a whole. Indeed some imports need not have served any western needs at all but were merely goods in transit. The most valuable of these (for a long time they were probably the most valuable of all imports) were the east European slaves. The slave traffic as a rule originated in and traversed other parts of Europe on its way to the countries of the moslem Levant.

The exports of western Europe to pay for the eastern imports were as a rule equally peripheral to its economy and its society. In some periods, more especially in the earlier centuries of the Middle Ages, the balance of trade was probably in favour of the East and therefore set up an outflow of currency and precious metals. Gold and silver apart, western Europe, especially in the earlier centuries, had little to sell to the East: some weapons, some horses, a little food, later some cloth and linen. In the aggregate, these exports were neither large nor very valuable and their procurement did not call for an outlay of labour or other resources on a scale large enough to exert a pressure on economic social processes in Europe, whether western or eastern.

However, from this point of view – that of economic and social processes – a distinction must be drawn between the two variants of the southern trade current. One of the currents was sea-borne and led from southern French, Catalan and above all Italian seaports across the Mediterranean to the Levant or North Africa; the other was mainly earth-bound and led from western Europe to the East across the land-mass of south-eastern Europe. Of the two variants, the maritime may have carried goods of greater worth and contributed to the development of the Italian city-states: a more conspicuous monument to its achievements than the goods and urban civilisations involved in the land route. But it was, geographically speaking, a one-step movement, a single link directly connecting the Mediterranean with Byzantium and the moslem East. It did not, therefore, draw to its traffic, or otherwise touch upon, any country or region of eastern Europe. On the other hand the land-borne route to and from the Orient went over the various territories of south-eastern Europe – mostly Slavic – and deposited in them some commodities and took from them some of their produce. For that reason alone, the various parts of continental Europe felt its impact and were bound to be influenced by it.

The countries thus drawn into the oriental trade of Europe were Bohemia, Hungary, South Poland (Malopolska), and, in the end, southern Russia. The order in which these regions have been arranged here is of course that of their relative positions in the west–east direction; but this purely geographical order also happens to coincide with the chronology of their economic development and the timing of their links with the transcontinental trade.

In this order, Bohemia and Moravia were the first regions to be drawn into the traffic. Indeed so early was Bohemia's economic development, compared with that of the more easterly regions, and so much of its development was influenced by German merchants and rulers, that from some points of view Bohemia, and in fact the whole of the area along the Sudeten and Carpathian belt, could with justice be considered as belonging to the western end of the east–west connection. In fact its trade connections and the network of its principal routes ran in every direction, not only to the east but also south to the Mediterranean via Vienna and Venice, to the north mainly by the Elbe, and to the west mainly to the Bavarian towns of Augsburg, Nuremberg and Rothenburg.

Bohemia's contacts with the world outside, to the west as well as to the east, were bound to quicken with the opening of her silver mines in the thirteenth century, when Jihtnovo and Kutna Hora grew to become very important sources of newly mined bullion. The range over which Bohemia's silver circulated, and the imports for which it paid, can only be guessed and cannot be precisely allocated. But it is a fair guess that until the turn of the fourteenth and fifteenth centuries, when the silver mines rapidly gave out, the supplies of bullion and the excellent silver currency based on it must have stimulated the long-distance exchanges with both East and West. It would, of course, be an exaggeration to ascribe the commercial development of the Bohemian economy in the thirteenth and fourteenth centuries and the growth of towns – Prague, Brno and Bratislava – wholly to the long-distance trade and more particularly to the trade along the southern routes to and from the Orient. But it must have been Prague's position along that route that drew to it, from the very earliest Middle Ages, merchants from both the moslem East and the West. It also provided an additional attraction to German urban settlers and merchants who flocked to Bohemian cities through-out the Middle Ages.

The regions immediately to the east and north-east of Bohemia – Silesia, Hungary, South Poland, and southernmost Russia – played a part in the east-bound traffic which differed from that played by Bohemia only in its timing and scale. Silesia developed somewhat later than Bohemia: the high-water mark of its economic expansion was in the four-teenth century. But that expansion also depended to some extent on the output of Silesian mines and on Silesia's position at the intersection of several important trade routes. Some of the latter led to the north-east into northern Poland and from there to western Russia, more particu-larly to the region of Volhynia; other routes led north and north-west into the German regions along the west Baltic Sea. Some of the routes, however, tapped and supplied the regions in the south-west. Above all Wrocław (Breslau) gathered to itself much of the trade from Bohemia, Hungary and South Poland, and indirectly also to and from Russia and the transpontine outposts of Byzantium. These channels carried eastern goods which were frequently re-exported farther west or north-west by local and Prussian merchants.

Next along the west–east route lay Hungary. Hungary's development, like that of other parts of eastern Europe, was predominantly agricultural, and its trade with other regions was largely based on the agricultural produce of its prairies, mainly grain, cattle and horses. But Hungarian trade also benefited from the opening up of the Transylvanian deposits of silver and copper, and from its geographical position on the way to the Danube valley and the shores of the Black Sea.

The geographical position on the approaches to southern Russia and the Black Sea also favoured the east-borne trade of southern Poland. Cracow, for long Poland's most important urban centre, rose to com-mercial eminence very early in the Middle Ages, possibly before the end of the first millennium. It appears to have harboured colonies of foreign merchants of oriental origin, Armenians, Jews and Greeks, in the very earliest periods of its history. We must assume that what drew these motley foreigners into Cracow was the facilities it provided for the im-portation and re-exportation of goods from other countries. Cracow's facilities for trade to the east eventually came to be shared and even excelled by the town of Lwow, a more easterly rival of Cracow which was greatly fostered by the Polish kings of the thirteenth century and even-tually became the most important entrepôt centre for trade to the plains of southern Russia and Moldavia. In general, South Poland served in the later Middle Ages as the principal approach to southern Russia and, above all, to the commercial centres at the estuaries of the Danube, Dnieper and Don. Eventually it was through these estuary towns and by way of the Polish termini that most of the eastern goods destined for the West were carried. The Polish involvement with the economic fortunes of south-west Russia became closer still with the conquest of a great part of this region by Casimir the Great in 1347.

The high-water mark of south Russian trade, or at any rate of the trade centred in the interior of southern Russia, was somewhat earlier, in the period between the tenth and early thirteenth centuries, when Kiev and the Kievan principality were at the height of their political power and economic development. From the very early centuries of Varangian rule in southern Russia, i.e. from the middle of the ninth century, Kievan Russia appeared to draw to itself large quantities of oriental luxuries: how large they were is shown by numerous archaeological finds of recent years. Literary sources also testify to the presence in Kiev at the earliest times of merchants from distant lands. It may well be that Kiev was not the sole Russian point of attraction for oriental goods or oriental merchants. According to a Russian chronicle, a ninth-century prince, Sviatoslav, extolled the attractions of Perejaslavl on the Dnieper in preference to Kiev as an emporium for eastern luxuries. Historians, however, have every reason for considering Kiev at the height of its prosperity, i.e. in the twelfth century, as the principal Russian terminus of the southern trade route by which eastern goods travelled to the West.

Kiev and Kievan Russia lost this role in the course of the late thirteenth and fourteenth centuries. For this, some blame must be attached to the political disorders brought about by the rivalries and wars between the south Russian principalities. The transfer of the political and economic centre of gravity of Russia to the north-east, to the regions of Vladimir and Suzdal, also contributed to the demise of Kiev. But it was the conquest of south Russia by the Tatars in the mid-thirteenth century that dealt the heaviest blow to the economic prosperity and commercial role of Kievan Russia.

The decline of Kiev as a terminus of the southern route did not, however, bring about any noticeable decline in the trade flowing along it. It merely enhanced the relative importance of alternative channels. Of the latter, the one which traversed the north of Europe and tapped the eastern supplies through the Volga and north-western Russia, will be dealt with later, in the context of northern trade. The other channel, however, was well to the south of Kiev, by the northern littoral of the Black Sea and the estuaries of the rivers flowing into it. On the estuary of the Dnieper there was the Byzantine outpost of Cherson (the Russian Korsun), on the estuary of the Don there was Tmutarakan, and on the Volga there was the Venetian factory of Tana.

More important than any of these was the Genoese port of Caffa on the Crimean coast with its satellites at the estuaries of the Danube and the Dniester in Moldavia. In the course of time the Genoese, harboured and protected as they were by the rulers of the Tatar Horde, and favoured by their powerful position in Byzantium and the Mediterranean, succeeded in building up Caffa as one of the largest, though also one of the least famed of medieval commercial centres. At the apogee of its development in the fourteenth century, its population may well have exceeded thirty thousand. Its exports comprised the entire gamut of south Russian products. Grain was apparently shipped to the eastern Mediterranean and occasionally to Italy; sylvan and other products of the Russian interior, such as furs and wax, also found their way there. But it was slaves who provided the mainstay of the trade and the bulk of its profits.

The importance of the trade and its volume can be judged from the fact that, according to literary sources at Cordoba in Spain, which was only one of many recipients of the human cargoes from Russia, the numbers of slaves at one time in the ninth century exceeded 14,000. And although the slave trade may have declined in the course of the late fourteenth and fifteenth centuries, a Portuguese traveller who visited Caffa in the fifteenth century, Pero Tafur, could still describe with great wonder the abundant volume of the slave traffic from the south Russian plains to Caffa and from there to the various countries of the Near and Middle East.

By that time, however, Caffa had already declined, and much of its erstwhile trade shifted to its Moldavian outposts of Akerman, Tighina and Kilia. In 1475 the Turkish conquest of the entire Pontine region, following the earlier Russian conquest and sack of the Venetian factory of Tana, wound up both the Italian termini of the southern route. But in the two or three centuries preceding the violent collapse of the Italian presence, that presence not only fed the transcontinental route across southern Europe with goods of oriental origin but also linked that route with its maritime alternative across the Mediterranean, and helped to create a single system of routes and exchanges binding the sources of oriental luxuries with their western markets.

To speak of this route as I have done here, region by region, each figuring mainly as a stage in the transcontinental progress of oriental goods, must distort the true story of economic development. To repeat what I have already pointed out, the bulk of the traffic circulating along the roads and rivers must to an overwhelming extent have been made up of goods which were, so to speak, indigenous, i.e. products of local agriculture, forestry and mining. Most of these goods served local markets within the regions themselves. Some of the local goods may have overflowed into long-distance channels, but the overflow was not great or powerful enough to influence the shape of indigenous economies and societies in any substantial way. If we consider the history of east-bound trade from the point of view of the impact it made upon economic development, the trade currents which circulated across northern Europe were of greater importance. They were closely bound up with the general eastward expansion of western European states, with the migration of population, with the opening up of the continental interior of central and eastern Europe and with the inauguration of large-scale exchanges of essential and bulky commodities. A trade thus rooted in general economic development was bound not only to affect the economic fortunes of the regions it traversed but also to be affected by them.

2. THE NORTHERN ROUTE: ECONOMIC GEOGRAPHY

The history of economic relations between eastern and western Europe across its northern and central regions is part of a more general movement of historical change. It reflects almost every aspect of medieval development: its geography, its economic processes, its political transformations, its institutional framework, its social system. Indeed, so wide was the spectrum of economic influences radiating from the north-west to the north-east, that any attempt to single out the history of trade may appear to simplify the situation to the point of distortion.

Most conspicuous of all were the changes in the geographical pattern of the east-borne trade of northern and central Europe, or rather in the territorial boundaries within which it operated and spread and in the routes along which it flowed. The frontiers marking off the trading areas and the routes linking them, were not wholly identical with political boundaries and were not always created by military conquest and political occupation. Yet there is little doubt that as the principalities of north-western Europe extended their military and political power to central and eastern Europe, the territorial range of medieval commerce expanded accordingly.

From this geo-political standpoint the history of north European trade falls into three clearly discernible stages. The initial stage coincides with the Dark Ages proper – the four or five centuries which followed the irruption and settlement of Germanic tribes in western Europe. During that period inter-regional trade was in all probability very meagre, and such little long-distance trade as northern and western Europe knew circulated almost wholly within the limits of the former Roman empire.

In general, documentary or archaeological evidence of the inter-regional commerce of northern Europe in the Dark Ages is sparse. We are told a little about the commercial activities of the Frisian inhabitants of the Rhine estuary, who provided some economic links between northern

Europe (England, the Low Countries and possibly Scandinavia) on the one hand, and southern Germany and perhaps northern Italy on the other. We are also told about Anglo-Saxon merchants trading with the regions across the narrow seas, and Scandinavian seafarers trading with England and Ireland. But of direct commercial contacts between north-west Europe and lands farther east we have hardly any evidence at all. Within eastern Europe the Scandinavians traded over long distances, though until the era of the Viking raids in the ninth and tenth centuries, their long-distance expeditions and trade were directed mainly south-eastwards to the markets of Byzantium and indirectly to those of the moslem Levant. The subjugation of Russia by the Swedish Varangians in the ninth century may or may not have been a wholly commercial venture, but it was undoubtedly bound up with Scandinavian trading voyages. In the subsequent two centuries the Scandinavians travelled and traded along the river routes across the plains of Russia, and in this way established commercial links with Constantinople and possibly also with other Byzantine regions in the Balkans and with the Hellenistic succession states between the Volga and the Caspian.

How great this eastward trade was is indirectly suggested by the vast hoards of coinage, mostly Arab, found buried in Scandinavian, mostly Swedish, sites and along the routes to the east frequented by the Scandinavians. In the area of Scandinavian domicile some 1700 hoards, containing on an average some 300 mostly eastern coins, have so far been found, and we must assume that the coins so hoarded formed only a proportion of the bullion and coinage the Scandinavians acquired in the course of their trade and voyages.

This trade was not focused in urban centres housing professional merchants to the same extent as it was to be in feudal Europe two or three centuries later. Some trading ports did, however, emerge on the Scandinavian trade routes. Whether they were real urban settlements or merely haphazard huddles of wattle cabins we do not know. Nor can we be certain that they were regularly visited by Scandinavians; some may have been no more than local trading stations frequented by local fishermen and sailors. But the town of Wisby on the Isle of Gotland was obviously a commercial centre, and is specifically described as a trading settlement in the Life of St Anskarius. So may also have been places such as Dortic, Haithabu, Birka on Lake Malar, the port of Volyn ('*in finibus Slavorum*'), Truso, visited at the end of the ninth century by an emissary of the king of Wessex, or Reric, possibly situated in the vicinity of the later city of Lübeck.

Some of these 'towns' were situated in Slavic lands, but how far the native population of principalities ruled by the Scandinavians, particularly the principality of Kiev, actively participated in transcontinental trade is difficult to tell. Between the tenth and the end of the twelfth century, as we have seen, Kiev had become an important trade centre. But there is very little evidence that other Slav principalities directly imported western merchandise or exported their own products to the West before the eleventh century; and there is little evidence of Kiev merchants engaging in long-distance trade. The only indigenous societies of eastern Europe to which early medieval documentary sources (mostly Arabic and Byzantine) impute a commercial role, were the Bulgars of the middle Volga and the Hazars of the lower Volga – the latter Jewish by religion and harbouring colonies of Jewish merchants.

Yet even the Hazar trade to the West was not considerable enough in quantity to leave a clear impression in the surviving evidence. Oriental goods from Byzantium and trans-Caspian Asia probably came in that way, but the export of slaves is virtually the only well-documented trade originating in the Volga regions. These regions probably formed the principal base from which, between the eighth and the eleventh centuries, but mainly in the tenth, the Jewish merchants (the Rhadanites) operated. According to Arab–Jewish sources of the period, the Rhadanites drove their caravans of slaves westwards across the entire continent of Europe to destinations as remote as Moslem Spain, or eastwards to central Asia and China.

We must therefore assume that, for all the romance clinging to trade routes and trading societies so remote in place and time, the commercial exchanges they supported were not and could not have been of very great importance to either western or eastern Europe and did very little to make them economically interdependent. Apart from slaves destined for moslem markets, the eastern exports by this route or similar exports by the southern route were probably confined to a few luxury goods of Byzantine and Near Eastern provenance. For its part, western Europe apparently sent very little of its own produce to the East. From the tenth century onwards, gold and silver, mostly coined, apparently formed north-western Europe's *quid pro quo* for such goods as reached it from or via eastern Europe. This, at any rate, is the conclusion to be drawn from the evidence provided by the vast coin hoards of this period, which have been found in Scandinavia and Scandinavian-dominated countries of eastern Europe. The evidence of the hoards also suggests that at some period before the middle of the eleventh century the Scandinavian trade changed its direction or its centre of gravity. For whereas in the earlier hoards (and we have seen how vast they were) coins of eastern provenance, mostly Arabic, predominated, the later hoards contain mainly western, largely English, coinage. It is probable, however, that much of the bullion in the later hoards came from booty or the proceeds of tributes, such as the English geld levied by Scandinavian conquerors. If so, the changed composition of the hoards may merely reflect the effect of the Norsemen's military and political activities in the West. We know, however, that in the eleventh century the supply of Arab coins dried up elsewhere as well, as a result of economic crises and political difficulties in the Arab empire.

Nevertheless, the very quantity of the hoarded gold and silver, whatever its origin, goes to demonstrate how one-sided the Scandinavian traffic must have been. Confined to rare and costly 'non-essential' commodities, it did not – indeed could not – do much to form or to transform the shape of Europe's economies or the structure of its societies. It is therefore not surprising that our records should be silent about merchants from the north-west voyaging to the Slav countries and beyond. Considered as networks of commercial connections, or what Germans call *Verkehrsgebiete*, the two areas – the western and the eastern – were to all intents and purposes self-contained spheres of commercial intercourse, brought into loose and intermittent contact by trade in slaves, luxuries and bullion.

Closer links between the two spheres, their eventual merger into a single commercial region, and the corresponding transformation of their internal economies and societies, were not to come until the next phase, roughly corresponding to what historians call the High Middle Ages, i.e. the period between the end of the tenth and the end of the thirteenth centuries. This was a period of manifold growth, favoured by several convergent factors. Relative stability came to Europe in the tenth century after 150–200 years of political disruption and of moslem, Magyar and Norse invasions and conquests. The feudal order which emerged by the eleventh century at the end of a turbulent period of anarchy, offered sufficient peace and stability to make it possible for populations to grow, for settlement and reclamation of marginal land to proceed, and for trade, both local and interregional, to revive.

Before long, the states and societies of north-western Europe began to expand beyond their eastern borders. The *Drang nach Osten* was at first political in motive. The political and military frontiers of western Europe were being continually pushed out to the east until they reached the fringes of what in modern times has come to be considered as Polish and Russian territory. But the military and political conquest merely anticipated and facilitated other movements of expansion. Of these movements, that of colonisation was probably the most far-reaching and enduring. But in the wake of conquering armies and colonising peasants came also the culture of north-western Europe, mainly derived from western Christianity and Latin or German speech and writing; and with the sword and the Holy Writ and the peasant's plough came the merchandise.

In this story of territorial expansion, the episodes best known to students of history (best known because they have been well told by chroniclers and are clearly reflected in the political map of Europe) were the military ones. The military conquests and political acquisitions in the east began while the Carolingian empire was still in its prime and while its objectives still lay within the Germanic homeland, mainly in the territories of the Saxon tribes, between the Weser and the Elbe. By the end of the tenth century or perhaps even a little earlier, the Saxon lands had been fully absorbed into Germanic society and the Frankish state. Indeed, so complete was the absorption that by the tenth century the whole focus of the German polity had shifted to the Saxon territories, and Saxon princes had come to lead it in their capacity as Holy Roman Emperors. No sooner, however, were the Saxon regions integrated into Romano-Germanic Europe than the latter began to push out beyond Saxony into the Slav lands across the Elbe. By the beginning of the thirteenth century the drive to the east had ended in the German conquest of the entire area between the Elbe in the west and the Vistula in the east, and between the eastern Baltic in the north and the Tyrolean passes into Italy in the south.

Considered as a military and political operation, the conquest was the work of princes and feudal 'bosses', men like Henry the Lion of Saxony. Its main objects, obviously, were to add to the power and glory of rulers, to establish new princely and knightly patrimonies and to acquire new lands capable of economic exploitation. The drive behind it, however, was not confined to princes and their military helpers. It owed much of its following and popular repute to its religious or missionary objectives. From its very beginning the conquest was presented as the 'Wendish crusade', a campaign against the Slav infidels; and the religious enthusiasm thus generated was sufficient to enlist the official support of the Holy See and also to divert the activities of the Teutonic Order from the conquest of the Holy Land to the allegedly similar enterprise in Prussia.

As a result of these military and missionary activities the Slav area between the Elbe and the Oder came to be parcelled out among a number of German principalities, and the whole of its population was Christianised. But probably the most remarkable result of the eastward conquests was the mass settlement of German immigrants, more especially in the parts which in modern times comprised the principalities of Brandenburg, Mecklenburg, Pomerania and western Silesia.

In the process of the settlement, the indigenous Slav population was not fully replaced. Some Slav communities may have been expelled or exterminated, but the extent to which the land was denuded of its native population can be easily exaggerated. It has been argued with good reason that in certain trans-Albingian regions, especially in Mecklenburg, the main core of Slav population survived the German conquest, and some of the Slav princes, such as those of Mecklenburg-Schwerin, continued to rule in the guise of a German dynasty. In the eastmost of the regions, particularly in East Prussia, and in the south-eastern territories of Silesia and Bohemia, the German settlement remained too thin to suppress the predominantly Slav character of civilisation and speech; and even farther west – a few miles from Berlin and in the neighbourhood of Leipzig – sermons were still preached in Slavonic languages in the eighteenth century. The main achievement of German colonisation and settlement was not so much to displace the existing Slav population as to introduce a large additional stratum of peasant immigrants, and thereby to create a wholly new agrarian economy on land hitherto unoccupied or else occupied very sparsely.

This political and economic expansion was accompanied and may even have been preceded by the commercial activities of German merchants. Long before the Wendish crusaders crossed the Elbe, i.e. all through the tenth and early eleventh centuries, German merchants from the steadily developing regions of the Rhine and the Weser had begun to reach out to the eastern fringes of the Saxon empire and to trade across the Elbe. Certain transcontinental routes, well defined on the map and frequently referred to in sources, were established by the end of the tenth century. The best known of them, the Hellweg, led from Soest and Dortmund in Westphalia to such crossing-points on the Elbe as Bardowiek and Magdeburg. The merchants most active on these routes were the men of Cologne; and men of Cologne they had to be, since the Rhine valley and Cologne at its head were the hub of such interregional trade as western Germany then knew. But from the very outset merchants from Westphalia and from Saxony east of the Rhine, especially from the former, also had a growing share in the trade. By the end of the twelfth century they had come to overshadow the merchants of Cologne and the other more westerly regions of old Germany, both as merchants and as mercantile colonisers. It fell to them to lead the movement of urban immigration and settlement which accompanied the colonising activities of princes, landlords and peasants.

In the end, the colonising merchants wove a whole network of new German towns and routes connecting them. Most of the towns were strung out along the south coast of the Baltic, but important commercial centres, like Toruń (Thorn) on the Vistula, also grew up on inland sites served by rivers and roads. At least one of these towns, Lübeck, originated as early as the end of the eleventh century as a trading station or 'factory', set up by German merchants within or alongside a pre-existing Slav town. To begin with, this particular 'factory' appeared to accommodate itself successfully to Slav rule and even to enjoy the protection of Slav princes. Before long, however, it turned to a colonising offensive. In the late thirties of the twelfth century, Adolph of Holstein invaded the land and burned the city, and in 1143 the Germans of Lübeck formally constituted themselves into a German town of the same name. This cuckoo-like procedure was not, however, followed everywhere, for most German towns in the Baltic regions apparently originated in new settlements, or in new German quarters attached to older Slav nuclei. One of the latest and most important, located on the estuary of the Vistula, was the town of Gdańsk (Danzig) which soon rose to a dominating position in the commerce of eastern Prussia and western Poland.

The effects of this urban colonisation on the power structure of the north European economies will be discussed later. From the point of view of economic geography, with which we have been dealing so far, its effect was to open up and to develop a maritime connection between western and eastern Europe and thereby to merge into a single commercial area the hitherto self-contained *Verkehrsgebiete* of north-western and of central and eastern Europe.

In this merger the merchants were not the sole agents. To adopt a phrase from a later age, 'trade followed the flag'. As the German princes and landlords spread their rule to the east, they created the political prerequisites for German activity beyond the Elbe and made it possible for the German merchants not only to sail unhindered along the coastal waters of the Baltic but also to establish permanent commercial settlements ('factories' and towns) in the interior.

The potentialities of the commercial settlements and their role in building up and sustaining the economic power of German merchants were reflected in their siting and the way they spread over the map. They were so placed as to form staging posts and entrepôts at regularly spaced points along the sea route and along the main inland routes to the sea. Most of them – above all Wismar, Rostock, Stettin and Gdańsk – were sited at places at which the north-flowing rivers of the German plain ran into the Baltic. Some, such as Reval, Riga or Dorpat, were seaports as well as administrative centres serving the Latvian and Livonian possessions of the knightly orders in the eastern Baltic. In addition, the two most important towns on the route, the neighbouring cities of Hamburg and Lübeck, benefited not only from their location at the Baltic end of the Elbe valley, tapping the wealth of the newly opened-up Wendish hinterland, but also from their position at the foot of the Jutland peninsula. For as long as the traffic to and from the west hugged the coasts and did not venture across the open seas, the Jutland peninsula was an impassable land barrier. Boats had to be unloaded at Hamburg on their way east and at Lübeck on their way west, and then carried across the peninsula and reloaded at the other side for a further voyage by water. In this way the two towns became unavoidable intermediaries in whatever traffic there was, and stood to benefit from all increases in the trade of other towns along the route. They derived advantages, too, from the great wealth of the fishing grounds off the nearby coast of southern Sweden (Skania), and were also able to draw on the wealth and importance of their Westphalian founder families. Thus favoured, Lübeck soon acquired a predominant role amidst other German towns trading to the Baltic, a role which eventually raised it to the position of an informal capital of the German Hanse.

Later in this essay I shall try to show how the new network of routes transformed the very composition of the trade and thereby helped to reshape the economies of the regions it served. The trade flowing up and down the rivers and along the Baltic route was, to an ever-increasing extent, to consist of goods producible and consumable in quantities large enough and at prices low enough to rank as 'essentials'. The Germans trading in the Baltic and across central and eastern Germany, and only they, were able to sustain the flow of these goods and to control their sources and markets. This made them all but indispensable in both East and West, and opened to them positions of power in places well beyond the natural termini of the Baltic sea-lanes.

Within the regions still ruled by the Slavs, native princes and merchants had to direct their exports to places dominated by the German merchants. The town of Novgorod on Lake Ilmen, connected with the Baltic by a short water route, housed a German 'factory' dominating the trade of the town and drawing to itself the entire foreign trade of north-eastern Europe. Farther south, the Russian towns of Smolensk, Pskov, Polotsk and Vitebsk, as well as others in Volhynia and Podolia, were not, like Novgorod, obviously dominated by German 'factories'. They nevertheless functioned as outlets through which Russian trade with Germany and the West was channelled. For their part Gdańsk and Toruń drew to themselves the bulk of the timber trade of eastern Poland and western Prussia.

The position of the German merchants in the West was for a time almost equally powerful. The essential commodities of eastern origin found large and expanding markets in western European countries. And as long as they were able to control the supply of these commodities, the German merchants were welcome and indeed irreplaceable, and were consequently able to obtain exclusive commercial privileges in several western countries. In most of these countries they established commercial 'factories' and trading stations, of which those of Bruges, London and Bergen were the most important. Eventually their commercial activities brought them into Italy as well; and the *Fondacho dei Tedeschi* in Venice became very nearly the sole south European outpost of east-to-west trade.

In this way the Baltic route had, by the end of the thirteenth century, become the principal single artery of north European commerce, and thereby one of the main sinews of economic power in eastern Europe. However, this system of east-to-west connections and influences was not destined to survive long beyond the second half of the fourteenth century. In the first place, political and demographic changes gradually reduced the impetus of the German drive to the east. The political vacuum in the Slav lands, which had enabled the Germans to conquer and occupy the territories of the western Slavs in the earlier Middle Ages, was eventually filled by the rising power of Slav states and in the first place by that of Jagiellonian Poland. In 1410 the political balance was finally redressed by the Polish victory over the Teutonic Order at Tannenberg.

The battle of Tannenberg put an end to German conquests, but even before this the German ability to fill the conquered territories with settlers had given out. The demographic pressure behind the flow of immigrants from western Germany and Flanders slackened in the four-teenth century and finally exhausted itself after the Black Death of 1348. As a result, the last eastern territories to be subjected to German political rule, such as eastern Silesia, Bohemia, Styria or the lake regions of eastern Prussia, were never fully germanised. The Germans who had established settlements there by the early fourteenth century were not reinforced by later drafts of colonists, and thus remained for ever mere enclaves of a linguistic and ethnic minority.

The slackening of German expansion and colonisation may or may not have reduced the actual volume of east-to-west trade (we do not possess sufficient evidence for measuring its turnover), but it certainly weakened the sway of the German merchants over it. And one of the reasons why this sway weakened is that the maritime route across the Baltic, and the land routes feeding it, were displaced in the course of the late fourteenth and fifteenth centuries, so losing their prime importance in east-to-west trade.

A striking feature in the economic geography of European trade in the late fourteenth and fifteenth centuries was the deflection of a large and a growing proportion of the trade away from the northernmost lanes. In this respect the changing role of the maritime lane across the Baltic was crucial. Recent historians of the Hanseatic League have raised objections to the tendency of some of their predecessors to build the whole history of north-western trade round the progress of the Baltic sea route and the towns along it. They rightly point out that the sea route was fed by the commercial currents flowing towards it from the interior, and that much, perhaps the bulk, of east European trade flowed between towns in the Baltic hinterland and along the trade routes traversing it in every direction. These objections notwithstanding, it is important, in considering the relations of eastern and western Europe, to bear in mind that throughout the Middle Ages waterways and especially sea-lanes provided by far the cheapest routes best suited to movements of bulky and inexpensive goods. And since large quantities of such goods were the distinguishing characteristic of east–west trade in northern Europe, the importance of the Baltic route and the Baltic towns in long-distance trade was bound to be greater than that of land routes and land-bound towns farther south. It was only in later centuries when, for reasons which were largely geo-political, the sea-borne trade was temporarily in decline, that the role of land routes and of the towns along them began to rival or even to exceed that of the Baltic Sea and the Baltic towns.

This phase of relative decline in the importance of the Baltic route was ushered in by several changes along it, and in the first place by the *Umlandfahrt* – a newly opened sea route round the Jutland peninsula. With the new, wholly maritime, lane open to navigation, it was no longer necessary to reload cargoes at Lübeck and Hamburg and direct sea voyages from the Low Countries to the eastern Baltic, by-passing the two towns, became possible and profitable.

The principal beneficiaries of the change were the Dutch. Their industry and commerce and, above all, their shipping had greatly advanced in the course of the late fourteenth and fifteenth centuries. They were now proving themselves to be efficient sailors, highly competitive carriers and agents of entrepôt trade. They were able, therefore, to exploit the new opportunities on the route and to challenge the German monopoly of Baltic shipping. To a somewhat smaller extent the English also began to compete in the Baltic. Having in the course of the late fourteenth and early fifteenth centuries developed a cloth-making industry, they tried to trade with eastern Europe directly, carrying their cloth to the Baltic and fetching from there important return cargoes.

It was very largely in order to ward off this Anglo-Dutch threat and to back up their threatened monopoly with political and naval action, that in 1367 the German towns, meeting in Stralsund to confer on their conflict with Scandinavia, converted their association, hitherto informal, into an overtly political organisation: the Hanseatic League. As a political and naval power this League survived until well into the modern era, but it could not reverse the unfavourable trend of geo-political change. The League's repeated attempts to beat down Dutch and English competition in the course of the fifteenth century merely succeeded, time after time, in destroying the peace on the high seas and thereby interrupting the flow of Baltic trade. Similarly, the Hanseatic attempts to enforce the League's monopoly in the West by repeated embargoes and boycotts, drove the trade away from centres in which the Germans were entrenched, especially Bruges, to centres not dominated by them, such as Antwerp. The northern route and its termini in most western parts of

Europe were becoming less reliable and less important, and, as their importance declined, alternative routes developed.

The most important of the alternative routes was a variant (or variants) of the southerly overland routes which, as we have seen, ran across Germany and the countries of south-eastern Europe to Poland and south Russia. These southern routes grew in importance not only because merchants were anxious to escape the Hanseatic stranglehold over Baltic trade, but also because southern Germany was becoming increasingly prosperous. The towns of Nuremberg, Augsburg and Regensburg do not appear to have suffered from the fifteenth-century depression to the same extent as most of the towns of western Germany. For one thing, the mining and metallurgical industries of southern Germany, which these towns served and controlled, revived towards the end of the Middle Ages. In addition, the evidence suggests that the main trade routes to Italy shifted eastwards to the advantage of the near-lying towns of southern Germany. Thus favoured, these cities seem to have entered on that upward path which they were destined to tread so successfully in the sixteenth and seventeenth centuries.

There may also have been corresponding development in the Slav areas. South-western Poland may have been less affected by the general depression which, in the closing centuries of the Middle Ages, lowered the tempo of interregional trade elsewhere. Hence the rising importance of south Polish connections and of the towns of Lwow and Cracow which benefited from the southward shift of western routes and grew in economic importance to the detriment of the northern Slav termini and of the Baltic route.

3. THE NORTHERN ROUTE: THE COMMODITIES

The southwards shift of the east-to-west routes was a geographical and economic transformation whose direct and immediate consequences were reflected mainly in the fortunes and policies of the Hanseatic League and in the powers of German cities over the regions they controlled. What appeared to be at stake was, first and foremost, the prosperity and the economic role of Lübeck, Hamburg, Gdańsk and Bruges, and the economic privileges which German merchants enjoyed in London, Scandinavia or the Low Countries. But, from the historical point of view, the most important results were the less conspicuous and more deeply hidden changes in the very composition of the trade which flowed along the great routes, both old and new. Indeed, the humdrum detail of the east-to-west traffic, i.e. of the commodities entering into it, holds the key to the proper understanding of the transformation which the trade wrought upon the economic system and social fabric of northern Europe.

The history of east-to-west trade, considered from the point of view of its material make-up, falls into several well-defined phases, roughly corresponding to those of its geo-political development. In its initial phase, that preceding the German expansion to the east, most of the commercial traffic of northern Europe to and from eastern Europe, like the trade of earlier centuries in southern Europe, was, from the purely economic point of view, supererogatory; that is to say, its commodities did not cater for the major needs of the regional economies and societies in either East or West. I have already pointed out that apart from slaves – and they were, so to speak, goods in transit – the western imports from the East consisted mostly of luxuries of eastern and Byzantine origin and were paid for partly by a few metal goods, such as weapons, and mainly in bullion.

In all probability both the quantity and the make-up of the commercial traffic between East and West changed in the initial phase of German expansion – the one which opened when the Saxon lands were conquered and absorbed, and the Westphalian and Saxon merchants appeared at the Elbe and its crossings. In that period trade was undoubtedly greater in volume than in the preceding epoch and probably brought both the West and the East a somewhat wider range of imports.

The eastern exports which, measured by value, must at that time have outweighed all the other commodities of eastern European origin, were furs. So far as we can gather from literary references and from pictorial representations, imported furs were articles of apparel ranking as semi-luxuries: relatively expensive but widely used. Ordinary peasants protected themselves from the rigours of winter by humble sheepskins, but men of greater substance in villages and in towns could afford other and better furs; and invariably they bought them, wore them and transmitted them with the rest of their heirlooms. These furs were relatively costly and, above all, differed in their cost (one fifteenth-century document put the value of a coat of ermine at sixty times that of a comparable coat of red fox), and thus were not merely utilitarian and convenient for men living in severe climates but could also be employed as status symbols and as objects of ostentatious display. Men bought and wore furs to suit their rank and wealth; indeed, this display function of furs became so generally accepted that, in the fifteenth and sixteenth centuries, national and municipal authorities in England and elsewhere thought it fit to regulate the ranking of men by the furs they wore. For these and other reasons furs, though not strictly essential commodities, came to represent a large and expanding market and to absorb considerable material resources.

Little is known about other imports from eastern Europe during the period. By inference from later evidence it appears that certain products of eastern woodlands which were to figure in the trade of the fourteenth and fifteenth centuries, such as beeswax and possibly honey, had begun to come in from the East in the eleventh and the twelfth centuries. Other commodities about which we hear in later periods – Baltic amber or goose-feathers and down – may also have begun to cross the Elbe in the eleventh and the twelfth centuries. Yet, in total, the trade in such commodities as these, though larger in volume and value than articles of *grande luxe* imported in the previous centuries, still remained on the periphery of medieval existence and could not have made much difference to the fundamental processes of economic life.

It was only in the final phases of medieval east-to-west trade, those beginning at the very end of the twelfth century, that the merchants who were engaged in it commenced dealing to an increasing extent in bulky commodities which served the common needs of ordinary people and involved large volumes of material resources and great numbers of men in their production. The historical factors behind this transformation in the composition of east–west trade have already been indicated. In the first place, there was the opening up of the east European interior; in the second, the Baltic route. The newly reclaimed and settled interior of eastern Europe yielded new commodities of an essential nature; the Baltic route made it possible to move these commodities over large distances and to place them in markets separated from their sources by the whole breadth of two seas.

Most of the 'essential' commodities were raw materials and foodstuffs. The raw materials, like the beeswax which began to arrive during the preceding period, were largely sylvan products: the natural yield of the vast forests of eastern Europe. Some of them were, so to speak, 'processed' or 'semi-manufactured': pitch, tar and resin drawn from the coniferous trees, and potash which was made by burning wood. However, by far the most important of the sylvan products of eastern Europe was timber, much of it shipped to the West in 'semi-manufactured' form, as boards or wainscoting. In the fifteenth century some timber was also sent to the West in the fully manufactured form of boat-hulls or complete ships. Most of the timber, however, came to the West unmilled and unwrought. In general, Baltic timber won its position in trade as raw material for the constructional and shipbuilding industry of the Low Countries, north-west Germany and England.

So great were the forested areas of eastern Europe and so abundant were its reserves of timber, that the ability of the Baltic regions to supply large quantities of exportable timber is easily explained. Equally easy to account for is eastern Europe's accessibility to trade: the forest lands of eastern Germany and western Poland and Russia were traversed by rivers, flowing into the sea, along which cut timber could be floated easily and cheaply. And by this time, there was a ready market for eastern timber in the countries of western Europe. The traditional picture of life in medieval Germany and even in medieval England, as set out in Grimm's fairy tales or the story of Robin Hood – a land of forests harbouring wolves and outlaws – is largely myth. In actual fact the forest lands of thirteenth-century Europe had been greatly reduced in the course of the preceding five or six hundred years of internal reclamation and colonisation. Some parts of western Europe, such as the uplands of south Germany and subalpine Swabia, Bavaria and Austria, or some areas in south-eastern and south-western France or the west midlands in England, still contained large areas of woodland. But in most other regions, especially those in which mixed farming prevailed, woodlands were now so small that usable timber was both scarce and very dear.

Moreover, it is doubtful whether domestic resources of timber would have met all western needs even had woodlands in the West remained intact. The characteristic home-grown timber of north-western Europe was hardwood, mainly oak and ash. It was valuable for many uses in building, shipbuilding and the manufacture of furniture and utensils. It was not, however, ideally suited for uses for which long poles, beams or struts were required. For these, softwoods were better, and for softwoods England, like much of the rest of western Europe, largely depended upon imports from regions where the pine and the yew grew well. When, at the end of the twelfth century, King John decided to construct a hunting-lodge in the heart of the Savernake forest, he apparently imported wood from Norway; and we must presume that he was not the only builder whose demand for timber could not be satisfied by the kind of oak which stood in the forest of Savernake.

In the twelfth century the softwoods needed in the West, as well as some other timbers, came mainly from Scandinavia. Specialised historical studies, such as Bugge's renowned book on the Norwegian timber trade, perhaps give a somewhat exaggerated picture of this trade; yet with all allowances made for the magnifying lens of the specialist, the fact remains that large quantities of timber were regularly shipped from Norway to England and that England was at that time greatly dependent on Norway for its supply of wood. It may well be that Scandinavian timber was somewhat less essential to other parts of western Europe. The timber of the south German woodlands may still have been floated down the Rhine and the Weser as it had been in the Dark Ages when that trade was in the hands of the Frisians. It is also possible that the south-western regions of France, or the French provinces bordering on Switzerland, or the parts of England along the Welsh marches, still disposed of sufficient supplies of home-grown timber and were not greatly dependent on foreign supplies. But most other regions had to tap the reserves of woodlands in Scandinavia or other forested regions of Europe to satisfy their most essential local needs.

The opening of the Baltic forest lands to west-borne trade did not, therefore, signify the beginning of the European timber trade, but rather its diversion to sources beyond the Elbe. Thus diverted, the trade was destined to grow in size and importance. On *a priori* grounds it appears obvious that Baltic timber would not have ousted Norwegian had it not been cheaper; and we must assume that, being cheaper, it was more widely used and was bought and sold in larger quantities than the timber available to the West in earlier times. On the same assumption, it is also possible to argue that the abundance of cheap softwoods of high quality favoured the innovation in the construction of western ship-hulls – those of north European 'hulks' and 'cogs' – which preceded and prepared for the technological advances in the design and construction of boats at the close of the Middle Ages. If this is so, it might not be fanciful to suggest that the shift in the timber trade to the Baltic contributed, albeit obliquely, to the great progress in shipping, ship-building and sea transport which we associate with the age of discovery and with Dutch, Portuguese and English navigation in the sixteenth and the seventeenth centuries.

The timber trade must also have had some impact on the economic activities of men in the Slav and east German forest lands. The timber had to be cut; some of it had to be worked and fashioned; all of it had to be floated to the sea. We know very little about the way in which this working and fashioning of timber was organised, or about the men employed in eastern Europe as woodcutters or shipwrights; and we have no direct means of estimating their numbers or their incomes. We have, however, a certain amount of evidence about river transport of timber and the manner in which it was conducted. In his classical treatise, now nearly a hundred years old, Theodore Hirsch described the rafts which were floated down the Russian and Polish rivers to Toruń and Gdańsk, so that we can at least imagine how medieval lumberjacks conducted their water-gipsy lives. The picture so imagined differs little from that of the west Russian lumber trade to the Baltic in the late nineteenth century. The trade created a type of employment, and favoured a mode of life, which must have been very similar in all periods, though naturally the scale of the operation in western Russia at the end of the nineteenth century was greater than in the fourteenth and fifteenth centuries.

However, of the different commodities entering the Baltic trade, the one which affected economic and social development the most was not timber. In sheer volume and value, as well as in its impact on the indigenous economy, the trade in timber was eventually outstripped by that in grain. The growing of grain in sufficient quantities and at low enough costs to make bulk exports practical, necessitated changes in agriculture which were bound to impress themselves deeply on the economic system as a whole. The activities of landlords, their relation to their tenants and labourers and, in a more general way, the condition of ordinary men, were intimately bound up with the fortunes of agriculture and thereby also with the development of exports.

Here again, some readers may wonder why any country in this period required and was able to absorb large volumes of imported grain, and how producing countries managed to yield them. Was not medieval agriculture, and, indeed, the medieval economy in general largely self-sufficient? Did not the overwhelming majority of medieval producers practise subsistence farming, and was not the grain trade, for this reason alone, both small and intensely local? This picture of medieval economy has, however, long been discarded. It is now well established that many households and regions in the Middle Ages did not produce enough to feed themselves, while others produced enough to provide surpluses. Indeed, so essential was the grain trade in medieval life that it appears to have formed the basis of the very pattern of regional settlement and regional specialisation.

This was certainly true of Scandinavia. It is difficult to imagine that western Norway, so ill-suited to the production of cereals, would have been occupied by its Germanic settlers except on the presumption that grain, some grain, could be obtained from outside. Certainly, in the twelfth and thirteenth centuries Norway was greatly dependent on imports of food, and England was the main source of grain. A much-quoted speech of King Haakon Hakonsen in 1138 underlines how indispensable, and therefore how welcome, English imports and importers were at that time. Similarly, it is difficult to imagine how Frisian society could have established itself and subsisted on the wet sands and the inundated pastures of the Rhine estuary before the ninth century had it not been able to import grain from higher and drier lands. When in the twelfth and thirteenth centuries Flanders developed its relatively highly industrialised economy, and when in the late fourteenth and fifteenth centuries Holland did likewise, they had to rely on food imports, mainly from the grain-growing regions of the lower Seine. We also know that as Gascony and Poitou developed their viticulture and became Europe's largest wine-producing and wine-exporting regions, they also lost the ability to feed themselves and had to import large quantities of grain, which in the late fourteenth and fifteenth centuries came mainly from or via England.

It would seem, therefore, that what the Baltic trade achieved was not the creation for the first time in the Middle Ages of an interregional grain trade, but rather a change in the geographical distribution of what had always been an important commercial commodity. Instead of coming from the middle Rhine valley or Picardy or England, the grain for

Europe's deficient regions now began to come from eastern European plains opened up in the process of colonisation east of the Elbe. In Scandinavian countries German imports displaced English grain, and German grain-importers became indispensable and hence also powerful. Above all, Flanders, and later the northern Netherlands (modern Holland), began to take their grain imports from the Baltic regions.

Moreover, the Baltic supplies were so abundant and reliable – and possibly also so cheap – that they were also shipped to places which did not regularly require imports of foodstuffs but were capable of putting cheap grain to other uses. In the later Middle Ages Hamburg developed a flourishing brewing industry based on corn imported from the Baltic; and in the fifteenth century Baltic grain also enabled the northern Netherlands to develop their brewing. Generally speaking, the economic growth and prosperity of the northern Netherlands in that century would have been impossible without regular supplies of Baltic grain. It is also probable that Baltic grain was shipped or transhipped to Bordeaux from Gdańsk in years in which English output was insufficient to supply Gascony.

Directly and indirectly, Baltic cereals were available to swell supplies of grain all over Europe and make up for its deficiencies at times when, and places in which, harvests fell short of requirements. It would not, therefore, be fanciful to suggest that availability of Baltic supplies may have been one of the reasons, albeit a subsidiary one, why grain prices all over Europe were relatively low in the late fourteenth and fifteenth centuries and why they were even sagging gently in the four or five decades before 1480.

The return cargoes, with which the westerners paid for Baltic goods, were not perhaps as indispensable as Baltic grain, but they were nevertheless bulk imports and were destined to be consumed in large quantities. The bulkiest and the most indispensable of the western imports to the East was salt, the principal food preservative and the principal raw chemical in the Middle Ages. To begin with, most of the salt shipped east came from the area of Lüneburg, west of the Elbe, and was shipped mainly from Hamburg. Lüneburg salt, however, was eventually displaced by the cheaper and more readily available salt of the Bay of Biscay (or, to be more exact, the Bay of Bourgneuf). In the fifteenth century, the great Bay fleets, sometimes made up of more than a hundred ships, regularly sailed with cargoes of salt from the west coast of France, past the Low Countries, to the herring fisheries off the south coast of Sweden (Skania) and off the north coast of Holland, and then beyond the Jutland peninsula to Gdańsk and even to Novgorod.

The Bay fleets also carried miscellaneous industrial goods of western manufacture, as did all ships trading with the Baltic. By far the most important of the manufactured goods was, of course, cloth. The imported cloth was very expensive by comparison with native linen textiles, or even with the coarser woollens made locally. Nevertheless, the quantities which could be absorbed by eastern European markets, including those of Russia, were very large; and eastern Europe consequently became one of the main outlets for the western European cloth industry.

At first, the bulk of the imported cloth came from Flanders. It was, as a rule, bought by German merchants in Bruges, and taken by them to the Baltic towns, from where it was distributed all over eastern Europe. At the end of the fourteenth century, however, the Flemish cloth industry declined, and that of England and Holland largely replaced it in the eastern markets. Some, perhaps most, of this cloth was also handled by Hanseatic importers, but throughout the fifteenth century the English and the Dutch, especially the former, tried to keep the marketing of their cloth in their own hands.

Most of the conflicts between England and the Hanseatic League, of which there were several in the fifteenth century, arose over the attempts of English merchants to establish themselves as importers of cloth in the Baltic area, more particularly in Gdańsk. To begin with, these attempts failed. Political conditions in England at the time of the Wars of the Roses were too unstable to provide English merchants with the political support they needed. The final defeat in the Hundred Years War also had a debilitating effect on England's political and naval power. Thus favoured, the Hanseatic League was able, for the time being, to smother English ambitions in the Baltic. But in the sixteenth century the greater political influence and naval power of the Tudor state, and the retreat of the Germans in Gdańsk and East Prussia before the advancing power of the Poles enabled England to revive her ambitions in the Baltic and to pursue them more successfully than before. Earlier still, the Dutch had fought successfully for their share in Baltic shipping and trade. In this way the cloth exports from western Europe to the East contributed to the geo-political changes of the fifteenth century which I have already described.

By comparison with salt and cloth, the other western exports were much less important. Metal goods of every kind came from Cologne and eastern Flanders, mostly Liège. Wine came from Burgundy and Gascony; cow hides, sheepskins, tin and pewter came from England; and (possibly) herring came from Swedish and later from Dutch fishing grounds.

In retrospect, however, even these important return cargoes did not have economic and social repercussions as far-reaching as exports from the east, and especially the flow of east European grain. If the adjective 'colonial' has any relevance to European conditions at the end of the Middle Ages, the export of cereals is one, perhaps the only, branch of trade which can conceivably be so classified: not only was it confined to unprocessed agricultural produce, i.e. grain and not malt or beer or flour, but it was largely paid for with manufactured imports; moreover, it was in the hands of outsiders, west European merchants and shippers, and it subjected the fortunes, the economic organisation and social structure of eastern economies to the requirements of western markets. There is little doubt that the grain trade, as it developed at the close of the Middle Ages and in the early centuries of the modern era, had an impact on economic conditions and social relations in eastern regions comparable to the impact of modern international commerce on under-developed countries exporting primary produce. To this impact we shall now pass.

4. THE SOCIAL IMPACT OF TRADING RELATIONS

Eastern Europe diverged widely from the West in its economic and social development. It would have diverged even if it had been unaffected by trade, since its economy and society were a product of recent conquest, immigration and new settlement. In any event, dissimilarities were not levelled out by east–west trade; on the contrary, the commercial exchanges between the two halves of Europe widened the economic and social divergence. The divergence had begun to reveal itself only by the end of the Middle Ages, but in some parts of eastern and central Europe it was already well under way by the end of the fifteenth century. In its medieval beginnings, as in its more modern phases, it derived much of its momentum from the pressures generated by trade.

In the early stages of German conquest and settlement the societies of West and East differed in detail and degree rather than in substance, more especially at their topmost levels. At these levels social structure conformed, broadly speaking, to what is now generally recognised as the feudal order. The role which the upper ranks of society in eastern Europe, mainly the owners of estates, were called upon to play in central and local government was in essence the same as that played by owners of fiefs in western Europe during the earlier centuries of the Middle Ages. The eastern European landowners, like the landed knights and nobility in the West, were a military class *par excellence*; and as such they bore the main burden in the conquest and occupation of the new territories. In the new territories, once they had been occupied and settled, the landowners as a rule continued to perform the military and administrative functions appropriate to members of the upper ranks of society. To this extent, the structure of state economy and society in the eastern half of Europe may be said to have been 'feudal' in the broadest sense of the term.

Nevertheless, eastern feudalism differed in several important respects from that in most western countries. It was less hierarchical than in certain parts of southern France (or, indeed, than in the Holy Land), and in some parts of the East it was more anarchical, less subordinated to the central power and less easily controlled by it. The duties, obligations and local powers of the noblemen and knights were not solely dependent upon an implied feudal contract between them and their suzerains (by no means all the large estates were in fact held on terms identical to those of western fiefs); rather, they sprang from their *de facto* positions as soldiers, owners of land and colonising *entrepreneurs*. As we shall see presently, this *de facto* feudalism may in later centuries have allowed individual landlords a freedom of action and opportunities for the exercise of their power which were all the greater for not being bound by the terms of an implied feudal contract.

Greater still were the differences in the conditions of lower men in the two halves of Europe. Everywhere in western Europe the manorial ties between landlords and peasant tenants were dissolving during the twelfth and the early thirteenth centuries. Larger numbers of manorial tenants saw their personal liberties enlarged and the burdens of their services and obligations lightened. In this way they were gradually approaching the condition of freeholders. Nevertheless, in most places in the twelfth century this process had not yet been completed; and except for relatively small groups of free peasants holding by allodial tenure, most peasants in western Europe still lived and held their lands in conditions of manorial dependency of some sort or another. Moreover, though the legal position of manorial peasants – their personal status and their tenurial obligations – was improving during the twelfth century and was to improve more radically still in the fourteenth and fifteenth centuries, their material level of life was low and sinking. Their poverty was due to purely physical causes, mainly the pressure of population. The ratio of land to hands and mouths was unfavourable, and peasant holdings were small. In most parts of Europe they were also becoming smaller as population increased and as reserves of reclaimable land dwindled.

By comparison, the condition of peasants in the East, especially the German immigrants, was much superior; it was freer, more prosperous, and seemingly more promising. In many places the trend was set not by German immigrants but by Flemish settlers. The Flemings were Europe's pioneers in land reclamation and, above all, in the draining and management of swampy lands; they were therefore sought after by the organisers of east European colonisation and attracted to the East by allurements of every kind. In the twelfth century Flemish peasants, unlike those of most parts of France or England, were personally free and held land by wholly free titles; and they had to be offered conditions of tenure equally free if they were to be enticed to the East. The total number of Flemings thus persuaded to move was probably quite small, but the Flemish version of free status and free tenure was also made available to the bulk of German immigrants. In order to attract settlers, landlords and colonising entrepreneurs promised and gave the German peasant settlers land to be held by 'Flemish law'.

Equally important was the quantity and quality of land made available to them. Land, and above all land recently reclaimed and thus unexhausted, was less scarce than in the West. Average holdings were therefore larger than average holdings in Franconia, Swabia or Westphalia, from where most of the immigrants had come. In this way, in eastern Germany and in the other Slav lands, where new immigrants predominated, a prosperous as well as a free peasant society was emerging.

Subsequent developments proceeded in diametrically opposite directions.. In the West, especially in England and France, the hold of the feudal landlords over state and society weakened as national governments consolidated themselves and as commerce expanded; in the East the power of the estate owners grew, while the peasants were brought to the very threshold of enslavement and impoverishment. In most parts of eastern and central Europe, the threshold was not passed until the sixteenth and seventeenth centuries. But in some parts, especially in the eastern fringes of Germany, such as the march of Brandenburg, it was approached very closely in the late fifteenth century.

The divergence between East and West was rooted in the origin of the eastern European states. From their beginnings, the princely states of eastern Europe differed from their western prototypes, though the differences were not mainly economic or social in origin, but political and constitutional. According to the commonly held view, the feudal landlords in western Europe established their power in the Dark Ages and increased it subsequently at the expense of the state and the princely authority, only to lose it in later centuries as and when princely powers and the authority of the state grew. This generalisation may not be universally applicable. In some countries, such as England or Normandy and some of the principalities of France, the feudal order was so to speak, 'nationalised'; it was adopted by the English kings, the Norman dukes and the kings of Norman Sicily as an instrument of their own authority, above all as an orderly system of military service and local administration. However, by degrees, in the course of the twelfth and thirteenth centuries in England, and at somewhat less definite points of time in France, the feudal hierarchy was ceasing to be the principal instrument of state government. The latter began to rely instead on civil servants and hired soldiers for the military, administrative and judicial services it required.

In the German principalities beyond the Elbe and in Prussia the government depended, from the very outset, on the support and services of its landowning knights and nobles – the *Junkers* as they eventually came to be known – for the exercise of its essential functions, and this dependence increased in the later centuries. The attempts by Ivan the Terrible of Russia in the sixteenth century to end the dependence of the state on the ancient nobility and to govern through the *Oprinchina* – a retinue of servants and police agents under the tsar's personal command – succeeded for a time in imposing upon the country a type of autocratic despotism. But it did not outlast Ivan's reign, and after him the new monarchy in Russia called into being a landowning class on which it could base its authority and from which it could draw its officers and administrators. In Poland, relations between the state and its landowners evolved somewhat differently. For one thing, the great magnates played an increasingly important role, and the powers of the state progressively weakened in the course of the early centuries of the modern era. In the late Middle Ages, and to some extent even later, the Polish monarchy had to draw on the landed estate and the landowning nobility for the machinery and the personnel of its administration and army.

The resurgence of feudalism, however, was clearest in the east German principalities. There, in the course of the later Middle Ages and the early centuries of the modern era, the powers of the feudal landowners grew. The principalities stood in great need of military service. They were, after all, frontier states; they administered and defended territories which were large and comparatively sparsely settled by medieval standards. Yet their administrative and military resources, above all their human cadres, were relatively meagre. In the absence of an old and powerful middle class, or of other nuclei of local power, the estates and their *Junker* owners were the only reserves of authority on which the state could draw and whose loyalty it had to keep.

This loyalty had to be kept, and services to the state had to be paid for, as they had been in the initial phases of western feudalism and in Tsarist Russia, by grants of land and by facilities for its profitable exploitation. In the conditions of eastern Europe, the means of exploitation were at least as important as the land itself, since the latter was relatively abundant and estates were, to begin with, easily carved out. But as long as population remained scarce, there were few hands to turn the land to use. Ownership of land did not, therefore, give sufficient remuneration in itself. In the initial phases of colonisation the most remunerative use for land was to settle it with people, and greater powers over other men were not what landowners needed in order to attract peasant settlers. In these conditions a society of free and prosperous peasants was wholly compatible with the interests of landlords. But the value of land to the landlord, and its use by him, changed when colonisation ceased and the corn trade developed. The large and growing market for grain offered great opportunities to owners of land for its profitable use. In eastern Germany and western Poland conditions were more favourable for the production of grain on a large scale and in large units than anywhere else at the end of the Middle Ages. Large corn-growing estates were thus becoming increasingly valuable, provided they could be worked, i.e. provided men could be found to work them.

Thus it became the policy of *Junkers* to obtain as much good land as possible and as many labourers as were needed to cultivate it. Much of the better land was already in the possession of peasant cultivators; hence, the acquisition of peasant land became the policy of profit-conscious landowners. Similarly, the peasants were the only possible source of manpower for working on the land. So far as we know, in the early phases of colonisation the number of smallholders or landless men willing to hire themselves to other men was very small. After the middle of the fourteenth century, when immigration petered out and population ceased to grow, or perhaps even began to decline, workers on the land became scarcer still, or, at least, more difficult to recruit.

Hence the *Bauernlegen* (the 'laying of peasants'): a double-headed weapon to match the twin purposes it served. Peasant land was seized by landlords for additional arable cultivation; peasants were deprived of their holdings or had their holdings reduced in order to compel them to work as labourers. The compulsion to work could be clothed in legal forms. The so-called *Gesindezwang*, a compulsory service for peasants as labourers, frequently received the sanction of law and could be enforced in courts. Other disabilities of a semi-servile character, restricting the peasant's freedom of movement and his status as the lords' equal in law, were also imposed on large sections of the peasant population. In this way the peasants in eastern Germany at the end of the fifteenth and in the sixteenth century (and in Poland and Russia at a somewhat later period) moved from freedom to serfdom at the very time when western society was shedding most of the constraints of medieval villeinage.

The divergence was thus complete and appeared to be irreversible. It was not, however, the result of spontaneous economic change; it was brought about by the exercise of landlords' power. Their influence and personal connections in the seats of central authority and the willingness of the central government to serve their interests, precluded any princely opposition to *Bauernlegen* or any policies in defence of peasants comparable to the anti-enclosure measures of the Tudor government in England.

Consequently, the *Junkers* were able to turn to account their great and increasing powers in central and local government and in the judiciary. This might have happened even if the corn trade had failed to develop: the *Junkers* might still have conceived it in their interest, and found it in their power, to reduce free peasants to serfdom. They did so in Russia in the seventeenth and eighteenth centuries even though Russian exports of grain at that time were as yet negligible. Nevertheless, there is no denying that the main reason why the *Bauernlegen* occurred in the other parts of eastern Europe earlier is that corn-trade exports were growing and appeared capable of further growth, and that landlords could not exploit the full potentialities of the trade so long as peasants owned much of the arable land and withheld their labour.

In this way one of the most tragic paradoxes of European history came to be enacted. In conventional histories, trade is often represented as a liberating force and as a solvent of serfdom and of feudal power: in this particular instance it enhanced the forces of resurgent feudalism. Trade is also said to be the great international leveller, capable of reducing the economic differences between regions and nations and extending common principles of social and economic organisation. But at the close of the Middle Ages, and still more in the two subsequent centuries, the corn trade widened the differences between the economy and society of the East and those of the West. Indeed, in the end it created along the river Elbe one of Europe's sharpest lines of social and economic demarcation. And yet this economic and social dividing-line occurred within the limits of a single European civilisation.

7

ITALIANS AND THE ECONOMIC DEVELOPMENT OF ENGLAND IN THE MIDDLE AGES*

I was asked to illustrate the effects of the economic leadership of advanced nations by an example drawn from English economic history in the Middle Ages. I have accordingly chosen the subject of Italian contribution to the economic development of medieval England. What prompted this choice was not only the contribution that the Italians in fact made but also the contribution that they are reputed to have made. Indeed their reputation for economic leadership interests me as much as their achievement. For if their reputation and their achievement are collated, something more interesting than a mere illustration of economic leadership may emerge. The illustration may well turn into a cautionary example. I hope I shall not appear immodest or perverse if I suggest that the Italian example may help to circumscribe the historical and the logical validity of the entire concept of nations as economic leaders. For the concept that appears to mean something in historical accounts of economic forms is apt to dissolve as soon as we reach out to the fundamental forces and processes of economic growth.

It is very largely because the founders of economic history in England were so largely concerned with outward forms of economic life that it did not occur to them to cast doubt either on the ability of the Italians to lead or on the need of the English to follow. In the text-books on which we were all brought up the problem was resolved very simply. We were told that in the earlier centuries of the Middle Ages Britain was, so to speak, on the fringes of Europe. The Anglo-Saxon conquest had wiped the slate clean of all survivals of Roman civilisation. For several centuries life was to remain simple and primitive – more so than in any other European regions west of the Rhine. Cities were slow to rise and to grow; commercial contacts with the outside world were very tenuous. The country was potentially rich, but her prospective wealth was in her agriculture, especially in her wool. It was not until foreigners began to

* This paper first appeared in *Journal of Economic History*, XI, 1951.

buy large quantities of English wool that England was able to start on that development which in the fullness of time made her the foremost economic power in the Western world.

The development, we are told, was initiated by the Italians. The Italians came to England to buy wool, and their purchases, their loans, and their investments gave a powerful stimulus to economic life. What is more, their precept and their example taught the indigenous merchants the arts of commerce and finance. By the second half of the fourteenth century the lesson was so well learned that the teacher could be dismissed. The act of formal dismissal, as described in books, bore every resemblance to the acts by means of which in more recent times the so-called 'backward' countries have tried to get rid of Western merchants and bankers. King Edward III defaulted on his vast obligations to the banking houses of Bardi and Peruzzi, and the consequent ruin of Italian merchants' houses in England enabled natives to take the place of the Italians in almost every branch of commerce and finance. The process was completed by a rapid industrialisation of the country, mainly by the development of a native cloth manufacture.

This is the accepted story, and no story could have been accepted by generations of scholars without some foundation in fact. It certainly fits what we all know about the Italian economy in the earlier centuries of the Middle Ages. Compared with other countries in Western Europe, including England, Italy was wealthy; her commercial and industrial arts were highly developed, her merchants experienced and well supplied with capital. They were to be found trading in every European region west of the Rhine, and no country in which they resided or with which they traded could fail to profit from their enterprise, from their investment and, above all, from their example of higher business technique and efficiency.

There is thus little doubt that the Italians were in a position to confer economic benefits on relatively laggard countries like England. What is more doubtful is whether the benefits were so great and continuous as to be a major factor in England's economic advance. The significant fact about England's economic progress in the Middle Ages – indeed about the economic progress of Europe as a whole – was that it was general and organic, in fact, that it was economic growth. As agricultural production increased, larger surpluses – wool and foodstuffs in England, foodstuffs and timber in eastern Europe – were available for export. As population increased, certain regions of Europe, especially the Netherlands, were able, in fact were compelled, to industrialise, and a natural symbiosis established itself between the industrial regions like Italy and the Netherlands and primary producers like England.

Growth so deeply rooted could not have been started or sustained except by forces of a simple and fundamental nature. The great agricultural development in England between the tenth century and the middle of the fourteenth, the growth of wool production in the same period, and the development of the cloth industry between the end of the fourteenth century and the fifteenth were possible only through greater supplies of labour, improved agricultural and industrial technique and continuous investment of capital.

What part did or could the Italians have played in all this? Did they supply the additional labour? Certainly not. Did they introduce or help to introduce new economic techniques? To some degree they probably did; but how great or small the degree was will not be apparent until we have looked into the problem a little more closely. It is easy enough to show that the Italian influence on agricultural technique was insignificant. In English agriculture, technical developments were of a kind that was common to all North European nations. The changeover from intermittent cultivation to two- and later three-field systems, the employment of heavier agricultural implements and larger plough teams, the improvement in the breeding of sheep and in the quality of their fleece, all these were, so to speak, autogenous skills – skills that the people of England acquired in the course of their own struggle with their own elements. A little borrowing from other nations of northern Europe there doubtless was. It is just possible that Flemish know-how in the control of floodwaters may have percolated into the eastern counties of England, for there was a great deal of Flemish settlement there. It is also possible that the Flemish and German advances in milling technique had been learned by English millwrights. It is highly probable that the growing of vines and most vegetables was introduced into England from France. And it is certain that the arts of curing white herring and brewing beer with hops were brought from other parts of Europe. But of direct Italian influence in any of these techniques there is not a trace; and yet it was in these techniques that the greatest advances, most essential to economic growth, took place.

Almost equally autogenous was England's industrial technique. England's major industry in the Middle Ages was cloth. A cloth industry of a kind and cloth exports abroad go back to the very early English history, to the times of Charlemagne and Offa. In the great development of the cloth industry, which took place in the fourteenth and fifteenth centuries, Flemish technique and example may have played a part, though perhaps not as great a part as was once thought. The notion that the industry was introduced to England by foreign weavers invited by Edward III is now taken for what it is: a simplification and an exaggeration. Some Flemish immigrants were invited, and more still gatecrashed, but the main branches of the industry were in English hands and were

managed by English clothmakers. The technical innovations in cloth-
making introduced from abroad were, as yet, small. England, until the
middle of the sixteenth century, continued to produce her traditional types
of cloth – the broadcloths and rays of her southern counties, the kerseys
and worsteds of her eastern counties. By far the most important, indeed a
revolutionary technical innovation, was the fulling mill, and Miss Carus
Wilson has taught us to regard the introduction of the fulling mill as the
turning point in the development of the English cloth industry in the
Middle Ages. Together with cheap wool, it gave the English clothmaker
an immense competitive advantage over the continental clothiers and
established the prosperity of the English clothmaking regions. But the
fulling mill by the village stream was a peculiarly English development,
part and parcel of England's social and political system in the Middle
Ages, which prevented the municipal government from interfering with
water-driven machinery and industrial settlement on agricultural estates.

More international in origin was the English technique of shipping and
navigation, yet it owed very little to Italian example. Until the second
half of the fifteenth century, the type of merchant ship that the English
seamen and merchants sailed, the hulk and the cog of northern design,
the sea lanes that they frequented, the methods of navigation they
favoured, were those they shared with other maritime nations in their
neighbourhood: the Dutch, the Scandinavians, the Germans. They did
not build Italian galleys or carracks and did not use Italian maps. On the
few rare occasions before the end of the fifteenth century when they
tried to sail into the Mediterranean they were heavily punished for their
audacity by the sailors and privateers of Genoa.

The only Italian example that the English imitated, both frequently
and faithfully, was that of office techniques. The English merchants who
sold or who bought from Italians, or who trafficked with them in foreign
currency or for credit, learned from the Italians how to cover bits of
parchment with business formulae, which were highly precise and universally understood. The particular form of Italian letter instructing payment abroad in foreign currency, the *tratta*, became the model for the
English letter of exchange. It is possible, though by no means certain, that
the contracts of 'sea loan' provided a prototype for such few contracts of
English maritime insurance as are to be found in the fourteenth and
fifteenth centuries. It is also probable that the English 'charter party'
conformed to the international usage and that that in its turn was very
largely formed on Italian prototypes.

Yet even these borrowings must not be overestimated. They were mostly
a matter of procedure, not of function. Long before the English merchants
adopted the standard form of the *tratta*, they wrote letters instructing
payment abroad in foreign currency. They often entered into partner-

ships with their agents abroad, even with their Italian agents, without observing the formalities or adopting the terminology of the Italian partnership contract. Throughout the Middle Ages the obligations of partners continued to be treated in English law as if they were those of servant and master, or receiver and master, actionable under the so-called 'Writ of Account'. The terminology, the formal correspondence and the book-keeping of partnerships all conformed to this legal doctrine. And so widely did the doctrine differ from that of the Italian *commenda* partnership that some legal historians unfamiliar with economic history have been led to believe that partnerships were unknown in medieval English commerce.

So much for technique. It now remains to inquire into the main and the least understood of Italian activities in England, that of investment. Evidence on this point is bound to be elusive and ambiguous. My own impression is that some Italian merchants' capital found its way into productive investment in England, but that on the whole its action was too feeble and too intermittent to make much difference to economic development.

This impression of mine is not only tentative and impressionistic but is also a composite one, for it begs at least two distinct questions: how much capital did Italians import into England? how much of the capital they imported found its way into productive employment? The first question might seem easy enough to answer. The great Italian mercantile and financial houses were very active during the thirteenth and the fourteenth centuries. Firms like the Riccardi and the Frescobaldi in the late thirteenth century, the Bardi and the Peruzzi in the early fourteenth, and the Medici in the late fourteenth and fifteenth greatly involved themselves in English finance, especially in government finance. The accumulated liability of the English Crown to the Bardi and Peruzzi in the first quarter of the fourteenth century must at times have greatly exceeded a quarter of a million pounds, a sum equivalent to Edward III's annual war budget at its highest. Royal debts of this magnitude must, in part, have been financed out of the capital resources belonging to Italians and imported from Italy. However much Villani exaggerated the ruin that Edward III's default brought upon the Florentine houses, there is probably little doubt that some Italian investors had suffered losses and that consequently some of the money that Edward III squandered in his wars on the continent might ultimately have come from Italian savings.

Some, but by no means all. Much, and at times most, of the capital that the Italians manipulated in this country came from domestic sources. It is probable that to some extent they used the deposits of wealthy Englishmen. Matthew of Paris alleges that the Jews, before their expulsion, operated with funds belonging to the great magnates. Mr E. B.

Fryde of the University College of Aberystwyth has recently described the deposits of the Dispencers and of one or two other fourteenth-century families with Italian bankers. However, this was hardly a practice sufficiently general to provide the Italians with a large proportion of their loanable capital in England. Much more important to them were the funds they raised by means of ecclesiastical taxes.

The business which in the first place brought Italian financiers to England was that of papal taxation. Their involvement with royal finance often followed from their activities as papal collectors. Professor Lunt has reminded us that in the thirteenth century the popes sometimes imposed their taxes with the express purpose of financing the English kings, but even the proceeds of taxes that were destined for the papal treasury stayed for a long time at home in the hands of collectors, and it was out of these transit funds that the Italians frequently made their loans to the Crown.

The contribution which the Italian savings and imports of capital made to the royal loans in this country was thus much smaller than the vast figures of royal indebtedness might suggest. Their contribution to productive investment was smaller still. Most of the loans were made to finance royal wars, and some of the funds advanced to the Crown were paid directly to the royal officials abroad, to his army treasurers, or to his garrisons in France. Compared with these advances, the Italian loans to the king's subjects were very small. Throughout the fourteenth and fifteenth centuries we find Italians lending money to nobles and to monasteries. Sometimes their loans took the form of advance payments on wool of future growth, and it is more than probable that some of the advance payments were invested in additional flocks and new pastures. There is, however, no evidence and no reason for connecting the great development in wool production with Italian loans. The growth of flocks and the expanding area of pasture can be followed in the records of the larger English estates, but the instances of additional flocks established by loans from wool merchants, Italian or English, are very few indeed.

The story of investment in wool is merely part of the general history of agricultural investment. Students of medieval agriculture agree in regarding the twelfth and thirteenth centuries as a period of great agricultural improvement and expansion. In the two hundred and fifty years between the Domesday Book and the Black Death, the acreage of land greatly increased. The number of agricultural holdings more than doubled. All this meant a vast accretion to the resources of British agriculture and represented a great new investment. But, very little – I am almost inclined to say none – of the capital thus invested came from mercantile sources, whether Italian or native. It was almost entirely created in the manner so beloved of the classical economists: by the abstinence or postponed consumption of a large number of ordinary people.

Thus the part the Italians played in economic development in England, so spectacular and conspicuous when seen reflected in the records of the counting-houses, becomes very secondary and relatively unimportant when set against the picture of national economy as a whole. Indeed, it may well be that where the impact of the Italians was most effective was neither in their direct investment nor in their lessons of higher technique, but in the part they played in helping the kings to unsettle the economic life of the country. Royal taxation and royal finance extracted from the landowning and land-working classes large amounts of wealth previously immobilised, and decanted it into the hands of merchants, financiers, contractors to the armies and war profiteers. In this way some of the wealth of the country which would otherwise have been hoarded was made available for commerce and industry.

However, much must not be made even of this. A very large proportion of the wealth thus extracted from the country was wasted on the battlefields of Europe. Indeed, the unsettlement that royal taxation and finance brought about in England's agriculture may well have helped to usher in the depression which began in the middle of the fourteenth century and was not to pass away until the end of the Middle Ages. From this point of view the Italians indirectly assisted not only in the economic growth in the thirteenth and early fourteenth centuries but also in the decline of the fourteenth and fifteenth.

This, more or less, concludes the cautionary argument. I may well have driven it much further than I should have done had my subject dealt with the nineteenth century when capital and skill happened to be distributed among the nations of the world much more unequally than in most other periods of European history. A set of concepts, which happens to fit the relations of Britain and the Bantu in the late nineteenth century or the U.S.A. and the South Americans in the mid-twentieth, will not help us to make much sense of the contacts of the Flemings and the Germans in the thirteenth century or the English and the Italians in the fourteenth. But, on the whole, this was the gist of my argument. My purpose was not to raise yet another objection to historical analogies but to suggest that similarities and distinctions revealed by the study of economic forms are not strictly relevant to the study of the more fundamental processes of economic growth.

8

THE MEDIEVAL WOOL TRADE*

I am told that it is a commonplace of English history as taught at school that wool, in the shape of fibre, as sheep grow it, or made up into cloth, was one of the mainstays of England's greatness throughout the centuries that separated the first arrival of the Anglo-Saxons in this island and the beginning of the cotton industry.

We are also told, and we know it is true, that wool could be found behind almost every manifestation of English economic and commercial activity in the Middle Ages and in the sixteenth, seventeenth and perhaps the early eighteenth centuries. Yet I wonder how many of us realise how really important English wool was to England and to countries abroad throughout the Middle Ages. The barons of England, sitting in Parliament, asserted in 1297 that wool represented half of England's wealth or, as they put it, 'half the value of the whole land'. Other medieval Englishmen, of course, were much more vague in their appraisal of the importance of wool. The merchants of the Staple might refer to it – it was the common way of referring to wool – as 'the jewel of this realm'. That particular reference to the jewel of the realm dates from about the middle of the fourteenth century, but two centuries earlier the chronicler Henry of Huntingdon referred to wool as Britain's main national endowment. A rich fourteenth-century merchant in the Home Counties scratched on his windows for all visitors to his house to behold that 'sheep had paid for it all' – glass, mullioned windows, tapestries and everything else.

Wool also paid for many other things. When Richard I was captured abroad, his ransom, a vast one, was paid in fifty thousand sacks of wool. When Edward I engaged in dynastic and military adventures abroad in the thirteenth century, wool paid for that too. When Edward III opened that great Hundred Years War, which was to last in fact for one hundred and sixty years, the entire cost of the war throughout the early stages was borne by the taxes on wool and by loans on wool. Later still, a considerable portion of the finance which made Crécy and Agincourt possible was levied from wool growers and wool merchants, directly or indirectly. No wonder the Chancellor sat on the Woolsack. That is where the majesty of England's power resided.

* A lecture given to the 'Wool Education Society', 29 February 1952.

The importance of English wool to the continent or, to be more exact, to certain parts of the continent of Europe, was in its own way almost as great. People do not always realise how early in the history of Europe there appeared industrial societies, regions wholly or mainly industrialised with the populations dependent on industry for their livelihood. In the twelfth century one region thus industrialised was Flanders and the Netherlands, just across the narrow seas. Another almost equally important region, with industrialisation almost equally thorough, was Italy, and above all that part of Italy round Florence, which became a centre of quite a number of industries, but primarily of a cloth industry.

Generally speaking, when I refer to industrialisation I merely mean industrialisation in the sense that the Indians and the Chinese understood the word until a few years ago: textiles. The one industry which was capable of being developed continually on the basis of expanding supplies of raw material was the cloth industry, very largely because an expanding source of raw materials was provided by England. However, English wool was, to begin with, not the only wool on which these industrial communities were reared. The prevailing impression, probably the correct one, is that at first the weavers of the Netherlands got most, or at least a very large proportion, of their wool from Burgundy, a country quite near to the south-east of the Low Countries. Some wool also came from Spain.

At some time early in the Middle Ages, exactly when we do not know, but as far as we can gather some time in the twelfth century, fine curly-haired merino sheep were introduced to Castile from, probably, North Africa. From that time onwards, merino wools of African-Castilian origin were sent either to Florence or to the north, but mainly to Florence. There was also that very curious type of wool which is described in medieval sources as Garbo, which also came from Spain, probably from southern Spain, and thus indirectly from North Africa. So for the time being English wool was merely one of several contributions to European supplies of wool. French and East German, Rhine and English wool kept Flanders or Central Italy going in the same way as foreign raw materials and foodstuffs keep this country ticking over in our own day.

It was only in the course of the late twelfth and thirteenth centuries that English wool began to displace all other competitors in the world markets, until by the end of the thirteenth and the beginning of the fourteenth centuries one could say that without English wool the wool industries of the highly-industrialised communities could not have existed.

How important wool had become by then you will realise if I remind you of the way in which whole regions of Europe could be brought to the brink of starvation and their economic life reduced to complete inactivity by the cessation for a year or a season of imports of English wool. In

1336, at the beginning of the Hundred Years War, when for a while English wool was very short in Flanders, Flemish weavers roamed the country and the north of France, begging and singing for their bread, as, you will remember, the Welsh miners did in the streets of London in the years of the coal crises in the twenties. And when, in 1297, English wool exports were stopped by royal decree, the country, as the chronicler puts it, 'just emptied out, and people deserted the towns in which neither employment nor nourishment could be obtained'.

This particular position, in which wool was the foundation on which England's majesty, like the Chancellor's body, rested, and also the position in which England could give or deny a livelihood to great parts of the continent of Europe, was not, of course, arrived at at once. There was a gradual expansion, a growth, both in the production of English wool and in English commerce. How far back the process goes, we do not know. The archaeologists, on whom we depend for all our information about early peoples, do not tell us much about sheep or wool. But we know that there were large flocks in Anglo-Saxon times.

When the Emperor Charlemagne ruled a united Europe in the seventh and eighth centuries, England must have clothed his armies with uniforms. That is how some people interpret a certain letter from the Emperor Charlemagne to King Offa of the Anglo-Saxons, complaining of the deterioration of the woollen cloaks which England manufactured and exported to the Carolingian Empire. These must have been made from home-grown wool. At any rate, that is an obvious presumption to make.

By the time of the Norman Conquest and in the eleventh and the twelfth centuries, England was already covered by a multitude of sheep runs and sheep farms. Not all the compilers of the Domesday survey were equally interested in sheep; with the result that most of what we know about sheep at that time relates only to eight counties: Suffolk, Norfolk, Essex, Cambridgeshire, Cornwall, Devon, Somerset and Dorset and with the exception of these last two, Somerset and Dorset, these were not really sheep farming counties. Nature never meant them to be. Nevertheless Domesday enumerates in those eight counties something like a quarter of a million sheep. It is not beyond the bounds of possibility or probability that between three and four million sheep were then to be found in the country as a whole.

Little as we know about that early period, what we know is that from then onwards the production of wool expanded almost without interruption until some point in the middle of the fourteenth century. Those of you who know a little about English agriculture of that period and have heard the words 'manor' and 'demesne' know that there were large estates which contained within them large home farms, which we sometimes describe by their technical term, demesne; and you will probably recall that the thirteenth century was the heyday of demesne farming.

On quite a number of estates there were large home farms, which were producing for the market. By the middle of the thirteenth century, which was the peak point of demesne farming, it is not at all difficult to find estates with scores of thousands of sheep on them. The Bishop of Winchester, for instance, who had his estates mostly in the downlands of Hampshire and Wiltshire and partly also in Berkshire, had at one time very nearly thirty thousand sheep. In surviving references to exports of wool in that period, the total figure sometimes approaches fifty thousand sacks. This figure covers only the amount of wool exported and, of course, only the best quality wool was exported. If you remember that one sack represents the produce of 240 sheep, it is not an exaggeration to estimate that the total number of sheep in this country at that particular time was between fifteen and eighteen million. If you watch in the newspapers the painfully slow way in which scores of thousands are being added to the sheep flocks of this country at the present time, you will realise what a remarkable wealth fifteen to eighteen million sheep must have represented.

With this particular growth in the volume of wool production, went also a change – an improvement if you like which I prefer to call a change for reasons I shall make clear later – in its quality.

As, until recently, the bones of medieval sheep were not the stock-in-trade of archaeologists, we do not know enough to generalise about the breeds of medieval sheep. But partly from archaeology, partly from Dr Power's posthumous book, and from such stray corroborative evidence as we have, we can guess that originally there were, broadly speaking, two breeds of sheep in this country. There was the short-wool sheep, mostly found on the uplands of the Welsh and Scottish borders, the Kerry, Shropshire and Cheviot Hills, the Yorkshire Moors, and also on the Chalk Downs in the south. Theirs was the short, soft, curly wool, useful only for the making of the kind of matted soft fabric that we call woollen cloth. Secondly, there was the long-wool breed, producing the long staple which had to be combed, and which goes nowadays into the making of worsteds and was employed for similar purposes in the Middle Ages. This long-staple wool was grown by a very small number of highly valuable flocks in the country somewhere between the Severn and the southern marches of Wales. These were the Ryelands of South Shropshire and Herefordshire. The men in the Middle Ages knew this wool by much more picturesque names, such as 'Leominster Ore', the Golden Fleece of England, which applied to all the wool grown in and round (and round was a vague term, it might have been thirty, forty or fifty miles) the cathedral city of Leominster.

There was also the long-staple sheep of Lincolnshire, and later of the Cotswolds. In Lincolnshire itself were the equally valuable small herds of the Lindsey Marshes. But at that time the indifferent breeds and inferior growths of all the other English shires were being slowly improved by breeding and crossbreeding with rams drawn from these two major sources of high quality wool. Above all, the great upland plateau of the Cotswolds, which was an almost empty country in the early twelfth century, was converted into pastures for a breed of long-staple sheep which obviously must have been improved by continuous importation of Lindsey rams. In manorial documents there are to be found references to purchases of Lindsey rams in those areas for the special purpose of breeding.

By the middle of the thirteenth century, which we have agreed was the heyday of demesne farming, that high quality, crossbred wool – I am using crossbred not in the modern technical sense, but merely to describe the process of breeding and crossbreeding that was going on – became the principal type of wool to be exported. It is that type of wool which was grown in quite a number of Midland counties and even in the southern counties, that came to be known abroad by the generic name of Cotswold wool. 'Cotts' – as it was described briefly – supplied the bulk, probably more than half, of English exports of wool.

Even then values differed and varied immensely. Tables of qualities were published by the government periodically, and in the fixed prices given, which are useful to historians as indicating the relative rates of wool, were those of wools which at one time fetched £12 per sack and of wools which at the same time fetched as little as £3 10s or even £3 5s. In the thirteenth century a travelling Italian merchant, Pegolotti had one set of clients who managed to get as much as £15 per sack for their wool, whereas others in the same list of Pegolotti's could get little more than about £3 or £3 10s.

Yet although there were at that time these great variations, the fact remains that more than half, possibly more than two-thirds of the wool exported was of the quality which enabled Englishmen to claim that they were sending abroad the great and famous English Cotswold wool: Puich wool, as the Dutch described it, the wool of the texture of down. It was this characteristic that the best Cotswold wool was supposed to possess.

By the time the quantity had risen to its peak and the quality had improved, changes were beginning to take place in the marketing, in the purely commercial side of the English wool trade. You will recall that earlier I described this period, the thirteenth century, as the heyday of demesne farming, the time when most of the marketable agricultural produce, whether it was wheat, rye, cheese, bacon or wool, came from large estates run, one might almost say, on commercial lines. Some of these estates were monastic. We know more about monastic estates, because the monasteries, being institutions, preserved their documents better. A large proportion came also from lay estates of various kinds. We can more or less assume that in that period the bulk of exportable wool came from large producers. Now as long as large producers supplied the bulk of the wool there was no necessity for developing the middleman function in the country. What happened was that the exporters, some of them Italian, some Flemish, and some English, got into direct contact with the big producers and obtained the wool on contract. The usual practice for an Italian was to have a contract for three, four, five, sometimes twelve years, with an important grower, and to get wool from that particular grower, year in, year out. Very often we find an Italian merchant, or a Flemish merchant, sometimes even an English exporter, advancing money to the grower, and so helping to finance investment in wool production.

You can consequently picture the entire wool trade as made up of large estates and their factors on the one hand, and the small but select group of high-class, wealthy, and if you want to use the term, capitalistic, wool exporters. Even then there were small quantities of wool grown here and there, but it is a curious thing to notice in documents that those small pockets of wool grown by smaller men, by substantial peasants or by smaller landowners, were usually collected by the great wool growers themselves. The contracts between exporters and the great nobles or monastic growers very often continued to make provision for what is known as the 'collecta'. In other words, the monastery, or the noble, or the Bishop of Winchester would undertake to collect wool in his area. In addition to, say, the sixty sacks of his own wool, he would supply five, ten or fifteen sacks of wool that he would gather from his tenants or from his neighbours.

This particular kind of organisation, with an international exporter dealing with a capitalist grower, could survive only as long as demesne farming flourished. It could not live a day longer after the demesne agriculture had broken up, and we know that in the late fourteenth and in the fifteenth century the whole structure and organisation of English agriculture changed. The large estate with the large home farm within it, run as a single commercial unit, was broken up into smaller tenancies. Of course I am generalising. At no time in English history did large estates, in that sense, disappear completely, but we can assume that by far the largest proportion of English agricultural production in the fifteenth century came not from large units, but from smaller ones, mostly from small holdings of twenty, thirty, forty or fifty acres, with a few head of sheep.

In order to get large quantities of wool it was now necessary to collect it all over the country, and there appear the men who were to become familiar figures in the English countryside from the late fourteenth century to the eighteenth century, the builders of so many beautiful houses, the founders and embellishers of so many churches, i.e. the wool brokers, as they were called at that time, the wool merchants of the smaller country towns and the more substantial villages. These brokers travelled in the wool growing areas, in Yorkshire, in Northamptonshire, in parts of Wiltshire, in parts of Dorset, in the Cotswolds and in Gloucestershire. Marks left by the wool merchant are found in many small towns, in houses as in Chipping Campden, or in churches or brasses as in Northleach, or in innumerable tombstones in practically every sheep-farming area of this country. We know roughly how he lived and how he traded. Surviving British records fortunately contain accounts of two or three families engaged in the wool trade. The best known was the Cely family, wool exporters, merchants of London with a country place in Essex. They were not wool merchants in the strict sense of the term, but they were in constant trading relations with three or four merchant houses in the Cotswolds, and mostly with two families at Northleach, those of Midwinter and Busshes. We can follow the activities of the Midwinters and the Busshes in constant business relations with practically every small wool grower in the country, advancing money, collecting a couple of fleeces here, a couple of fleeces there, sending out travelling agents called chapmen, who sold trinkets and bought wool, sold salt and textiles and obtained again fleeces and lambs'-wool and all the other varieties of wool grown in the country. We also see the Busshes and the Midwinters collecting the wool, packing it, assembling it in samples, delivering it to the Celys under contract, sometimes participating in the profits. Very often they participated in many other not necessarily commercial interests, as when they married their daughters to their clients or placed their sons in their firms. In fact, they became an essential part of the business community of England.

This particular change in the marketing of wool within England was followed and to some extent accompanied by changes among the wool exporters.

When one thinks about the thirteenth century there is perhaps a tendency to idealise it, but it now begins to appear to us very much as does the Victorian era: a time about which we know very little that is precise, but about which we can say now that while it lasted things grew, and were, broadly speaking, free. It was a process of development which was unregulated and uncontrolled, and for that reason alone we know so little about it. When I was still a young man learning my history, some of the people who taught me used to say, 'Of course, there must have been very little trading in that particular period, as there are very few documents.' That is the kind of argument a historian ten centuries, or five centuries hence might produce about the Victorian Age. They might say, 'there was not really a Victorian Age; people had no bread at all, certainly no butter, because they had no coupons'.

The fact is that the earlier centuries bred no documents because governments, municipalities, or other authorities took little cognisance of trade, with the result that we have to guess much more than we know. Unfortunately we know very much more about some of the later centuries like the fifteenth, in which everything was regulated and controlled and one could not sell a pound of wool or lend a mark of silver, without leaving almost its worth in parchment as a record, a testimony to the transaction.

Consequently what we think about the thirteenth century may be to some extent unsubstantial owing to scarcity and paucity of documentation. But what we are inclined to think about it at present is that it was a period when trade was very largely unregulated, uncontrolled, and the export trade was free to all-comers, and the all-comers were foreign and English alike. There may have been as many foreigners as there were Englishmen among them. We know more about the foreigners than about the Englishmen, because they were the only merchants who had to get permission of entry and a licence to trade. But both Englishmen and foreigners were engaged in that particular branch of export trade.

This free and open structure of the export trade was gradually replaced by a monopoly which was on the one hand a national one, open only to native English merchants, and at the same time a monopoly which was restricted to a relatively small group of people. The growth of that monopoly is described in history as the rise of the Staple. The Company of the Staple was a regulated company which acquired exclusive rights of wool exports. Some historians, perhaps rightly, connect the growing power and the maturity of English commercial leadership in foreign markets with the appearance and development of this monopolist Company of the Staple.

I do not want to enter into a discussion as to how far that particular connection is justified. All I want to suggest is that at the end of the fourteenth and the beginning of the fifteenth centuries, when the Staple was finally established, the overwhelming bulk of the English wool trade was already in the hands of the English merchants, who as members of the company could trade in wool. In that particular period England's exports of wool no longer were at the high level of thirty or forty thousand sacks. The English wool exports had been declining slowly for some time before the machinery of the Staple came into existence, and went on declining for some time after the organisation had appeared.

Why it declined is, of course, a debatable question. If I were to try to answer it I should get myself, I am afraid, involved in all the controversies about the history of English society and agricultural economy in the later Middle Ages. What I am going to tell you now is to a large extent a matter of surmise. I want to suggest two things. First there was a general decline in agricultural production. England was becoming a poorer and a smaller country in the later Middle Ages. It may have been due to the Hundred Years War. It may have been some of those mysterious hidden processes in population movement, the behaviour of people, their attitude to economic matters, or perhaps their attitude to marrying and setting up families. Perhaps all these things happened more or less together. But whatever the cause, there undoubtedly occurred in the late fourteenth and the fifteenth centuries, and continued until about the 60s or 70s of the fifteenth century, a general decline in agricultural production. Contrary to what you may have heard when you were at school, the decline in arable farming did not necessarily result in increased pasture. Pasture and arable as a rule declined together and there was a general decline in the production of wool. An American, Professor Gray, who tried to work these figures out, and two or three others, have concluded that between the middle of the thirteenth and the middle of the fifteenth centuries the total output of wool must have declined.

There is no doubt at all that exports declined very drastically. In the thirteenth and early fourteenth centuries as much as forty or forty-five thousand sacks could be exported in a single year, while the average exports in the middle of the fifteenth century were only from eight to twelve thousand sacks. The average export declined in the middle of the fifteenth century to roughly one quarter or one third of what it had been about two centuries earlier.

The decline in exports cannot be put down wholly to the economic condition of the country. We can find a very obvious and specific cause, royal taxation. I have already told you that wool paid for it all, and one of the ways in which wool could be made to pay for the war was by taxing it; and taxed it was. In various customs taxes and subsidies some exporters, especially foreigners, at times paid as much as £3 10s or £4 per sack of wool. For some qualities of wool it was a tax of very nearly eighty per cent. Even for the Cotswold wool, which by that time had dropped in price to somewhere about £8 a sack, there was a forty per cent export tax, and this tax made it impossible for cheap cloth to be made out of English wool either in Florence or in Flanders. Wool at that price, carrying a tax of that magnitude, could be worked up only in expensive luxury cloths. In general, those who study Florentine history admit that there was a general decline in the total volume of production, and that the Flemish and Florentine cloth makers were concentrating on the making of much smaller quantities of very much more expensive cloths. Cloth was ceasing to be the article of mass consumption and becoming a luxury textile.

Such a heavy tax must also have discouraged domestic producers and may have been responsible for some of the decline in English production which we have already mentioned. By the middle of the fifteenth century, perhaps even by the end of the fourteenth century, a situation had developed in which the foreigner could not buy all the wool he would have bought had it been cheaper, and the domestic producer was not growing all the wool he would have grown had he been able to sell it abroad at its full economic value.

In this picture of excessive taxation, monopoly and decline, decline both in England and abroad, there is perhaps one redeeming feature. The tax, £4, or £3, or £2 10*s*, per sack of wool, which inhibited exports, also favoured the use of wool at home. The domestic user of wool, the man who wanted to spin it into yarn in England and make it up into cloth in England, was now able to obtain this indispensable, invaluable, irreplaceable English Cotts fleece. He could obtain it for roughly thirty to fifty per cent below the price which the foreigner had to pay for it. It is very largely because of this unexpected, unpremeditated and unplanned competitive advantage which the English clothmaker obtained at the expense of the foreign clothmaker, under the protection of an unplanned tariff system, that the domestic manufacturer of cloth began to forge ahead. By the end of the fourteenth century and the early fifteenth century English cloth production had outstripped by a very wide margin the small quantities of cloth which England made in the earlier period.

In your text-books, and in my text-books when I was young, we read about the good King Edward III who woke up one morning with a very bright idea of inviting the Flemish weavers to this country. Why should they go on weaving cloth in Flanders if they could weave it here? He invited John Kempe, a Flemish weaver, who came with his wife and his children, his implements and his workers, and started English cloth production on the road on which it travelled from that time onwards until the revolution in the English industry in the eighteenth century. I do not know whether it was Edward III who invited Kempe. There is in fact a letter in the records admitting him and his family to England, as there are hundreds, perhaps thousands, of other letters admitting other Flemings to England before and after this period. I am quite prepared to believe that Edward III thought it was a good idea, but what the text-books do not tell us is why Kempe thought it a good idea to accept the invitation. Someone else might have and probably did invite Flemish weavers in an earlier century; but why did they not accept then but accept so readily now?

The crux of the matter is that England was now a desirable country to gate-crash into, not merely to come by invitation, because England was the country in which it was possible to get wool, and to get it cheaply.

This, of course, is not the entire story, for there were other advantages as well. England had developed some mechanical aids to the fulling of cloth. Owing to the strength of royal power and the weakness of town municipalities, it was possible to establish rural centres of industry where the making of cloth could develop without much interference from guilds, or urban authorities.

All this played its part, but what I really wanted to emphasise was that the particular story of decline which appears to be such a sad ending to the history of English commerce, did not pass unrelieved. The very same causes which had brought down the export of English wool and reduced the importance of England's trade in foreign industrial areas, enabled a very flourishing industry to be established in this country.

9
ENGLISH STUDIES OF THE CUSTOMS ACCOUNTS*

1

I hope you will forgive me if I begin with a personal remark. I abandoned the study of trade for other researches some years ago. However, I often look back with nostalgia to my early work on commercial topics. Compared with my present researches on rural society and demography the work I then did in collaboration with other historians was simple and direct and produced clear and incontestable results. It was a real *terra firma*: and what gave it its solidity was its foundation in customs accounts. Of all the sources of English economic history, the customs accounts of the fourteenth and fifteenth centuries appear the fullest, the firmest and the easiest to interpret.

I believe that the customs accounts for the last two centuries of the Middle Ages form a much more abundant series than the sources which serve the study of medieval trade in other countries. For the period in which I am interested we have annual summaries (enrolments) of imports and exports subject to dues for each port and for almost every year. In addition to these summaries (Enrolled Accounts), we have detailed lists, the so-called Particular Accounts, which give details of imports and exports, ship by ship. Unfortunately the latter series are not complete for every port, but, for the years and the ports for which they are available, they give the names of ships and captains, complete descriptions of the merchandise, the names of the merchants who had despatched it, as well as the dates of arrival and departure of the boats. In addition, for many years and for several ports, we have collections – literally by the bundle – of miscellaneous documents which complement the customs accounts: individual receipts for the payment of dues (called 'cockets'), royal licences whenever those were needed, and documents concerning inquests or occasional official searches of cargoes. These additional documents are so numerous that most of them have never been studied and are not even known. When a young historian who helped Eileen Power in her

* First published in the *Actes du Quatrième Colloque Internationale d'histoire maritime*, Paris, 1962.

researches tried to examine some of the collections of cockets she had to give it up almost immediately on the advice of her doctor. The bundles were so thickly covered with dust which had been quietly accumulating since the fourteenth or fifteenth centuries that she went down with bronchitis within a week of starting work. When she untied the mid-fourteenth-century bundle I was afraid that she would release into the world the germs of the Black Death.

However, even if this enormous mass of documents, not only the additional ones, but also the two principal series of Enrolled and Particular accounts had remained intact under its layer of dust, its existence has always been known. Royal officials and lawyers consulted the customs from time to time, although until the seventeenth century they had not subjected them to any systematic search. Here, as in many other cases, the lawyers and antiquaries of the seventeenth and early eighteenth centuries were the pioneers, but they were content with no more than mere samples just sufficient to reveal the workings of medieval government.

Such was the main interest of Sir Edward Coke, the great jurist of the early seventeenth century, of Sir John Davies (another man of law who published a work on the Customs in 1656), of Sir Matthew Hale, a historian alive in 1660, and of Sir Thomas Madox, the great antiquary. Of all those who dipped into the customs accounts, Hale was the first to base a systematic study on them; but he, too, appears to have been content with a simple 'sounding' and remained almost completely indifferent to the commercial aspects of the accounts.

The first study of the customs accounts to be modern and global was that by Hubert Hall (1885)[1] an officer of the Public Record Office and a well-known scholar. He described the different kinds of documents, but concerned himself above all with the early period and with the origins. He also examined in some detail the administration of the customs. Then, next in chronological order, came the study of the customs by the American historian, N. S. B. Grass (1918).[2] He, also, was primarily interested in the origins, but included a detailed study of the Particular accounts of different ports and published several of them in an appendix to his book.

The first truly economic and statistical study of the customs accounts to concern itself with the information they contained about English trade and not merely with the light they cast on government was that of a German historian, G. Schanz.[3] But Schanz concerned himself mainly with the post-medieval period, and limited himself to the Enrolled accounts. Individual merchants and ships and the composition of their

---

[1] H. Hall, *A History of the Customs Revenue in England*, 2 vols. (1885).
[2] N. S. B. Gras, *The Early English Customs System* (Cambridge, Mass., 1918).
[3] G. Schanz, *Englische Handelspolitik*, 2 vols. (Leipzig, 1881).

cargoes did not interest him greatly. For this we must turn to the important work of Professor H. L. Gray.

In a famous article in the *English Historical Review*[4] on the exports of English wool and cloth in the fourteenth century, he made great use of customs accounts. The results he obtained were so important and so wide-ranging that they encouraged at least one distinguished English historian to continue this quest into the fifteenth century. Around the years 1925–6 Eileen Power brought together a group of young historians specialising in economic history, among whom were Miss Carus Wilson and myself, and began the lengthy researches which led in 1933 to the publication of figures for the fifteenth century extracted from the customs accounts and of studies of trade in the same century.[5]

Miss Power's seminar comprised eight to fifteen students, some young, some not so young, who included at different times, apart from Miss Carus Wilson and myself, Miss Sylvia Thrupp, Miss M. Dale, Miss Winifred Haward, Mr Philippe Wolff, Alfred Neumann, Mr de Sturler, Miss Leech, Miss Payne and others, as well as visitors, like Dr H. J. Smit, who was at that time assembling material for his great collection of sources connected with Anglo-Dutch trade.[6] Professor Gray, who came to England each spring and summer, also participated in it for more than ten years. After the war the work was taken up again and was continued by Miss Carus Wilson and members of her seminar.

Practically the whole of the first two or three years of the seminar's work was devoted to examining the customs accounts from the point of view of their accuracy and their use as a source of information. The fact that the beginning of the seminar's activities coincided with the publication of Miss Carus Wilson's study exposing the inexactitude of the Aulnager's accounts[7] and with the general criticism of medieval statistics by Professor Tout, confirmed Eileen Power and me in our decision not to proceed with a detailed use of the accounts before making sure of the nature and especially the reliability of the documentary information.

These preliminary investigations were above all devoted to examining the administration of the customs and of the various controls which were set up in the fourteenth and fifteenth centuries by government and merchants. The results of our investigations were that the customs were not trustworthy and were very difficult to use in their early years, i.e. in the thirteenth century and the beginning of the fourteenth century, the period when the series is fragmentary and during which the administration was

[4] *Economic History Review*, xxxix (1929).
[5] E. E. Power and M. M. Postan (eds.), *Studies in English Trade in the Fifteenth Century* (London, 1933).
[6] *Bronnen tot de Geschiedenis van den Handel met England, Schotland en Ireland (1150–1485)*, 4 vols. (The Hague, 1928).
[7] *Economic History Review*, ii (1929).

still inexperienced and the direct control of the State was frequently replaced by farming out. But we also arrived at the conclusion that from the last quarter of the fourteenth century until the reintroduction of the system of farming in the sixteenth century the customs accounts were, on the whole, remarkably reliable, especially for the four main groups of commodities: wool, cloth, wine and the miscellaneous merchandise subject to the Petty Custom and the Subsidy of Poundage.

2

The grounds on which these conclusions were founded with special reference to cloth, wine and miscellaneous merchandise have been dealt with by Miss Carus Wilson. I shall therefore limit myself to wool. For obvious reasons the temptation to evade payment of customs by falsifying entries and departures and by fraud was greater for wool than for all other merchandise, since from the last quarter of the fourteenth century the various taxes on the export of wool were levied at a very high rate, sometimes as high as 20 to 35 per cent of the value of the merchandise. As, nevertheless, contraband on a large scale appears to have been rare (infractions of lesser importance were naturally more frequent) and the customs accounts seem to give exact figures of wool exports, we must attribute this to the manner in which the customs were administered and controlled at the end of the fourteenth and beginning of the fifteenth centuries.

In each of the principal ports the levying of customs dues on wool was in the hands of a group of men the most important of whom were the Collector and the Controller. One of them was, as a general rule, a royal officer, usually a lawyer recruited from among the employees of the Exchequer or the King's Chamber; the other was almost invariably a merchant. Originally, the Collector and the Controller had to keep separate registers, but in fact only the Collector's register was kept regularly and has survived until our day.

In addition, in each port, there were officials occupied in what we should now call customs police: searchers and their assistants. Their job obliged them to visit ships in the principal ports, and even in creeks and smaller ports, to assure themselves that merchandise was not being embarked illegally. During the greater part of the fifteenth century, the activities of the searchers were very frequently supervised by their superiors the Surveyors of Search. In all ports they were assisted by workers or sailors. When John Pole, Searcher of Southampton, of whom I would like to say more later, went out to visit a ship, he was accompanied by a troop of twelve to twenty men.

Such a method of administration and control and the proliferation of officials rendered fraud and smuggling not so much difficult as costly. Indeed, taken together the Collectors and Controllers, with their deputies and their clerks, the Searchers with their supervisors and their employees (not to mention the personnel of harbours – weighers, checkers, trovers) were an enormous crowd of men, all or most of whom would have had to be 'bought' by any captain or shipper who wished to indulge in contraband or fraud. The number and omnipresence of officers must have greatly limited attempts at clandestine lading.

The greatest obstacle to the fraudulent transport of wool was provided by the existence of the Company of the Staple and by the control which it exercised over trade. There are two reasons why, near the end of the fourteenth century, the Company of the Merchants of Staple should have assumed the form in which we know it. It existed, in the first place, in order to canalise the wool trade through a single channel so as to facilitate its supervision and control, and in the second place, in order to apply the agreement entered into with the government, according to which the Staple advanced to the Crown some of the revenue of the taxes on wool and recovered it from receipts at the ports. The advantage the Staplers obtained in exchange for the facilities thus offered to the government was the monopoly of trade and the powers which they were given to enforce it.

This meant that a ship owner who tried to evade the customs dues came into conflict with the collective interests of the English wool merchants. It would have been impossible to transport large quantities of wool without the knowledge of the other exporters and of the foreign merchants to whom it was destined. The chief producers of wool at home and the country merchants who collected wool from them and sold it wholesale to the exporting Staplers, and, finally, the Dutch, Flemish, Italian or Genoese merchants who transported the wool from the Staple town (in the fifteenth century this was Calais) to Bruges, Antwerp or Middelburg, all combined to form a close network of firms and mutual relationships. In modern terminology it was a 'market' whose transactions were public and open. And in such a market secret sales and clandestine movements on a large and regular scale were unthinkable. When in the somewhat similar conditions, which were to prevail in the cloth trade of England in the sixteenth and seventeenth centuries, many interlopers regularly transgressed the Merchant Adventurers' monopoly, their activities were known to all. By contrast, the documents do not retain the slightest trace of large-scale evasions similarly known and tolerated in the wool trade of the fifteenth century.

The reason why they were not tolerated and could not exist was the fact that each lading trying to escape the customs infringed not only the monopoly of the Staple, but also prevented the latter from fulfilling the

GRAPH 9.1 *English wool exports, 1279–1547*

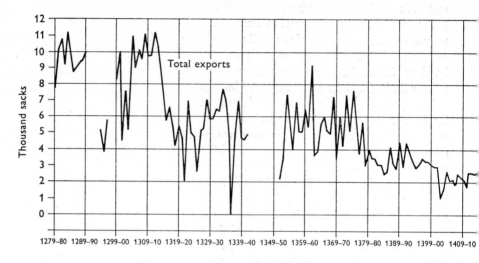

contract which it had concluded with the Crown. It is thus not surprising that the collective machinery of the Staple on the one side, and the public pressure exercised by the wool merchants on the other, and finally the publicity which inevitably surrounded all important transactions would have rendered regular and far-reaching deception impossible. In the few instances – perhaps one or two – where individual merchants as well known as Stocker or Horn transported, or were suspected of transporting, large quantities of wool without paying customs dues, their names re-appeared ceaselessly in the complaints and requests addressed to the Crown. The guilty men themselves became the objects of accusations and complaints of which traces can be found in the records of the Exchequer and the Chancery.

Needless to say illicit ladings on a small scale – a sack here or there – were easier to conceal and could have been more frequent. In her study of the English wool trade in the fifteenth century Eileen Power cites a certain number of contemporary references to unauthorised ladings. Eileen Power, myself, and other members of the seminar, have found in the Memoranda Rolls or in other miscellaneous records of the Exchequer a considerable number of references to minor cases of contraband or fraud. There is no doubt that many similar cases remain unknown. Nevertheless, it would be erroneous to conclude that the total of cases so far concealed from view was larger than the number of those which

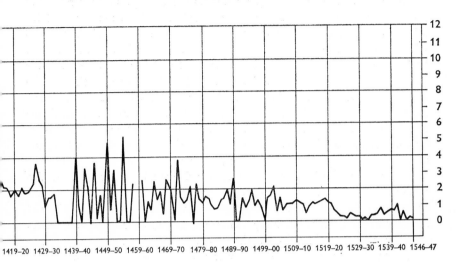

the Exchequer documents reveal. On the contrary, it is probable that in the cases mentioned in our documents, the offences were exaggerated. Most of those to which Eileen Power refers, precede the attempts of the Staple to obtain the right of search in the ports (a right which the Mayor of the Staple had in fact obtained in the year 1440) and may be considered as propaganda in support of the Staplers' case. Indeed they decrease in number after the Mayor of the Staple had obtained the right to search; and its decrease was to some extent due to the efficiency of his searchers. Other examples bear witness to the excessive zeal of the searchers; such zeal is easily understood when one realises that these men were, in principle, remunerated by confiscated goods in a proportion which often reached one-third of the value of the merchandise. Our documents provide many examples of these over-conscientious searchers who believed they had uncovered offences even where none had been committed. The most abundant collection of documents relating to these false or excessive accusations is preserved in the well-known dossier of John Pole, a searcher of Southampton to whom I have already referred. This official had the luck to 'discover' thousands – I use the word thousands advisedly – of pieces of cloth, legally exported but secretly loaded, in the great port of Southampton on ships as considerable as those of carracks from Genoa. However, he was not lucky enough to convince the local authorities in Southampton, or, for all we know, the officers of the Exchequer, of the illegality of these shipments.

In the Chancery Proceedings several similar examples of excessive and not entirely disinterested zeal can be found. For these reasons, and for others, we have been led to conclude that the accounts of contraband which we have been able to establish from the records of the Exchequer both under- and over-estimated the extent of real frauds. But even if the cases of fraud and contraband shipment had been several times more numerous than those revealed in our documents they would still not have amounted to a very significant total. The total was probably minimal: 20, 30, or perhaps 50 sacks a year. Even if these figures were multiplied by ten, this would hardly add up to more than one per cent of the average annual exports in the fifteenth century.

That the cases of contraband and fraud were in fact so few is also shown by the private documents we possess. The correspondence and accounts of the Cely family, covering the business of two generations of Staplers in the fifteenth century, contain large numbers of private letters full of small talk and gossip, but they do not make the smallest allusion to fraudulent ladings of wool either by one of the Staplers or by any other merchant, whereas they sometimes speak of minor swindles and double dealing. The Chancery Proceedings have also preserved for us many references to ladings of wool made by individuals and on at least five occasions it has been possible to verify these ladings by referring to the customs accounts. Finally, records from Leyden contain a large quantity of references to and of regulations concerning purchases of English wool; yet not a single mention is to be found among them of export, departure or import of English wool outside the official channels, at least in appreciable quantities.

INDEX

Subjects of essays and their inclusive page references are in **bold** type, references to statistical tables are in *italic* type. MA means Middle Ages.